MEMORY CONSOLIDATION

MEMORY CONSOLIDATION

Essays in Honor of James L. McGaugh

EDITED BY PAUL E. GOLD AND
WILLIAM T. GREENOUGH

AMERICAN PSYCHOLOGICAL ASSOCIATION
WASHINGTON, DC

Published by
American Psychological Association
750 First Street, NE
Washington, DC 20002
www.apa.org

To order   Tel: (800) 374-2721, Direct: (202) 336-5510
APA Order Department   Fax: (202) 336-5502, TDD/TTY: (202) 336-6123
P.O. Box 92984   Online: www.apa.org/books/
Washington, DC 20090-2984   Email: order@apa.org

In the U.K., Europe, Africa, and the Middle East, copies may be ordered from
American Psychological Association
3 Henrietta Street
Covent Garden, London
WC2E 8LU England

Typeset in Berkeley Book by EPS Group Inc., Easton, MD

Printer: Automated Graphics Systems, White Plains, MD
Dust jacket designer: Nini Sarmiento, Baltimore, MD
Technical/Production Editor: Jennifer Powers

The opinions and statements published are the responsibility of the authors, and such opinions and statements do not necessarily represent the policies of the American Psychological Association.

Library of Congress Cataloging-in-Publication Data
Memory consolidation : essays in honor of James L. McGaugh / edited by Paul E. Gold, William T. Greenough.
        p. cm.—(Decade of behavior)
    Includes bibliographical references and index.
    ISBN 1-55798-783-1 (alk. paper)
        1. Memory.   I. McGaugh, James L.   II. Gold, Paul E.
    III. Greenough, William T.   IV. Series.

    BF371 .M4484 2001
    153.1′2—dc21

                                                                        2001018926

British Library Cataloguing-in-Publication Data
A CIP record is available from the British Library.

Printed in the United States of America
First Edition

APA Science Volumes

Attribution and Social Interaction: The Legacy of Edward E. Jones

Best Methods for the Analysis of Change: Recent Advances, Unanswered Questions, Future Directions

Cardiovascular Reactivity to Psychological Stress and Disease

The Challenge in Mathematics and Science Education: Psychology's Response

Changing Employment Relations: Behavioral and Social Perspectives

Children Exposed to Marital Violence: Theory, Research, and Applied Issues

Cognition: Conceptual and Methodological Issues

Cognitive Bases of Musical Communication

Cognitive Dissonance: Progress on a Pivotal Theory in Social Psychology

Conceptualization and Measurement of Organism–Environment Interaction

Converging Operations in the Study of Visual Selective Attention

Creative Thought: An Investigation of Conceptual Structures and Processes

Developmental Psychoacoustics

Diversity in Work Teams: Research Paradigms for a Changing Workplace

Emotion and Culture: Empirical Studies of Mutual Influence

Emotion, Disclosure, and Health

Evolving Explanations of Development: Ecological Approaches to Organism– Environment Systems

Examining Lives in Context: Perspectives on the Ecology of Human Development

Global Prospects for Education: Development, Culture, and Schooling

Hostility, Coping, and Health

Measuring Patient Changes in Mood, Anxiety, and Personality Disorders: Toward a Core Battery

Occasion Setting: Associative Learning and Cognition in Animals

Organ Donation and Transplantation: Psychological and Behavioral Factors

Origins and Development of Schizophrenia: Advances in Experimental Psychopathology

APA Decade of Behavior Volumes

Contents

Contributors

Patricia G. Ardenghi, Memory Center, Department of Biochemistry, University of Rio Grande do Sul, Porto Allegre, Brazil

Daniela M. Barros, Memory Center, Department of Biochemistry, University of Rio Grande do Sul, Porto Allegre, Brazil

Federico Bermúdez-Rattoni, Neuroscience Department, National University of Mexico, Mexico, D.F.

Lia Bevilaqua, Memory Center, Department of Biochemistry, University of Rio Grande do Sul, Porto Allegre, Brazil

Edwin C. Clayton, Department of Psychiatry, University of Pennsylvania, Philadelphia

Paul E. Gilbert, Department of Psychology, University of Utah, Salt Lake City

Paul E. Gold, Department of Psychology, University of Illinois at Urbana–Champaign

William T. Greenough, Department of Psychology, University of Illinois at Urbana–Champaign

Humberto Gutiérrez González, Neuroscience Department, National University of Mexico, Mexico, D.F.

Iván Izquierdo, Memory Center, Department of Biochemistry, University of Rio Grande do Sul, Porto Allegre, Brazil

Luciana A. Izquierdo, Memory Center, Department of Biochemistry, University of Rio Grande do Sul, Porto Allegre, Brazil

Robert A. Jensen, Department of Psychology, Southern Illinois University, Carbondale

Raymond P. Kesner, Department of Psychology, University of Utah, Salt Lake City

Donna L. Korol, Department of Psychology, University of Illinois at Urbana–Champaign

Philip W. Landfield, Department of Pharmacology, University of Kentucky College of Medicine, Lexington

Keng Chen Liang, Department of Psychology, National Taiwan University, Taipei

Christa McIntyre, Center for the Neurobiology of Learning and Memory, University of California at Irvine

Ewan McNay, Department of Psychology, Yale University, New Haven, CT

Jorge H. Medina, Institute of Cell Biology and Neuroscience, Faculty of Medicine, University of Buenos Aires, Argentina

Tadeu Mello e Souza, Memory Center, Department of Biochemistry, University of Rio Grande do Sul, Porto Allegre, Brazil

María Isabel Miranda, Neuroscience Department, National University of Mexico, Mexico, D.F.

Mark G. Packard, Department of Psychology, Yale University, New Haven, CT

Patricia Pereira, Memory Center, Department of Biochemistry, University of Rio Grande do Sul, Porto Allegre, Brazil

Steven P. R. Rose, Brain and Behavior Research Group, Open University, Milton Keynes, UK

Mark R. Rosenzweig, Department of Psychology, University of California at Berkeley

Aryeh Routtenberg, Department of Psychology, Northwestern University, Evanston, IL

Marcia M. de Souza, Memory Center, Department of Biochemistry, University of Rio Grande do Sul, Porto Allegre, Brazil

Mark Stefani, Department of Psychiatry, Yale University School of Medicine, New Haven, CT

Oswald Steward, Reeve–Irvine Research Center, Department of Anatomy and Neurobiology, and Department of Neurobiology and Behavior, University of California at Irvine

Olivier Thibault, Department of Pharmacology, University of Kentucky College of Medicine, Lexington

Monica R. M. Vianna, Memory Center, Department of Biochemistry, University of Rio Grande do Sul, Porto Allegre, Brazil

Christopher S. Wallace, Department of Biology, Whitman College, Walla Walla, WA

Norman M. Weinberger, Center for the Neurobiology of Learning and Memory and Department of Neurobiology and Behavior, University of California at Irvine

Cedric L. Williams, Department of Psychology and Graduate Program in Neuroscience, University of Virginia, Charlottesville

Paul F. Worley, Department of Neuroscience, Johns Hopkins School of Medicine, Baltimore

Foreword

In early 1988, the American Psychological Association (APA) Science Directorate began its sponsorship of what has become an exceptionally successful activity in support of psychological science—the APA Scientific Conferences program. This program has showcased some of the most important topics in psychological science, and the conference participants have included many leading figures in the field.

As we enter a new century, it seems fitting that we begin with a new face on this book series—that of the Decade of Behavior (DoB). The DoB is a major interdisciplinary initiative designed to promote the contributions of the behavioral and social sciences to address some of our most important societal challenges and will occur from 2000 to 2010. Although a major effort of the initiative will be related to informing the public about the contributions of these fields, other activities will be put into place to reach fellow scientists. Hence, the series that was the "APA Science Series" will be continued as the "Decade of Behavior Series." This represents one element in APA's efforts to promote the DoB initiative as one of its partner organizations.

Please note the DoB logo on the inside jacket flap and the full title page. We expect this logo will become a familiar sight over the next few years. For additional information about DoB, please visit http://www.decadeofbehavior.org.

As part of the sponsorship agreement with APA, conference organizers commit themselves not only to the conference itself but also to editing a scholarly volume that results from the meeting. This book is such a volume. Over the course of the past 12 years, we have partnered with 44 universities to sponsor 60 conferences on a variety of topics of interest to psychological scientists. The APA Science Directorate looks forward to continuing this program and to sponsoring other conferences in the years ahead.

We are pleased that this important contribution to the literature was supported in part by the Scientific Conferences program. Congratulations to the editors and contributors on their sterling effort.

Richard McCarty, PhD
Executive Director for Science

Virginia E. Holt
Assistant Executive Director for Science

Acknowledgments

The authors of the chapters in this book participated in a meeting at the Center for the Neurobiology of Learning and Memory at the University of California at Irvine, to honor Jim McGaugh for his many contributions to the field of memory consolidation and to plan this festschrift. We were fortunate to obtain significant support for the meeting from many sources. We are very grateful to the American Psychological Association, which sponsored the meeting and has published this book, and for additional financial support for the meeting received from Academic Press. We are especially grateful for support we received from the University of California at Irvine; from the chancellor, Dr. Ralph J. Cicerone; the executive vice-chancellor, Dr. William J. Lillyman; and the dean of biological sciences, Dr. Shin Lin.

We are also very grateful to the staff at the Center for the Neurobiology of Learning and Memory at the University of California at Irvine. Nan Collett, Lynn Brown, Jacquie Weinberger, and Lori Metherate painstakingly arranged the details of the meeting and ensured that this would be an event at which both the scientific and social aspects would be outstanding. This meeting could not have happened without their extraordinary assistance. We are also grateful for the assistance of Aubrey Marks and Kathy Bates at the University of Illinois at Urbana–Champaign.

About James L. McGaugh

James L. McGaugh is a distinguished psychologist and neuroscientist who has nearly 500 publications spanning areas as diverse as social psychology (a textbook), methods in chromatography, developmental psychobiology, biological psychiatry, and aging. His contributions to the neurobiology of learning and memory have been both fundamental and monumental, truly transforming the field from its primitive state in the 1960s when he began work in the area to its contemporary focus on the protracted cellular and molecular processes now known to underlie the memory process. What is known about these processes is covered in detail in chapters 1–4 and also forms the underpinnings or deep rationale for work described in the later chapters.

Jim received his PhD from the University of California at Berkeley and did postdoctoral research in neuropharmacology in Rome, Italy (with Nobel Laureate Dr. Daniel Bovet) before going to the University of California at Irvine (UCI) in 1964 as the founding chair of the Department of Neurobiology and

Behavior (formerly Psychobiology). At UCI, he has also served as dean of the School of Biological Sciences and executive vice-chancellor. He is a member of the U.S. National Academy of Sciences and the Brazilian Academy of Sciences and a Fellow of the American Academy of Arts and Sciences. He is a William James Fellow and past president of the American Psychological Society. He received the John P. McGovern Award from the American Association for the Advancement of Science and the American Psychological Association Distinguished Scientific Contribution Award. At UCI, Jim received the Distinguished Faculty Award for Research, the Extraordinarious Award, and the UCI Medal.

All those who have worked closely with Jim have come to appreciate his attitude that a principal goal of doing research is to have a good time at it. As Jim has conveyed this to us, having a good time includes total commitment to the intellectual issues involved in the research, intense investment of time and energy, and constant questioning of all of the work in the area by others, by ourselves, and even by Jim himself. Jim also encouraged broad participation in the research process—his laboratory was, for example, nearly overrun with undergraduates working on various projects. The number of individuals brought into scientific careers by contact with Jim is hard to estimate but clearly exceeds the 150 people present at the festschrift meeting. Even now he continues to train students at all levels in his current position of research professor in the Department of Neurobiology and Behavior, which he founded as the Department of Psychobiology in a temporary trailer in 1964, and director of the Center for the Neurobiology of Learning and Memory, which he founded in 1983.

MEMORY
CONSOLIDATION

Introduction:
Evolution of Memory Consolidation

Paul E. Gold
William T. Greenough

W hen James L. McGaugh began his graduate work in the Department of Psychology at the University of California, Berkeley, most of what we knew about the neurobiology of memory was that treatments like electroconvulsive shock produced retrograde amnesia (Duncan, 1949). Although theories of the brain mechanisms of learning and memory were much older (Ramon y Cajal, 1893; Tanzi, 1893), relevant data were not available. Application of methods and principles of biochemistry, physiology, and anatomy to questions of learning and memory would come a bit later. Simply put, before the 1960s, the brain of a trained rat looked just like the brain of an untrained rat in all respects. There was no anatomical plasticity, no long-term potentiation, no N-methyl-d-aspartate receptor—there was no glutamate as a neurotransmitter! It was not until 1969 that changes in the fine anatomy of the brain— reactive synaptogenesis—were evident after lesions (Raisman, 1969) and not until the 1970s that evidence emerged showing that the fine anatomy of the (undamaged) brain changed with experience (e.g., Volkmar & Greenough, 1972; West & Greenough, 1972).

McGaugh's classic (1966) article identified the main issues in this field, showed the world not only that drugs could impair memory but also that some drugs could *improve* memory, and crystallized the importance of posttraining designs for studies of memory. Within the framework of the early 1960s, the conclusion we accept so readily now—that drugs administered after training can enhance memory formation—was not an especially reasonable one. Indeed, the initial papers, first rejected and later published in the *Journal of Comparative and Physiological Psychology* (Breen & McGaugh, 1961; McGaugh, Westbrook, & Burt, 1961; McGaugh, Westbrook, & Thomson, 1962), were met with great skepticism by reviewers and editors alike. Although much of the prior and coming research on memory consolidation dealt with retrograde amnesia, it was

3

the establishment of retrograde enhancement of memory that led directly to modulation of memory as we characterize it today, with some hormonal and neurotransmitter systems playing important roles in both up- and down-regulating memory formation.

Although the empirical findings related to retrograde enhancement and impairment of memory are of great importance, there is another key element of Jim's early work that we often now take for granted. Jim's work provided a conceptual leap in our understanding of how we should study memory formation processes. The importance of the posttraining design to developing procedures in which one can most clearly show specific effects on memory has been critical to the development of studies of memory. In the course of showing that memory formation could be both facilitated and impaired by treatments applied *after learning had taken place,* he championed the view that retrograde temporal gradients provided the best way to show that the treatments acted on memory—not on attention, not on motor or sensory functions, not on later retrieval—but on *memory formation.* This idea must rank right along side of—and is probably inseparable from—the demonstrations of memory facilitation.

With electroconvulsive shock and other amnestic treatments, early consolidation theory developed to deal with issues of short- and long-term memory. An important component of early studies in memory consolidation was the belief that the time course of the retrograde amnesia gradient, and later the retrograde enhancement gradient as well, would represent how long it took for memory to be made. This time parameter would be a critical bit of information for the underlying neurobiology of learning and memory, constraining the putative mechanisms to fit that time frame. If only it had been that easy! As memory consolidation studies grew, so, too, did the number of temporal gradients, until it became clear that there were many gradients for retroactive effects on memory. In determining the meaning of these multiple gradients, Jim and his colleagues led an evolution of consolidation theory into a theory that identified times of "susceptibility to modification" (McGaugh & Dawson, 1971). This theory was a necessary antecedent to the later views that extended consolidation of memory to modulation of memory (Gold & McGaugh, 1975). Modulation of memory emphasized that retrograde enhancement and impairment of memory reflected actions of endogenous responses, such as release of some hormones and neurotransmitters after training, to regulate the brain mechanisms of memory formation.

It is rather extraordinary that the early findings and views of memory consolidation Jim gave us could anticipate so well contemporary issues in neurobiology of memory. Importantly, the fuzzy time parameter and the logic of early consolidation and later modulation have acquired new sense as the neurobiology of memory has evolved to include a rather large set of cellular and molecular events that take *times*, not time but *times*, to begin and to reach completion. The fact that posttraining treatments could enhance (and impair) memory also led directly to a second era of this research, the view that endogenous hormonal and neurotransmitter responses to an experience could regulate later memory for that experience. Current research based on these foundations can be seen in chapters in this volume by Paul E. Gold and colleagues (chapter 12), Robert A. Jensen (chapter 7), Mark G. Packard (chapter 11), and Cedric L. Williams and Edwin C. Clayton (chapter 8). In addition, the definition of time-dependent memory processes provides the basis for studies of the cellular and molecular mechanisms underlying memory, for example by offering the deep rationale for examination of time-dependent gene expression well after a learned experience has ended. That underlying rationale is evident in chapters in this volume by William T. Greenough (chapter 4), Iván Izquierdo and colleagues (chapter 5), Steven P. R. Rose (chapter 6), Aryeh Routtenberg (chapter 2), and Oswald Steward and colleagues (chapter 3). Together, the use of the posttraining design for reasons of experimental clarity and for reasons of neurobiological understanding continues to have major impact on contemporary experiments in and beyond the specific field of pharmacology of learning and memory.

During the course of preparing this volume, it quickly became evident that Jim McGaugh's career spanned almost exactly the 40 years that represent the development of the neurobiology of learning and memory. The primary focus of this book is the development of learning and memory during those 40 years, with special attention given to the evolution of studies of memory consolidation through that time. Chapter 1 by Jim himself sets the background for the early studies conducted by Jim and his colleagues and provides the context for research on memory consolidation over the next 40 years.

Throughout this book, we ask the question, How will we view regulation of the neurobiology of memory storage in the next decade? The varied answers and varying levels of analysis offered by Jim's students and colleagues are the focus of the chapters included herein. The chapters lead from molecular to systems to theoretical views of the neurobiology of learning and memory. Chapters 2–6 describe investigations, with underlying bases in memory consolidation, into molecular and cellular processes that form memories over time after an experience. Chapters 7–14 describe pharmacological bases of memory consolidation, with obvious direction of this research area into questions of organization of neural systems responsible for regulating and storing new memories. Chapters 15 and 16 offer new perspectives that integrate research on learning and memory into new views of memory formation. Our hope is that taking this collection as a whole will enable future researchers and students to begin to answer the question posed above—how will we view the neurobiology of memory storage in the future?

References

Breen, R. A., & McGaugh, J. L. (1961). Facilitation of maze learning with posttrial injections of picrotoxin. *Journal of Comparative and Physiological Psychology, 54*, 498–501.

Duncan, C. P. (1949). The retroactive effect of electroshock on learning. *Journal of Comparative and Physiological Psychology, 42*, 32–42.

Gold, P. E., & McGaugh, J. L. (1975). A single trace, two process view of memory storage processes. In D. Deutsch & J. A. Deutsch (Eds.), *Short term memory* (pp. 355–390). New York: Academic Press.

McGaugh, J. L. (1966). Time-dependent processes in memory storage. *Science, 153*, 1351–1358.

McGaugh, J. L., & Dawson, R. G. (1971). Modification of memory storage processes. In W. K. Honig & P. H. R. James (Eds.), *Animal memory* (pp. 215–242). New York: Academic Press.

McGaugh, J. L., Westbrook, W., & Burt, G. (1961). Strain differences in the facilitative effects of 5-7-diphenyl-1-3-diazadamantan-6-ol (1757 I.S.) on maze learning. *Journal of Comparative and Physiological Psychology, 54*, 502–505.

McGaugh, J. L., Westbrook, W. H., & Thomson, C. W. (1962). Facilitation of maze learning with posttrial injections of 5-7-diphenyl-diazadamantan-6-ol (1757 I.S.). *Journal of Comparative and Physiological Psychology, 55*, 710–713.

Raisman, G. (1969). Neuronal plasticity in the septal nuclei of the adult rat. *Brain Research, 14*, 25–48.

Ramon y Cajal, S. (1893). Neue Darstellung vom histologischen Bau des Centralnervoius system [New findings about the histological structure of the central nervous system]. *Archives of Anatomical Physiology (Anat.)*, pp. 319–428.

Tanzi, E. (1893). I fatti e le induzioni nell'odierna istologia del sistema nervoso [Facts and inductions in current histology of the nervous system]. *Rivista Sperimentale di Freniatria e Medicina Legale Delle Mentali Alienazioni, 19*, 419–472.

Volkmar, F. R., & Greenough, W. T. (1972). Rearing complexity affects branching of dendrites in the visual cortex of the rat. *Science, 176*, 1445–1447.

West, R. W., & Greenough, W. T. (1972). Effect of environmental complexity on cortical synapses of rats: Preliminary results. *Behavioral Biology, 7*, 279–284.

CHAPTER 1

Orchestration of Consolidation:

Overture and Coda

James Lafayette McGaugh

To say that I was stunned to learn about the publication of this festschrift is a gross understatement. I thank Paul Gold and Bill Greenough for planning and editing this volume and the authors for contributing the chapters.

My role in all of this probably began when I was an undergraduate student majoring in psychology at San Jose State College (now a university) and read about Mueller and Pilzecker's (1900) consolidation hypothesis in Woodworth's *Experimental Psychology* (1938). I should perhaps confess that my initial interests in college were drama and music. Those interests linger and sometimes find expression in metaphors such as those in the title of this chapter. The Korean War erupted at the end of my freshman year. As student deferments from the draft were in those days based on college grades, the incentive to do well in college was clear. In summer 1953 I graduated, and my student deferment ended. I enlisted as an officer in the Air Force, although about a month later a cease-fire was signed, and I was, fortunately, no longer needed. So, instead of going to Korea, I went to the University of California at Berkeley as a graduate student in the Department of Psychology. It seemed a reasonable alternative.

On my arrival at Berkeley in 1953, I was given a teaching assistant's position and assigned to assist Edward Tolman and David Krech. Their influences on my conceptual and methodological approaches to research on learning and memory were profound and permanent. Later my interest in physiological approaches was stimulated when I served as a teaching assistant to Mark Rosenzweig and by taking seminars on brain chemistry and behavior offered by Krech, Rosenzweig, and colleagues. There I had the good fortune to meet and interact with a remarkable group of graduate students that included John Garcia, Robert Bolles, and Lewis Petrinovich (who provided a particularly strong influence because, as a more advanced graduate student, he "knew the ropes"). In particular, I was quick to note (and found it hard to believe) that Petrinovich had already published articles (coauthored with Bolles) in our then scientific "bible," the *Journal of Comparative and Physiological Psychology*. Petrinovich and I collaborated in preparing a review paper for the "Brain Chemistry and Behavior" seminar summarizing all published findings concerning the effects of drugs on learning and memory. It had about 100 references. We continued to revise and update it in subsequent years but found that a hopeless task. This area of research was growing so rapidly that we could not continue to claim that the review was comprehensive. Finally (mercifully), we published it a decade later (McGaugh & Petrinovich, 1965).

Tuning Up

In preparing that review for the seminar we discovered a paper by Karl Lashley (1917) reporting that maze learning was enhanced by strychnine. Petrinovich and I found that interesting for three reasons. First, the paper was authored by Lashley, who was doubtless the most influential physiological psychologist of the first half of the 20th century. Second, although many drugs were reported to impair learning, strychnine was the only drug reported to enhance learning. Intuitively (but not necessarily logically) such findings seemed to us to be more difficult to interpret as being due to nonspecific influences unrelated to learning. Third, there was evidence at that time (very probably wrong) suggesting that strychnine is an acetylcholinesterase (ACh) inhibitor. As the brain chemistry and behavior research program initiated by Krech and Rosenzweig focused on ACh, and Petrinovich and I were both involved in that research program, that suggested mechanism of strychnine caught our attention. So, Petrinovich and I conducted an "in principle" replication of Lashley's study. We gave rats daily intraperitoneal injections of saline or various doses of strychnine sulphate a few minutes before they were trained in an alley maze with a food reward. Simply put, we replicated Lashley's findings. Buoyed by our success we submitted an article reporting our findings to the "bible" that was at that time edited by Harry Harlow. Petrinovich and I were greatly disappointed that the paper was rejected. Moreover, we were astonished and dismayed by Harlow's assessment of our creative work. He wrote (among other dismal points in several pages of uninterrupted and unrestrained criticism), "The results of your paper upset a fundamental pharmacological assumption that no drug improves behavior." Additionally, he concluded, "I think there is every reason to doubt that strychnine improves maze learning, and the data presented in your paper are by no means convincing. . . . I regret that I cannot publish your paper, but I have no alternative." Well, *we* certainly thought that he had an alternative that we would have greatly preferred. Eventually, several years later, we published the paper elsewhere (McGaugh & Petrinovich, 1959).

Solo and Consolidation Reprise

Tolman taught me (and all who have read his works) that it is absolutely critical to distinguish *learning* from *performance*. Performance is observed; learning is inferred. It is, of course, difficult to make inferences about the effects of a drug on learning on the basis of rats' performance while they are under the influence of the drug. A drug can, of course, have many influences on performance in addition to or instead of the wished-for effect on learning. Although Harlow was thus correct in concluding that our findings (McGaugh & Petrinovich, 1959) were not convincing, he did not offer the learning–performance issue in rejecting our paper. In retrospect, he should have.

Fortunately, experimental findings from other laboratories and a book published in 1949 suggested a way to deal with this complicated issue. Duncan (1949) resurrected the consolidation hypothesis in interpreting his finding that electroconvulsive shock given to rats after training in an active avoidance task produced retrograde amnesia. In his influential book, Hebb (1949) proposed that a short-term fragile memory trace is converted into a lasting trace by synaptic changes resulting from reverberating neural activity occurring after an experience. Gerard (1949) obtained similar findings and proposed a similar hypothesis.

The evidence of retrograde amnesia and the dual-trace hypothesis suggested that it might be possible to enhance memory by injecting stimulant drugs shortly after training, that is, during the early stage of memory consolidation (Mueller & Pilzecker, 1900). These ideas fueled my enthusiasm for testing the effects of posttraining injections. My thesis advisor at the time, Krech, was less enthusiastic. *Much* less. But, his lack of enthusiasm ("Bad idea, forget it") did not restrain me because he promptly departed for a sabbatical leave in Norway. In his absence, as part of my PhD thesis, I examined the effects on learning, of injections of strychnine administered immediately after rats were given a daily training trial in the same alley maze used in the previous study. I was delighted (and very surprised!) to find that the posttraining injections enhanced learning, or memory, as the performance measure was errors made on each trial, 24 hours after the previous injection. Memory was, of course, inferred from the performance. But as the animals were drug free when tested, the reduction in errors (compared to saline control animals) could not be attributed to a direct influence of the drug on performance. Rosenzweig, who was now my thesis advisor, approved my thesis. Krech returned from Norway and was enthusiastic about my findings despite his earlier admonishment. The findings of this experiment greatly influenced most of the research I have done with my students and colleagues in subsequent years. The use of posttraining treatments has been and is a common feature of experiments from my laboratory because it provides an effective means of solving the learning–performance problem when studying the effects of various treatments on memory consolidation (McGaugh, 1989b).

San Jose Reprise

I returned in 1957 to my undergraduate alma mater as an assistant professor in the Department of Psychology, where I established an animal research laboratory in a large, abandoned basement room. It was easy to understand why it had been abandoned, as it was (until we got the problem fixed) occasionally flooded with 2 or 3 inches of water. There, with the help of energetic undergraduate and graduate students (including William Westbrook, William Hudspeth, and Millard Madsen), we set up a laboratory and began a series of studies examining the effects of other central nervous system (CNS) stimulants as well as the generality of the effects of posttraining injections tested in different learning tasks. The first evidence that posttraining injections of the GABAergic antagonist picrotoxin enhances memory (Breen & McGaugh, 1961) was obtained in that laboratory, as was the evidence that posttraining injections of strychnine enhance delayed response alternation (Petrinovich, Bradford, & McGaugh, 1965) and latent learning (Westbrook & McGaugh, 1964). We also initiated experiments using 1-trial inhibitory avoidance tasks that had been originally developed in Tolman's laboratory and refined by Murray Jarvik (1964).

Several years after arriving at San Jose I received some mixed news. I learned that I had been nominated for a National Academy of Sciences–National Research Council Senior Postdoctoral Fellowship. I also learned that Harry Harlow was on the selection committee (along with Frank Beach and Karl Pribram). I then learned that I was selected for an interview and that Harlow was to interview me. He did. He asked me about my research and the stack of unpublished manuscripts that I brought with me to the interview, saying, "Didn't I publish these?" I said, "No." He then said, "Then it is time that I publish them." And, he did. He also recommended that I receive the fellowship, which I did.

Allegro Ma Non Troppo

David Krech told me that he had just returned from Rome, Italy, where he had learned that Daniel Bovet, a recent Nobel Laureate (for discovery of the antibiotic sulfa drugs and antihistamines) had developed a series of new stimulant drugs and was interested in my research findings. I wrote to Bovet to ask if I could come to his laboratory to do postdoctoral work. Unfortunately, I could not read his reply as it was, of course, in Italian, so I assumed that he agreed, and I wrote him a letter telling him that I would arrive in September 1961. In

Rome I was able to continue my studies in collaboration with Bovet and Vincenzo Longo. Additionally, and importantly, my fellowship enabled me to travel throughout Europe to visit laboratories of interest to me. The contacts that I made in Europe resulted in my meeting many internationally recognized scientists and subsequently being invited to speak at many international meetings. I do not think it is possible to overemphasize the importance of my postdoctoral fellowship with Bovet on my subsequent academic research career.

As most readers of this chapter know, the heading of this section, roughly translated is, "fast but not too fast." My research was interrupted (although enormously aided, of course) by the move with my wife Becky and two young children (Douglas and Janice) to Rome and then from Rome to Eugene, Oregon, where I joined the Department of Psychology. In Eugene I started a new laboratory, again with the aid of enthusiastic students, including William Greenough (the coeditor of this volume), who was an undergraduate student. Midway through my second year at Eugene I received an offer to move to the yet-to-be-established University of California at Irvine (a yet-to-be-established city) as founding chair of the Department of Psychobiology in the School of Biological Sciences. For many obvious reasons the offer was much too tempting to ignore despite the fact that I greatly enjoyed my work and appreciated the opportunities at the University of Oregon. So, we moved again. And, again, *allegro, ma non troppo*.

My colleague Larry Cahill pointed out that there are three stages of evaluation of one's research. First, "it isn't true," then "it isn't new," and finally "it isn't you." As noted above, Harlow provided the first stage. The second occurred shortly after I arrived at Irvine in 1964 with several graduate students from Oregon (including Marvin Luttges, the first student to enroll at the new university). We left lush and verdant Oregon for the dry, brown, rocky spot where cows grazed and set up a laboratory in a temporary building (which, of course, is still in use, several decades later, for other purposes). While the new Irvine campus buildings were being constructed. Becky and I settled nearby and have remained here for almost four decades. Our third child, Linda, was born during those early days.

At the new laboratory our first order of business was to provide additionally convincing evidence that drugs do, in fact, enhance memory when administered posttraining and, additionally, do so in several kinds of learning tasks. Thus, we conducted massive experiments with many drugs, doses, and times of injections before and after training Although the reviewers and editors now said, "it isn't new," the papers were published (e.g., Krivanek & McGaugh, 1968, 1969; Luttges & McGaugh, 1971; McGaugh & Krivanek, 1970). Other graduate students (including Philip Landfield and Steven Zornetzer) as well as postdoctoral students (including Paul Gold, coeditor of this volume) also joined the laboratory. Although the evidence of posttraining enhancement of memory by drugs was, by this time, well established (McGaugh, 1973; McGaugh & Herz, 1972; McGaugh, Zornetzer, Gold, & Landfield, 1972), the origins of the idea and evidence are perhaps obscured by the mists of time, or as one of my colleagues once put it, "the great sludge of history." We reached the third stage.

Accelerando

Our findings (and those of many other laboratories), that it is relatively easy to enhance memory consolidation with drugs administered posttraining, raised an interesting and important question. Are there endogenous neuromodulatory systems that normally regulate memory consolidation? This question has guided most of the research in my laboratory for the past three decades. The initial study by Gold conducted in my laboratory (Gold & van Buskirk, 1975) investigating this issue found that, as with CNS stimulants, memory is enhanced by posttraining injections of epinephrine, an adrenal medullary hormone normally released following training. Modulation of memory storage is initiated out in the body.

This finding stimulated a cascade of studies examining the effects of epinephrine and other hormones (Introini-Collison & McGaugh, 1991; McGaugh, 1983, 1989b; McGaugh & Gold, 1989; McGaugh et al., 1982) including, more recently, glucocorticoids released from the adrenal cortex (Roozendaal, 2000). These findings raised the obvious question of where and how the hormones act in the brain to influence memory consolidation. As Gold and I were also investigating the effects of amygdala stimulation on memory in the mid-1970s (McGaugh & Gold, 1976), this area became a prime target of inquiry as a possible site of influences of drugs and hormones on memory consolidation. In an extensive series of studies, graduate and postdoctoral students in my laboratory found that many hormones and drugs regulate memory consolidation through influences involving the release of norepinephrine in the amygdala and that a subregion of the amygdala is critically important in mediating such influences (McGaugh et al., 1990). Moreover, the effects involve activation of memory storage in other brain regions. Gold also subsequently found evidence indicating that epinephrine effects are mediated, in part, by activating the release of glucose. As these issues are the topics of many of the chapters in this volume and are reviewed in several papers (Cahill & McGaugh, 1998; McGaugh, 2000; McGaugh, Cahill, Ferry, & Roozendaal, 2000; McGaugh, Cahill, Parent, et al., 1995; McGaugh, Cahill, & Roozendaal, 1996; McGaugh, Ferry, Vazdarjanova, & Roozendaal, 2000; McGaugh, Roozendaal, & Cahill, 1999; Packard, Williams, Cahill, & McGaugh, 1995), I will not discuss the details in this brief chapter.

Coda

This completes the overture. I have tried to provide some background and context for some of the research reported in the following chapters. Much, but not all, of the work reported in this volume is in some way derived from or related to the early finding from my laboratory reported in the 1950s, 1960s, and 1970s. The work of my former (and present) students and colleagues reported in the chapters in this volume is remarkable in its breadth, originality, and impact. The findings provide significant understanding of mechanisms underlying processes only imagined by Mueller and Pilzecker, Hebb, and Gerard. This *coda* is only for the first century of research on the systems regulating memory. As the findings reported in this volume indicate, the players are clearly tuning up for the overture to the second century.

References

Breen, R. A., & McGaugh, J. L. (1961). Facilitation of maze learning with posttrial injections of picrotoxin. *Journal of Comparative and Physiological Psychology, 54*, 498–501.

Cahill, L., & McGaugh, J. L. (1998). Mechanisms of emotional arousal and lasting declarative memory. *Trends in Neuroscience, 21*, 294–299.

Duncan, C. P. (1949). The retroactive effect of electroshock on learning. *Journal of Comparative and Physiological Psychology, 42*, 32–42.

Gerard, R. (1949). Physiology and psychiatry. *American Journal of Psychiatry, 106*, 225–230.

Gold, P. E., & van Buskirk, R. (1975). Facilitation of time-dependent memory processes with posttrial epinephrine injections. *Behavioral Biology, 13*, 145–153.

Hebb, D. O. (1949). *The organization of behavior*. New York: Wiley.

Introini-Collison, I. B., & McGaugh, J. L. (1991). Interaction of hormones and neurotransmitter systems in the modulation of memory storage. In R. C. A. Frederickson, J. L. McGaugh, & D. L. Felten (Eds.), *Peripheral signaling of the brain: Role in neural immune interactions, learning and memory* (pp. 275–302). Toronto: Hogrefe & Huber.

Jarvik, M. (1964). The influence of drugs upon memory. In H. Steinberg, A. V. S. deReuck, & J. Knight (Eds.), *Animal Behaviour and Drug Action* (pp. 4–61). London: Churchill.

Krivanek, J., & McGaugh, J. L. (1968). Effects of pentylenetetrazol on memory storage in mice. *Psychopharmacologia, 12*, 303–321.

Krivanek, J. A., & McGaugh, J. L. (1969). Facilitating effects of pre- and posttrial amphetamine administration on discrimination learning in mice. *Agents and Actions, 1*, 36–42.

Lashley, K. S. (1917). The effect of strychnine and caffeine upon rate of learning. *Psychobiology, 1*, 141–170.

Luttges, M. W., & McGaugh, J. L. (1970). Facilitating effects of bemegride on retention of a visual discrimination task. *Agents and Actions, 1*, 234–239.

McGaugh, J. L. (1973). Drug facilitation of learning and memory. *Annual Review of Pharmacology, 13*, 229–241.

McGaugh, J. L. (1983). Hormonal influences on memory. *Annual Review of Psychology, 34*, 297–323.

McGaugh, J. L. (1989a). Dissociating learning and performance: Drug and hormone enhancement of memory storage. *Brain Research Bulletin, 23*, 339–345.

McGaugh, J. L. (1989b). Involvement of hormonal and neuromodulatory systems in the regulation of memory storage. *Annual Review of Neuroscience, 12*, 255–287.

McGaugh, J. L. (2000). Memory: A century of consolidation. *Science, 287,* 248–251.

McGaugh, J. L., Cahill, L., Ferry, B., & Roozendaal, B. (2000). Brain systems and the regulation of memory consolidation. In J. J. Bolhuis (Ed.), *Brain, perception, memory: Advances in cognitive neuroscience* (pp. 233–252). London: Oxford University Press.

McGaugh, J. L., Cahill, L., Parent, M. B., Mesches, M. H., Coleman-Mesches, K., & Salinas, J. A. (1995). Involvement of the amygdala in the regulation of memory storage. In J. L. McGaugh, F. Bermudez-Rattoni, & R. A. Prado-Alcala (Eds.), *Plasticity in the central nervous system: Learning and memory* (pp. 17–40). Hillsdale, NJ: Erlbaum.

McGaugh, J. L., Cahill, L., & Roozendaal, B. (1996). Involvement of the amygdala in memory storage: Interaction with other brain systems. *Proceedings of the National Academy of Sciences, 93*, 13508–13514.

McGaugh, J. L., Ferry, B., Vazdarjanova, A., & Roozendaal, B. (2000). Amygdala: Role in modulation of memory storage. In J. P. Aggleton (Ed.), *The amygdala: A functional analysis* (pp. 391–424). London: Oxford University Press.

McGaugh, J. L., & Gold, P. E. (1976). Modulation of memory by electrical stimulation of the brain. In M. R. Rosenzweig & E. L. Bennett (Eds.), *Neural mechanisms of learning and memory* (pp. 549–560). Cambridge, MA: MIT Press.

McGaugh, J. L., & Gold, P. E. (1989). Hormonal modulation of memory. In R. B. Brush & S. Levine (Eds.), *Psychoendocrinology* (pp. 305–339). New York: Academic Press.

McGaugh, J. L., & Herz, M. J. (1972). *Memory consolidation.* San Francisco: Albion.

McGaugh, J. L., Introini-Collison, I. B., Nagahara, A. H., Cahill, L., Brioni, J. D., & Castellano, C. (1990). Involvement of the amygdaloid complex in neuromodulatory influences on memory storage. *Neuroscience and Biobehavioral Reviews, 14*, 425–431.

McGaugh, J. L., & Krivanek, J. (1970). Strychnine effects on discrimination learning in mice: Effects of dose and time of administration. *Physiology and Behavior, 5*, 1437–1442.

McGaugh, J. L., Martinez, J. L., Jr., Messing, R. B., Liang, K. C., Jensen, R. A., Vasquez, B. J., & Rigter, H. (1982). Role of neurohormones as modulators of memory storage. In E. Costa & M. Trabucchi (Eds.), *Regulatory peptides: From molecular biology to function* (pp. 123–130). New York: Raven Press.

McGaugh, J. L., & Petrinovich, L. (1959). The effect of strychnine sulphate on maze-learning. *American Journal of Psychology, 72,* 99–102.

McGaugh, J. L., & Petrinovich, L. F. (1965). Effects of drugs on learning and memory. *International Review of Neurobiology, 8,* 139–196.

McGaugh, J. L., Roozendaal, B., & Cahill, L. (1999). Modulation of memory storage by stress hormones and the amygdaloid complex. In M. Gazzaniga (Ed.), *Cognitive neuroscience* (2nd ed., pp. 1081–1098). Cambridge, MA: MIT Press.

McGaugh, J. L., Zornetzer, S. F., Gold, P. E., & Landfield, P. W. (1972). Modification of memory systems: Some neurobiological aspects. *Quarterly Reviews of Biophysics, 5,* 163–186.

Mueller, G. E., & Pilzecker, A. (1900). Experimentelle Beitraege zur Lehre vom Gedaechtnis [Experimental contributions to the study of memory]. *Z. Psychol. Ergaenzungband, 1,* 1–300.

Packard, M. G., Williams, C. L., Cahill, L., & McGaugh, J. L. (1995). The anatomy of a memory modulatory system: From periphery to brain. In N. E. Spear, L. Spear, & M. Woodruff (Eds.), *Neurobehavioral plasticity: Learning, development and response to brain insults* (pp. 149–184). Hillsdale, NJ: Erlbaum.

Petrinovich, L., Bradford, D., & McGaugh, J. L. (1965). Drug facilitation of memory in rats. *Psychonomic Science, 2,* 191–192.

Roozendaal, B. (2000). Glucocorticoids and the regulation of memory consolidation. *Psychoneuroendocrinology, 25,* 213–238.

Westbrook, W. H., & McGaugh, J. L. (1964). Drug facilitation of latent learning. *Psychopharmacologia, 5,* 440–446.

Woodworth, R. S. (1938). *Experimental psychology.* New York: Henry Holt.

CHAPTER 2

It's About Time

Aryeh Routtenberg

It was apparent to Gerhard Muller and Adolph Pilzecker nearly a century ago that insults to the brain that caused amnesia could be effective depending on the time interval between the insult and the learning (see Glickman, 1961; McGaugh, 1966, for reviews). What this meant then was that there were two processes important for memory storage: perseveration of neural activity followed by consolidation of that perseverative trace. These initial views at the turn of the century were based on clinical information that the perseverative process appeared susceptible to head trauma so that recent events were lost from memory. But more distant memories that had entered the consolidation phase were not susceptible and so survived.

An interesting parallel exists with normal aging in which recent events are more susceptible and seem difficult to store, while older memories persist and may appear to be resurrected ("reminiscence") and gain strength. An individual from such a cohort, due to the weakening of the perseverative process, can also forget the act of such recollection, repeating the sweet memories of youth that give such reminiscent pleasure to the old and consternating impatience to the young.

This two-stage process also is at the heart of the neurophysiological postulate advanced by D. O. Hebb (1949) insofar as the "repeated and persistent activity" represented perseveration and "growth process and metabolic change" the consolidation phase. Here I find that my own academic history brushes up against those of some early pioneers. Having taken my first course in psychology from Hebb, I was sent to Northwestern by Peter Milner to study with Steve Glickman for 3 years, and with Jim Olds in Ann Arbor. Taking my one and only faculty position at Northwestern, (*vide supra* re reminiscence), I found myself across the hall from Carl Duncan who demonstrated in the same year as Hebb articulated his two-stage theory the time-dependent memory loss using electroconvulsive shock at different intervals after learning (Duncan, 1949). The translation of such early studies to more modern ones was spurred by one of Hebb's students, Glickman (1961), who carried out brain stimulation experiments to understand the brain locales where the perseverative process might take place, focusing on the reticular formation, a region of the brain studied by Don Lindsley, a physiological psychologist at Northwestern before Glickman. When Glickman left Northwestern for an Ann Arbor faculty position, I moved back to Northwestern from Ann Arbor in 1965, fortunate to have been instructed and surrounded by a rich tradition of studies on the process of memory formation.

I distinctly recall that at this period I had read this article on memory as a time-dependent process that had the effect of focusing these early efforts, a galvanizing moment that remains to this day the articulate statement of the concept that memory storage is a time-dependent process. Written by the man we honored at a meeting in 1998 (which became the foundation of this book), this seminal review clearly demonstrated, using disruptive and facilitative treatments in both negative and positive reinforcing situations, the time-dependent nature of memory (McGaugh, 1966).

As others will discuss these findings and their fruitfulness for current research, at that level of analysis, I have chosen to focus my remarks on the following concept: that memory-manipulating agents have their site of action on molecular events requiring protein kinase participation, each of which has an identifiable onset and termination time point. Thus, while the experience of events and the memories formed may be continuous, the underlying molecular processes, it will be shown, are clearly discontinuous and have unexpected but clearly defined time courses.

Molecular Events Ordered on a Time Scale

A few years ago, Colley and I (1993) advanced what was, to our knowledge, the first and perhaps still the only effort to schematize long-term potentiation (LTP), a physiological model of information storage (Bliss & Collingridge, 1993), as a series of sequential and parallel molecular events occurring over time in both presynaptic and postsynaptic compartments. This "synaptic dialogue" model of plasticity was recently shown to have application to the logic of the Hebb synapse (Routtenberg, 1999). It takes as its starting point transmitter release and receptor activation, focusing on the glutamate system. (It is surprising how few studies on regulation of the glutamate system have been carried out in relation to studies of memory in contrast to the multitude of studies of glutamate and LTP, with some notable exceptions; see Morris, 1989.) The efficacy of such neurotransmission will depend on the state of that synapse prior to the invasion of the action potential. So we begin the "plasticity time line" with the pre-event time point.

One theme that emerges in this review is that protein kinases play a central role in regulating the amplitude and kinetics of the response, ultimately deter-mining whether the information is stored. Even though these enzymes are ar-chitects for the orchestration of nanosecond biochemical responses to millisec-ond electrophysiological signals, as seen later, they can also play a central role in memory storage processes that last for days.

Stage 1: Immediately Prior to Event

There are a variety of state-dependent conditions that regulate the intensity and duration of the neurotransmitter response. Thus, the phosphorylation state of proteins regulating calcium channels in the presynaptic terminal, the amount of calcium bound to exocytotic protein machinery (EPM; Sudhof, 1995) prior to activation of the terminal, will determine the rate and extent of transmitter release. We know from studies on NMDA (n-methyl-D-aspartate) receptor an-tagonists such as APV (l-amino-5-phosphonovaleric acid) that if that receptor is not available at the time of the event (behavioral learning or electrical tetanus) that behavioral change does not occur. We also know from the series of studies of Gold and McGaugh (1989) that regulating the state with adrenergic agents has a powerful impact on what will be stored. We know from biochemical studies dating back to the Nobel prize-winning work of Earl Sutherland (Suth-erland & Robinson, 1969) that adrenergic agents regulate the kinase cascade that determines the rate of glucose and glycogen metabolism.

Even the sodium channel is subject to regulation by kinases. To understand the cellular role of protein kinase C (PKC), David Linden and I (1988) studied sodium and calcium channels regulated by lipid-activated PKC. To our surprise we found a 30–40% reduction in both these currents. Although it is well known that calcium channels are closely associated with synaptic change (Grover & Teyler, 1990) and memory (Deyo & Straube, 1989), it is only re-cently appreciated how sodium channels present in the dendritic arbor may also regulate the malleability of synapses (Golding & Spruston, 1998; Linden, & Routtenberg, 1988).

The induction is clear: The state of kinase activity prior to the event de-termines the initial neuronal response; the amplitude and kinetics of the acti-vation will, in turn, determine whether memory storage will occur. Because memory-manipulating drugs also affect postevent processes, it is important to recognize the possibility that the same agent may act on different molecular events depending on the time of drug manipulation. Thus, we can cast in molecular terms evidence from memory modulator studies: that one target of these modulators are the protein kinases that can regulate (a) transmitter bio-synthesis by phosphorylating rate-limiting enzymes necessary for transmitter biosynthesis; (b) release of transmitter by phosphorylating calcium channels; and (c) transmitter receptor kinetics by phosphorylating, for example, the glutamate receptors, AMPA (alpha-amino-3-hydroxy-5-methyl-isoxazole-4-propionic acid), NMDA, and mGluR (metabotropic glutamate receptor).

It is now possible to show, using transgenic mice, that altering the phosphorylation state of a protein substrate of a protein kinase prior to the behavioral learning or the tetanus of a pathway can have a major impact on the response (e.g., Routtenberg, Serrano, Cantallops, Zaffuto, & Namgung, 2000). Whether this effect is directly related to altered regulation of transmitter function has not yet been established. In the future it should be possible to design constructs for transgenic mice to answer this question. What is clear at the present is that the pre-event state of phosphorylation of proteins that are targets for protein kinases will determine the amplitude and kinetics of the response to the learning event.

Stages 2 and 3: During and Immediately After the Event

We can start by differentiating between the Stages 2 and 3 in the context of the participation of such molecules as the NMDA receptor, which is explicitly required for the initiation of the plastic response (Stage 2), but once initiated, plays no further role. This is likely to apply to the AMPA receptor as well, another glutamate receptor with different ion-gating properties. The metabotropic receptor, particularly those located presynaptically, are likely to be downstream of these initial events. It is instructive to note that the role of calmodulin kinase II also appears to be important in Stage 2 but not at this subsequent stage (Otmakhov, Griffith, & Lisman, 1997). This contrasts with the PKC enzyme, which appears to refrain from participation in Stages 2 and 3 but engages at the time of Stage 4. In general, then, Stage 2 can be differentiated from Stage 3 by the fact that certain agents work before but not immediately after the event. The class of drugs that are effective immediately after the event in Stage 3 but not during the event in Stage 2, to my knowledge, has not been identified.

Stage 4: A Few Minutes After the Event

When the idea that kinases could modify proteins already present within the synapse to effect change emerged (Routtenberg, 1979), it was with the view that these were synaptic transmission processes set into motion by the event itself. It was thus a watershed moment in my laboratory when we found that certain kinase inhibitors were effective for a time-limited duration after the event occurred. Specifically, PKC inhibitor effects on LTP suggested that the enzyme was recruited after the tetanus and the potentiated response occurred and appeared to be active at about 30–60 minutes but not thereafter. Although there remains some debate in defining these time frames, the basic finding has remained clear. Moreover, this evidence opened the door to the notion that the experience of an external event was setting into motion a sequence of parallel molecular events that could have time courses essentially of any duration and initiated at any time, even days after the event. Although this seemed a guess at that time, studies reviewed below strongly support to this early notion.

PKC is a signal-transducing enzyme that converts external signals to internal biochemical events (Nishizuka, 1995). Using LTP as a model, we found that PKC inhibitors could perform a feat that no other kinase inhibitor could do: PKC was effective after the potentiated response was established. Importantly, when the inhibitor was given before the tetanus, the potentiated response still persisted for 15 minutes afterward and only then began to decay (Colley et al., 1990). It was suggested that PKC activity might thus be necessary for information storage during the period between 5 minutes and 1 hour after the event. Izquierdo and his group demonstrated, indeed, that PKC inhibitors blocked 1-trial step-down avoidance in a time-dependent fashion, consistent with our LTP results (see Jerusalinsky et al., 1994). Moreover, we had observed that PKC translocation occurred not 1 minute but 30 and 60 minutes after LTP (Akers, Lovinger, Colley, Linden, & Routtenberg, 1986). Similarly, the substrate protein phosphorylated by PKC, GAP-43, was also not increased in its phosphorylation 1 minute after LTP but was obvious 15 minutes after tetanus, when the level of its phosphorylation correlated directly with the level of enhancement (Routtenberg, Lovinger, & Steward, 1985).

The purpose of this chapter is to focus on the time-dependent nature of molecular events underlying information storage processes; it is not my intent here to document the evidence for the specific role of particular kinases and their substrates in the process. Readers who wish to explore that terrain can see Benowitz and Routtenberg (1997).

At the time of these observations on PKC inhibitors we were puzzled because it meant that there was a process recruited at some time after the event but not initiated directly by the tetanus. Now we would say that PKC activation was downstream of transmitter release. Perhaps we should have not been so puzzled given the multitude of studies demonstrating posttrial disruption of memory consolidation. But the prevailing view was that the process disrupted had its onset at the time of the event, not initiated at some time thereafter. These considerations are relevant to the hoary question of whether molecular events underlying memory storage are initiated simultaneously with different decay kinetics for different molecular processes (parallel model) or alternatively that different events are recruited at different times (serial model) and can have similar or different decay properties (see, for example, Matthies, 1982, for an example of the parallel model). Clearly, comparison of the effects of NMDA receptor antagonists with the effects of PKC inhibitors strongly favor the serial model. Also, the model in Colley and Routtenberg (1993, see Figure 1 in that paper) suggests that there are several serial processes occurring in parallel.

It is now clear that one can identify a particular molecular process with highly defined temporal characteristics. Especially relevant in this regard was the report of Colley and myself (1989), who studied the effect of PKC activation by phorbol esters on LTP expression. Although we replicated our initial observations (Routtenberg, Colley, Linden, Lovinger, & Murakami, 1986) that PKC activation at low doses facilitates LTP (it would be interesting to know if it facilitates learning), we also found that at higher doses of the phorbol ester, given prior to tetanus, actually blocked LTP. This result was consistent with our biochemical studies, taking the conclusion one step further. Not only is PKC activated after the event, it is explicitly inactivated at the time of the tetanus and shortly thereafter, because if it were active, then the plastic response would not occur. For example, PKC can regulate NMDA receptor function; if it were to decrease its function at the time of the tetanus or behavioral event, then it would be inhibitory rather than facilitatory. Thus, its inhibition by endogenous factors (Routtenberg, 1993) is an appealing thought.

It would be instructive to consider other kinases, calmodulin kinase and cAMP-dependent kinases, in the process, but given limitations of space, suffice to say that there is evidence for their involvement at particular time points. In contrast to calmodulin kinase, cAMP kinases may be responsible only for more persistent aspects of the response, inhibitors having their effect at the 4–6 hour time point, possibly on transcription factor function, to be discussed. The available evidence suggests that tyrosine kinases may be effective at the time of the tetanus (Grant et al., 1992).

In summary of this section, as suggested over 20 years ago (Holian, Brunngraber, & Routtenberg, 1972; Routtenberg, 1979). modification of existing proteins already positioned at synapses to be modified solves the problem of synaptic specificity (Frey & Morris, 1997), because rapid changes in protein function can occur at the site of change. What has been learned in recent years is that the enzymes are recruited at different points in time and so are susceptible to blockade only at that time at which they are recruited.

It may be surprising to imagine that in the first 15 minutes after an event occurs transcription factors, proteins that bind to the noncoding region of the DNA, are also being regulated by kinases. In the same way that we think of the rapid change of synapses occurring due to rapid phosphorylation of synaptic proteins, so to is it necessary to think about the phosphorylation of transcription factors as regulating gene expression from the "get go."

This statement is suggested by a few experiments in our laboratory that were initiated because of evidence that gene regulation through transcription factors was mediated by phosphorylation of transcription factors. Our initial study cast a wide net hunting for transcription factors that would rapidly respond to a brief experience, one that would be overwhelming for a rat living in relative austerity in a plastic amber cage, with wire roof overhead and sawdust on the floor. Taking the animal's perspective, we refer to the experiment as the "Grand Canyon Study." In fact, we simply exposed rats to an 8-arm radial maze for 4 minutes, and then 5, 10, 30 and 60 minutes thereafter we removed the dorsal hippocampus and performed an electrophoretic mobility shift assay (EMSA) to study transcription factor binding to recognition elements (consensus nucleotide sequences of DNA that are located in the 5′ non-coding region of the eukaryotic gene that bind a particular transcription factor). We studied nine different recognition elements, CRE and AP-1 among them. Kinney and I (1993) found that CREB (the cyclic AMP recognition element binding protein) was altered in its binding to CRE (the cyclic AMP recognition element). This was also the case for AP-1 (the Fos-Jun recognition element).

We were initially surprised to find how rapid the increase in binding was after the rats had seen the grand canyon. The binding of CREB to its recognition element had the following time course: After the brief 4-minute exposure, there was no detectable increase in binding at 5 or 15 minute after the event. There was an increase in binding at 30 minutes. At 1 hour an increase in binding was observed in other bands, which is discussed in the next section. (As pointed out by Guzowski and McGaugh [1997], these time-dependent processes are inaccessible in knock out studies of CREB; see Bourtchuladze et al., 1994.)

What could account for this narrow window of activation of the CREB transcription factor? We suggested, based on the evidence that protein kinase can regulate CREB activity (Montminy, 1997), that binding was turned on by CREB phosphorylation and turned off by CREB dephosphorylation. Why the delay until 30 minutes? One attractive possibility is that events at the synapse send signals to the nucleus that lead to phosphorylation of CREB. We return to this idea when considering another kinase regulated TF, NF-kB, where its subcellular location makes it an attractive signal.

Although the narrow time frame of CREB activation was surprising, one other result took us aback yet again. With the thought to increase the size of the effect, as in more is better, instead of 4 minutes we exposed the animals to the maze for 15 minutes. This additional 11 minutes of exposure to the maze completely turned off the increased binding. After shaking our heads, we returned to our ethological roots observing the behavior of the animal. We saw with our eyes that after 4–8 minutes of vigorous exploration, the animal, at the 15-minute time point, was essentially immobile in a shady part of the environment. Clearly the maze was now no longer novel, possibly even approaching boring, during the last 5 minutes of the 15-minute time period in the maze. We speculated that during the last 5-minute period, CREB, which was phosphorylated during the first 4 minutes and remained so until 30 minutes, was actively dephosphorylated at 10–15 minutes, and thus no detectable effect was observed.

These findings make it clear that TFs that bind to recognition elements on DNA located in the nucleus regulating gene expression can reflect and react to different states of the organism nearly on a minute-to-minute basis. Whether this is solely mediated by phosphorylation remains to be determined. But it is thus to be emphasized that environmentally sensitive gene regulation can occur without the synthesis of immediate early genes but rather by the posttranslational modification of existing transcription factors.

Although I have used CREB as an example, it is important to emphasize that TFs work only because of their combinatorial properties (Struhl, 1991). That is, TFs binding to each other and to recognition elements form supramolecular complexes of several different proteins, which then provide the combination necessary to trigger transcription. Thus, at various sites along the DNA promoter sequence possibly hundreds of protein brothers, sisters, and distant relatives (enhancers, repressors, terminators, etc.) bind to recognition elements to determine gene expression. To illustrate this point, if one carries out a computer search on the first 1,000 base pairs of the GAP-43 promoter, there are over 50 consensus sequences for known recognition elements. Only recently has any attempt been made to identify sites on the promoter that in fact regulate GAP-43 transcription (Chiarmello, Neuman, Peavy, & Zuber, 1996; Kinney, McNamara, Valcourt, & Routtenberg, 1996).

It is safe to say, then, that CREB alone cannot be sufficient for DNA transcription and for any physiological process such as memory storage. Moreover, when necessity for a particular protein is decided on the basis of evidence from the so-called single-gene knockout approach, one is in a precarious position as there are many interpretive difficulties, thus precluding a firm conclusion (Routtenberg, 1995, 1996). In the case of the CREB knockout, the issue of dominant negative effects is of concern. When determined by antisense techniques (Guzowski & McGaugh, 1997), it demonstrates CREB participation, but only in the sense that it is one part of the key that opens the transcriptional door. One other sobering thought: If there are 100,000 genes, each with their own promoter, one wonders what percentage contain a CREB recognition site. Thus, the manipulation can have widespread influence, and identifying the key elements would be a very large task indeed.

One other point on the CREB issue bears on the general question of phylogenetic generality of molecular mechanisms. Subsequent to our initial work on CREB, a series of articles appeared that suggested involvement of CREB in nervous system plasticity in a range of animals from fruit fly to rat. This generality was touted by the various authors to point to the inherent fundamental importance of this mechanism (see Frank & Greenberg, 1994). I could not disagree more with this point of view. Indeed, were it the case that CREB activation is central to the production of both fly and mouse memory, then one wonders what mechanism confers the unique properties of mammalian, or, indeed, vertebrate, memory. Those memory processes possessed by the mouse and not by the fly, one would infer, do not involve the CREB mechanism. Put another way, what should be sought are not only these basic processes but also those that are unique to the vertebrate order. The argument used by these authors resurrects reasoning that was used to justify the study of memory in the aplysia, the so-called "alphabet of memory." Now that alphabet has transmogrified into transcription factor acronyms.

Stage 5: One Hour After the Event

Because kinase inhibitors applied to the region of the synapse cease to become effective at 1 hour after LTP is initiated, one is led to believe that this time frame occupies an important transition. Two transcription factors that we have recently studied, because they may be regulated by PKC, are NF-kB and the E-box family (otherwise known as the basic helix–loop–helix [bHLH] family) of transcription factors.

We have found that synthesis of the mRNA (messenger ribonucleic acid) of the NF-kB subunits (known as p50 and p65) are increased 1 hour after an LTP tetanus. But they are also increased after low frequency stimulation. Nonetheless, we have evidence, similar to that for *c-fos* and for TFIIIA (transcription factor IIIA), that increased synthesis of p50 and p65 is a consistent response of brain cells to increased activation. But, because a more rapid response can be effected by kinase modification, what is the reason for the rapid synthesis following the phosphorylation event? As proposed earlier (Meberg, Barnes, McNaughton, & Routtenberg, 1993), those proteins that are phosphorylated are utilized and thus send a signal to the nucleus to make more of that protein. If this proposal has generality it means that the increase in synthesis is not the first step and it is not propelling the target gene synthesis but is replenishing that which has been used. The moniker "immediate, early gene" may be more spin than temporal reality.

Although what has been discussed so far could be taken to mean that more of a transcription factor means more transcription and then more target protein, this could not be further from the truth. The increased synthesis of repressors, regulators, and terminators would necessarily lead to decreased synthesis. Moreover, decreased binding of one of these negative regulators would lead to increased synthesis. A suggested example of this comes from our work on the binding of hippocampal transcription factors to the E-box (Kinney et al., 1996), in which decreased binding is correlated with increased GAP-43 mRNA in a variety of different situations and different in vivo and in vitro systems.

Importantly for the main theme of this chapter, E-box binding decreased 1 hour but not 5 minutes after LTP. Thus the decrease in binding may actually be necessary for an increase in transcriptional activity. This conclusion may be warranted given the report that LTP can alter GAP-43 mRNA even 1 hour after the LTP response.

Ultimately it is the binding of the "combinatorial TFs" to the display of REs on the DNA that determines transcription. At about 1 hour after a brief event there are a multitude of promoter related events that can be identified just from the studies carried out recently in this laboratory. Kinney and I (1994) observed an increase in binding of different CREB bands and of different AP-1 bands after the grand canyon experience, an increased synthesis of NF-kB subunit elements after LTP (Meberg, Kinney, Valcourt, & Routtenberg, 1996) and a decrease in binding to the E-box 1 hour after LTP (Kinney et al, 1996). Thus, we have identified 4 different TFs that are likely to be active at 1 hour after the event; importantly, they are not active before and they are not active 1 hour later. This illustrates two key points: Transcription factors are likely to work in combination never in isolation (also see Xiao et al., 1995, on this point). One can identify molecular events that have a circumscribed time point in which the combination occurs, defining a particular time point in the memory storage process. These specific time points then become targets for drugs that can be selective in time for manipulating that molecular event.

These different events could nonetheless be caused by a single prior event. In particular, I propose that protein kinase activation leads to the recruitment of these different transcription factors. Thus, transmembrane signaling through protein phosphorylation cascades can lead to the multiplicity of events we have witnessed at the same 1-hour time point. It is interesting that posttrial manipulations previously used suggest that by 1 hour, memory disruption is no longer observed. The transition to consolidation is likely occurring at this point in time as the different transcription factors, some of which we have just considered, are mobilized by signal transduction pathways.

Stage 6: Six Hours After the Event

We can also see that there is a time frame about 6 hours after the event that may herald another transition point. Here we find two studies with widely disparate methods pointing to this time point. Guzowski and McGaugh (1997) studied the effect of antisense oligonucleotides to CREB on learning a Morris water maze, and Meberg, Kinney, et al. (1996) observed the effect of kainic acid on E-box binding in hippocampus. The latter study was carried out because it had previously been shown that kainic acid induced GAP-43 mRNA 24 hours after its administration (*vide infra*). We wished to know what would cause such a delay, particularly because we had observed a small but significant increase in GAP-43 mRNA 1 hour after LTP. We assumed that the kainate induction might involve synthesis of transcription factors, followed by prolonged binding, leading to prolonged synthesis (mRNA levels were elevated 10 days after the initial kainate acid administration). What we found was that binding decreased after kainate, nearly significantly so at 6 hours and then significantly at 24 hours. Because the trend was clear, it is safe to say, given the inherent variability in the EMSA, that the process had been set into motion at 6 hours. Interestingly, we only begin to see the elevation of GAP-43 mRNA at 24 hours.

The parallel with the Guzowski and McGaugh (1997) result is clear. The decrease in levels of CREB occur at 6 hours, but the deficiency in retrieval is observed later: The authors report impairment at 48 hours.

Stage 7: Twenty-Four Hours Later

As mentioned earlier, we found that kainic acid induces GAP-43 mRNA in the granule cells of the dorsal hippocampus 24 hours after administration, but not before. Here the function appears to be to promote growth, as can be seen 48 hours after kainate. Although this is an induction event, and hence a special case, because there is normally no GAP-43 in granule cells in the adult, these findings buttress the conclusion warranted earlier: that each external event that is a potential memory to be stored sets into motion signaling pathways that have specific times of onset and termination. Additionally, these events are then subject to manipulation by agents that can facilitate or inhibit the process set into motion, but only at the time of that process.

Stage 8: Two Days Later

We have observed that transcriptional activation of GAP-43 occurs in hilar neurons 48 and 72 hours after LTP but not before at 6, 12, and 24 hours. (Namgung, Matsuyama, & Routtenberg, 1997). As with the kainate study we are faced with the question of the sequence of processes that spans the 48-hour time frame and only begins to emerge 48 hours after the event. It should be noted that at 72 hours we also observe an increase in both transcriptional activation and GAP-43 mRNA, so that it is the case in this instance that the increase in promoter activity leads to an increase in mRNA. (A recent study in our laboratory studying primary transcripts using intronic probes in relation to mRNA levels points to another approach in studying these gene regulatory events; see Namgung & Routtenberg, 2000.) Thus, transcription can be terminated at any point in the reading off of the primary transcript by proteins known as antiterminators (Greenblatt, Nodwell, & Mason, 1993). Thus, while transcription proceeds, mRNA levels remain low. In the case of normal adult hippocampal granule cells, GAP-43 transcription may be prematurely terminated.

If it were assumed that the increase in mRNA points to an increase in protein, it is interesting that at 3 days after LTP we had observed an increase in protein phosphorylation, which we considered to be related to an increase in kinase or substrate synthesis (Lovinger, Akers, Nelson, Barnes, & Routtenberg, 1985). The evidence might suggest that there is an increase in substrate

3 days after the event. Alternatively, there may be an increase in PKC synthesis and no change in GAP-43.

The 2–3 day delay in promoter activation and mRNA synthesis raise the issue, hoary to be sure, of the role of protein synthesis and memory. It is probably safe to say that the prevailing view is that protein synthesis leads to structural changes that are the physical substrate for long-term, lasting memories. I advocate a different view: that protein synthesis occurs in response to need; it is activated when replenishment is required. As such, those proteins synthesized after learning are essentially acting as a reporter for those that have been utilized, i.e., posttranslationally modified. This should be distinguished from the view that protein synthesis is constitutive, because this view refers to the inexorable production of proteins independent of input that are necessary to maintain the cell *qua* cell. The replenishment model points to those proteins utilized in the service of information storage and thus represent a specific recruitment of gene regulatory events that are input dependent.

Stage 9: Weeks, Months, and Years Later

What maintains memories for a lifetime? Here we have little data, although one could marshal evidence from chick imprinting (Meberg, McCabe, & Routtenberg 1996; Sheu, McCabe, Horn, & Routtenberg, 1993) and birdsong learning (Chew, Vicario, & Nottebohm, 1996) to find clues. In the case of imprinting, the initial event can last a lifetime; in the case of birdsong learning, it can last for 1 year. These studies point the way to consideration of molecular events that are capable of spanning years.

Conclusion

It was proposed here that synaptic plasticity leading to information storage requires a dialogue between presynaptic and postsynaptic elements. This dialogue takes place over time: The opening line is glutamate release, then the NMDA receptor dependent retort of retrograde signaling, leading to modification of presynaptic release processes, followed by the answered alteration in postsynaptic receptor sensitivity; this alteration in sensitivity in turn sends a strong message to the presynaptic terminal to then signal the nucleus via retrograde axonal signals, thereby regulating gene expression of presynaptic proteins to be shipped to the terminal. Available evidence, as well as decorous and restrained speculation about the pivotal role of protein kinases in each stage, can be mobilized to indicate how McGauvian manipulations that demonstrate time-dependent memory storage processes would necessarily interfere with different stages of the synaptic dialogue recruited in the service of knowledge acquisition.

Following are a few generalizations to be gleaned from this chapter:

1. There is no particular time point that can be identified as involved with STP and LTP. There is a molecular process occurring at every time after the event, and thus a memory stage is continuous behaviorally, but discontinuous and overlapping, at the molecular level.

2. Protein synthesis is not important for memory formation. Its requirement is based on the need to replenish proteins that have been utilized, posttranslationally modified, translocated, and proteolytically cleaved.

3. Synaptic tagging is not required, because all the events necessary to maintain the synapse in an altered state are transported to that region and recruited in a use-dependent manner.

4. No single transcription factor, for example, CREB, is responsible for regulating transcription, much less memory. Moreover, a decrease in its level does not mean that there is a decrease in transcription. Quite the opposite may be the case.

5. Collating data from our laboratory over the past 10 years, I can safely say that particular molecular events can be tracked over the course of the first 10 days.

6. Learning recruits a series of distinct molecular events that lead to information storage. Each event can be initiated at any time and can be terminated at any time after learning. The cohort of events overlap so that as a superordinate there are no apparent time gaps.

7. Time points of vulnerability to different agents depends wholly on the point in time when that molecular event targeted by that agent is engaged.

My intent in this brief chapter was to point out that an event sets into motion a sequence of parallel and serial processes, signaling pathways, that extend out probably for the lifetime of the individual, but we can track it for at least a few days after the event. Although I have taken work from this laboratory to illustrate the main conclusion, it is likely that others could review their own contributions in the "It's about time" frame of mind and arrive at the same conclusion. I hope that this contribution will encourage such an enterprise.

It is remarkable indeed that, while events rapidly pass before us as we stare out the window at the passing landscape that is the sequence of our life experiences, each event must somehow set into motion a molecular sequence of events that remains intact. How could the single cell keep these molecular events lined up in temporal order? There are principles yet to be discerned to answer this question.

The recent report by Frey and Morris (1997) is a first valiant effort to answer this question. I have argued elsewhere (1999) that the second effort would require consideration of both sides of the synapse. Indeed, although I have made a perfunctory bow to this issue, the issue was not more deeply considered. Now there is good reason to believe that the "synaptic dialogue" model may help understand facilitation of learning by GAP-43 overexpression in transgenic mice (Routtenberg et al., 2000), but some caution is always required when using gene targeting (Routtenberg, 1996). One needs to consider the alternative models before addressing this issue: One model states that protein synthesis leads to a product that consolidates the synapse, changes its structure, and so promotes long-term memory. The other model, which I favor currently, is that synaptic change requires posttranslational modification and that protein synthesis is recruited to replenish utilized macromolecules. Evidence from this laboratory and others exists to support this latter view (Namgung et al., 1997).

At the beginning of this chapter I noted briefly the pleasures of reminiscence, certainly an example of lifetime memories, that may gain strength as the capacity to form new memories diminishes. This book, and the meeting that inspired it, give me hope that I might sustain both: the pleasure of a friendship that has spanned many years and thus is suitable grist for ample wandering dialogue and the pleasure of the present where we can form new memories replenishing and adding to that cherished repository of reminiscences.

References

Akers, R., Lovinger, D., Colley, P., Linden, D., & Routtenberg, A. (1986). Translocation of protein kinase C activity after long-term potentiation may mediate synaptic plasticity. *Science, 231,* 587–589.

Benowitz, L. I., & Routtenberg, A. (1997). GAP-43: An intrinsic determinant of neuronal development and plasticity. *Trends in Neuroscience, 20,* 84–91.

Bliss, T. V. P., & Collingridge, G. L. (1993). A synaptic model of memory: LTP in the hippocampus. *Nature, 361,* 31–39.

Bliss, T. P. V., Douglas, R. M., Errington, M. L., & Lynch, M. A. (1986). Correlation between long-term potentiation and release of endogenous amino acids from dentate gyrus of anaesthetized rats. *Journal of Physiology (London), 377,* 391–408.

Bourtchuladze, R., Frenguelli, B., Blendy, J., Cioffi, D., Schutz, G., & Silva, A. J. (1994). Deficient long-term memory in mice with a targeted mutation of the cAMP-responsive element-binding protein. *Cell, 79,* 59–68.

Cantallops, I., & Routtenberg, A. (1996). Rapid induction by kainic acid of both axonal growth and F1/GAP-43 protein in the adult rat hippocampal granule cells. *Journal of Comparative Neurology, 366*, 303–319.

Chew, S. J., Vicario, D. S., & Nottebohm, F. (1996). Quantal duration of auditory memories. *Science, 274*, 1909–1914.

Chiaramello, A., Neuman, T., Peavy, D. R., & Zuber, M. X. (1996). The GAP-43 gene is a direct downstream target of the basic helix–loop–helix transcription factors. *Journal of Biological Chemistry, 271*, 22035–22043.

Colley, P. A., & Routtenberg, A. (1989). Dose-dependent phorbol ester facilitation or blockade of hippocampal long-term potentiation: Relation to membrane/cytosol distribution of protein kinase C activity. *Brain Research, 495*, 205–216.

Colley, P. A., & Routtenberg, A. (1993). Long-term potentiation as synaptic dialogue. *Brain Research Reviews, 18*, 115–122.

Colley, P. A., Sheu, F.-S., & Routtenberg, A. (1990). Inhibition of protein kinase C blocks two components of LTP persistence leaving initial potentiation intact. *Journal of Neuroscience, 10*, 3353–3360.

Deyo, R. A., & Straube, K. T. (1989). Disterhoft JF Nimodipine facilitates associative learning in aging rabbits. *Science, 243*, 809–811.

Duncan, C. P. (1949). The retroactive effect of electroshock on learning. *Journal of Comparative and Physiological Psychology, 42*, 32–44.

Frank, D. A., & Greenberg, M. E. (1994). CREB: A mediator of long-term memory from mollusks to mammals. *Cell, 79*, 5–8.

Frey, U., & Morris, R. G. M. (1997). Synaptic tagging and long-term potentiation. *Nature, 385*, 533–536.

Glickman, S. E. (1961). Perseverative neural processes and consolidation of the memory trace. *Psychological Bulletin, 58*, 218–233.

Gold, P. E., & McGaugh, J. L. (1975). A single-trace, two process view of memory storage processes. In D. Deutsch & J. A. Deutsch (Eds.), *Short-term memory* (pp. 355–378). New York: Academic Press.

Golding, N. L., & Spruston, N. (1998). Dendritic sodium spikes are variable triggers of axonal action potentials in hippocampal CA1 pyramidal neurons. *Neuron, 21*, 1189–1200.

Grant, S. G., O'Dell, T. J., Karl, K. A., Stein, P. L., Soriano, P., & Kandel, E. R. (1992). Impaired long-term potentiation, spatial learning, and hippocampal development in fyn mutant mice. *Science, 258*, 1903–1910.

Greenblatt, J., Nodwell, J. R., & Mason, S. W. (1993). Transcriptional antitermination. *Nature, 364*, 401–406.

Grover, L. M., & Teyler, T. J. (1990). Two components of long-term potentiation induced by different patterns of afferent activation. *Nature, 347*, 477–479.

Guzowski, J. F., & McGaugh, J. L. (1997). Antisense oligodeoxynucleotide-mediated disruption of hippocampal CREB protein levels impairs memory of a spatial task. *Proceedings of the National Academy of Sciences (USA), 94*, 2693–2698.

Hebb, D. O. (1949). *Organization of behavior.* New York: Wiley.

Holian, O., Brunngraber, E. G., & Routtenberg, A. (1971). Memory consolidation and glycoprotein metabolism: A failure to find a relationship. *Life Sciences, 10,* 1029–1035.

Jerusalinsky, D., Quillfeldt, J. A., Walz, R., Da Silva, R. C., Medina, J. H., & Izquierdo, I. (1994). Post-training intrahippocampal infusion of protein kinase C inhibitors causes amnesia in rats. *Behavioral and Neural Biology, 61,* 107–109.

Kinney, W. R., McNamara, R. K., Valcourt, E. G., & Routtenberg, A. (1996). Prolonged alteration in E-box binding after a single systemic kainate injection: Potential relation to F1/GAP-43 gene expression. *Molecular Brain Research, 38,* 25–36.

Kinney, W., & Routtenberg, A. (1993). Brief exposure to a novel environment enhances binding of hippocampal transcription factors to DNA. *Molecular Brain Research, 20,* 147–152.

Linden, D. J., & Routtenberg, A. (1988). Cis-fatty acids, which activate protein kinase C, attenuate voltage-dependent Na+ current in mouse neuroblastoma cells. *Journal of Physiology (London), 419,* 95–119.

Linden, D. J., & Routtenberg, A. (1989). The role of protein kinase C in long-term potentiation: A testable model. *Brain Research Reviews, 14,* 279–296.

Lovinger, D. M., Akers, R., Nelson, R., Barnes, C. A., & Routtenberg, A. (1985). A selective increase in hippocampal protein F1 phosphorylation directly related to three-day growth of long-term synaptic enhancement. *Brain Research, 343,* 137–143.

Matthies, H.-J. (1982). Stages of memory formulation. In C. A. Marsden & H. Matthies (Eds.), *Mechanisms and models of neural plasticity* (Proceedings of the 11th International Neurobiology IBRO Symposium on Learning and Memory, Vol. 9, pp. 17–24). New York: Raven Press.

McGaugh, J. L. (1966). Time-dependent processes in memory storage. *Science, 153,* 1351–1358.

McNamara, R. K., Namgung, U., & Routtenberg, A. (1996). Distinctions between mouse and rat hippocampus: Protein F1/GAP-43 gene expression, promoter activity, spatial memory. *Molecular Brain Research, 40,* 177–187.

Meberg, P. J., Barnes, C. A., McNaughton, B. L., & Routtenberg, A. (1993). Protein kinase C and F1/GAP-43 gene expression in hippocampus inversely related to synaptic enhancement lasting 3 days. *Proceedings of the National Academy of Sciences (USA), 90,* 12050–12054.

Meberg, P. J., Kinney, W. R., Valcourt, E. G., & Routtenberg, A. (1996). Gene expression of the transcription factor NF-κB in hippocampus: Regulation by synaptic activity. *Molecular Brain Research, 38,* 179–190.

Meberg, P. J., McCabe, B. J., & Routtenberg, A. (1996). MARCKS and protein F1/GAP-43 RNA in chick brain: Effects of imprinting. *Molecular Brain Research, 35,* 149–156.

Mellor, H., & Parker, P. J. (1998). The extended protein kinase C superfamily. *Biochemical Journal, 332,* 281–292.

Montminy M. (1997). Transcriptional regulation by cyclic AMP. *Annual Review of Biochemistry, 66,* 807–822.

Morris, R. G. (1989). Synaptic plasticity and learning: Selective impairment of learning rats and blockade of long-term potentiation in vivo by the N-methyl-D-aspartate receptor antagonist AP5. *Journal of Neuroscience, 9,* 3040–3057.

Namgung, U., Matsuyama, S., & Routtenberg, A. (1997). Long-term potentiation activates the GAP-43 promoter: Selective participation of hippocampal mossy cells. *Proceedings of the National Academy of Sciences (USA), 94,* 11675–11680.

Namgung, U., & Routtenberg, A. (2000). Transcriptional and post-transcriptional replication of a brain growth protein: Regional differentiation and repenetration insuction of GAP-43. *European Journal of Neuroscience, 12,* 3124–3136.

Namgung, U., Valcourt, E., & Routtenberg, A. (1995). Long-term potentiation *in vivo* in the intact mouse hippocampus. *Brain Research, 689,* 85–92.

Nishizuka, Y. (1995). Protein kinase C and lipid signaling for sustained cellular responses. *Journal of the Federation of Experimental Societies for Experimental Biology, 9,* 484–496.

Otmakhov N., Griffith L. C., & Lisman, J. E. (1997). Postsynaptic inhibitors of calcium/calmodulin-dependent protein kinase type II block induction but not maintenance of pairing-induced long-term potentiation. *Journal of Neuroscience, 17,* 5357–5365.

Routtenberg, A. (1979). Anatomical localization of phosphoprotein and glycoprotein substrates of memory. *Progress in Neurobiology, 12,* 113.

Routtenberg, A. (1993). Resisting memory storage: Activating endogenous protein kinase C inhibitors. In L. A. Horrocks (Ed.), *Phospholipids and signal transmission* (pp. 151–162). Berlin, Germany: Springer-Verlag.

Routtenberg, A. (1995). Knockout mouse fault lines. *Nature, 374,* 314–315.

Routtenberg, A. (1996). Reverse piedpiperase: Is the knockout mouse leading neuroscientists to a watery end? *Trends in Neuroscience, 19,* 471–472.

Routtenberg, A. (1999). Tagging the Hebb synapse. *Trends in Neuroscience, 22,* 255–256.

Routtenberg, A., Colley, P., Linden, D., Lovinger, D., & Murakami, K. (1986). Phorbol ester promotes growth of synaptic plasticity. *Brain Research, 378,* 374–378.

Routtenberg, A., Lovinger, D. M., & Steward, O. (1985). Selective increase in phosphorylation state of a 47kD protein (F1) directly related to long-term potentiation. *Behavioral and Neural Biology, 43,* 3–11.

Routtenberg, A., Serrano, P., Cantallops, I., Zaffuto, S., & Namgung, U. (2000). Enhanced learning by genetic overexpression of a brain growth protein. *Proceedings of the National Academy of Science, 97,* 7657–7662.

Sheu, F. S., McCabe B. J., Horn G., & Routtenberg A. (1993). Learning selectively increases protein kinase C substrate phosphorylation in specific regions of the chick brain. *Proceedings of the National Academy of Sciences (USA), 90,* 2705–2709.

Struhl, K. (1991). Mechanisms for diversity in gene expression patterns. *Neuron, 7,* 177–181.

Sudhof, T. C. (1995). The synaptic vesicle cycle: A cascade of protein–protein interactions. *Nature, 375,* 645–653.

Sutherland, E. W., & Robinson, R. D. (1969). The role of cyclic AMP in the control of carbohydrate metabolism. *Diabetes, 18,* 797–819.

Xiao, B., Smerdon, S. J., Jones, D. H., Dodson, G. G., Soneji, Y., Aitken, A., & Gamblin, S. J. (1995). Structure of a 14-3-3 protein and implications for coordination of multiple signalling pathways. *Nature, 376,* 188–191.

CHAPTER 3

Synapse-Specific Gene Expression of the IEG Arc:

Insights Into Molecular Processes in Memory Consolidation

Oswald Steward

Christopher S. Wallace

Paul F. Worley

If one were to lay out an obvious strategy for defining the cellular and molecular mechanisms of memory, the first step would probably be to identify the sites of the modifications that underlie memory storage. Then one could go on to determine the cellular and molecular mechanisms that mediate these changes. This systematic strategy has in fact been used to define the cellular mechanisms underlying simple forms of learning in invertebrate systems. This approach has been successful because both the learning and the neural circuits that mediate the learning are simple. Hence, in these "simple systems," it is possible to trace the entire circuit activated during a learning experience from the sensory input to the motor output, assess patterns of activity at each station along this circuit before and after a learning experience, and determine the sites where there was a transformation of input/output patterns that could account for the final change in system output.

In studying the mechanisms of memory in vertebrate systems, the simple systems approach has been much more difficult to apply. The reason is the complexity of the neural systems that mediate even the simplest forms of mem-

The authors thank Christine Duncan, Paula Falk, Debbie Keelean, and Leanna Whitmore for technical assistance. Supported by National Institutes of Health (NIH) Grant NS12333 to O. Steward; National Science Foundation Grant IBN92-22120 to O. Steward; NIH Grant MH 53603 to P. F. Worley; and NIH/National Institute of Neurological Diseases and Stroke Individual NRSA NS0973 to C. S. Wallace.

ory. It is difficult and perhaps impossible to trace all of the circuits activated during a learning experience because of the extent of divergence and parallel transmission in the central nervous system (CNS). Also, it is difficult to determine which routes of information flow are essential to the learning process and which are ancillary. Finally, it is an enormous technical challenge to assess patterns of activity at each station along these circuits to evaluate information transfer before and after a learning experience. For this reason, much of the research on cellular and molecular mechanisms of learning in vertebrates has used more indirect strategies.

Among the indirect strategies, one of the most common is to search for candidate cellular and molecular mechanisms with features that seem consistent with a memory mechanism. It is useful to state explicitly what some expected features are, because they provide an indication of how we would recognize a cellular and molecular mechanism of information storage if one were found. We state these in the following postulates:

1. *Long-term memory storage is mediated by synaptic modifications.* Most current hypotheses posit that memory storage is mediated by some enduring change in synaptic function. It is important to recognize that there are other possibilities, however. For example, there could be a change in the integrative function of a single neuron altering its input/output function. Nevertheless, the idea that the engram is synaptically localized is pervasive. One reason is theoretical; storage capacity is much greater if the unit of the underlying modification is the synapse rather than the entire neuron. The other reasons are that the memory mechanisms defined so far in invertebrates are synaptically based. The key implication of this assumption is that candidate mechanisms that seem most plausible to us at this time are those involving long-term synaptic plasticity.

2. *Modifications that underlie memory are triggered by patterns of activity over the circuits that are modified.* The focus on activity-induced changes in circuits highlights a key implicit assumption—that the mechanism for information storage must be an activity-dependent process. This assertion is based on a simple fact. From the nervous system's point of view, "experience" is represented exclusively by patterns of neuronal activity. Information about the environment reaches the brain in one and only one form—patterns of action potentials carried over sensory pathways. Thus, modifications arising as a result of experience must come about as a result of a particular pattern of action potentials in various pathways. Hence, candidate mechanisms for memory storage must occur as a result of patterns of activity.

3. *Modifications that underlie long-term memory take time to establish.* This is a simple statement of the consolidation hypothesis (Mc-Gaugh, 1966). The conclusion that it takes time for memories to be "consolidated" is based on a host of studies indicating that memory can be disrupted or enhanced by manipulations during a critical time window that extends for several hours after the training event. After that critical period, memory is highly resistant to disruption or modification and is said to be "consolidated." The important conclusion is that candidate mechanisms for long-term memory storage should exhibit a similar time-dependent consolidation process.

It is important to emphasize that candidate mechanisms must not only exhibit a time dependence but also exhibit a transition from labile to stable phases. Moreover, this transition should occur with the same timing as the transition from labile to stable memory. Thus, time-dependent consolidation should be considered a key criterion for a candidate memory mechanism. It is in this context that the work of McGaugh and colleagues has special relevance, because it defines in detail the key temporal features that must be fulfilled by any candidate mechanism.

4. *Modifications that underlie long-term memory require gene expression and new protein synthesis.* This conclusion is based on the fact that blockade of transcription or translation during a critical time window after a training event disrupts memory consolidation. This feature is closely related to the consolidation hypothesis. Hence, cellular events that are induced by activity and that occur during a critical time window after the inducing event warrant special attention.

LTP: Cellular Analog of Memory Mediated by Mechanisms Underlying Memory Storage

The above conclusions are why long-term potentiation (LTP) is considered to be a plausible cellular analog of memory; indeed, there is considerable speculation that the cellular and molecular mechanisms that underlie LTP may also underlie at least some forms of memory storage. Features of LTP that make it an attractive candidate mechanism have been discussed extensively and include (a) its associative nature, (b) its long-lasting nature, (c) its synapse specificity, (d) the fact that it can be induced by patterns of activity that are actually exhibited by CNS neurons, and (e) the fact that the late stages of LTP apparently require new protein synthesis (for recent reviews, see Bailey, Bartsch, & Kandel, 1996; Mayford et al., 1996; Nguyen & Kandel, 1996).

There is considerable information regarding the mechanisms of induction of LTP and the early cellular and molecular events that may be involved in bringing about the initial change in synaptic strength. Much less is known, however, about the molecular and cellular events that may underlie the later, protein synthesis-dependent phase of the synaptic modification. Probably the most important clue is that the establishment of enduring synaptic modifications can be interrupted by inhibiting protein synthesis. Although there are numerous possible interpretations of this general finding, a widely accepted view is that appropriate patterns of activity at individual synapses induce the synthesis of particular proteins that then are critical for establishing enduring modifications. These modifications involve select populations of synapses (synapse specificity) and occur during a critical time window that extends for several hours after the triggering event. Hence, in molecular terms, the epoch of consolidation involves stepwise molecular modifications that are precisely timed and that occur selectively in certain populations of synapses (the ones that experienced the appropriate patterns of activity).

The steps involved in bringing about the protein synthesis-dependent phase of synaptic modification are not known. A dependence on protein synthesis could indicate that the proteins required for enduring synaptic modifications are made from messenger ribonucleic acids (mRNAs) that are present constitutively or mRNAs that are synthesized as a consequence of transcriptional activation. If the required proteins are made using existing mRNAs, one would expect there to be some mechanism for regulating translation via synaptic activity. If new gene expression is required to bring about activity-dependent synaptic modifications, there must be some mechanism that allows signaling from the synapse to the transcriptional machinery of the neuron. This could be directly mediated by signal transduction events triggered specifically by the synapses to be modified or could be a general signal related to postsynaptic activity. Both the initial and the later occurring modifications apparently occur selectively as a function of the history of activity at individual synapses, indicating that there must be some means to assure synapse specificity. The newly synthesized proteins critical for modification could be delivered selectively to the synapses that are to be modified, or could be widely distributed, with synapse specificity being conferred by some interaction between the newly synthesized proteins and other molecules at synapses that had been modified by synaptic activity. This is the idea of synaptic tagging put forth by Frey and Morris (1997).

Based on these considerations, it is reasonable to be vigilant for molecular processes that (a) can be triggered by the patterns of activity that lead to enduring synaptic modification; (b) involve the induction of gene expression in response to synaptic activation; (c) involve the synthesis of new protein during a critical time window that extends for a few hours after the inducing stimulus; (d) could lead to selective modifications of the synapses that had experienced a particular pattern of activity; and (e) can be induced in neurons by behavioral experience.

Are there molecular mechanisms with these features? The answer is a definite yes. Several signal transduction pathways have been identified that could regulate translation or mediate signaling from the synapse to the transcriptional machinery of the neuron. Many of these signal transduction pathways have been shown to be activated in situations that lead to enduring synaptic modification. Also, there are clearly several ways that newly synthesized gene products can be delivered to particular synapses in a way that would assure synapse specificity. But for maximal economy, it is reasonable to pay special attention to mechanisms that can mediate several of the required functions simultaneously.

In what follows, we focus on the mechanism that neurons possess that allows "synapse-specific gene expression"; this mechanism allows a particular subset of proteins to be synthesized locally at individual postsynaptic sites. We focus especially on recent findings regarding a unique immediate early gene (IEG) known as Arc, or activity-related cytoskeleton-associated protein, and also known as Arg 3.1. This gene is induced by activity; the newly synthesized mRNA is rapidly delivered into dendrites, where it comes to be selectively localized at synapses that had been activated; the mRNA mediates the synthesis of a protein that is part of the synaptic junctional region. The induction of gene expression, delivery of the mRNA to dendrites, and synthesis of the protein occur during the first few hours after the inducing event—to a first approximation, the same time period in which protein synthesis-dependent synaptic modifications are occurring. Finally, the gene is induced, and the mRNA is delivered into dendrites following a brief behavioral experience. Although it remains to be established that Arc itself plays a role in synaptic modifications, the cellular mechanisms that Arc has revealed have the characteristics predicted above for a molecular mechanism of consolidation.

Synapse-Specific Gene Expression

Synapse-specific gene expression refers to the capability that neurons have for transporting particular mRNAs to synaptic sites on dendrites where the mRNAs can be locally translated. This idea had its roots in the discovery of "synapse-associated polyribosome complexes" (SPRCs)—polyribosomes and associated membranous cisterns that are selectively localized beneath postsynaptic sites on the dendrites of CNS neurons (Steward, 1983; Steward & Fass, 1983; Steward & Levy, 1982). Based on the assumption that form implies function, the highly selective localization of SPRCs beneath synapses suggested the following working hypotheses: (a) that the machinery might synthesize key molecular constituents of the synapse and (b) that translation might be regulated by activity at the individual postsynaptic site. As discussed below, these working hypotheses have been confirmed, and the idea that these elements may be involved in synaptic plasticity has been reinforced and refined.

Many of the mRNAs that are present in dendrites have been identified, and there is now evidence that these mRNAs do enable a local, intradendritic, synthesis of the encoded proteins (Steward, Falk, & Torre, 1996; Steward & Singer, 1997). Table 3.1 lists the mRNAs that extend for several hundred μm from the cell body. There are also certain other mRNAs that are localized primarily in cell bodies but extend slightly into proximal dendrites (e.g., the mRNAs for two protein kinase C substrates, F1/GAP43 and RC3; Laudry, Watson, Handley, & Campagnoni, 1993).

There are several other mRNAs that are detectable by in situ hybridization in the dendrites of young neurons developing in vitro that are not evident in the dendrites of mature neurons in vivo (e.g., the mRNAs for BDNF and trkB receptors). Finally, there are also other "possible" dendritic mRNAs for which in situ hybridization evidence for dendritic localization has not yet been reported (e.g., the mRNA for a "Fragile X" related protein, see below). Taken together, the existing evidence allows several generalizations:

1. There are several different patterns of mRNA distribution. Some mRNAs are present at relatively high levels throughout dendrites, whereas other mRNAs are concentrated in particular dendritic domains (Paradies & Steward, 1997). Also, the degree to which certain mRNAs are localized in dendrites varies across neuron types (Paradies & Steward, 1997). Table 3.1 lists only those mRNAs that have a distinctly dendritic distribution in most of the neuron types that express the genes in question.

2. All of the dendritic mRNAs that have been identified so far are expressed differentially by different types of neurons. This is especially evident when considering the mRNAs that are present in the dendrites of forebrain neurons versus cerebellar Purkinje cells.

3. The proteins encoded by the dendritically localized mRNAs include different classes of protein (cytoplasmic, cytoskeletal, integral membrane, and membrane associated). These proteins have different functions. This means that it is unlikely that there will be a single purpose for mRNA localization in dendrites (for additional discussion of this point, see Steward, 1997).

The fact that a different mixture of mRNAs is present in the dendrites of

TABLE 3.1

mRNAs Shown to Be Localized Within Dendrites of Neurons in Vivo by in Situ Hybridization

mRNA	CELL TYPE	LOCALIZATION IN DENDRITES	CLASS OF PROTEIN	PROTEIN FUNCTION
MAP2[a]	Cortex, hippocampus, dentate gyrus	Proximal 1/3–1/2	Cytoskeletal	Microtubule associated
CAMII kinase[b] alpha subunit	Cortex, hippocampus, dentate gyrus	Throughout	Membrane-associated postsynaptic density	Multifunctional kinase Ca++ signaling
ARC/ARG 3.1[c]	Cortex, hippocampus, dentate gyrus depending on inducing stimulus	Throughout (when induced)	Cytoskeleton associated	Actin-binding synaptic junctional protein
Dendrin[d]	Hippocampus, dentate gyrus, cerebral cortex	Throughout	Putative membrane	Unknown
G-Protein[e] gamma subunit	Cortex, hippocampus, dentate gyrus, striatum	Throughout	Membrane associated	Metabotrophic receptor signaling
Calmodulin[f]	Cortex, hippocampus, Purkinje cells	Proximal-middle (during synaptogenesis)	Cytoplasm and membrane associated	Ca++ signaling in conjunction with CAMII kinase
NMDAR1[g]	Dentate gyrus	Proximal-middle	Integral membrane	Receptor
Glycine receptor[h] alpha subunit	Motoneurons	Proximal	Integral membrane	Receptor
Vasopressin[i]	Hypothalamo–hypophyseal	Proximal-middle	Soluble	Neuropeptide
Neurofilament protein 68[j]	Vestibular neurons	Proximal-middle	Cytoskeletal	Neurofilament
InsP3 receptor[k]	Purkinje cells	Throughout (concentrated proximally)	Integral membrane (endoplasmic reticulum)	Ca++ signaling
L7[l]	Purkinje cells	Throughout	Cytoplasmic	Homology to PDGF oncogene signaling
PEP19[l]	Purkinje cells	Proximal one third	Cytoplasmic	Ca++ binding

Note. [a]Garner, Tucker, & Matus. (1988); [b]Burgin et al. (1990); [c]Link et al. (1995), Lyford et al. (1995); [d]Herb et al. (1997); [e]Watson et al. (1994); [f]Berry & Brown (1996); [g]Gazzaley, Benson, Huntley, & Morrison (1997); [h]Racca, Gardiol, & Triller (1997); [i]Prakash, Fehr, Mohr, & Richter (1997); [j]Paradies & Steward (1997); [k]Furuichi et al. (1993); [l]Bian, Chu, Schilling, & Oberdick (1996).

different cell types and even different dendritic regions of individual neurons has important implications for understanding the cell biological significance of local protein synthesis. For example, although several mRNAs are present in the dendrites of cortical neurons, hippocampal pyramidal cells, and dentate granule cells, the patterns of expression and subcellular distributions of the mRNAs are different. The mRNAs for CAMII kinase, dendrin, and Arc (when induced) are localized throughout the neuropil layers. In contrast, MAP2 mRNA is concentrated in proximal dendrites and is not detectable in distal dendrites.

The mRNAs that are present in the dendrites of Purkinje cells also exhibit different localization patterns; the mRNA for the InsP3 receptor is present throughout dendrites but is concentrated in the proximal one third of the dendrite, whereas L7 mRNA appears to be more uniformly distributed in Purkinje cell dendrites (Bian, Chu, Schilling, & Oberdick, 1996). These findings indicate that the capability exists for a different mixture of proteins to be synthesized locally in different neuron types and different dendritic domains.

Regulation of mRNA Translation at the Synapse

The selective localization of SPRCs at synapses provides a potential mechanism for locally regulating the production of key proteins that are necessary for synaptic modification. In particular, the proteins necessary for synaptic modification could be synthesized during the period that the synaptic modification was being consolidated into a durable form. This local synthesis could involve mRNAs already in place, and/or mRNAs that are induced by synaptic activity and delivered into dendrites. Until recently, there was no evidence of a linkage between synaptic activation and either the transport of mRNAs into dendrites or the local translation of these mRNAs on site. However, recent data establish that a linkage does exist, and that synaptic activation may both modulate translation of mRNAs already in place, and trigger the transport of new mRNA transcripts to synaptic sites.

In the case of mRNAs already in place, modulation of the production of proteins during a particular time window would require translational regulation. Is there evidence for such translational regulation of mRNAs at synapses? The answer is a provisional yes. For example, studies involving hippocampal slices have revealed that afferent stimulation (activation of the Schaffer collateral system), in conjunction with activation of muscarinic acetylcholine receptors, leads to increases in protein synthesis in the activated dendritic laminae (stratum radiatum). This study evaluated the distribution of newly synthesized protein using autoradiographic techniques after pulse labeling of hippocampal slices with a 3H-labeled protein precursor. Although the results suggest local synthesis within dendrites, the possibility of rapid transport of the newly synthesized proteins from the cell body in these intact neurons cannot be excluded in these experiments.

Other evidence indicating synaptic regulation of translation within dendrites comes from studies that use synaptoneurosome preparations (a subcellular fraction containing terminals and dendrites isolated by filtration techniques). Both depolarization and neurotransmitter activation lead to an increase in the proportion of mRNA associated with polysomes and in the levels of protein synthesis within cell fragments in the preparation (Weiler & Greenough, 1991, 1993). An especially interesting line of evidence has come from the study of Fragile X mental retardation protein (FMRP) and its homologs. FMRP is encoded by a gene called FMR1 that is affected in human Fragile X syndrome. Recent evidence suggests that the protein plays some role in the mechanism through which certain mRNAs are translated at synaptic sites on the dendrites of CNS neurons (Feng et al., 1997; Weiler et al., 1997; see also Greenough, chapter 4, this volume). This evidence has led to the idea that the neuronal dysfunction that is part of Fragile X syndrome may result from a disruption of local synthesis of protein at synapses, which in turn would disrupt synaptic function, especially the capability to undergo long-lasting forms of synaptic plasticity (Comery et al., 1997; Weiler et al., 1997).

Synaptic Regulation of mRNA Trafficking in Dendrites

Evidence that synaptic activation triggers the transport of new mRNA transcripts to the synapse comes from studies of the IEG (immediate early gene) Arc. Arc was initially discovered in screens for novel IEGs, defined as genes that are induced by activity in a protein synthesis-independent fashion (Link et al., 1995; Lyford et al., 1995). Like other IEGs, Arc expression is strongly induced by neuronal activity. However, in dramatic contrast to the mRNAs of other IEGs, Arc mRNA rapidly migrates throughout the dendritic arbor of the neuron in which it is induced.

Arc is also noteworthy because unlike most other IEGs, its protein product is not a nuclear transcription factor. Analysis of a synthetic peptide (based on the sequence deduced from the mRNA) indicated that the protein associates with the cytoskeleton and that this association is regulated by $Ca++$ (Lyford et al., 1995). Also, immunocytochemistry using antibodies against the synthetic peptide demonstrated that the newly synthesized protein was localized in dendrites and was not targeted to the nucleus as is the case of IEG transcripton factors (Lyford et al., 1995). Interestingly, these same studies revealed the existence of other IEGs that encode proteins that are not transcription factors. Nevertheless, Arc is so far unique among IEGs in terms of the dendritic trafficking of its mRNA. The nature of the other nontranscription factor IEGs is being further explored (see, e.g., Tsui et al., 1996).

More recent studies have revealed that Arc protein is especially highly concentrated at the synapse. Evidence in support of this conclusion is of two sorts:

1. Immunostaining of hippocampal neurons in culture reveals intense punctate staining for Arc at the heads of some, but not all, dendritic spines (Figure 3.1A). In the spines that exhibit staining, the Arc-positive puncta colocalize with punctate staining for CAMKII (Figure 3.1B). Other studies have revealed that the CAMKII-stained puncta coincide with postsynaptic sites that are apposed by presynaptic terminals. These postsynaptic sites also contain accumulations of glutamate receptors and other synaptic junctional constituents. It is not clear why Arc protein is localized selectively in a subset of spines, but it is tempting to speculate that these synapses may be undergoing some form of growth or activity-dependent modification.

FIGURE 3.1

Immunocytochemical evidence for Arc localization at synaptic sites on the dendrites of hippocampal neurons in culture.

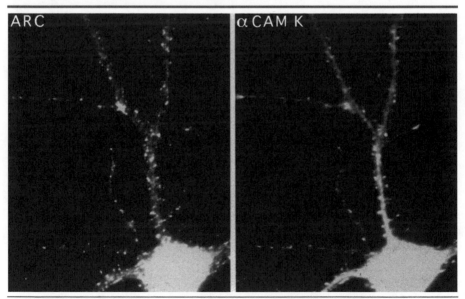

(A) illustrates the immunofluorescent staining pattern for Arc in a hippocampal neuron in culture. Note the intense immunofluorescence associated with what appear to be the heads of dendritic spines and the relatively lower level of immunofluorescence in the shaft of the dendrite. (B) illustrates the same neuron immunostained using an antibody against the alpha subunit of CAMKII. Note again the intense immunofluorescence in what appear to be spine heads and the relatively higher overall level of immunofluorescence in the dendritic shaft.

2. Subcellular fractionation experiments have revealed that Arc protein is highly concentrated in the synaptic junction. In the experiment illustrated in Figure 3.2, subcellular fractions were prepared according to the procedure of Cotman and Taylor (1972). This procedure yields fractions enriched in various types of cellular membranes: Band 1 contains myelin, Band 2 contains nonspecialized plasma membrane, Band 3 contains synaptic plasma membranes, and the pellet contains mitochondria. When Band 3 is treated with a detergent that removes membrane lipids and solu-

FIGURE 3.2

Evidence from subcellular fractionation experiments that Arc protein is concentrated at the synaptic junction.

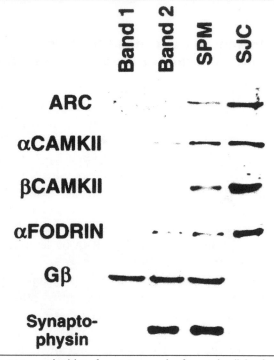

The figure illustrates a slot blot of protein samples from subcellular fractions prepared according to the procedure of Cotman and Taylor (1972) that have been stained with various antibodies. Band 1 contains myelin, Band 2 contains nonspecialized plasma membrane, and Band 3 contains synaptic plasma membranes (SPM). Synaptic junctional complex (SJC) is the detergent insoluble fraction that remains after treatment of Band 3 with detergent. Note that Arc protein is present at the highest relative levels in the synaptic plasma membrane fraction and SJC fractions, as is also true of the alpha and beta isoforms of CAMKII and fodrin. Other markers are enriched in other bands.

bilizes integral membrane proteins, the remaining insoluble residue represents a fraction that is highly enriched in the insoluble proteins of the synaptic junction—the so-called synaptic junctional complex (SJC). Analyses of these subcellular fractions using antibodies for Arc protein and other synaptic molecules reveals that Arc protein is present at the highest relative levels in the synaptic plasma membrane fraction and at even higher concentration in the SJC fraction. This is the same distribution seen for other known components of the postsynaptic junction, like CAMKII.

Taken together, these immunocytochemical and subcellular fractionation data indicate that Arc protein is highly concentrated in the postsynaptic junctional region of certain spine synapses. It remains to be established whether the newly synthesized Arc protein that is induced following synaptic activation (see below) is also targeted to the synaptic junctional region and, if so, over what time course.

Arc mRNA Is Present in Dendrites When Protein Synthesis-Dependent Synaptic Modifications Occur

The fact that Arc mRNA is normally expressed at low levels and is strongly induced by synaptic activity provides an opportunity to evaluate the kinetics of the transport and localization processes. Arc was initially discovered because it was induced after a single electroconvulsive seizure (ECS). ECS was used because it induces a period of intense neuronal activity within a discrete time window. In this way, the pattern of gene induction after a discrete episode of activity can be evaluated. Initial studies revealed that a single ECS caused Arc mRNA to migrate into dendrites within 15–30 minutes of the inducing stimulus and to remain in place for several hours. These data yielded the first estimate of transport rate for an individual dendritic mRNA (at least 300 μm/hour; see Wallace, Lyford, Worley, & Steward, 1998).

The evaluation of Arc expression at various times following ECS defined the interval between the onset of synaptic activation and the arrival of newly synthesized mRNA in dendrites and also revealed that Arc mRNA was present in dendrites only transiently. Peak levels of Arc mRNA were seen 1–2 hours after a single ECS; thereafter, the levels of Arc mRNA declined, returning to near control levels after about 6 hours. To a first approximation, this time interval corresponds to the period during which synaptic modifications are sensitive to inhibition of protein synthesis. Hence, the timing of Arc delivery is synchronous with the protein synthesis-dependent phase of synaptic modification.

Arc mRNA is also induced in dentate granule cells following the induction of LTP in the perforant path (Link et al., 1995; Lyford et al., 1995). Although not evaluated in detail, the kinetics of induction and dendritic delivery appear to be comparable following ECS and the induction of LTP.

Newly Synthesized Arc mRNA Is Targeted to Activated Synapses

Recent studies have revealed a remarkable additional feature of the trafficking of Arc mRNA (Steward, Wallace, Lyford, & Worley, 1998). It was found that patterned synaptic activation both induces Arc expression and causes the newly synthesized mRNA to localize selectively at the synapses that had been activated.

The experiments that demonstrated activity-dependent localization of Arc mRNA involved stimulation of the perforant path projections from the entorhinal cortex (EC) to the dentate gyrus (Figure 3.3). The perforant path inner-

FIGURE 3.3

Newly synthesized Arc mRNA is selectively targeted to dendritic domains that have been synaptically activated.

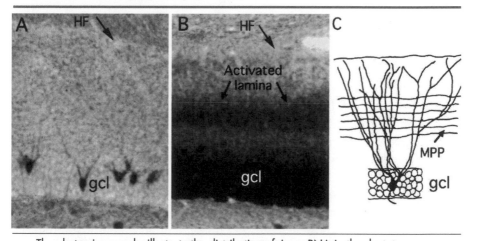

The photomicrographs illustrate the distribution of Arc mRNA in the dentate gyrus as revealed by nonisotopic in situ hybridization. (A) Distribution of Arc mRNA in the dentate gyrus on the control (nonstimulated) side of the brain. In this animal, there were an unusually large number of heavily-labeled granule cells on the control side. The likely reason is the experience of the animal just before preparation for the physiology experiment (see later). Note the labeled dendrites extending from heavily-labeled cell bodies. (B) Induction of ARC and dendritic delivery of Arc mRNA after 2 hours of high frequency stimulation of the perforant path. The band of labeling occurs in the dendritic zone in which the medial perforant path terminates. (C) The drawing illustrates the distribution of the dendrites of the dentate granule cells in the molecular layer and the pattern of termination of medial perforant path projections from the entorhinal cortex. Gcl = granule cell layer; MPP = medial perforant path.

vates the outer two thirds of the molecular layer of the dentate gyrus. Within that zone, the medial EC projects to the middle molecular layer, whereas the lateral EC projects to the outer molecular layer (see Figure 3.3C, which schematically illustrates the pattern of termination of the projections from the medial EC). Hence, by positioning a stimulating electrode in the medial EC, it is possible to selectively activate a band of synapses that terminate on mid-proximo–distal dendrites.

The medial perforant path was activated for different periods of time using a stimulation paradigm that is typically used to induce LTP in the dentate gyrus (400 Hz trains, 8 pulses per train, delivered at a rate of 1/10 seconds). When stimulation was delivered for 1–2 hours, there was a striking band of labeling for newly synthesized Arc mRNA in the middle molecular layer. This is exactly the location of the band of synapses that had been activated (cf. Figure 3.3A, which illustrates the resting levels of Arc mRNA in the nonactivated dentate gyrus contralateral to the stimulation, and Figure 3.3B, which illustrates the distribution of Arc mRNA following 2 hours of stimulation of the medial perforant path). The degree to which labeling is concentrated in the activated lamina is illustrated in the graph of optical density (OD) across the molecular layer.

The Pattern of Localization of Arc mRNA Depends on Activated Afferents

Different afferent projections to the dentate gyrus terminate in different laminae in the molecular layer. Hence it was of interest to determine whether Arc mRNA could be differentially targeted by activating synapses that terminate at various proximo–distal levels on the dendrite. Figure 3.4 illustrates an experiment in which the commissural projection to the dentate gyrus was stimulated at high frequency for 2 hours. The synapses of the commissural pathway are excitatory and terminate in the inner one third of the molecular layer. However, stimulation of this pathway also evokes strong GABAergic inhibition, and the induction of LTP in this pathway requires that this inhibition be blocked (Steward, Tomasulo, & Levy, 1990). Hence, for this experiment, we used the same strategy previously used to permit LTP in which a recording micropipette contained 40 mM bicuculline. The diffusion of the bicuculline from the pipette blocks GABAergic inhibition locally in an area of about 1 mm diameter, thus enabling the induction of LTP (Steward et al., 1990).

As illustrated in Figure 3.4A, stimulation of the commissural pathway strongly induced Arc expression in a small region around the bicuculline-filled micropipette. Moreover, in the area in which Arc was induced, there was a highly defined band of labeling for newly synthesized Arc mRNA in the inner molecular layer—exactly the layer in which the commissural pathway termi-

FIGURE 3.4

Targeting of newly synthesized Arc mRNA to proximal dendritic regions after activation of dentate commissural projections.

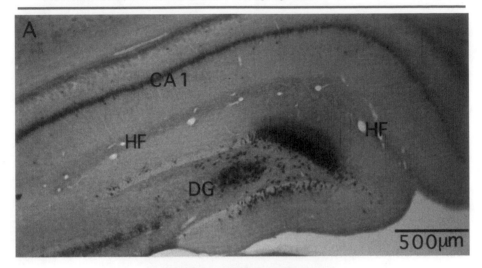

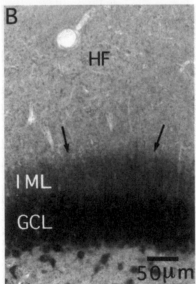

Stimulation of the commissural pathway strongly induced Arc expression in a small region around the bicuculline-filled micropipette and caused the newly synthesized mRNA to localize selectively a discrete band in the inner molecular layer—exactly the layer in which the commissural pathway terminates. DG = dentate gyrus; CA1 = CA1 region of the hippocampus. From "Synaptic Activation Causes the mRNA for the IEG Arc to Localize Selectively Near Activated Postsynaptic Sites on Dendrites," by O. Steward, C. S. Wallace, G. L. Lyford, and P. F. Worley, 1998, *Neuron, 21,* 741–745. Copyright 1998 by Cell Press. Used with permission of the authors.

nates. Note the sharp distal boundary of labeling, representing the sharp boundary between the area of the molecular layer innervated by the commissural pathway, and the middle molecular layer, which is innervated entorhinal cortex. Other studies revealed that newly synthesized Arc mRNA could also be selectively targeted to the outer molecular layer following activation of projections from the lateral entorhinal cortex, which terminate on more distal dendritic segments.

Localization of Arc mRNA in Activated Dendritic Laminae Is Associated With Local Accumulation of Arc Protein

Immunostaining of tissue sections from stimulated animals using an Arc-specific antibody revealed a band of newly synthesized protein in the same dendritic laminae in which Arc mRNA was concentrated. The fact that synaptic activation leads to the selective targeting of both recently synthesized mRNA and protein suggests that the targeting of the mRNA underlies a local synthesis of the protein.

The selective targeting of the newly synthesized mRNA to synapses that had been activated reveals the existence of a previously unknown mechanism that is ideally suited to mediate protein synthesis dependent, synapse-specific, long-term plasticity. It is important to emphasize, however, that our experiments do not establish a direct link between the induction and synaptic localization of Arc mRNA and the induction of enduring LTP. Establishing this link will require an evaluation of whether the patterns of activation that are necessary and sufficient to induce LTP are also necessary and sufficient to induce mRNA localization. The fact that newly synthesized Arc protein accumulates selectively in the dendritic laminae in which Arc mRNA is localized also suggests that targeting of the mRNA underlies a local synthesis of the protein. It remains to be established whether local synthesis of Arc protein plays a role in the protein synthesis-dependent phase of LTP.

Arc mRNA Is Strongly Induced by a Novel Behavioral Experience

The final piece of the puzzle pertains to the inducibility of Arc in behaviorally relevant situations. If Arc induction and dendritic targeting play a role in the synaptic modifications that underlie memory storage, then Arc must be induced and its mRNA must be delivered into dendrites in response to behavioral experience. Indeed, previous studies have revealed that Arc, along with other

IEGs, is induced in certain behavioral settings (Gall, Hess, & Lynch, 1998). What had not been established was whether newly synthesized Arc mRNA and protein were in fact also delivered into dendrites in neurons in which the gene had been induced.

To determine whether behavioral experience can regulate the dendritic transport of Arc mRNA, we evaluated Arc mRNA localization using nonisotopic in situ hybridization techniques, which can definitively reveal the presence of the mRNA in dendrites. In one approach, rats were allowed to explore a novel, toy-filled environment for 15 minutes to 2 hours. This is the environmental complexity paradigm, originally devised by Hebb (1949) and subsequently used by numerous others to demonstrate the capacity of experience to alter brain structure and synaptic organization (Black, Isaacs, Anderson, Alcantara, & Greenough, 1990; Chang & Greenough, 1984; Comery, Shah, & Greenough, 1995; Greenough & Volkmar, 1973; Sirevaag & Greenough, 1985).

After brief (15 minutes–2 hours) experience in a novel complex environment, Arc mRNA was strongly induced in a variety of neuron types throughout the forebrain (Figure 3.5). The pattern of induction (in terms of the neurons exhibiting increased expression) appeared qualitatively similar to that reported previously for the mRNA encoding the immediate early gene transcription factor NGFI-A (i.e., neocortex, striatum and hippocampal formation; Wallace et al., 1995).

The patterns of experience-dependent induction were particularly interesting in the hippocampal formation. For example, levels of expression were dramatically higher in the vast majority (perhaps all) pyramidal neurons in the CA1 subfield. Compare Figure 3.5A control with Figure 3.5B which illustrates the pattern of labeling 2 hours afterexposure to the novel environment. After 15 minutes of exploration, Arc was strongly induced in neuronal cell bodies (Figure 3.5C) but there was little dendritic labeling. At 1 hour, however, there was a clear increase in labeling for Arc mRNA throughout the dendritic laminae of CA1 (Figure 3.5D), indicating dendritic localization of the mRNA. The overall level of labeling appeared to decrease somewhat by 2 hours but dendritic labeling was still evident (Figure 3.5E).

In the CA3 region, however, the pattern was different. Many but by no means all hippocampal neurons exhibited increased expression. Moreover, the extent of dendritic labeling was much less than in CA1. A still different pattern of induction was seen in the dentate gyrus. In animals that remain in the home cage, a small number of dentate granule cells exhibit a high level of labeling. In animals exposed to the novel environment, the number of heavily labeled granule cells increases, especially in the dorsal blade of the dentate gyrus. Nevertheless, these changes were restricted to a very small percentage of the total population of granule cells; the vast majority of granule cells exhibited no increases in labeling.

FIGURE 3.5

Brief experience in a novel environment induces Arc expression, and results in the delivery of newly synthesized Arc mRNA into dendrites.

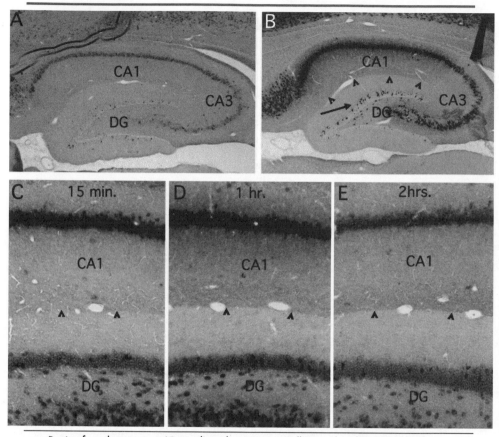

Brains from home cage (Control) and environmentally stimulated (ECS) animals were bisected and half brains from each group were mounted together on microscope slides. The distribution of Arc mRNA was evaluated using nonisotopic in situ hybridization using dioxygenin-labeled antisense cRNA probes. Exposure to the novel environment dramatically increased Arc mRNA levels in neuron types throughout the forebrain, especially in the cortex and hippocampus (A control vs. B, 2 hours after initial exposure to the novel environment). In the hippocampus, the vast majority of CA1 pyramidal neurons exhibited increased labeling, and there was prominent labeling throughout the dendritic layers of CA1, reflecting dendritic transport of the newly synthesized mRNA (A vs. B). In CA3, many but not all pyramidal neurons exhibited increased labeling, but there was minimal labeling over the dendritic laminate. Within the dentate gyrus, Arc expression was restricted to a small subset of granule cells, but the number present in the dorsal blade of the dentate gyrus was increased significantly after exposure to EXP (see long arrow in B). CA1 and CA3 = hippocampal subfields; DG = dentate gyrus; arrows indicate hippocampal fissure. C, D, and E illustrate higher magnification views of the pattern of labeling at 15 minutes, 1 hour, and 2 hours after initial exposure to the novel environment.

The significance of the cell-type specific pattern of Arc induction and dendritic transport is not yet clear. Nevertheless, our findings demonstrate that Arc is strongly induced, and its mRNA is delivered into dendrites in response to a brief behavioral experience. Indeed, this behavioral induction was surprising both in its pattern and magnitude.

In terms of the pattern of expression, we were surprised that Arc was induced strongly in the cortex and hippocampus, but that induction was limited to a small percentage of dentate granule cells. This is surprising because ECS leads to a strikingly selective induction of Arc expression in dentate granule cells. Hence, multiple types of neurons have the capacity to deliver newly synthesized Arc mRNA to their dendrites, but that this translocation is invoked in different activational contexts depending on the neuron type.

The magnitude of the induction was surprising in terms of the number of neurons in which Arc was induced. If Arc induction marks neurons in which synaptic modifications are taking place, then the synaptic modifications induced by a brief period of exploration in a novel environment are remarkably widespread. It will probably be necessary to study Arc induction following a more controlled behavioral experience to further explore the relationship between Arc induction and synaptic modification.

The transient induction of Arc represents a distinctly different mode of dendritic mRNA supply than is the case for the dendritic mRNAs that are expressed constitutively. After an inducing stimulus, levels of Arc mRNA rise dramatically within dendrites (probably by several orders of magnitude) but then return to control levels within a few hours. Hence, between episodes of massive delivery of Arc mRNA to dendrites are intervals where the mRNA is scarce. In contrast, the mRNAs stationed in dendrites constitutively provide a substrate for synthesizing new proteins, but any regulation would have to be at the level of translation of the mRNA. For these mRNAs, the potential exists for an uncoupling of nuclear transcription and local synaptic translation. In this way, the mixture of proteins that can be synthesized within dendrites varies as a function of the mRNAs that are present.

The transient presence of a dendritic mRNA might allow a protein involved in a specialized physiological adaptation to be present selectively at a critical period during its production/degradation cycle. This would be consistent with a special role for this protein during a particular phase of synaptic modification. Again, it is intriguing that the time window when Arc mRNA is present in dendrites is similar to the period during which protein synthesis must occur for synaptic modifications to be consolidated (Frey, Krug, Reymann, & Matthies, 1988; Krug, Lossner, & Ott, 1984; Otani & Abraham, 1989; Otani, Marshall, Tate, Goddard, & Abraham, 1989).

Lessons From the Study of Arc: A Candidate Mechanism for Protein Synthesis-Dependent Synaptic Modification

The material summarized above regarding Arc reveals the existence of a heretofore unknown candidate mechanism for the consolidation process:

1. The expression of the Arc gene is triggered by the patterns of synaptic activity that lead to enduring synaptic modification.

2. Arc mRNA encodes a protein that is targeted to the synapse.

3. The activity-dependent induction of Arc protein occurs during a time window that extends for a few hours after the inducing stimulus.

4. The selective delivery of Arc mRNA and protein to synapses that had experienced particular patterns of activity could certainly be a mechanism for synapse-specific modifications.

5. Arc is induced and its mRNA is delivered into dendrites in response to the sorts of brief behavioral experience that can lead to long-lasting synaptic modifications.

6. Finally, Arc mRNA is induced in neuron types that are thought to participate in enduring synaptic modification in response to behavioral experience (neurons in the hippocampus and cerebral cortex).

There are several pieces of the puzzle that are still missing, however. First, it remains to be established whether Arc in fact plays a role in activity-induced synaptic modification. Additional clues about the actual role of the protein will likely come from studies of the protein itself and its interactions with other functional molecules of the synaptic junctional region. But even if Arc does turn out to be a "red herring," the way that Arc is handled by neurons reveals the existence of previously unknown RNA trafficking mechanisms that could be used for sorting other mRNAs that do play a key role in bringing about activity-dependent modifications.

The fascinating properties of Arc should not make us lose sight of the fact that other mRNAs are present in dendrites constitutively, including the mRNAs for molecules that have already been strongly implicated in activity-dependent synaptic modification (the mRNA for the alpha subunit of CAMII kinase, for example). These mRNAs that are present constitutively provide an opportunity for local regulation of the synthesis of key signaling molecules (via translational regulation). Hence, gene expression at individual synapses may be regulated in a complex fashion, first through the regulation of the mRNAs available for translation (i.e., Arc) and then by regulation of the translation of the mix of mRNAs that are in place, including those present constitutively (a model of which might be the translational regulation of Fragile X; see Greenough, chapter 4, this volume; Weiler et al., 1997). How this is coordinated and how all of these molecules actually fit in to the molecular consolidation process remain to be established.

References

Bailey, C. H., Bartsch, D., & Kandel, E. R. (1996). Toward a molecular definition of long-term memory storage. *Proceedings of the National Academy of Sciences, 93,* 13445–13452.

Berry, F. B., & Brown, I. R. (1996). CaM I mRNA is localized to apical dendrites during postnatal development of neurons in the rat brain. *Journal of Neuroscientific Research, 45,* 565–575.

Bian, F., Chu, T., Schilling K., & Oberdick, J. (1996). Differential mRNA transport and the regulation of protein synthesis: Selective sensitivity of Purkinje cell dendritic mRNAs to translational inhibition. *Molecular Cell Neuroscience, 7,* 116–133.

Black, J. E., Isaacs, K. R., Anderson, B. J., Alcantara, A. A., & Greenough, W. T. (1990). Learning causes synaptogenesis, whereas motor activity causes angiogenesis, in cerebellar cortex of adult rats. *Proceedings of the National Academy of Sciences, 87,* 5568–5572.

Burgin, K. E., Washam, M. N., Rickling, S., Westgate, S. A., Mobley, W. C., & Kelly, P. T. (1990). In situ hybridization histochemistry of CA++/calmodulin-dependent protein kinase in developing rat brain. *Journal of Neuroscience, 10,* 1788–1798.

Chang, F.-L. F., & Greenough, W. T. (1984). Transient and enduring morphological correlates of synaptic activity and efficacy change in the rat hippocampal slice. *Brain Research, 309,* 35–46.

Comery, T. A., Harris, J. B., Willems, P. J., Oostra, B. A., Irwin, S. A., Weiler, I. J., & Greenough, W. T. (1997). Abnormal dendritic spines in fragile X knockout mice: Maturation and pruning deficits. *Proceedings of the American Academy of Sciences, 94,* 5401–5404.

Comery, T. A., Shah, R., & Greenough, W. T. (1995). Differential rearing alters spine density on medium-sized spiny neurons in the rat corpus striatum: Evidence for association of morphological plasticity with early response gene expression. *Neurobiology of Learning and Memory, 63,* 217–219.

Cotman, C. W., & Taylor, D. (1972). Isolation and structural studies on synaptic complexes from rat brain. *Journal of Cell Biology, 55,* 696–710.

Feng, Y., Gutekunst, C.-A., Eberhart, D. E., Yi, H., Warren, S. T., & Hersch, S. M. (1997). Fragile X mental retardation protein: Nucleocytoplasmic shuttling and association with somatodendritic ribosomes. *Journal of Neuroscience, 17,* 1539–1547.

Frey, U., Krug, M., Reymann, K. G., & Matthies, H. (1988). Anisomycin, an inhibitor of protein synthesis, blocks late phases of LTP phenomena in the hippocampal CA1 region in vitro. *Brain Research, 452,* 57–65.

Frey, U., & Morris, R. G. M. (1997). Synaptic tagging and long-term potentiation. *Nature, 385*, 533–536.

Furuichi, T., Simon-Chazottes, D., Fujino, I., Yamada, N., Hasegawa, M., Miyawaki, A., Yoshikawa, S., Guenet, J.-L., & Mikoshiba, K. (1993). Widespread expression of inositol 1,4,5-trisphosphate receptor type 1 gene (Insp3r1) in the mouse central nervous system. *Receptors and Channels, 1*, 11–24.

Gall, C. M., Hess, U. S., & Lynch, G. (1998). Mapping brain networks engaged by, and changed by, learning. *Neurobiology of Learning and Memory, 70*, 14–36.

Garner, C. C., Tucker, R. P., & Matus, A. (1988). Selective localization of messenger RNA for cytoskeletal protein MAP2 in dendrites. *Nature, 336*, 674–677.

Gazzaley, A. H., Benson, D. L., Huntley, G. W., & Morrison, J. H. (1997). Differential subcellular regulation of NMDAR1 protein and mRNA in dendrites of dentate gyrus granule cells after perforant path transection. *Journal of Neuroscience, 17*, 2006–2017.

Greenough, W. T., & Volkmar, F. R. (1973). Pattern of dendritic branching in occipital cortex of rats reared in complex environments. *Experimental Neurology, 40*, 491–504.

Hebb, D. O. (1949). *The organization of behavior.* New York: Wiley.

Herb, A., Wisden, W., de Catania, M. V., Marechal, D., Dresse, A., & Seeberg, P. H. (1997). Prominent dendritic localization in forebrain neurons of a novel mRNA and its product, dendrin. *Molecular Cell Neuroscience, 8*, 367–374.

Krug, M., Lossner, B., & Ott, T. (1984). Anisomycin blocks the late phase of long-term potentiation in the dentate gyrus of freely moving rats. *Brain Research Bulletin, 13*, 39–42.

Laudry, C. F., Watson, J. B., Handley, V. W., & Campagnoni, A. T. (1993). Distribution of neuronal and glial mRNAs within neuronal cell bodies and processes. *Society for Neuroscience Abstracts, 19*, 1745.

Link, W., Konietzko, G., Kauselmann, G., Krug, M., Schwanke, B., Frey, U., & Kuhl, K. (1995). Somatodendritic expression of an immediate early gene is regulated by synaptic activity. *Proceedings of the National Academy of Sciences, 92*, 5734–5738.

Lyford, G., Yamagata, K., Kaufmann, W., Barnes, C., Sanders, L., Copeland, N., Gilbert, D., Jenkins, N., Lanahan, A., & Worley, P. (1995). Arc, a growth factor and activity-regulated gene, encodes a novel cytoskeleton-associated protein that is enriched in neuronal dendrites. *Neuron, 14*, 433–445.

Mayford, M., Bach, M. E., Huang, Y.-Y., Wang, L., Hawkins, R. D., & Kandel, E. R. (1996). Control of memory formation through regulated expression of a CaMKII transgene. *Science, 274*, 1678–1683.

McGaugh, J. L. (1966). Time-dependent processes in memory storage. *Science, 153*, 1351–1358.

Nguyen, P. V., & Kandel, E. R. (1996). A macromoleular synthesis-dependent late phase of long-term potentiation requiring cAMP in the medial perforant pathway of rat hippocampal slices. *Journal of Neuroscience, 16*, 3189–3198.

Otani, S., & Abraham, W. C. (1989). Inhibition of protein synthesis in the dentate gyrus, but not the entorhinal cortex, blocks maintenance of long-term potentiation in rats. *Neuroscience Letter, 106,* 175–180.

Otani, S., Marshall, C. J., Tate, W. P., Goddard, G. V., & Abraham, W. C. (1989). Maintenance of long-term potentiation in rat dentate gyrus requires protein synthesis but not messenger RNA synthesis immediate post-tetanization. *Neuroscience, 28,* 519–526.

Paradies, M. A., & Steward, O. (1997). Multiple subcellular mRNA distribution patterns in neurons: A nonisotopic in situ hybridization analysis. *Journal of Neurobiology, 33,* 473–493.

Prakash, N., Fehr, S., Mohr, E., & Richter, D. (1997). Dendritic localization of rat vasopressin mRNA: Ultrastructural analysis and mapping of targeting elements. *European Journal of Neuroscience, 9,* 523–532.

Racca, C., Gardiol, A., & Triller, A. (1997). Dendritic and postsynaptic localizations of glycine receptor alpha subunit mRNAs. *Journal of Neuroscience, 17,* 1691–1700.

Steward, O. (1983). Polyribosomes at the base of dendritic spines of CNS neurons: Their possible role in synapse construction and modification. *Cold Spring Harbor Symposium on Quantitative Biology, 48,* 745–759.

Steward, O. (1997). mRNA localization in neurons: A multipurpose mechanism. *Neuron, 18,* 9–12.

Steward, O., Falk, P. M., & Torre, E. R. (1996). Ultrastructural basis for gene expression at the synapse: Synapse-associated polyribosome complexes. *Journal of Neurocytology, 25,* 717–734.

Steward, O., & Fass, B. (1983). Polyribosomes associated with dendritic spines in the denervated dentate gyrus: Evidence for local regulation of protein synthesis during reinnervation. *Progressive Brain Research, 58,* 131–136.

Steward, O., & Levy, W. B. (1982). Preferential localization of polyribosomes under the base of dendritic spines in granule cells of the dentate gyrus. *Journal of Neuroscience, 2,* 284–291.

Steward, O., & Singer, R. H. (1997). The intracellular mRNA sorting system: Postal zones, zip codes, mail bags, and mail boxes. In J. B. Hartford & D. R. Morris (Eds.), *mRNA metabolism and post-transcriptional gene regulation* (pp. 127–146). New York: Wiley-Liss.

Steward, O., Tomasulo, R., & Levy, W. B. (1990). Blockade of inhibition in a pathway with dual excitatory and inhibitory action unmasks a capability for LTP that is otherwise not expressed. *Brain Research, 516,* 292–300.

Steward, O., Wallace, C. S., Lyford, G. L., & Worley, P. F. (1998). Synaptic activation causes the mRNA for the IEG Arc to localize selectively near activated postsynaptic sites on dendrites. *Neuron, 21,* 741–751.

Tsui, C. C., Copeland, N. G., Gilbert, D. J., Jenkins, N. A., Barnes, C., & Worley, P. F. (1996). Narp, a novel member of the pentraxin family, promotes neurite outgrowth and is dynamically regulated by neuronal activity. *Journal of Neuroscience, 16,* 2463–2478.

Wallace, C. S., Lyford, G. L., Worley, P. F., & Steward, O. (1998). Differential intracellular sorting of immediate early gene mRNAs depends on signals in the mRNA sequence. *Journal of Neuroscience, 18,* 26–35.

Wallace, C. S., Withers, G. S., Ivan, J. W., George, J. M., Clayton, D. F., & Greenough, W. T. (1995). Correspondence between sites of NGFI-A induction and sites of morphological plasticity following exposure to environmental complexity. *Molecular Brain Research, 32,* 211–220.

Watson, J. B., Coulter, P. M., Margulies, J. E., de Lecea, L., Danielson, P. E., Erlander, M. G., & Sutcliffe, J. G. (1994). G-protein gamma7 subunit is selectively expressed in medium-sized neurons and dendrites of the rat neostriatum. *Journal of Neuroscience Research, 39,* 108–116.

Weiler, I. J., & Greenough, W. T. (1991). Potassium ion stimulation triggers protein translation in synaptoneuronsomal polyribosomes. *Molecular Cell Neuroscience, 2,* 305–314.

Weiler, I. J., & Greenough, W. T. (1993). Metabotropic glutamate receptors trigger postsynaptic protein synthesis. *Proceedings of the National Academy of Sciences, 90,* 7168–7171.

Weiler, I. J., Irwin, S. A., Klintsova, A. Y., Spencer, C. M., Brazelton, A. D., Miyashiro, K., Comery, T. A., Patel, B., Eberwine, J., & Greenough, W. T. (1997). Fragile X mental retardation protein is translated near synapses in response to neurotransmitter activation. *Proceedings of the National Academy of Sciences, 94,* 5395–5400.

CHAPTER 4

Morphological and Molecular Studies of Synaptic Memory Mechanisms:

Links to the Fragile X Mental Retardation Syndrome

William T. Greenough

I was one of Jim McGaugh's first undergraduate research assistants, joining his laboratory in 1963 under the aegis of the National Science Foundation Undergraduate Research Participant program. Jim had just discovered that events occurring after learning could both facilitate and impair memory at later points in time. This meant that (a) the memory process took time, (b) scientists could study and understand memory at the brain level in terms of the kinds of treatments that affected it, and (c) potentially measurable phenomena occurred in response to learning that subsequently mediated memory—the ultimate direction my own work has followed. These were heady times for an undergraduate, with Jim regularly going to important conferences and visitors arriving to discuss his research and talk about their own. It took me years to realize that the life of a researcher was not always this event-filled or exciting and that most scientists waited months to years for the telephone to ring. I completed what then seemed to be an important study—one that helped to clarify that when strychnine facilitated memory it did so by acting back in time on the memory formation process rather than forward in time on the recall/recognition process (Greenough & McGaugh, 1965). In subsequent work, I attempted to understand the effects of experience on the developing brain both from a structural perspective (e.g., Greenough, Fulcher, Yuwiler, & Geller, 1970) and in terms of possible modulation of memory storage processes (e.g., Greenough, Yuwiler, & Dollinger, 1973) and metabolism (Yuwiler, Greenough, & Geller, 1968). Through this, inspired by the work of Bennett, Rosenzweig, and colleagues (e.g., Bennett, Diamond, Krech, & Rosenzweig, 1964) and the now firmly established concept of a time-requiring memory consolidation process (McGaugh, 1966), my post-PhD work focused increasingly on the effects of experience and learning on brain anatomy. Jim and I communicated regularly while I was in graduate school a few miles north of Irvine at University of California, Los Angeles. Facilitated by a stint as a visiting faculty member at Irvine in 1973 (when I also got to know Paul Gold), the relationship has remained strong, with both research and professional advice always readily available from Jim.

I focus in this chapter on the perspective that has evolved from that beginning, which emerged first from recognizing that there might be important similarities between the mechanisms that encoded experience effects on early sensory development and those that encoded memory, as suggested by the early work of Steven Rose (e.g., 1967) and Brian Cragg (e.g., 1967). It subsequently became apparent that, although there indeed seemed to be common mechanisms, there were also important differences between the processes of early sensory development and those of more adult-like learning, a point I return to later.

An important thing I learned from Jim was the value of allowing undergraduate students to play significant roles in research. Undergraduates have been seriously involved in about half of my work. One early example was Fred Volkmar, who found that rats reared from weaning in a complex, toy-filled group environment (EC) had more extensive visual cortex dendritic fields than did rats reared individually (IC) or in pairs (SC) in standard laboratory cages (Greenough & Volkmar, 1973; Volkmar & Greenough, 1972). This result indicated that the EC rats' neurons had more space for synapses and, subsequently, Turner and Greenough (1983, 1985) showed that EC rats had more visual cortex synapses per neuron than did SC or IC rats. This finding implied that experience drove synapse formation and provided one of the earliest pieces of evidence that the formation of new synapses might underlie brain information storage. West and Greenough (1972) found synapses in layer IV of the visual cortex to be larger in EC than in IC rats, a finding replicated by Sirevaag and Greenough (1985), which was among the earliest indications that structural modification of synapses might also be involved in brain information storage. Another structural modification, perforations in the postsynaptic density, is increased in EC rats (Greenough, West, & DeVoogd, 1978); these perforations have been subsequently shown also to increase in the dentate gyrus following long-term potentiation (LTP) induction and kindling (e.g., Geinisman, deToledo-Morrell, & Morrell, 1991).

It is important to note that the effects of exposure to a complex environment were not restricted to neurons: Capillary branching and astrocytic processes were greater in rats reared in EC than in SC or IC environments (e.g., Black, Sirevaag, & Greenough, 1987; Sirevaag & Greenough, 1991). These nonneuronal changes remind us that the brain adapts as a whole to its experience and, although only some of those changes fit the traditional definitions of memory, the broader pattern of brain adaptation is a more complete description of how the brain allows the organism to adapt to the demands of its environment.

Parallel work (e.g., LeVay, Wiesel, & Hubel, 1980) has shown that the developing feline and primate visual systems were exquisitely sensitive to experience, and other work has indicated that the developing visual system produced more synapses than it ultimately retained (Boothe, Greenough, Lund, & Wrege, 1979; Cragg, 1975; Huttenlocher, 1979). Theorists (e.g., Changeux & Danchin, 1976) noted that the overproduction could allow for synapses to be selected on the basis of functional utility, a view supported by subsequent research (e.g., Hata & Stryker, 1994). This suggested that there might be two separate mechanisms whereby experience directed the patterning of synaptic connections: (a) an early developmental mechanism in which selection from an overproduced population of synapses was guided by experience (termed "experience-expectant" synaptogenesis) and (b) a lifelong mechanism in which the formation of synapses was under the control of experience (termed "experience-dependent" synaptogenesis; Greenough, 1984, 1985). This concept has been explored in some detail elsewhere (e.g., Black & Greenough, 1986, 1998) and is not further pursued here. One point that subsequently becomes important is that, during development when overproduction and selection is taking place, postsynaptic elements, particularly spines, are more commonly marked by polyribosomal aggregates, that is, protein translational organelles of the cell, indicating that protein is being actively produced at these synapses.

Case for Synapse Formation and Modification as Memory Mechanisms

Much of my laboratory's additional work has examined the relationship between learning and synapse formation. Earlier work focused principally on light microscopic measures of dendritic plasticity, whereas more recent work has emphasized electron microscopic quantification of synapses. Studies of EC versus IC rats indicated that essentially the same dendritic changes seen in weanlings occurred in rats placed in a complex environment in adulthood (Juraska, Greenough, Elliott, Mack, & Berkowitz, 1980). An indication that learning was important was the finding that rats trained on a series of complex maze patterns exhibited altered visual cortical dendritic branching compared to nontrained, handled control rats (Greenough, Juraska, & Volkmar, 1979; see Figure 4.1). Moreover, when the corpus callosum was cut to block interhemispheric communication, restriction of visual experience principally to the contralateral hemisphere by use of eye occluders restricted these dendritic changes to that hemisphere, as shown in Figure 4.1 (Chang & Greenough, 1982), indicating

FIGURE 4.1

Effect of unilateral Hebb–Williams maze training on branching of apical dendrites of layer V pyramidal neurons in split brain (corpus collotomized) rats.

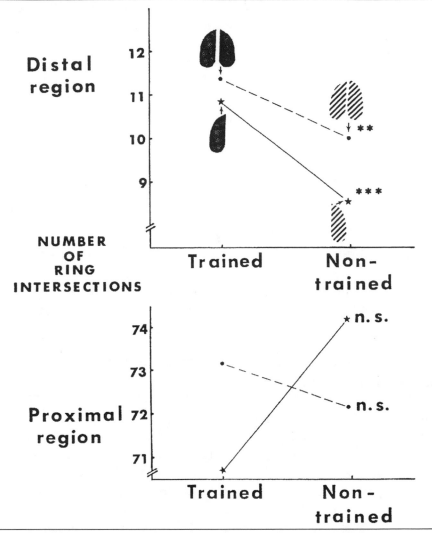

Trained designates a trained hemisphere connected to an open eye, and Nontrained designates a nontrained hemisphere, connected to an occluded eye or in an untrained animal. Effects were confined to the upper, more distal region of the dendrite. Hemispheres receiving visual input from the maze exhibit effects of training, compared to nonexposed hemispheres. From "Lateralized Effects of Monocular Training on Dendritic Branching in Adult Split-Brain Rats," by F.-L. Chang and W. T. Greenough, 1982, *Brain Research, 232,* p. 287. Copyright 1982 by Elsevier Science. Reprinted with permission.

that the changes were related to processing information from the training and not to general hormonal or metabolic consequences of the training procedure. Similar work using a task in which rats learned to reach into a small opening for bits of food showed that dendritic changes were restricted to the somatosensory–motor forelimb region of the hemisphere opposite the trained forelimb (Greenough, Larson, & Withers, 1985). Taken together, these studies indicated that the morphological effects of training were specifically associated with training-related neural activity, but they did not rule out the possibility that neural activity, rather than learning, was responsible for the morphological effects.

To examine the relative contributions of activity versus learning to neuronal and nonneuronal morphological responses to experience, Black, Isaacs, Anderson, Alcantara, and Greenough (1990) devised a paradigm to independently vary learning and neural activity. Four groups were run: (a) a "learning" group (AC; "Acrobat Condition") that acquired motor skill by traversing an elevated obstacle course that maximized learning while minimizing physical activity; (b) a "Forced eXercise" (FX) activity group that maximized physical exercise while minimizing learning by running on a treadmill; (c) a "Voluntary eXercise" (VX) group that maximized physical exercise while minimizing learning by running at their own pace in standard activity wheels attached to their cages; and (d) an "Inactive Condition" (IC—also known as "cage potatoes") that remained in their cages except for a brief daily period of handling to equate for the handling involved in the AC and FX tasks. We examined both capillary density and the number of synapses per Purkinje cell nucleus in the molecular layer of the cerebellar paramedian lobule, a brain region known to be activated during running exercise and to be involved in skilled movements of the head and limbs. The results, as shown in Figure 4.2, were very clear: The VX and FX exercise conditions increased capillary density with no statistically detectable effect on synapse number, whereas the AC learning condition increased synapse number with no effect on capillary density. Synapse formation occurred with learning, whereas capillary formation occurred with exercise. Taken with the prior findings, this result strongly suggests that synapse formation mediates at least some of the effects of learning.

Subsequent studies have clarified aspects of the relationship of synapse formation to learning in the cerebellum. Kleim, Vij, Ballard, and Greenough (1997) found that the training-induced synapse number changes—and the associated behavioral skills—both persisted for at least 4 weeks in the absence of additional training. Anderson, Alcantara, and Greenough (1996) and Kleim, Swain, et al. (1998) found that the principal synaptic change was in parallel fiber synapses, long regarded by modelers of cerebellar plasticity as the likely "plastic" connection (e.g., Albus, 1971; Fujita, 1982; Ito, 1984). Kleim, Swain, et al. (1997) found that inhibitory interneurons also changed with training,

FIGURE 4.2

Effect of motor skill learning on an elevated obstacle course (ACrobat), Forced eXercise on a treadmill (FX), Voluntary eXercise (VX) in an activity wheel attached to the cage, or InaCtivity (IC) on the density and number of synapses per Purkinje neuron in the cerebellar paramedian lobule.

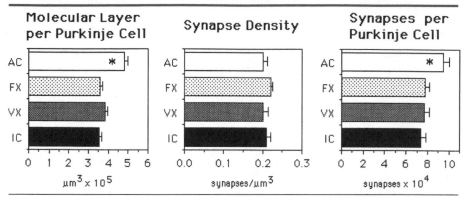

Note that only the learning condition increased the number of synapses, illustrated in the right panel. By contrast (data not shown), the two exercise conditions increased the density of blood vessels, whereas the AC condition did not differ from IC in blood vessel density. From "Learning Causes Synaptogenesis, Whereas Motor Activity Causes Angiogenesis, in Cerebellar Cortex of Adult Rats," by J. E. Black, K. R. Isaacs, B. J. Anderson, A. A. Alcantara, and W. T. Greenough, 1990, *Proceedings of the National Academy of Sciences, 87*, p. 5571. Copyright 1990 by the National Academy of Sciences. Reprinted with permission of the authors.

suggesting that plasticity was not limited to the excitatory inputs to the Purkinje cells, the only output cell of the cerebellar cortex. Federmeier, Kleim, and Greenough (2001) found that the new parallel fiber to Purkinje cell synapses tended to occur between cells that were already connected, apparently strengthening preexisting pathways, rather than recruiting new Purkinje cells into learning circuits, a result that modelers might well wish to consider. Kleim, Pipitone, Czerlanis, and Greenough (1998) found that the synaptic organization of the dentate nucleus, the cerebellar region to which the paramedian lobule output primarily projects, was statistically unaffected by training—it is the cerebellar cortex alone that exhibits plasticity in this system. A possible analogy that provides understanding is to think of the output nucleus as a piano on which the plastic cerebellar cortex plays; the response of the piano must remain stable if the cerebellar cortical player's learning is to have its desired effect.

The cerebellar results were mirrored in studies of the effects of motor skill training on the motor cortex. Kleim, Lussnig, Schwarz, Comery, and Greenough (1996) found that synapse numbers increase gradually across the 3-week period of training and that the expression of the immediate early transcription factor gene c-fos was elevated early in training but not subsequently when most synapse formation had been completed. Particularly interesting in the motor cortex were modifications in synapse structure: Both synaptic perforations and the size of the postsynaptic density appeared to change independently of changes in synapse number (Kleim, McNamee, Blankstein, & Greenough, 2001). This result indicates that these effects really do represent structural alterations in synapses and are not merely artifacts of the selective formation of synapses with these properties (see Wallace, Hawrylak, & Greenough, 1991, for an elaboration of this argument). Thus, there is evidence for two independent kinds of morphological synaptic plasticity in this paradigm: (a) plasticity of synapse number and (b) plasticity of synapse structure. It is interesting that there may be more than one cellular mechanism whereby neurons accomplish learning and memory. Although they could mediate something as simple as memories of different durations, it is tempting to suggest that mammals, having invested both in a metabolically expensive brain and in the additional metabolic expense of keeping it warm enough to be rapidly activated regardless of the conditions of the external environment, must rely heavily on the brain's reliability as an information-capturing device. Hence, it may be that multiple cellular functions have evolved in the service of the fidelity of memory.

In addition to demonstrating a unique association between structural changes and learning, delineating their involvement in memory involves demonstrating that they bring about functional changes in the organization of the nervous system consonant with the changes that occur in neural organization and in behavior. As a first step toward this, Ivanco, Churchill, Patel, Norr, and Greenough (2001) have shown, both in the complex environment paradigm and in the reach training paradigm described above, that changes in the response to various forms of intracortical stimulation occur as a consequence of training. This work remains incomplete but clearly indicates at this point that synaptic structural changes induced by training are accompanied by changes in the functional organization of the brain areas in which the structural changes occur.

Taken together, these results make a powerful argument for synapse formation, as well as structural synapse modification, as mammalian memory mechanisms, at least in the case of "real" memory as opposed to models of it, such as LTP. Interestingly, despite arguments to the contrary (Sorra & Harris, 1998), there is growing evidence for involvement of new synapse formation (e.g., Shi et al., 1999), as well as synapse modification (Geinisman et al., 1991, discussed above), in at least some forms of LTP. How or whether these forms of structural plasticity might relate to changes at the receptor expression/occlusion level proposed to be involved in LTP is not clear at this point.

Possible Molecular Mechanisms of Synaptic Development and Plasticity

I turn briefly now to studies that were directed at the molecular mechanisms underlying these plastic changes in synapse morphology. I noted earlier that polyribosomal aggregates (PRAs), the protein synthesis organelles of the cell, were observed more frequently at synapses during developmental periods when synapse formation and elimination were occurring. Prior to this, Steward (1983) had shown elevated PRA levels at synapses during deafferentation-induced synaptogenesis in the dentate gyrus. Greenough, Hwang, and Gorman (1985) found a similar elevation in synaptic PRA levels in the visual cortex of rats reared in complex environments compared to cage-housed counterparts, as shown in Figure 4.3. This suggested that protein synthesis at the synapse could be involved in synaptic plasticity.

Subsequently, we used a cortical synaptoneurosome preparation depicted in Figure 4.4 to detail aspects of a postsynaptic signaling pathway that leads from synaptically released glutamate activation of metabotropic receptors to the assembly of PRAs and the synthesis of protein in the postsynaptic compartment (Angenstein, Greenough, & Weiler, 1998; Angenstein et al., 2001; Weiler & Greenough, 1991, 1993, 1999). In this novel enzyme "cascade," activated protein kinase C (PKC) appears to bind directly to the receptor for activated C kinase (RACK-1), which in turn is bound to the messenger ribonucleic acid (mRNA) complex via poly-adenosine binding protein, as illustrated in Figure 4.5.

In parallel work, Weiler et al. (1997) demonstrated that one of the proteins apparently translated by these postsynaptic polyribosomes is the Fragile X mental retardation protein (FMRP). This protein is absent in the Fragile X mental retardation syndrome, due to a genetic error that results in suppression of transcription of the FMR-1 gene into mRNA (Hagerman & Cronister, 1996). Weiler et al. (1997; see also Figure 4.5) showed that FMR-1 mRNA was taken up into polyribosomal translation complexes and that FMRP levels were increased in a synaptoneurosome preparation in response to treatment with metabotropic glutamate receptor agonists.

A possible in vivo correlate of this synaptic stimulation effect is seen in immunocytochemical studies of regional brain expression of FMRP in animals subjected to behavioral stimulation. Irwin, Christmon, et al. (2001) and Irwin, Swain, et al. (2000) report that animals that were (a) subjected to exposure to an EC environment, (b) provided the opportunity for motor skill learning in the AC training apparatus, and (c) provided the opportunity to run ad libitum in an activity wheel attached to the home cage (VX) all exhibited enhanced FMRP expression in relevant brain areas (visual cortex for EC animals, forelimb motor cortex for AC and VX animals). This work leads to two conclusions:

FIGURE 4.3

The number of dendritic spines, the postsynaptic component of most excitatory inputs, exhibiting polyribosomal aggregates (PRAs; cellular protein synthesis organelles) in the head and stem regions was increased in Environmental Complexity–reared (EC) rats compared with rats reared socially in pairs (SC) or in individual cages (IC).

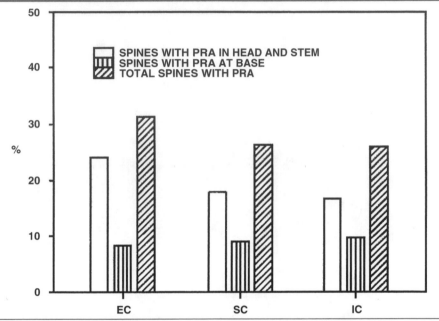

Data from "The Possible Role of Experience-dependent Synaptogenesis, or Synapses on Demand, in the Memory Process," by W. T. Greenough, 1985, in *Memory Systems of the Brain: Animal and Human Cognitive Processes,* edited by N. M. Weinberger, J. L. McGaugh, and G. Lynch, New York: Guilford Press. Copyright 1985 by Guilford Press. Adapted with permission of the publisher.

(a) as FMRP expression occurs in the VX group, for which there is no evidence for synaptogenesis or for much learning, the expression of FMRP does not appear to be closely coupled to learning per se, and (b) FMRP expression appears to be driven by peripheral and associated central neural activity. Of course, detection of cells that were active could be an important aspect of any process in which learning is encoded into memory by the brain.

We have also addressed the function of FMRP, using, in particular, a "knockout" mouse model in which the FMR-1 gene has been inactivated such that a full-length mRNA and protein cannot be produced (Dutch–Belgian Fragile X Consortium, 1994). These animals exhibited mild learning deficits as well as some of the physical characteristics of the human syndrome, such as macro-orchidism (e.g., Dutch–Belgian Fragile X Consortium, 1994; Kooy et al., 1996).

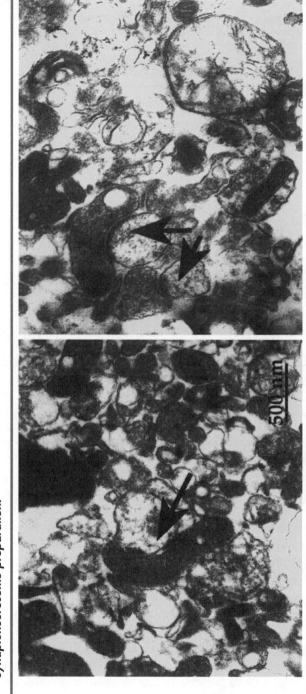

FIGURE 4.4

Synaptoneurosome preparation.

Arrows indicate transversely sectioned synapses. Only a proportion of synapses present would appear transversely oriented in the arbitrary section plane of a single micrograph. However, many nonsynaptic elements, such as mitochondria and fragments of membrane, are also present. Unpublished photograph courtesy of Anna Klintsova, University of Illinois at Urbana-Champaign. Used with permission.

FIGURE 4.5

Schematic depiction of elements theorized to lead from metabotropic glutamate receptor activation via protein kinase C (PKC) to the synthesis of proteins at the synapse.

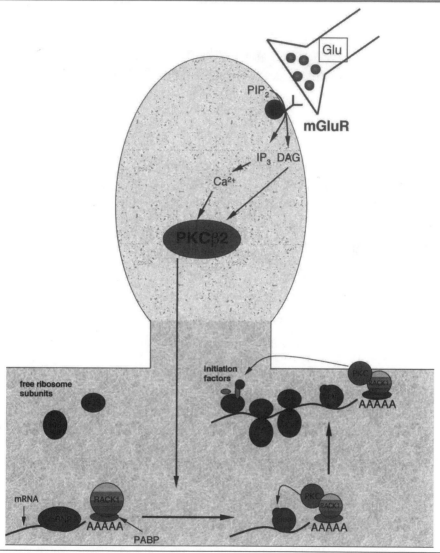

Glu = glutamate; MgluR = metabotropic glutamate receptor; PIP_2 = phosphoinositol diphosphate; IP_3 = inositol triphosphate; DAG = di-actyl glycerol; Ca^{2+} = ionic calcium; PKCβ2 = protein kinase C, beta-2; RACK-1 = receptor for activated c-kinase 1; PABP = poly-A binding protein; AAAAA = poly-A; mRNA = messenger ribonucleic acid. One of the proteins synthesized in response to receptor activation is FMRP, the protein that is absent in the Fragile X mental retardation syndrome. Unpublished figure courtesy of Frank Angenstein, University of Illinois at Urbana–Champaign. Used with permission.

FIGURE 4.6

Dendritic spines of apical shaft layer V pyramidal neuron synapses in the Fragile X syndrome adult autopsy temporal neocortex more commonly exhibited an elongated, immature-appearing morphology, compared to the predominant short spines characteristic of control brain tissue.

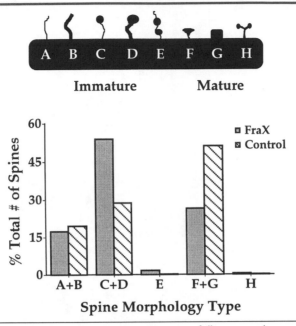

Unpublished figure courtesy Scott Irwin, University of Illinois at Urbana–Champaign. Used with permission.

Studies of these mice have revealed a possible function of FMRP as well as some consequences to the brain of developing without it. First, following on original studies of human autopsy tissue (Hinton et al., 1991; Rudelli et al., 1985; Wisniewski, Segan, Miezejeski, Sersen, & Rudelli, 1991), we have shown that knockout mice have spines on cortical pyramidal neurons that frequently exhibit an immature-like form, elongated and thin as opposed to the normally thick and shorter spines of the adult (Comery et al., 1997; Irwin, Idupulapati, et al., 2001). Similarly, in autopsy tissue, Irwin, Patel, et al. (2001) have confirmed the presence of excess immature-appearing spines, as shown in Figure 4.6, and also found that the density of spines along dendrites was higher in the affected individuals, a rare case of a mentally retarded population with a greater apparent number of synapses than is found in unaffected controls. Thus, a working hypothesis that is elaborated further below is that

FMRP is involved in some way in the process of maturation and pruning of synapses.

Second, in pursuing the function of FMRP, we have examined the stimulation of protein synthesis in the cortical synaptoneurosome preparation by K+ depolarization and metabotropic glutamate receptor-specific analogs in knockout versus wild type mice. Our results indicate that the protein synthesis response is essentially absent in the knockout mouse (Spangler et al., 2001) whether depolarization or receptor activation is the stimulus. Assuming that this result reflects the state at synapses in vivo, it indicates that potentially critical locally synthesized proteins other than FMRP are not produced in the absence of FMRP. This could lead to failure of normal synaptic development and result in the morphological immaturity of synapses seen in the knockout mice and the human syndrome. In addition, using electron microscopy of visual cortex fixed in vivo, we found that the number of cortical synapses with polyribosomal aggregates present postsynaptically in the knockout mice was less than half the wild type level at 15 and at 25 days of age, developmental points when these protein synthesizing organelles are normally present at high levels. This result corroborates in vivo the absence of local synaptic protein synthesis in the knockout mouse synaptoneurosome preparation and is compatible with the finding that neurotransmitter-activated protein synthesis at the synapse is substantially reduced in the developing FMR-1 knockout mouse. Together these results strongly suggest that proteins normally produced at the synapse are not produced there in Fragile X knockout mice and that this may be a key aspect of the mental retardation associated with the human Fragile X syndrome.

The events relating brain activation to the synthesis of FMRP at the synapse is illustrated in Figure 4.7. A tentative hypothesis consonant with these results is that one or more of the proteins whose synthesis at the synapse is enabled by the presence of FMRP plays a critical role in the synapse maturation process. Given the continuing ability of the brain to synthesize FMRP in adulthood and given the ability of behavioral activity to up regulate FMRP synthesis, it remains possible that FMRP synthesis could play a role in the cellular mechanisms mediating synapse addition or modification in the memory process as well. Also, due to the debilitating effects of the Fragile X mental retardation syndrome and the fact that it is the largest inherited form of mental retardation, it is important to determine what proteins are dependent for synaptic synthesis on the presence of FMRP and what their functions are at the synapse. It may well be that these steps will bring us closer to treatments for the disorder as well as to an understanding of the cellular mechanisms underlying memory.

FIGURE 4.7

Schematic depiction of events leading to synthesis of FMRP at synapses.

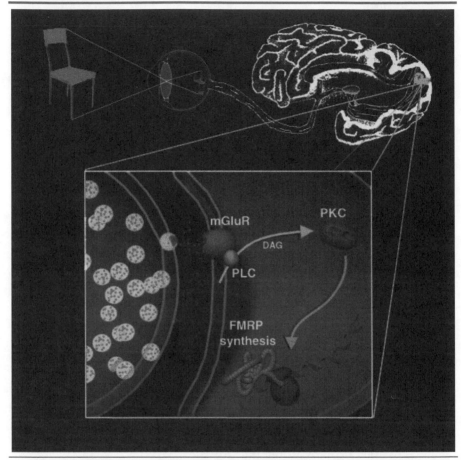

PLC = phospholipase C; FMRP = Fragile X mental retardation protein; MgluR = metabotropic glutamate receptor; DAG = di-actyl glycerol; PKC = protein kinase C. Sensory-driven activity activates glutamatergic synapses, driving protein synthesis via metabotropic glutamate receptors. Unpublished figure courtesy of William Greenough, University of Illinois at Urbana–Champaign.

References

Albus, J. S. (1971). A theory of cerebellar function. *Mathematical Biosciences, 10,* 25–61.

Anderson, B. J., Alcantara, A. A., & Greenough, W. T. (1996). Motor skill learning: Changes in synaptic organization of the rat cerebellar cortex. *Neurobiology of Learning and Memory, 66,* 221–229.

Angenstein, F., Greenough, W. T., & Weiler, I. J. (1998). Metabotropic glutamate receptor-initiated translocation of protein kinase p90rsk to polyribosomes: A possible factor regulating synaptic protein synthesis. *Proceedings of the National Academy of Sciences, 95,* 15078–15083.

Angenstein, F., Settlage, B., Kacharmina, J. E., Moran, S. T., Ling, S.-C., Klintsova, A. Y., Eberwine, J., Hunt, D., & Greenough, W. T. (2001). *RACK-1, a receptor for activated C kinase, links metabotropic glutamate receptor activation with dendritic translational control.* Manuscript in preparation, University of Illinois at Urbana–Champaign.

Bennett, E. L., Diamond, M. C., Krech, D., & Rosenzweig, M. R. (1964). Chemical and anatomical plasticity of brain. *Science, 146,* 610–619.

Black, J. E., & Greenough, W. T. (1986). Induction of pattern in neural structure by experience: Implications for cognitive development. In M. E. Lamb, A. L. Brown, & B. Rogoff (Eds.), *Advances in developmental psychology* (Vol. 4, pp. 1–50). Hillsdale, NJ: Erlbaum.

Black, J. E., & Greenough, W. T. (1998). Developmental approaches to the memory process. In J. Martinez & R. Kesner (Eds.), *Neurobiology of learning and memory* (pp. 55–88). New York: Academic Press.

Black, J. E., Isaacs, K. R., Anderson, B. J., Alcantara, A. A., & Greenough, W. T. (1990). Learning causes synaptogenesis, whereas motor activity causes angiogenesis, in cerebellar cortex of adult rats. *Proceedings of the National Academy of Sciences, 87,* 5568–5572.

Black, J. E., Sirevaag, A. M., & Greenough, W. T. (1987). Complex experience promotes capillary formation in young rat visual cortex. *Neuroscience Letters, 83,* 351–355.

Boothe, R. G., Greenough, W. T., Lund, J. S., & Wrege, K. S. (1979). A quantitative investigation of spine and dendrite development of neurons in the visual cortex (area 17) of Macaca nemestrina monkeys. *Journal of Comparative Neurology, 186,* 473–490.

Chang, F.-L., & Greenough, W. T. (1982). Lateralized effects of monocular training on dendritic branching in adult split-brain rats. *Brain Research, 232,* 283–292.

Changeux, J.-P., & Danchin, A. (1976). Selective stabilization of developing synapses as a mechanism for the specification of neuronal networks. *Nature, 264,* 705–712.

Comery, T. A., Harris, J. B., Willems, P. J., Oostra, B. A., Irwin, S. A., Weiler, I. J., & Greenough, W. T. (1997). Abnormal dendritic spines in Fragile X knockout mice: Maturation and pruning deficits. *Proceedings of the National Academy of Sciences, 94,* 5401–5404.

Cragg, B. G. (1967). Changes in visual cortex on first exposure of rats to light: Effect on synaptic dimensions. *Nature, 215,* 251–253.

Cragg, B. G. (1975). The development of synapses in the visual system of the cat. *Journal of Comparative Neurology, 160,* 147–166.

Dutch–Belgian Fragile X Consortium (1994). FMR1 knockout mice: A model to study Fragile X mental retardation. *Cell, 78,* 23–33.

Federmeier, K. D., Kleim, J. A., & Greenough, W. T. (2001). *Multiple synapse formation in the cerebellar cortex after complex motor learning.* Manuscript in preparation, University of California, San Diego.

Fujita, M. (1982). Adaptive filter model of the cerebellum. *Biological Cybernetics, 45,* 195–206.

Geinisman, Y., deToledo-Morrell, L., & Morrell, F. (1991). Induction of long-term potentiation is associated with an increase in the number of axospinous synapses with segmented postsynaptic densities. *Brain Research, 566,* 77–88.

Greenough, W. T. (1984). Structural correlates of information storage in the mammalian brain: A review and hypothesis. *Trends in NeuroSciences, 7,* 229–233.

Greenough, W. T. (1985). The possible role of experience-dependent synaptogenesis, or synapses on demand, in the memory process. In N. M. Weinberger, J. L. McGaugh, & G. Lynch (Eds.), *Memory systems of the brain: Animal and human cognitive processes* (pp. 77–103). New York: Guilford Press.

Greenough, W. T., Fulcher, J. K., Yuwiler, A., & Geller, E. (1970). Enriched rearing and chronic electroshock: Effects on brain and behavior in mice. *Physiology and Behavior, 5,* 371–373.

Greenough, W. T., Hwang, H.-M., & Gorman, C. (1985). Evidence for active synapse formation, or altered postsynaptic metabolism, in visual cortex of rats reared in complex environments. *Proceedings of the National Academy of Sciences, 82,* 4549–4552.

Greenough, W. T., Juraska, J. M., & Volkmar, F. R. (1979). Maze training effects on dendritic branching in occipital cortex of adult rats. *Behavioral and Neural Biology, 26,* 287–297.

Greenough, W. T., Larson, J. R., & Withers, G. S. (1985). Effects of unilateral and bilateral training in a reaching task on dendritic branching of neurons in the rat motor–sensory forelimb cortex. *Behavioral and Neural Biology, 44,* 301–314.

Greenough, W. T., & McGaugh, J. L. (1965). The effect of strychnine sulphate on learning as a function of time of administration. *Psychopharmacologia (Berlin), 8,* 290–294.

Greenough, W. T., & Volkmar, F. R. (1973). Pattern of dendritic branching in rat occipital cortex after rearing in complex environments. *Experimental Neurology, 40,* 491–504.

Greenough, W. T., West, R. W., & DeVoogd, T. J. (1978). Sub-synaptic plate perforations: Changes with age and experience in the rat. *Science, 202,* 1096–1098.

Greenough, W. T., Yuwiler, A., & Dollinger, M. (1973). Effects of post-trial eserine administration on learning in "enriched" and "impoverished" reared rats. *Behavioral Biology, 8,* 261–272.

Hagerman, R. J., & Cronister, A. (1996). *Fragile X syndrome: Diagnosis, treatment, and research* (2nd ed.). Baltimore: Johns Hopkins University Press.

Hata, Y., & Stryker, M. P. (1994). Control of thalamocortical afferent rearrangement by postsynaptic activity in developing visual cortex. *Science, 265,* 732–735.

Huttenlocher, P. R. (1979). Synaptic density in human frontal cortex—Developmental changes and effects of aging. *Brain Research, 163,* 195–205.

Hinton, V. J., Brown, W. T., Wisniewski, K., & Rudelli, R. D. (1991). Analysis of neo-cortex in three males with the Fragile X syndrome. *American Journal of Medical Genetics, 41,* 289–294.

Irwin, S. A., Christmon, C. A., Swain, R. A., Galvez, R., Weiler, I. J., & Greenough, W. T. (2001). *Fragile-X mental retardation protein immunoreactivity is increased in vivo in areas that exhibit active synaptogenesis in response to motor-skill learning and motor activity.* Manuscript in preparation, University of Illinois at Urbana–Champaign.

Irwin, S. A., Idupulapati, M., Gilbert, M. E., Harris, J. B., Chakravarti, A. B., Rogers, E. J., Crisostomo, R. A., Larsen, B. P., Mehta, A., Alcantara, C. J., Patel, B. A., Swain, R. A., Weiler, I. J., & Greenough, W. T. (2001). *Dendritic spine and dendritic field characteristics of layer V pyramidal neurons in the visual cortex of Fragile-X knock-out mice.* Manuscript in preparation, University of Illinois at Urbana–Champaign.

Irwin, S. A., Patel, B., Idupulapati, M., Harris, J. B., Cristostomo, R., Kooy, F., Willems, P. J., Cras, P., Kozlowski, P. B., Weiler, I. J., & Greenough, W. T. (2001). Abnormal dendritic spine characteristics in the temporal and visual cortices of patients with Fragile-X syndrome: A quantitative examination. *Medical Genetics, 98,* 161–167.

Irwin, S. A., Swain, R. A., Christmon, C. A., Chakravarti, A., Weiler, I. J., & Greenough, W. T. (2000). Evidence for altered Fragile-X mental retardation protein expression in response to behavioral stimulation. *Neurobiology of Learning and Memory, 73,* 87–93.

Ito, M. (1984). *The cerebellum and neural control.* New York: Raven Press.

Ivanco, T. L., Churchill, J. D., Patel, S., Norr, D., & Greenough, W. T. (2001). *Physio-logical measures indicate that motor learning influences basal synaptic efficacy and LTP induction in the rat motor cortex.* Manuscript in preparation, University of Illinois at Urbana–Champaign.

Juraska, J. M., Greenough, W. T., Elliott, C., Mack, K. J., & Berkowitz, R. (1980). Plasticity in adult rat visual cortex: An examination of several cell populations after differential rearing. *Behavioral and Neural Biology, 29,* 157–167.

Kleim, J. A., Lussnig, E., Schwarz, E. R., Comery, T. A., & Greenough, W. T. (1996). Synaptogenesis and Fos expression in the motor cortex of the adult rat following motor skill learning. *Journal of Neuroscience, 16,* 4529–4535.

Kleim, J. A., McNamee, D., Blankstein, E., & Greenough, W. T. (2001). *Structural cor-relates of motor skill learning: Multiple changes in synapse morphology in the rat motor cortex suggest multiple forms of plastic change.* Manuscript in preparation, University of Illinois at Urbana–Champaign.

Kleim, J. A., Pipitone, M. A., Czerlanis, C. M., & Greenough, W. T. (1998). Structural stability within the lateral cerebellar nucleus of the rat following complex motor learning. *Neurobiology of Learning and Memory, 69,* 290–306.

Kleim, J. A., Swain, R. A., Armstrong, K. E., Napper, R. M. A., Jones, T. A., & Greenough, W. T. (1998). Selective synaptic plasticity within the cerebellar cortex following complex motor skill learning. *Neurobiology of Learning and Memory, 69,* 274–289.

Kleim, J. A., Swain, R. A., Czerlanis, C. M., Kelly, J. L., Pipitone, M. A., & Greenough, W. T. (1997). Learning dependent dendritic hypertrophy of cerebellar stellate cells: Plasticity of local circuit neurons. *Neurobiology of Learning and Memory, 67,* 29–33.

Kleim, J. A., Vij, K., Ballard, D. H., & Greenough, W. T. (1997). Learning dependent synaptic modifications in the cerebellar cortex of the adult rat persist for at least four weeks. *Journal of Neuroscience, 17,* 717–721.

Kooy, R. F., D'Hooge, R., Reyniers, E., Bakker, C. E., Nagels, G., De Boulle, K., Storm, K., Clincke, G., De Deyn, P. P., Oostra, B. A., & Willems, P. J. (1996). Transgenic mouse model for the Fragile X syndrome. *American Journal of Medical Genetics, 64,* 241–245.

LeVay, S., Wiesel, T. N., & Hubel, D. H. (1980). The development of ocular dominance columns in normal and visually deprived monkeys. *Journal of Comparative Neurology, 191,* 1–51.

McGaugh, J. L. (1966). Time-dependent processes in memory storage. *Science, 153,* 1351–1358.

Rose, S. P. R. (1967). Changes in visual cortex on first exposure to light. *Nature, 215,* 253–255.

Rudelli, R. D., Brown, W. T., Wisniewski, K., Jenkins, E. C., Laure-Kamionowska, M., Connell, F., & Wisniewski, H. M. (1985). Adult Fragile X syndrome: Clinico–neuropathologic findings. *Acta Neuropathologica (Berlin), 67,* 289–295.

Shi, S.-H., Hayashi, Y., Petralia, R. S., Zaman, S. H., Wenthold, R. J., Svoboda, K., & Malinow, R. (1999). Rapid spine delivery and redistribution of AMPA receptors after synaptic NMDA receptor activation. *Science, 284,* 1811–1816.

Sirevaag, A. M., & Greenough, W. T. (1985). Differential rearing effects on rat visual cortex synapses: II. Synaptic morphometry. *Developmental Brain Research, 19,* 215–226.

Sirevaag, A. M., & Greenough, W. T. (1991). Plasticity of GFAP-immunoreactive astrocyte size and number in visual cortex of rats reared in complex environments. *Brain Research, 540,* 273–278.

Sorra, K. E., & Harris, K. M. (1998). Stability in synapse number and size at 2 hr after long-term potentiation in hippocampal area CA1. *Journal of Neuroscience, 18,* 658–671.

Spangler, C. C., Klintsova, A. Y., Bertaina-Anglade, V., Base, C. K., Weiler, I. J., & Greenough, W. T. (2001). *Fragile X mental retardation protein enables transmitter-actuated synaptic translation.* Manuscript submitted for publication.

Steward, O. (1983). Polyribosomes at the base of dendritic spines of CNS neurons: Their possible role in synapse construction and modification. *Cold Spring Harbor Symposia on Quantitative Biology, 48,* 745–759.

Turner, A. M., & Greenough, W. T. (1983). Synapses per neuron and synaptic dimensions in occipital cortex of rats reared in complex, social, or isolation housing. *Acta Stereologica, 2* (Suppl. 1), 239–244.

Turner, A. M., & Greenough, W. T. (1985). Differential rearing effects on rat visual cortex synapses: I. Synaptic and neuronal density and synapses per neuron. *Brain Research, 329,* 195–203.

Volkmar, F. R., & Greenough, W. T. (1972). Rearing complexity affects branching of dendrites in the visual cortex of the rat. *Science, 176,* 1445–1447.

Wallace, C. S., Hawrylak, N., & Greenough, W. T. (1991). Studies of synaptic structural modifications following LTP and kindling: Context for a molecular morphology. In M. Baudry & J. Davis (Eds.), *LTP: A debate of current issues* (pp. 189–232). Cambridge, MA: MIT Press.

Weiler, I. J., & Greenough, W. T. (1991). Potassium ion stimulation triggers protein translation in synaptoneurosomal polyribosomes. *Molecular and Cellular Neurosciences, 2,* 305–314.

Weiler, I. J., & Greenough, W. T. (1993). Metabotropic glutamate receptors trigger postsynaptic protein synthesis. *Proceedings of the National Academy of Sciences, 90,* 7168–7171.

Weiler, I. J., & Greenough, W. T. (1999). Synaptic synthesis of the Fragile X protein: Possible involvement in synapse maturation and elimination. *American Journal of Medical Genetics, 83,* 248–252.

Weiler, I. J., Irwin, S. A., Klintsova, A. Y., Spencer, C. M., Brazelton, A. D., Miyashiro, K., Comery, T. A., Patel, B., Eberwine, J., & Greenough, W. T. (1997). Fragile X mental retardation protein is translated near synapses in response to neurotransmitter activation. *Proceedings of the National Academy of Sciences, 94,* 5395–5400.

West, R. W., & Greenough, W. T. (1972). Effect of environmental complexity on cortical synapses of rats: Preliminary results. *Behavioral Biology, 7,* 279–284.

Wisniewski, K. E., Segan, S. M., Miezejeski, C. M., Sersen, E. A., & Rudelli, R. D. (1991). The Fra(X) syndrome: Neurological, electrophysiological, and neuropathological abnormalities. *American Journal of Medical Genetics, 38,* 476–480.

Yuwiler, A., Greenough, W. T., & Geller, E. (1968). Biochemical and behavioral effects of magnesium pemoline. *Psychopharmacologia (Berlin), 13,* 174–180.

CHAPTER 5

Consolidation of Short- and Long-Term Memory

Iván Izquierdo, Patricia G. Ardenghi, Daniela M. Barros, Lia Bevilaqua,
Luciana A. Izquierdo, Jorge H. Medina, Tadeu Mello e Souza,
Patricia Pereira, Marcia M. de Souza, and Monica R. M. Vianna

A seminal article in modern memory research appeared in 1966 by Jim McGaugh in the journal *Science*. In that article, McGaugh reformulated Müller and Pilzecker's (1900) concept of memory consolidation in terms amenable to biological investigation; established the use of posttraining treatments as a tool in memory research; and brought forward under a new light the old question (James, 1890) of whether short-term memory (STM) and long-term memory (LTM) are serial or parallel processes. In addition, McGaugh greatly contributed to the establishment of one-trial inhibitory avoidance as a paradigm particularly useful to measure time-dependent processes in memory storage, including the distinction between STM and LTM. Here we comment on recent findings from our group that stem directly from McGaugh's (1966) article.

Consolidation of Long-Term Memory: Role of CA1

McGaugh's (1966) concept of consolidation derived from Gerard's (1961) idea that some form of neural activity must underlie the setting down of memory traces. It is easier to view this as a truism today than it was in 1961 or 1966. Gerard thought of consolidation as the product of reverberation in circuits processing recently acquired information. Indeed, rapid reverberation in the CA1-subiculum-entorhinal cortex-dentate gyrus-CA3–CA1 circuit does occur (Iijima

This research was supported by Programa Nacional de Núcleos de Excelencia, Brazil. Jorge H. Medina is at the Instituto de Biología Celular y Neurociencia Eduardo de Robertis, at the Facultad de Medicina, Universidad de Buenos Aires and his participation was supported by Ministerio de Salud Publica of Argentina, Brazil.

et al., 1996), and all components of this circuit are known to be crucial for consolidation of a great variety of tasks (Eichenbaum, Schoenbaum, Young, & Bunsey, 1996; Ferreira, da Silva, Medina, & Izquierdo, 1992; Ferreira, Wolfman, et al., 1992; Izquierdo & Medina, 1995, 1997a, 1997b; Saucier & Cain, 1995).

In 1993, Bliss and his coworkers discovered long-term potentiation (LTP) in the dentate gyrus and in the CA3–CA1 pathway (Bliss & Collingridge, 1993). LTP is an obvious model of memory, and it was proposed early on as the actual basis of memory (e.g., Lynch & Baudry, 1984; Matthies, 1989). Again, it is easier to dismiss this assertion today than it was in 1984 or 1989. Morris, Anderson, Lynch, and Baudry (1986) observed that the intracerebroventricular administration of the glutamate NMDA (N-methyl d-aspartate) receptor antagonist, AP5 (aminophosphonopentanoic acid), at doses or concentrations capable of blocking CA1 LTP impairs spatial learning in the Morris water maze, a task that requires the integrity of CA1. This finding opened the way for a detailed study of the role of glutamatergic transmission and its biochemical consequences in CA1 in memory formation (Izquierdo & Medina, 1995, 1997a, 1997b; Riedel, 1996; Wilson & Tonegawa, 1997). Now we know that probably no form of memory relies on a single burst of stimuli to one set of fibers and that even memory of a task as deceivingly simple as one-trial inhibitory avoidance requires the integrated activity of many brain cortical and subcortical structures (Izquierdo, Quillfeldt, et al., 1997; Van der Zee, Douma, Bohus, & Luiten, 1994), in some cases simultaneously (Brioni, 1993; Izquierdo, da Cunha, et al., 1992; Izquierdo, Izquierdo, et al., 1998), in others sequentially (Ferreira et al., 1992; Izquierdo, Quillfeldt, et al., 1997), and in others without any participation of NMDA receptors (Izquierdo, Izquierdo, et al., 1998).

The biochemical chain of events underlying LTP involves

- initial activation of NMDA (n-methyl-0-aspartate), AMPA (aminohydroxymethylisoxazole), and metabotropic glutamate receptors (Bliss & Collingridge, 1993)

- sustained enhancement of AMPA receptor function in the next 2–3 hours (Sergueeva, Fedorov, & Reymann, 1993), maintained by phosphorylation of its GluR1 subunit by calcium/calmodulin-dependent protein kinase II (CaMKII; Barria, Muller, Verkach, Griffith, & Soderling, 1997)

- activation of presumably postsynaptic protein kinase G (PKG; Zhuo, Hu, Schultz, Kandel, & Hawkins, 1994), of pre- and postsynaptic protein kinase C (PKC; Colley & Routtenberg, 1993), of postsynaptic CaMKII (Barria et al., 1997), of the Erk/Ras system (English & Sweat, 1996), and of postsynaptic protein kinase A (PKA; Abel et al., 1998; Matthies & Reymann, 1993)

- phosphorylation of CREB (camp response element binding protein; Silva, Kogan, Frankland, & Lida, 1998)
- consequent synthesis of proteins, among which some are believed to be involved in cell adhesion changes (Lüthi, Laurent, Figurov, Muller, & Schachner, 1994) and in morphological changes of the synapses that have been activated (see Martin & Kandel, 1996).

The biochemical steps underlying memory formation in CA1 in rats were studied in detail by our group in the one-trial inhibitory avoidance paradigm. The studies centered on neurotransmitter systems and on the major enzymatic pathways known to be activated by them. The strategy was to study the effect on memory of specific agonists and antagonists of various neurotransmitters and of enzyme inhibitors given at various times after training and to study the effect of training on the properties of those neurotransmitters and enzymes and the substrates of the latter, also at different times after training (Izquierdo & Medina, 1997a). The biochemical steps of memory processing in rat CA1 turned out to be essentially those of LTP, with a few important differences (Izquierdo & Medina, 1995, 1997b).

The major similarities are

1. the early role of NMDA, AMPA, and metabotropic glutamate receptors (Bianchin et al., 1994; Izquierdo, da Cunha, et al., 1992; Jerusalinsky et al., 1992)

2. the sequential participation of PKA (Bernabeu, Bevilaqua, et al., 1997), PKG (Bernabeu, Schröder, et al., 1997), PKC (Cammarota, Paratcha, et al., 1997; Jerusalinsky, Quillfeldt, et al., 1993, 1994), and CaMKII (Cammarota, Bernabeu, Levi de Stein, Izquierdo, & Medina, 1997; Wolfman et al., 1994) in the first 3 hours (Izquierdo & Medina, 1995, 1997a)

3. the enhancement of AMPA receptor binding properties during those 3 hours by phosphorylation of the GluR1 subunit by CaMKII (Cammarota, Bernabeu, et al., 1997); and a second, late cAMP/PKA-dependent phase at 3–6 hours from training that activates the transcription factor family CREB and leads to protein synthesis (Bernabeu, Bevilaqua, et al., 1997; Bernabeu, Schmitz, Faillace, Izquierdo, & Medina, 1996; Izquierdo & Medina, 1997a, 1997b). Consolidation becomes effectively completed only after this late transcription-dependent phase and its consequences are over. Among these consequences are the need of neural cell adhesion molecules some time between the 5th and the 7th hour after training (Doyle, Nolan, Bell, & Regan, 1992) and the occurrence of late morphological synaptic changes (O'Connell, O'Malley, & Regan, 1997).

The differences between the mechanisms of LTP and of LTM formation in CA1 are

1. The synaptic messengers NO (nitric oxide), CO (carbon oxide), and the platelet-activating factor play an important role in CA1 for LTM formation (Izquierdo & Medina, 1995, 1997a, 1997b) but this role is less clear for LTP (Bliss & Collingridge, 1993; Izquierdo & Medina, 1995).

2. LTM formation can be made nondependent on NMDA receptors by preexposure to the apparatus or by pretraining (Roesler et al., 1998).

3. An early, immediate posttraining peak of PKA activity coupled with a very rapid increase of nuclear P-CREB in CA1 is essential for LTM formation (Bernabeu, Bevilaqua, et al., 1997; Izquierdo & Medina, 1997a; Vianna, Izquierdo, Barros, Medina, & Izquierdo, 1999). There is a similar early need of protein synthesis for memory formation in chicks (Freeman, Rose, & Scholey, 1995). This early peak has not been described as essential for LTP (see Bliss & Collingridge, 1993; Frey & Morris, 1998; Huang, Li, & Kandel, 1994; Matthies & Reymann, 1993).

4. The second cAMP/PKA-P-CREB peak in CA1 at 3–6 hours from training is modulated not only by dopaminergic D1 receptors, as in CA1 LTP (Huang & Kandel, 1995), but also and importantly by β-noradrenergic and by 5HT1A receptors (Ardenghi et al., 1997; Bernabeu, Bevilaqua, et al., 1997; Bevilaqua et al., 1997; Izquierdo, Medina, Ardenghi, et al., 1998). This multiple monoamine modulation lasts for hours and takes place simultaneously in the entorhinal and posterior parietal cortex (Ardenghi et al., 1997).

5. The Erk/Ras system intervenes at different times in LTM and in LTP and, in the former case, participates in several brain areas in parallel (Van der Zee et al., 1994; Walz et al., 2000).

Aside from these differences, the coincidence of the nature and the timing of the biochemical steps of LTM formation of the one-trial task and LTP in the CA1 region is remarkable (Izquierdo & Medina, 1995, 1997a, 1997b). Many of these steps have been shown to play a role in LTM formation of other tasks in rodents (glutamate receptors—Riedel, 1996; Walz et al., 2000; Wilson & Tonegawa, 1997; PKC—Nogués, Micheau, & Jaffard, 1994; CaMKII—Mayford et al., 1996; Tan & Liang, 1996; PKA—Abel et al., 1998; P-CREB—Bourchuladze et al., 1994; and late protein synthesis, cell adhesion, and morphological changes—O'Connell et al., 1997; Roullet, Mileusnic, Rose, & Sara, 1997) and in other species, including the fruit fly (Yin & Tully, 1996), the honeybee (Menzel & Müller, 1996), the mollusk *Aplysia* (Carew, 1996), and the chick (Roullet et al., 1997).

One-trial inhibitory avoidance in the chick has been the task most comprehensively studied besides one-trial inhibitory avoidance in the rat. In spite of anatomical differences, the coincidences are remarkable, from the early involvement of glutamate receptors (Bourchuladze & Rose, 1992) and PKC (Bourchuladze, Potter, & Rose, 1990) to a bimodal requirement of protein synthesis (Freeman et al., 1995) and cell adhesion molecules (Scholey, Mileusnic, Schachner, & Rose, 1995). Further, several of the biochemical steps underlying LTM formation or LTP take place in the nucleus accumbens in the development of drug addiction (Kalivas, Sorg, & Pierce, 1998).

This renders the question of whether "LTP equals memory" (Stevens, 1998) somewhat irrelevant. Clearly, the sequence of biochemical chains of events underlying CA1 LTP is very similar to that used by the same area in LTM formation, or to that used by neurons elsewhere to develop long-term plastic changes; but this simply means that neurons "do" synaptic plasticity by way of that sequence of events, not that one event is equal to any other. Not surprisingly, because many of the steps involved in LTP and memory formation in CA1 overlap, LTP of sufficient intensity may saturate those mechanisms and block memory formation (Moser, Krobert, Moser, & Morris, 1998).

The specificity of the LTMs formed cannot rely on any biochemical step of the chain used for developing plasticity. The PKA/P–CREB step in particular is obviously common to many forms of chronic plasticity (Impey et al., 1996), from cell development to cell survival, from spermatogenesis to circadian rhythms, and from drug addiction to memory (Finkbeiner et al., 1997; Ginty et al., 1993; Silva et al., 1998). The specificity of LTMs must rely on what synapses are ultimately changed in each case (Izquierdo & Medina, 1997a) rather than on a general molecular switch; that is, the code must be anatomical rather than transcriptional. The search for a role of changes in cell adhesion molecules taking place hours after behavioral training (O'Connell et al., 1997; Scholey et al., 1995) and eventually leading to morphological changes at specific synapses (O'Connell et al., 1997) appears therefore particularly promising. LTP data have suggested that the link between the recent activation and the subsequent long-lasting change of synapses must rely on their tagging by posttranscriptional changes of local preexisting proteins (Frey & Morris, 1998).

Consolidation of Long-Term Memory: Role of Other Brain Regions

The hippocampus does not act in isolation in producing LTM consolidation. As mentioned, the early steps of its participation require the functional integrity of the prefrontal (Izquierdo, Izquierdo, et al., 1998) and entorhinal cortex (Willner et al., 1993) and are modulated by the amygdala (Cahill & McGaugh, 1996, 1998) and other areas, notably the medial septum (Izquierdo, da Cunha, et al., 1992). Any information arriving at the hippocampus from the prefrontal areas in charge of working memory (WM; Goldman-Rakic, 1991) and from sensory and associative areas of the cortex must relay on the entorhinal cortex (Van Hoesen, 1985; Witter, Groenewegen, Lopes da Silva, & Lohman, 1989).

In addition, the entorhinal and parietal cortex play a late role in consolidation as well. Blockade of NMDA receptors by AP5 or GABAergic stimulation by muscimol between 0.5 and 3–4 hours after training in the entorhinal cortex, or between 1 and 3–4 hours after training in the posterior parietal cortex, results in full retrograde amnesia (Ferreira, da Silva, et al., 1992; Ferreira, Wolfman, et al., 1992; Izquierdo, Quillfeldt, et al., 1997). Pharmacological data suggest that PKC in the entorhinal cortex (Jerusalinsky, Quillfeldt, et al., 1993) and the cAMP/PKA pathway both in the entorhinal and the parietal cortex are necessary for LTM formation hours after training (see next section).

Late Memory Modulation

The early literature on LTM consolidation dwells on whether it lasts seconds or minutes; few ventured that it could extend any longer than that (Gold & McGaugh, 1975; McGaugh, 1966, 1968). However, findings on the biochemistry of LTM have clearly established that events that take place in CA1 and associated structures much later (up to 6 hours after training) are essential for storage (Izquierdo & Medina, 1995, 1997a, 1997b). Indeed, the crucial step seems to be the late peak of cAMP/PKA activity/nuclear P-CREB levels that occurs 3–6 hours after training (Bernabeu, Schröder, et al., 1997) without which there is no LTM consolidation (Bourchuladze et al., 1994). These late events are modulated by monoaminergic pathways related to affect, mood, and emotion (Ardenghi et al., 1997; Bevilaqua et al., 1997). Serotoninergic, dopaminergic, and noradrenergic fibers innervate the hippocampus, entorhinal, and parietal cortex, and 5HT1A, dopamine D1, and β-adrenergic receptors are present in those structures (Ardenghi et al., 1997; Bevilaqua et al., 1997). 5HT1A receptors inhibit, and dopamine D1 and β-adrenergic receptors stimulate, adenylyl cyclase, the enzyme that mediates cAMP synthesis.

Considering that the cAMP/PKA phase of LTM formation takes several hours, we studied the effect on memory of various substances acting on this metabolic pathway by infusing them bilaterally into dorsal CA1 (Figure 5.1), the amygdala (Figure 5.2), the entorhinal cortex (Figure 5.3), or the posterior parietal cortex (Figure 5.4) 0–9 hours after step-down inhibitory avoidance training (Ardenghi et al., 1997; Bevilaqua et al., 1997; Izquierdo, Medina, Ardenghi, et al., 1998). The drugs were 8-Br-cAMP, the stimulator of adenylyl cyclase, forskolin, the specific D1 agonist, SKF38393, and the specific D1 antagonist, SCH23390, norepinephrine, the β-blocker, timolol, the 5HT1A agonist, 8-HO-DPAT, and the 5HT1A antagonist, NAN-19, and the PKA inhibitor KT5720. The drugs were dissolved in a vehicle (20% dimethyl sulfoxide in saline) and infusion volume was 0.5 μl in all cases (doses of the drugs are given in the legends to Figures 5.1–5.4). They were the same for the four brain structures, and were established from Ki or Km values in in vitro experiments assuming a diffusion volume of 1 mm^3 (Ardenghi et al., 1997; Bevilaqua et al., 1997; Izquierdo, Medina, Ardenghi, et al., 1998).

At 0 hours after training, only norepinephrine had an effect on memory when given into CA1 (Figure 5.1); this has been described before (Izquierdo, da Cuhna, et al., 1992) and is attributable to a synaptic interaction with regular excitatory transmission. All other treatments given into CA1 were ineffective when given 0 or 1.5 hours after training. When given into this area 3 or 6 hours posttraining, SKF38393, norepinephrine, 8-Br-cAMP, forskolin, and NAN-190 enhanced LTM of the task measured on the next day, and KT5720, SCH23390, timolol, and DPAT were amnestic. These findings correlate with the late peak of CA1 cAMP levels (Bernabeu et al., 1996) and CREB-P and PKA activity (Bernabeu, Bevilaqua, et al., 1997), and indeed suggest that activation of the cAMP/PKA signaling pathway 3–6 hours posttraining may result from the activation of noradrenergic and dopaminergic pathways, and perhaps the inhibition of serotoninergic pathways.

When given into the entorhinal cortex 0, 3, or 6 hours posttraining, 8-Br-cAMP, forskolin, SKF 38393, and norepinephrine caused LTM facilitation, and KT5720, SCH23390, and 8-HO-DPAT caused retrograde amnesia (Figure 5.2). Timolol was amnestic depending on the time at which it was administered into the entorhinal cortex.

When given into the posterior parietal cortex 0, 3, or 6 hours after training, KT5720 was amnestic; when given into this structure 3 or 6 but not 0 or 9 hours posttraining 8-Br-cAMP, forskolin, and norepinephrine caused memory facilitation and KT5720, SCH23390, and timolol caused retrograde amnesia (Figure 5.3). As in CA1 (Figure 5.1) or entorhinal cortex (Figure 5.2), no effects were seen when drugs were given 9 hours after training in the parietal area.

With the exception of an immediate posttraining retrograde facilitatory effect of norepinephrine that had been described before (Izquierdo, da Cunha, et al., 1992) and was attributed to interactions with excitatory synaptic transmission at the time of training (Izquierdo, da Cunha, et al., 1992), LTM was insensitive to the infusion of any of the drugs given 0, 3, or 6 hours after training into the amygdala (Figure 5.4).

The data point to a role of cAMP/PKA-dependent mechanisms in LTM formation in the entorhinal cortex 0, 3, and 6 hours after training, and in CA1

FIGURE 5.1

Effects of substances infused bilaterally in the CA1 region on long-term memory of the step-down inhibitory avoidance task (0.3 mA foot shock).

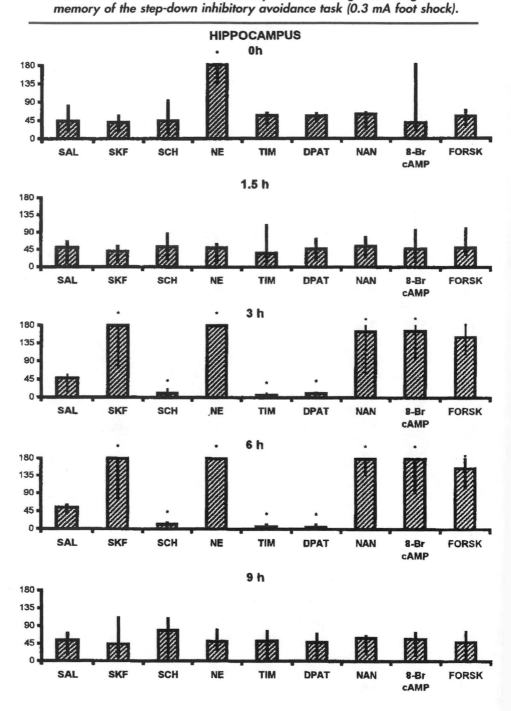

and in the parietal cortex 3–6 hours after training, as well as to a strong modulation of these mechanisms by dopaminergic D1, β-adrenergic, and 5HT1A receptors in these structures but not in the amygdala (Ardenghi et al., 1997).

The timing of the intervention of the entorhinal and parietal cortex in consolidation (Izquierdo, Quillfeldt, et al., 1997) is different from that of their participation in the modulation of memory (see above and Figures 5.2 and 5.3). There is a long-lasting modulatory intervention of dopaminergic D1, β-adrenergic, and 5HT1A mechanisms in all these structures that are independent of the amygdala and from the NMDA receptor-dependent role of these areas in memory formation (see above).

The amygdala appears to be involved in events related to alertness, stress, or high-pitched but transient emotional aspects of memory at the onset of the consolidation process; for example, those that may be at the crux of "flashbulb" memories (Cahill & McGaugh, 1998). The late-acting monoaminergic pathways acting on CA1, the entorhinal, and parietal cortex may instead be related to mood, affect, anxiety, or longer lasting emotional changes that affect our daily life and whose failure underlies a variety of mental disorders (Izquierdo, Medina, Ardenghi, et al., 1998).

Things That Happen to Memories Late After Training

Exposure to a novel environment 1 hour after induction but not 5 minutes before or 24 hours later reverses LTP in rat hippocampus (Xu, Anwyl, & Rowan,

(continued from previous page)
The ordinates express median (interquartile range) test session latency, in seconds. Rats were infused bilaterally in the dorsal CA1 region, 0, 1.5, 3, 6, or 9 hours after training, with saline, 8-HO-DPAT, 2.5 μg/side (DPAT); NAN-190, 2.5 μg/side (NAN); norepinephrine, 0.3 μg/side (NE); timolol, 0.3 μg/side (TIM); SKF38383, 7.5 μg/side (SKF); SCH23390, 0.5 μg/side (SCH); 8-Br-cAMP, 1.25 μg/side (cAMP); a vehicle (20% dimethylsulfoxide in saline, SAL), KT-5720, 0.5 μg/side (KT); and forskolin, 0.5 μg/side (FORSK). Asterisks indicate significant differences in Mann–Whitney U tests, two-tailed, at $p < .002$ level with the saline control group (all drugs except KT and FORSK), and with the vehicle group (KT and FORSK). $n = 9$–12 per group. Note that when treatments were given immediately after training (0 hours), NE caused retrograde memory facilitation and KT caused retrograde amnesia. When given 1.5 or 9 hours after training, all treatments were ineffective. When infused 3 or 6 hours posttraining, NAN, NE, SKF, cAMP, and FOR induced a pronounced facilitation; and DPAT, TIM, SCH, and KT caused full retrograde amnesia. From "Drugs Acting Upon the Protein Kinase A/CREB Pathway Modulate Memory Consolidation When Given Late After Training Into Rat Hippocampus but Not Amygdala," by L. Bevilaqua, P. Ardenghi, N. Schröder, E. Bromberg, P. K. Schmitz, E. Schaeffer, J. Quevedo, M. Bianchin, R. Walz, J. H. Medina, and I. Izquierdo, 1997, *Behavioural Pharmacology, 8*. Copyright 1997 by Lippincott, Williams & Wilkins. Adapted with permission of the publisher.

FIGURE 5.2

Effects of substances infused bilaterally in the central/basolateral area of the amygdala on long-term memory of the step-down inhibitory avoidance task (0.3 mA foot shock).

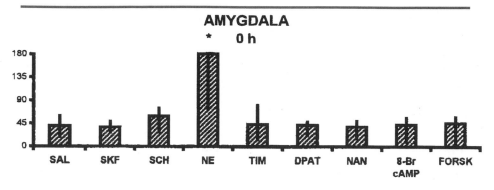

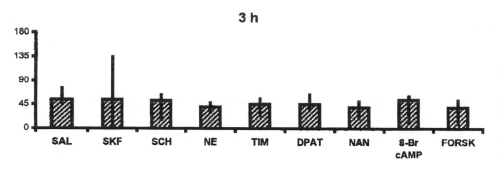

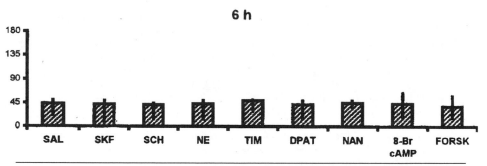

The ordinates express median (interquartile range) test session latency, in seconds. Rats were infused bilaterally in the central/basolateral area of the amygdala, 0, 1.5, 3, 6, or 9 hours after training, with saline, 8-HO-DPAT, 2.5 μg/side (DPAT); NAN-190, 2.5 μg/side (NAN); norepinephrine, 0.3 μg/side (NE); timolol, 0.3 μg/side (TIM); SKF38383, 7.5 μg/side (SKF); SCH23390, 0.5 μg/side (SCH); 8-Br-cAMP, 1.25 μg/side (cAMP); a vehicle (20% dimethylsulfoxide in saline, SAL), KT-5720, 0.5 μg/side (KT); and forskolin, 0.5 μg/side (FORSK). Asterisks indicate significant differences in Mann–Whitney U tests, two-tailed, at $p < .002$ level with the saline control group, and with the vehicle group (KT and FORSK).

1998). Morris (1998) thought it critical to see whether novelty similarly affects hippocampus-dependent one-trial learning. As recently shown by Izquierdo, Schröder, Netto, and Medina (1999), it does.

Rats were trained in step-down inhibitory avoidance and tested 24 hours later for LTM. Either 5 minutes before training, or 1 or 6 hours after training, the animals were placed for 2 minutes in an open field and left to explore it freely for 2 minutes. Crossing of black lines drawn on the floor of the open field were taken as a measure of exploration. There was habituation of this exploration, measured by a significant decrease in the number of crossings of lines drawn on the floor of the open field between the 1st and 2nd minute of their permanence in the open field.

Five groups of 10 rats were trained in the avoidance task using a 0.4 mA shock. One was exposed just to this task; others were exposed to novelty 5 minutes before, or 1 or 6 hours after, avoidance training; and the 5th group was exposed to 2 minutes of handling 1 hour after avoidance training. Two other groups were trained using a 1.0 mA shock. One was and the other was not exposed to the novelty 1 hour after training. The first 4 groups were tested at 9, 24, 48, 72, and 96 hours from training; the last 3 were tested only at 24 hours. Novelty 1 hour after training abruptly enhanced forgetting of the avoidance task regardless of whether this was acquired with a 0.4 or a 1.0 mA shock. Novelty presented 5 minutes before or 6 hours after avoidance training or handling had no effect on the retention of avoidance or its extinction rate. Avoidance did not affect habituation, even at the higher shock level (Izquierdo, Schröder, et al., 1999).

The findings agree not only with Morris's (1998) prediction but also with previous experiments in which we described a similar effect of various forms of novelty (an open field, a small box, a Y maze, repeated tones, etc.) on active or inhibitory avoidance acquired 2 but not 22 hours before (Cahill, Brioni, & Izquierdo, 1986; Netto, Dias, & Izquierdo, 1985). As suggested for its effect on LTP (Morris, 1998; Xu et al., 1998) perhaps novelty (or habituation to novelty) blocks memory of the one-trial task because it resets its biochemical chain of events at the wrong time, i.e., much before it consolidates (Izquierdo & Medina, 1997a, 1997b). Indeed, the retrograde amnestic effect of novelty 1

Infusions were carried out 0, 3, or 6 hours after step-down inhibitory avoidance training (0.3 mA foot shock). NE given 0 hours posttraining caused retrograde memory facilitation. All other treatments were ineffective. $n = 8$–12 per group. From "Late and Prolonged Memory Modulation in Entorhinal and Parietal Cortex by Drugs Acting on the cAMP/Protein Kinase A Signalling Pathway," by P. Ardenghi, D. Barros, L. A. Izquierdo, L. Bevilaqua, N. Schröder, J. Quevedo, C. Rodrigues, M. Madruga, J. H. Medina, & I. Izquierdo, 1997, *Behavioural Pharmacology, 8.* Copyright 1997 by Lippincott, Williams & Wilkins. Adapted with permission of the publisher.

FIGURE 5.3

Effects of substances infused bilaterally in the entorhinal cortex on long-term memory of the step-down inhibitory avoidance task (0.3 mA foot shock).

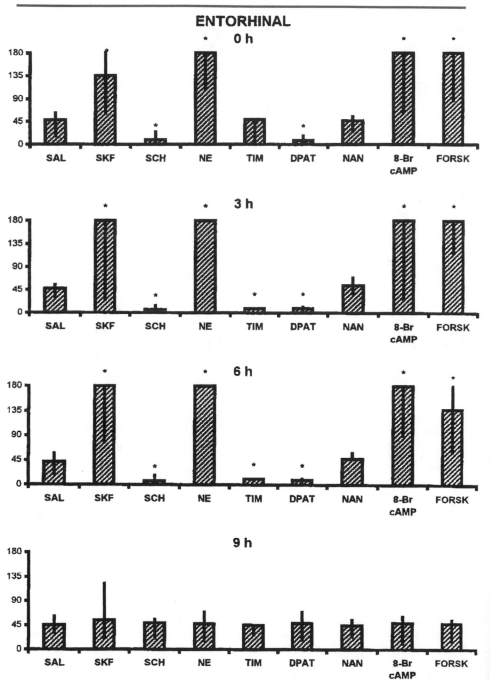

hour after training is prevented by the intrahippocampal infusion of the NMDA receptor antagonist, AP5, or the inhibitor of calcium-calmodulin-dependent protein kinase II, KN-62 (Izquierdo, Schröder, et al., 1999). Memory of habituation to novelty indeed uses many of these biochemical steps in the first few minutes after acquisition (Izquierdo & Medina, 1995, 1997a). As in the LTP experiment of Xu et al. (1998), stress (Netto et al., 1985), or hippocampal saturation (Moser et al., 1998) is not likely to be a factor. First, posttraining stress usually enhances retention of one-trial avoidance (Izquierdo, 1987). Second, this task is indeed stressful (more so with the 1.0 mA foot shock), induces much larger and longer lasting biochemical changes in the hippocampus than habituation (Izquierdo & Medina, 1997a), and has no influence on the latter (Figure 5.1)

Short- and Long-Term Memory

McGaugh (1966) distinguished "three memory trace systems: one for immediate memory . . . one for STM (which develops in a few seconds or minutes and lasts for several hours); and one which consolidates slowly and is relatively permanent." Immediate memory lasting seconds or a few minutes (Jacobsen, 1936) has now been identified with working memory (WM; Goldman-Rakic, 1991, 1996) and indeed is often the only way to measure it (Goldman-Rakic, 1991; Izquierdo, Izquierdo, et al., 1998). WM and the other memory types (STM and LTM) pertain to entirely different categories of phenomena. WM is primarily dependent on the electrical activity of cells of the

---

(continued from previous page)
The ordinates express median (interquartile range) test session latency, in seconds. Rats were infused bilaterally in the entorhinal cortex, 0, 1.5, 3, 6, or 9 hours after training, with saline, 8-HO-DPAT, 2.5 μg/side (DPAT); NAN-190, 2.5 μg/side (NAN); norepinephrine, 0.3 μg/side (NE); timolol, 0.3 μg/side (TIM); SKF38383, 7.5 μg/side (SKF); SCH23390, 0.5 μg/side (SCH); 8-Br-cAMP, 1.25 μg/side (cAMP); a vehicle (20% dimethylsulfoxide in saline, SAL), KT-5720, 0.5 μg/side (KT); and forskolin, 0.5 μg/side (FORSK). Asterisks indicate significant differences in Mann–Whitney U tests, two-tailed, at $p < .002$ level with the saline control group (all drugs except FORSK), and with the vehicle group (KT and FORSK). Infusions were carried out 0, 3, 6, or 9 hours after training. 8-Br-cAMP, FORSK, SKF, and NE caused retrograde facilitation; and KT, SCH, and DPAT caused retrograde amnesia when given 0, 3, or 6, but not 9, hours posttraining. TIM was amnestic when given 3 or 6 hours posttraining. NAN had no effect at any time. n = 9–12 per group. From "Late and Prolonged Memory Modulation in Entorhinal and Parietal Cortex by Drugs Acting on the cAMP/Protein Kinase A Signalling Pathway," by P. Ardenghi, D. Barros, L. A. Izquierdo, L. Bevilaqua, N. Schröder, J. Quevedo, C. Rodrigues, M. Madruga, J. H. Medina, & I. Izquierdo, 1997, *Behavioural Pharmacology, 8.* Copyright 1997 by Lippincott, Williams & Wilkins. Adapted with permission of the publisher.

FIGURE 5.4

Effects of substances infused bilaterally in the posterior parietal cortex on long-term memory of the step-down inhibitory avoidance task (0.3 mA foot shock).

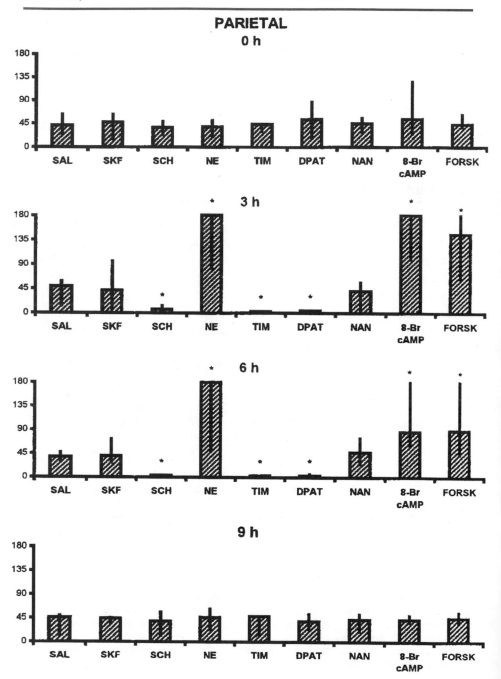

prefrontal cortex (Goldman-Rakic, 1991, 1996) linked to that of other regions (Goldman-Rakic, 1996; Salmon et al., 1996). Its persistence over a few seconds or minutes is accounted for by off responses of the neurons in charge of WM (Goldman-Rakic, 1991, 1996). Unlike STM and LTM, WM is not an archive of individual memories but rather a "manager" of moment-to-moment cognitive events that may relate to information that is already stored or that may be stored (see Izquierdo, Izquierdo, et al., 1998).

Because WM subserves an entirely different function from STM or LTM as described by McGaugh (1966), it makes no sense to call processes that take place between the end of WM and the effective consolidation of LTM "intermediate," as was in fashion some decades ago (McGaugh, 1968). Both the term and the existence of an intermediate type of memory were brought into question by Markowitsch (1997). Thus, as originally proposed by McGaugh (1966), here we use STM to designate memory "that develops within a few seconds or minutes and lasts for several hours," whereas the consolidation of LTM proceeds "slowly."

Separation of Short- and Long-Term Memory

The question of whether STM and LTM involve separate or consecutive processes was first raised by McGaugh (1966) and is one of the central questions of memory research. This question applies regardless of whether one chooses to examine STM as a whole or as something that can be divided into pieces (McGaugh, 1966, 1968; Gold & McGaugh, 1975).

(continued from previous page)
The ordinates express median (interquartile range) test session latency, in seconds. Rats were infused bilaterally in the posterior parietal cortex, 0, 1.5, 3, 6, or 9 hours after training, with saline, 8-HO-DPAT, 2.5 μg/side (DPAT); NAN-190, 2.5 μg/side (NAN); norepinephrine, 0.3 μg/side (NE); timolol, 0.3 μg/side (TIM); SKF38383, 7.5 μg/side (SKF); SCH23390, 0.5 μg/side (SCH); 8-Br-cAMP, 1.25 μg/side (cAMP); a vehicle (20% dimethylsulfoxide in saline, SAL), KT-5720, 0.5 μg/side (KT); and forskolin, 0.5 μg/side (FORSK). Asterisks indicate significant differences in Mann–Whitney U tests, two-tailed, at $p < .002$ level with the saline control group (all drugs except FORSK), and with the vehicle group (FORSK). Infusions were carried out 0, 3, 6, or 9 hours after training. KT was amnestic when given 0, 3, or 6, but not 9, hours posttraining. 8-Br-cAMP, FORSK, and NE caused retrograde memory facilitation; and KT, SCH, TIM, and DPAT caused retrograde amnesia when given 3 or 6 hours, but not 0 or 9 hours, posttraining. n = 9–12 per group. From "Late and Prolonged Memory Modulation in Entorhinal and Parietal Cortex by Drugs Acting on the cAMP/Protein Kinase A Signalling Pathway," by P. Ardenghi, D. Barros, L. A. Izquierdo, L. Bevilaqua, N. Schröder, J. Quevedo, C. Rodrigues, M. Madruga, J. H. Medina, & I. Izquierdo, 1997, *Behavioural Pharmacology, 8.* Copyright 1997 by Lippincott, Williams & Wilkins. Adapted with permission of the publisher.

The critical experiments to determine whether STM and LTM are parallel or consecutive have shown that STM can be canceled without affecting LTM for the same task in the same subject (Izquierdo, Barros, et al., 1998; Izquierdo, Izquierdo, et al., 1998; Izquierdo, Medina, Ardenghi, et al., 1998; Izquierdo, Medina, Izquierdo, et al., 1998). Had this been impossible, one would have to assume that STM is merely a step toward LTM (Izquierdo, Medina, Ardenghi, et al., 1998; Izquierdo, Medina, Izquierdo, et al., 1998). Early attempts to conduct these experiments (see Cherkin, 1968; Freeman et al., 1995; Gold & McGaugh, 1975; Sara, 1974) failed because the treatments used in those days to block memory of one or the other type (protein synthesis inhibitors, electroconvulsive shock, hypoxia, etc.) were both too intense and too nonspecific and ended up affecting performance and often the general health of the experimental animals as well. Further, many of the early experiments were based on the false premise that memory measured 1 or a very few minutes after acquisition was STM. Now we know that it reflects, rather, WM (Goldman-Rakic, 1991, 1996). Experiments in which treatments preserve STM but cancel LTM (e.g., Bourchuladze et al., 1994; Sara, 1974; Yin & Tully, 1996) are uninformative as to their sequential or consecutive nature; as are those that preserve short-term potentiation (STP) but block LTP (Bliss & Collingridge, 1993; Colley & Routtenberg, 1993; Frey & Morris, 1998).

Emptage and Carew (1993) found that the nonspecific 5HT antagonist cyproheptadine blocks the short- (2–6 minutes) but not the long-lasting (24 hours) facilitation of a monosynaptic response in *Aplysia* induced by 5HT. We decided to repeat this finding using one-trial step-down inhibitory avoidance in rats, with a longer training–test interval to measure STM (1.5–3 hours, see below) in order to avoid "contamination" by WM.

There is no direct way to extricate the biochemistry of the first 3–6 hours of LTM from that of STM, because both take place simultaneously (Izquierdo, Barros, et al., 1998). The only way to address this question is to use drugs that are known to affect those biochemical events and whose action is rapidly reversible. We used immediate posttraining infusions into definite brain regions of drugs of known biochemical effects whose influence on LTM had been well established (see previous sections). We chose a training foot shock level (0.3–0.4 mA) that yields retention scores well above floor and well below ceiling (see Figures 5.1–5.5). The animals were tested twice: first at 1.5 hours for STM, and then again at 24 hours for LTM (Bianchin et al., 1999; Izquierdo, Barros, et al., 1998; Izquierdo, Izquierdo, et al., 1998; Izquierdo, Medina, Ardenghi, et al., 1998; Izquierdo, Medina, Izquierdo, et al., 1998; Vianna et al., 1999).

One concern was whether testing the animals twice might alter LTM either by extinction (i.e., Figure 5.5) or by a reminder effect (Roesler et al., 1998; Sara, 1973). This was ruled out by two facts. First, there were no significant differences in control groups between STM and LTM performance in any of our studies (Figures 5.6–5.8; Bianchin et al., 1999; Izquierdo, Barros, et al., 1998; Izquierdo, Izquierdo, et al., 1998; Izquierdo, Medina, Ardenghi, et al., 1998; Izquierdo, Medina, Izquierdo, et al., 1998; Vianna et al., 1999). Second, all treatments studied affected LTM retention scores equally regardless of whether there was a preceding STM test or not (Table 5.1). There was no evidence for any Kamin-like effect either. First, the Kamin effect (a nonassociative inhibition of retrieval that takes place between 1 and 4–6 hours training) has been described in active avoidance tasks using high intensity and repeated foot shocks, but not in inhibitory avoidance (Anisman, 1973; Kamin, 1963). Further, the effects we observed with scopolamine on STM and LTM (see below) are incompatible with those described for this drug on the Kamin effect (Anisman, 1973).

The drugs used, their doses, and the results obtained are shown in Figures 5.6 and 5.7. The drugs were the glutamate AMPA receptor blocker, CNQX; the glutamate NMDA receptor antagonist, AP5; the glutamate metabotropic receptor antagonist, MCPG; the GABA$_A$ receptor agonist, muscimol; the muscarinic receptor antagonist, scopolamine; the dopamine D1 receptor agonist, SKF38393; the D1 antagonist, SCH23390; norepinephrine; the β-adrenoceptor antagonist, timolol; the 5HT1A receptor agonist, 8-HO-DPAT; the 5HT1A antagonist, NAN-190; the CaMKII inhibitor, KN-62; the PKC inhibitor, staurosporin; the inhibitor of Tyr kinases at low doses and of PKG at higher doses, lavendustin A; the inhibitor of guanylyl cyclase, LY83583; the selective PKG inhibitor, KT5823; the selective inhibitor of MAPKK (MAP kinase kinase), PD098059; 8-Br-cAMP; the stimulator of adenylyl cyclase, forskolin; and the PKA inhibitor, KT5720. (The doses are shown in the legends to Figures 5.6–5.8.) These drugs at the same doses had been previously shown to affect LTM when given after training (see above, Izquierdo & Medina, 1997a, 1997b; Walz et al., 2000; and Table 5.1).

Figure 5.5 shows the results obtained with drugs infused into CA1. Several of the treatments blocked both STM and LTM: AP5, CNQX, MCPG, muscimol, scopolamine, and KT5720. This suggests a link between STM and LTM at the glutamate receptor level (Izquierdo, Barros, et al., 1998; Izquierdo, Izquierdo, et al., 1998), at the level of modulation by GABA$_A$ and muscarinic receptors (Izquierdo, Barros, et al., 1998; Izquierdo, Izquierdo, et al., 1998; Izquierdo, Medina, Ardenghi, et al., 1998), and at the level of the need for PKA activity immediately posttraining (Vianna et al., 1999). The effects of 8-Br-cAMP and forskolin agree with the latter suggestion (Vianna et al., 1999). Some treatments had no effect on either STM or LTM (timolol and NAN-190). Others affected selectively LTM: norepinephrine, which enhanced it; and KN-62, staurosporin, lavendustin at the higher dose, and KT5823. This suggests that, in CA1, STM, like STP (Bliss & Collingridge, 1993; Izquierdo & Medina, 1995), does not require CaMKII, PKC, or PKG activity (Izquierdo, Medina, Ardenghi, et al.,

FIGURE 5.5

Effects of bilateral infusion into CA1 area of the hippocampus.

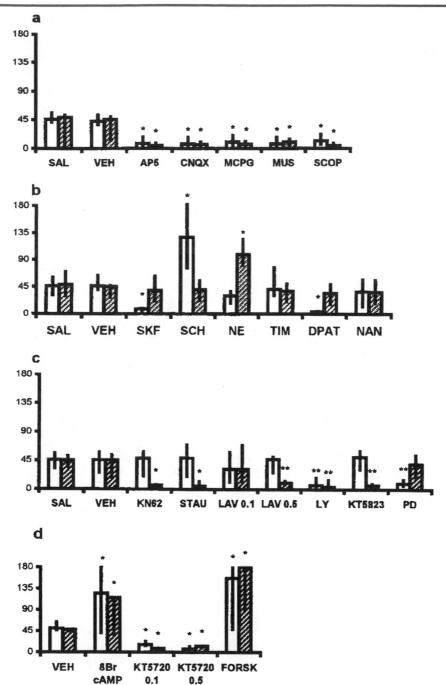

1998). Finally, and most importantly, three of the treatments given into CA1 selectively blocked STM while leaving LTM untouched: SKF38393 (Izquierdo, Medina, Izquierdo, et al., 1998), 8-HO-DPAT (Izquierdo, Barros, et al., 1998), and PD098059.

Figure 5.6 shows the results obtained with drugs infused into the entorhinal cortex. Only two of the treatments tested blocked STM and LTM simultaneously: staurosporin and KT5720. SCH23390 depressed LTM selectively. Several drugs had opposite effects on both memory types: 8-HO-DPAT and PD098059 enhanced STM while leaving the animals amnestic in terms of LTM; and SKF38393 depressed STM but simultaneously left LTM enhanced. It is important to note here that, as occurs with many bodily functions (blood pressure is an archetypal example), similar regulatory mechanisms (those that regulate the Erk/Ras pathway, Walz et al., 2000; brain monoamines, Izquierdo, Medina, Izquierdo, et al., 1998) may simultaneously exert physiologically opposite effects on different parts of the brain. Therefore, from the point of view of what monoaminergic influences related to mood or emotion do to STM or LTM at any given moment, the outcome is not easily predictable. Clinical studies will surely contribute to that. So far, it is common knowledge that in depressive patients STM may fail selectively, and that in delirium it does consistently, to the point of that being a diagnostic criterion.

The effect on STM and LTM of drugs given into posterior parietal and

---

(continued from previous page)
Memory of the step-down task was measured 1.5 hours after training (short-term memory) and again at 24 hours (long-term memory).

Data are included from Izquierdo, Barros, et al. (1998); Izquierdo, Izquierdo, et al. (1998); Izquierdo, Medina, Ardenghi, et al. (1998); Izquierdo, Medina, Izquierdo, et al. (1998); and Vianna, Izquierdo, Barros, Medina, & Izquierdo (1998). $n = 10$ per group, except for the control groups of a, b, and c, in which $n = 20$. Infusion volume was 0.5 (l in all cases).

The following treatments were applied by bilateral infusion into the CA1 area of the hippocampus: (a) Saline (SAL), vehicle (20% dimethylsulfoxide); AP5 (5 μg/side); CNQX (0.5 μg/side); MCPG (2.5 μg/side); muscimol (MUS, 0.5 μg/side); and scopolamine HBr (SCOP, 2 μg/side). (b) SAL, VEH, SKF38393 (SKF, 7.5 μg/side); SCH23390 (SCH, 0.5 μg/side); norepinephrine ClH (NE, 0.3 μg/side); timolol ClH (TIM, 0.3 μg/side); 8-HO-DPAT (DPAT, 2.5 μg/side); and NAN-190 (NAN, 2.5 μg/side). (c) SAL, VEH, KN-62 (KN, 3.6 μg/side); staurosporin (STAU, 2.5 μg/side); lavendustin A (LAV, 0.1 and 0.5 μg/side); LY83583 (LY, 2.5 μg/side); KT5823 (2.0 μg/side); and PD 098059 (0.05 μg/ side). (d) VEH, 8-Br-cAMP (8-Br, 1.25 μg/side); KT5720 (KT, 0.1 and 0.5 μg/ side); and forskolin (FORSK, 0.5 (μg/side). *Indicates significant difference from control values at $p < .001$ level and ** same, at $p < .02$ level. AP5, CNQX, MUS, SCOP, LY, and KT5720 caused amnesia both for short-term memory (STM) and long-term memory (LTM). SKF, DPAT, and PD caused selective amnesia for STM, leaving LTM intact. KN-62, STAU, and the higher dose of LAV caused amnesia only for LTM but not for STM. 8-Br-cAMP and FORSK enhanced both memory types. SCH enhanced STM selectively and NE enhanced LTM selectively.

FIGURE 5.6
Effects of bilateral infusion into entorhinal cortex.

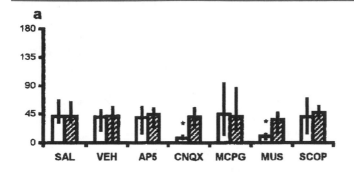

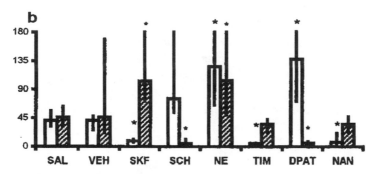

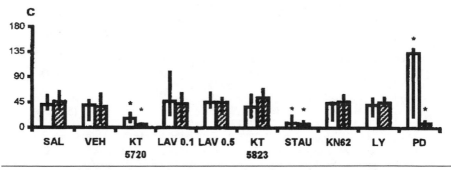

Memory of the step-down task was measured 1.5 hours after training (short-term memory) and again at 24 hours (long-term memory). Several of the drugs were infused bilaterally into the entorhinal cortex 0 hours after training. The ordinates express median (interquartile range) test session latency, in seconds. Rats were infused bilaterally in the dorsal CA1 region, 0, 1.5, 3, 6, or 9 hour after training, with saline, 8-HO-DPAT, 2.5 μg/side (DPAT); NAN-190, 2.5 μg/side (NAN); norepinephrine, 0.3 μg/side (NE); timolol, 0.3 μg/side (TIM); SKF38383, 7.5 μg/side (SKF); SCH23390, 0.5 μg/side (SCH); 8-Br-cAMP, 1.25 μg/side (cAMP); a vehicle (20% dimethylsulfoxide in saline, VEH), KT-5720, 0.5 μg/side (KT); and forskolin, 0.5 μg/side (FORSK). Asterisks indicate significant differences in Mann–Whitney U tests, two-tailed, at $p < .002$ level with the saline control group anterolateral prefrontal cortex (Izquierdo, Izquierdo, et al., 1998) and amygdala (Bianchin, Mello e Souza, Medina, & Izquierdo, 1999) is shown in Figure 5.7. Scopolamine blocked LTM when given into any of the three areas; in the parietal cortex it inhibited, in addition, STM. CNQX and muscimol given into the parietal cortex blocked STM selectively, as they did in the entorhinal cortex (Izquierdo, Izquierdo, et al., 1998). Interestingly, AP5 given into the parietal or prefrontal cortex has no effect on either STM or LTM. None of the treatments that were given into the amygdala (which included several of the drugs used in the other structures plus picrotoxin, 0.08 (μg/side) had any effect on STM; all had an effect on LTM, that being the reason why they were chosen for this study to begin with (Bianchin et al., 1999).

Nine of the treatments studied selectively depressed STM; eight of them did so while leaving LTM intact (SKF38393, 8-HO-DPAT, and PD098059 in CA1, Figure 5.5; CNQX, muscimol, timolol, and NAN-190 given into the entorhinal cortex, Figure 5.6; and CNQX and muscimol given into the parietal cortex, Figure 5.7), and one blocked STM and simultaneously left LTM enhanced (SKF38393 given into the entorhinal cortex, Figure 5.7). Thus, the mechanisms of STM are clearly separate from those of LTM formation, at least with regard to the systems affected by the treatments mentioned (Izquierdo, Barros, et al., 1998; Izquierdo, Izquierdo, et al., 1998; Izquierdo, Medina, Ardenghi, et al., 1998; Izquierdo, Medina, Izquierdo, et al., 1998; Vianna et al., 1999). Still another set of treatments must be added to this list: The infusion of KT5720 into CA1 at 22, 45, or 90 minutes after training selectively hinders STM but not LTM, suggesting a dual influence of PKA, certainly on different substrates, in the regulation of STM and LTM (Vianna et al., 1999). Indeed, this finding with the PKA inhibitor does not favor the idea that STM as studied here may be in any way subdivided into phases: The effect of KT5720 on STM was exactly the same at any of the infusion times and regardless of whether the animals were tested at 90 or 180 minutes from training.

The effects we observed on STM with the various treatments are not due to influences on retrieval or performance. None of the treatments that affected STM when given posttraining influenced retention test performance when given

---

(all drugs except KT and FORSK), and with the vehicle group (KT and FORSK). Here n = 20 in all the control groups and n = 10 for all other groups.

Data are included from Izquierdo, Barros, et al. (1998); Izquierdo, Izquierdo, et al. (1998); Izquierdo, Medina, Ardenghi, et al. (1998); Izquierdo, Medina, Izquierdo, et al. (1998); and Vianna, Izquierdo, Barros, Medina, & Izquierdo (1998). CNQX, MUS, SKF, TIM, and NAN selectively blocked short-term memory (STM); SKF actually simultaneously enhanced long-term memory (LTM), while the other treatments did not affect it. KT5720 and STAU hindered both STM and LTM. DPAT, LY, and PD enhanced STM while causing amnesia for LTM. NE enhanced both STM and LTM.

FIGURE 5.7

Effects of bilateral infusion into posterior parietal cortex, anterolateral prefrontal cortex, and amygdala.

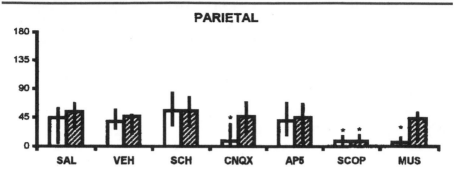

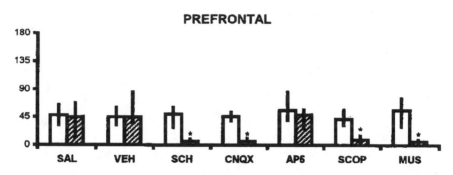

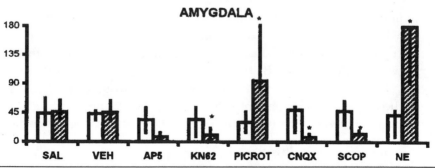

Memory of the step-down task was measured 1.5 hours after training (short-term memory) and again at 24 hours (long-term memory). Some of the drugs were infused bilaterally into the posterior parietal cortex, the anterolateral prefrontal cortex, and the amygdala. The ordinates express median (interquartile range) test session latency, in seconds. Rats were infused bilaterally in the dorsal CA1 region, 0, 1.5, 3, 6, or 9 hours after training, with saline, 8-HO-DPAT, 2.5 μg/side (DPAT); NAN-190, 2.5 μg/side (NAN); norepinephrine, 0.3 μg/side (NE); timolol, 0.3 μg/side (TIM); SKF38383, 7.5 μg/side (SKF); SCH23390, 0.5 μg/side (SCH); 8-Br-cAMP, 1.25 μg/side (cAMP); a vehicle (20% dimethylsulfoxide in saline, VEH), KT-5720, 0.5 μg/side (KT); and forskolin, 0.5 μg/side (FORSK).

5 minutes prior to the STM test or 1.5 hours prior to the LTM test (Izquierdo, Izquierdo, et al., 1998; Izquierdo, Medina, Ardenghi, et al., 1998; Izquierdo, Medina, Izquierdo, et al., 1998; Vianna et al., 1999).

The intimate biochemistry of STM, and its regulation by monoaminergic, cholinergic, and eventually other systems, requires further study before it can be spelled out as clearly as that of LTM (see above and Izquierdo & Medina, 1997a, 1997b). Suffice it to say here that they take place at the same time as those of LTM, and to a large extent in many of the same brain regions (except the prefrontal cortex and the amygdala), but are indeed different.

Pharmacological Observations on Working Memory

The only way to measure WM in a task like this, which is learned in seconds, is to measure immediate memory (Goldman-Rakic, 1991). Figure 5.8 shows the effect on WM of the step-down task of several of the drugs whose influence on STM and LTM is shown in Figures 5.5–5.7. The drugs were administered into posterior parietal, anterolateral prefrontal or entorhinal cortex, dorsal CA1, or the amygdala 5 minutes prior to training. The WM test was carried out 3 seconds after the foot shock. CNQX and muscimol blocked WM when given into any of the cortical regions, indicating that regular AMPA receptor-mediated glutamatergic transmission, susceptible to GABAergic inhibition, is necessary for WM processing in the four areas. Scopolamine blocked WM when given into parietal or entorhinal cortex or into CA1, and SCH23390 blocked WM when given into the prefrontal region, as shown by Goldman-Rakic (1996) and her group, but also when given into the parietal cortex or into CA1. AP5 had no effect on WM in any of the brain regions studied. None of the treatments influenced WM when given into the amygdala, strongly suggesting that this nucleus plays no role in WM, as the data of Figure 5.6 suggest for STM as well (Bianchin et al., 1999).

The results of Figures 5.5–5.8 suggest links between WM and LTM in prefrontal cortex, and between WM and STM in parietal and entorhinal cortex

---

Asterisks indicate significant differences in Mann–Whitney *U* tests, two-tailed, at *p* < .002 level with the saline control group (all drugs except KT and FORSK), and with the vehicle group (KT and FORSK).

Data are from Bianchin, Mello e Souza, Medina, & Izquierdo (1999), and Izquierdo, Izquierdo, et al. (1998). When given into parietal cortex, SCOP blocked both short-term memory (STM) and long-term memory (LTM), whereas CNQX and MUS selectively blocked STM without altering LTM. When given into the prefrontal cortex, SCH, CNQX, SCOP, and MUS had no effect on STM but left the animals amnestic for LTM. When given into the amygdala, none of the drugs had any effect on STM, but all affected LTM: AP5, KN-62, CNQX, and SCOP blocked it; and picrotoxin (PICROTOX, 0.08 μg/side) and NE enhanced it.

FIGURE 5.8

Effect of several drugs on working memory.

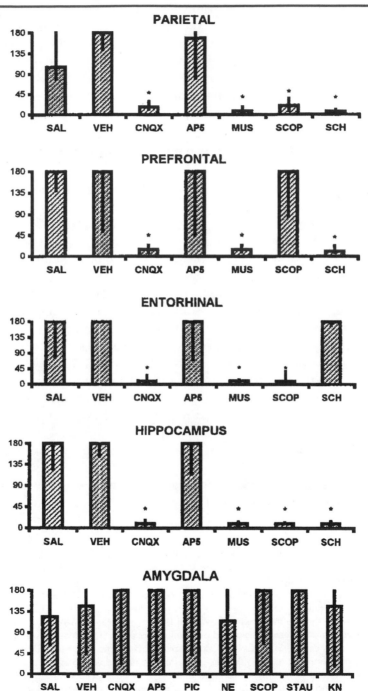

and CA1. Of course, several of the results point to links between STM and LTM (Izquierdo, Izquierdo, et al., 1998). However, at the same time, they indicate that the pharmacological "spectrum" of WM, STM, and LTM is different, and that, clearly, each of the three memory types obey unique combinations of biochemical mechanisms. This is true even if the same cells in some of the structures end up processing all three. The sorting out of the intracellular metabolic pathways that are involved in each memory type should be at the post-receptor level. One possibility that may deserve study is that the recently described protein complex of postsynaptic deusities (Craven & Bredt, 1998) may be involved in this. Another is that mechanisms related to the (hitherto biochemically undefined) "synaptic tagging" process described by Frey and Morris (1998) may be involved.

Summary and Conclusion

Here we reviewed data on the three main issues raised by McGaugh (1966): memory consolidation; the modulation of consolidation; and the subdivision of memory into time-dependent types. Our work is a tribute to Jim's extraordinary contribution to memory research.

We established the major metabolic pathways leading to consolidation of a one-trial task in the CA1 area of the hippocampus (Izquierdo & Medina, 1997a, 1997b). These turned out to be rather similar to those of LTP in that region (Izquierdo & Medina, 1995) and their activity lasts several hours (Bernabeu, Bevilaqua, et al., 1997; Cammarota, Bernabeu, et al., 1997). In memory formation, however, unlike in LTP, CA1 interacts strongly with other brain structures and the involvement of these is essential (Izquierdo, Quillfeldt, et al., 1997).

Among the systems that interact with the hippocampus in memory for-

---

(continued from previous page)
The ordinates express median (interquartile range) test session latency, in seconds. Rats were infused bilaterally in the dorsal CA1 region, 0, 1.5, 3, 6, or 9 hours after training, with saline, 8-HO-DPAT, 2.5 μg/side (DPAT); NAN-190, 2.5 μg/side (NAN); norepinephrine, 0.3 μg/side (NE); timolol, 0.3 μg/side (TIM); SKF38383, 7.5 μg/side (SKF); SCH23390, 0.5 μg/side (SCH); 8-Br-cAMP, 1.25 μg/side (cAMP); a vehicle (20% dimethylsulfoxide in saline, VEH), KT-5720, 0.5 μg/side (KT); and forskolin, 0.5 μg/side (FORSK). Asterisks indicate significant differences in Mann–Whitney U tests, two-tailed, at $p < .002$ level with the saline control group (all drugs except KT and FORSK), and with the vehicle group (KT and FORSK). Drugs were given 5 minutes prior to training. CNQX and MUS blocked working memory (WM) when given into posterior parietal, prefrontal, or entorhinal cortex or into the CA1 area of the dorsal hippocampus. AP5 had no effect on WM. SCOP blocked WM when given into parietal or entorhinal cortex or into CA1. SCH blocked WM when given into parietal or prefrontal cortex or into CA1. None of the treatments given into the amygdala had any effect on WM.

TABLE 5.1

Effect of Drugs on the LTM of One-Trial Avoidance Measured Alone or After Having Measured STM in the Same Animals (Median Test–Training Step-Down Latency in Seconds)

DRUGS	CA1		ENTORHINAL CORTEX		AMYGDALA	
	ALONE	AFTER STM	ALONE	AFTER STM	ALONE	AFTER STM
AP5 (5.0)[a]	−1*[1]	2*[13]	51[2]	40[13]	2*[1]	8*[19]
CNQX (0.5)	4*[2]	5*[11]	42[2]	40[11]	4*[2]	8*[19]
MCPG (2.5)	7*[4]	5*[18]			44[4]	
Muscimol (0.03–0.5)[a]	3*[1]	3*[12]	53[5]	42[11]	2*[1]	
Picrotoxin (0.08)	180*[1]		40[6]	42[13]	180*[1]	102*[18]
Scopolamine (2.0)	0*[1]	1*[13]	6*[9]	3*[10]	4*[1]	12*[18]
8-OH-DPAT (2.5)	50[8]	38[10]	42[9]	40[10]		
NAN-190 (2.5)	45[8]	40[10]	120*[9]	100*[10]		
SKF38393 (7.5)	42[8]	45[10]	7*[9]	5*[10]		
SCH23390 (0.5)[a]	41[7]	42[10]				
Norepinephrine (0.3)	153*[1,8]	101*[10]	180*[9]	96*[10]	180*[1]	180*[18]
Timolol (0.3)	48[7]	42[10]	35[9,18]	41[10]	38[8,9]	
8-Br-cAMP (1.25)	38[7,8]	40[18]	180*[9]	80*[12]	36[8,9]	
KT5720 (0.5)	1*[7,8]	6*[12]	0*[9]	6*[12]		
KN-62 (0.0035)	3*[3,19]	6*[12]			4*[3,19]	7*[12]
Staurosporin (1.0)	4*[16]	4*[12]			4*[19]	8*[12]
LY83583 (2.5)	0*[15]	5*[12]		38[12,18]		
PD098059 (50 M)	45[17]	38[12]	2*[17]	6*[12]		

LTM = long-term memory; STM = short-term memory; [a] AP5, muscimol, and SCH23390 were also studied in the posterior parietal cortex and found to have no effect on LTM measured with or without a preceding STM test.[13,14] *Significant enhancing or depressant effect when compared with controls at $p < .02$ level or less; [1] Izquierdo, da Cunha, et al. (1992); [2] Jerusalinsky et al. (1992); [3] Wolfman et al. (1994); [4] Bianchin et al. (1994); [5] Ferreira, da Silva, Medina, & Izquierdo (1992); [6] Ferreira, Wolfman, et al. (1992); [7] Bernabeu, Bevilaqua, et al. (1997); [8] Bevilaqua, Ardenghi, et al. (1997); [9] Ardenghi et al. (1997); [10] Izquierdo, Izquierdo, et al. (1998); [11] Izquierdo, Izquierdo, et al. (1998); [12] Izquierdo, Medina, Ardenghi, et al. (1998); [13] Izquierdo, Izquierdo, et al. (1998); [14] Izquierdo, Quillfeldt, et al. (1997); [15] Bernabeu, Schröder, et al. (1997); [16] Jerusalinsky et al. (1993); [17] Walz et al. (1998); [18] Bianchin et al. (1998); [19] Izquierdo, Barros, et al. (1998).

mation, several exert in addition modulatory influences. There are two major sets of posttraining modulatory influences: those acting at or through the amygdala, which are crucial in the first few minutes of the consolidation process and are related to alertness, anxiety, or stress (Cahill & McGaugh, 1996, 1998); and those that act in the hours that follow, which involve monoaminergic pathways acting simultaneously on the hippocampus, and the entorhinal and the parietal cortex, but not the amygdala as these systems are related to mood, affect, and emotion (Ardenghi et al., 1997; Izquierdo, Medina, Ardenghi, et al., 1998).

Finally, we have shown a distinction between the mechanisms of the three memory types suggested by McGaugh (1966): immediate memory (which later become identified as WM), STM (which extends from a few seconds or minutes to a few hours), and LTM (Izquierdo, Barros, et al., 1998; Izquierdo, Izquierdo, et al., 1998; Izquierdo, Medina, Ardenghi, et al., 1998; Izquierdo, Medina, Izquierdo, et al., 1998; Vianna et al., 1999).

References

Abel, T., Nguyen, P. V., Bard, M., Deuel, T. A. S., Kandel, E. R., & Bourchuladze, R. (1998). Genetic demonstration of a role for PKA in the late phase of LTP and in hippocampus-based long-term memory. *Cell, 88,* 615–626.

Anisman, H. (1973). Cholinergic mechanisms and alterations in behavioral suppression as factors producing time dependent changes in avoidance performance. *Journal of Comparative and Physiological Psychology, 83,* 465–467.

Ardenghi, P., Barros, D., Izquierdo, L. A., Bevilaqua, L., Schröder, N., Quevedo, J., Rodrigues, C., Madruga, M., Medina, J. H., & Izquierdo, I. (1997). Late and prolonged memory modulation in entorhinal and parietal cortex by drugs acting on the cAMP/protein kinase A signalling pathway. *Behavioural Pharmacology, 8,* 745–751.

Barria, A., Muller, D., Verkach, V., Griffith, L. C., & Soderling, T. R. (1997). Regulatory phosphorylation of AMPA-type glutamate receptors by CaM-KII during long-term potentiation. *Science, 276,* 2042–2045.

Bernabeu, R., Bevilaqua, L., Ardenghi, P., Bromberg, E., Schmitz, P., Bianchin, M., Izquierdo, I., & Medina, J. H. (1997). Involvement of hippocampal D1/D5 receptor —cAMP signaling pathways in a late memory consolidation phase of an aversively-motivated task in rats. *Proceedings of the National Academy of Sciences (USA), 94,* 7041–7046.

Bernabeu, R., Schmitz, P. K., Faillace, M. P., Izquierdo, I., & Medina, J. H. (1996). Hippocampal cGMP and cAMP are differentially involved in memory processing of an inhibitory avoidance learning. *NeuroReport, 7,* 585–588.

Bernabeu, R., Schröder, N., Quevedo, J., Cammarota, M., Izquierdo, I., & Medina, J. H. (1997). Further evidence for the involvement of a hippocampal cGMP/cGMP-dependent protein kinase cascade in memory consolidation. *NeuroReport, 8,* 2221–2224.

Bevilaqua, L., Ardenghi, P., Schröder, N., Bromberg, E., Schmitz, P. K., Schaeffer, E., Quevedo, J., Bianchin, M., Walz, R., Medina, J. H., & Izquierdo, I. (1997). Drugs acting upon the protein kinase A/CREB pathway modulate memory consolidation when given late after training into rat hippocampus but not amygdala. *Behavioural Pharmacology, 8,* 331–338.

Bianchin, M., Fin, C., Schmitz, P. K., da Silva, R. C., Medina, J. H., & Izquierdo, I. (1994). Memory of inhibitory avoidance in rats is regulated by glutamate metabotropic receptors in the hippocampus. *Behavioral and Neural Biology, 5,* 356–359.

Bianchin, M., Mello e Souza, T., Medina, J. H., & Izquierdo, I. (1999). The amygdala is involved in the modulation of long-term memory but not in working or short-term memory. *Neurobiology of Learning and Memory, 71,* 127–131.

Bliss, T. V. P., & Collingridge, G. R. (1993). A synaptic model of memory: Long-term potentiation. *Nature, 361,* 31–39.

Bourchuladze, R., Frenguelli, B., Blendy, J., Cioffi, F. D., Schutz, G., & Silva, A. J. (1994). Deficient long-term memory in mice with a targeted mutation of the cAMP-responsive element-binding protein. *Cell, 79,* 59–68.

Bourchuladze, R., Potter, J., & Rose, S. P. R. (1990). Memory formation in the chick depends on membrane-bound protein kinase C. *Brain Research, 535,* 131–138.

Bourchuladze, R., & Rose, S. P. R. (1992). Memory formation in day-old chicks requires NMDA but not non-NMDA glutamate receptors. *European Journal of Neuroscience, 4,* 533–538.

Brioni, J. D. (1993). Role of GABA during the multiple consolidation of memory. *Drug Development Research, 28,* 3–27.

Cahill, L., Brioni, J. D., & Izquierdo, I. (1986). Retrograde memory enhancement by diazepam: Its relation to anterograde amnesia and some clinical implications. *Psychopharmacology, 90,* 454–456.

Cahill, L., & McGaugh, J. L. (1996). Modulation of memory storage. *Current Opinion in Neurobiology, 6,* 237–242.

Cahill, L., & McGaugh, J. L. (1998). Mechanisms of emotional arousal and lasting declarative memory. *Trends in Neuroscience, 21,* 294–299.

Cammarota, M., Bernabeu, R., Levi de Stein, M., Izquierdo, I., & Medina, J. H. (1997). Learning-specific, time-dependent increases in hippocampal Ca2+/calmodulin-dependent protein kinase II activity and AMPA GluR1 subunit immunoreactivity. *European Journal of Neuroscience, 10,* 2669–2676.

Cammarota, M., Paratcha, G., Levi de Stein, M., Bernabeu, R., Izquierdo, I., & Medina, J. H. (1997). B-50/GAP-43 phosphorylation and PKC activity are increased in rat hippocampal synaptosomal membranes after an inhibitory avoidance training. *Neurochemical Research, 22,* 499–505.

Carew, T. J. (1996). Molecular enhancement of memory formation. *Neuron, 16,* 5–8.

Cherkin, A. (1968). Kinetics of memory consolidation: Role of amnesic treatment parameters. *Proceedings of the National Academy of Sciences (USA), 63,* 1094–1101.

Colley, P. A., & Routtenberg, A. (1993). Long-term potentiation as synaptic dialogue. *Brain Research Reviews, 18,* 115–122.

Craven, S. E., & Bredt, D. S. (1998). PDZ proteins organize synaptic signaling pathways. *Cell, 93,* 495–498.

Doyle, E., Nolan, P. M., Bell, R., & Regan, C. (1992). Intraventricular infusions of anti-neural cell adhesion molecules in a discrete posttraining period impair consolidation of a passive avoidance response in rats. *Journal of Neurochemistry, 59,* 1569–1570.

Eichenbaum, H., Schoenbaum, G., Young, B., & Bunsey, M. (1996). Functional organization of the hippocampal memory system. *Proceedings of the National Academy of Sciences (USA), 93,* 13500–13507.

Emptage, N. J., & Carew, J. (1993). Long-term facilitation in the absence of short-term facilitation in aplysia neurons. *Science, 262,* 253–256.

English, J. D., & Sweat, J. D. (1996). Activation of p42 mitogen-activated protein kinase in hippocampal long-term potentiation. *Journal of Biological Chemistry, 271,* 24329–24332.

Ferreira, M. B. C., da Silva, R. C., Medina, J. H., & Izquierdo, I. (1992). Late posttraining memory processing by entorhinal cortex: Role of NMDA and GABAergic receptors. *Pharmacology, Biochemistry, and Behavior, 41,* 767–771.

Ferreira, M. B. C., Wolfman, C., Walz, R., da Silva, R., Zanatta, M. S., Medina, J. H., & Izquierdo, I. (1992). BMDA-dependent GABA-A-sensitive role of the entorhinal cortex in posttraining memory processing. *Behavioural Pharmacology, 3,* 387–394.

Finkbeiner, S., Tavazole, S. F., Maloratsky, A., Jacobs, K. M., Harris, K. M., & Greenberg, M. E. (1997). CREB: A major mediator of neuronal neurotrophin responses. *Neuron, 19,* 1031–1047.

Freeman, F. M., Rose, S. P. R., & Scholey, A. B. (1995). Two time windows of anisomycin-induced amnesia for passive avoidance training in the day-old chick. *Neurobiology of Learning and Memory, 63,* 291–294.

Frey, U., & Morris, R. G. M. (1998). Synaptic tagging: Implications for late maintenance of hippocampal long-term potentiation. *Trends in Neurosciences, 21,* 181–187.

Gerard, R. W. (1961). The fixation of experience. In A. Fessard, R. W. Gerard, J. Konorski, & J. F. Delafresnaye (Eds.), *Brain mechanisms and learning* (pp. 21–36). Oxford, England: Blackwell.

Ginty, D. D., Kornhauser, J. M., Thompson, M. A., Bading, H., Mayo, K. E., Takahashi, J. S., & Greenberg, M. E. (1993). Regulation of CREB phosphorylation in the suprachiasmatic nuclei by light and a circadian clock. *Science, 260,* 238–241.

Gold, P. E., & McGaugh, J. L. (1975). A single-trace, two-process view of memory storage processes. In D. Deutsch & J. A. Deutsch (Eds.), *Short-term memory* (pp. 355–378). New York: Academic Press.

Goldman-Rakic, P. (1991). Prefrontal cortical dysfunction in schizophrenia: The relevance of working memory. In B. J. Carroll & J. E. Barrett (Eds.), *Psychopathology and the brain* (pp. 1–23). New York: Raven Press.

Goldman-Rakic, P. (1996). Regional and cellular fractionation of working memory. *Proceedings of the National Academy of Sciences (USA), 93,* 13473–13480.

Huang, Y. Y., & Kandel, E. R. (1995). D1/D5 receptor agonists induce a protein-synthesis-dependent late potentiation in the CA1 region of the hippocampus. *Proceedings of the National Academy of Sciences (USA), 92,* 2446–2450.

Huang, Y. Y., Li, C. X., & Kandel, E. R. (1994). CAMP contributes to mossy fiber LTP by initiating both a covalently mediated early phase and macromolecular synthesis-dependent late phase. *Cell, 79,* 69–79.

Iijima, T., Witter, M. P., Ichikawa, M., Tominaga, T., Kajiwara, R., & Matsumoto, G. (1996). Entorhinal-hippocampal interactions revealed by real-time imaging. *Science, 272,* 1176–1179.

Impey, S., Mark, M., Villacres, E. C., Poser, S., Chavkin, C., & Storm, D. R. (1996). Induction of CRE-mediated gene expression by stimuli that generate long-lasting LTP in area CA1 of the hippocampus. *Neuron, 16,* 973–982.

Izquierdo, I. (1987). On leaving drunks alone. *Trends in Pharmacological Sciences, 8,* 161–162.

Izquierdo, I., Barros, D. M., Mello e Souza, T., de Souza, M. M., Izquierdo, L. A., & Medina, J. H. (1998). Separate but linked mechanisms for short- and long-term memory in the rat. *Nature, 393,* 635–636.

Izquierdo, I., da Cunha, C., Rosat, R., Ferreira, M. B. C., Jerusalinsky, D., & Medina, J. H. (1992). Neurotransmitter receptors involved in memory processing by the amygdala, medial septum, and hippocampus of rats. *Behavioral and Neural Biology, 58,* 16–25.

Izquierdo, I., Izquierdo, L. A., Barros, D. M., Mello e Souza, T., de Souza, M. M., Quevedo, J., Rodrigues, C., Sant'Anna, M. K., Madruga, M., & Medina, J. H. (1998). Differential involvement of cortical receptor mechanisms in working, short- and long-term memory. *Behavioural Pharmacology, 9,* 421–427.

Izquierdo, I., & Medina, J. H. (1995). Correlation between the pharmacology of long-term potentiation and the pharmacology of memory. *Neurobiology of Learning and Memory, 63,* 19–32.

Izquierdo, I., & Medina, J. H. (1997a). The biochemistry of memory and its regulation by modulatory processes. *Psychobiology, 25,* 1–9.

Izquierdo, I., & Medina, J. H. (1997b). Memory formation: The sequence of biochemical events in the hippocampus and its connection to activity in other brain structures. *Neurobiology of Learning and Memory, 68,* 285–316.

Izquierdo, I., Medina, J. H., Ardenghi, P. G., Barros, D. M., Bevilaqua, L., Izquierdo, L. A., Mello e Souza, T., Quevedo, J., & Schröder, N. (1998). Memory processing and its shifting maps: Interactions between monoamines and events dependent on glutamatergic transmission. In R. Beninger, T. Archer, & T. Palomo (Eds.), *Interactive monoaminergic basis of brain disorders* (pp. 517–547). London: Farrand.

Izquierdo, I., Medina, J. H., Izquierdo, L. A., Barros, D. M., de Souza, M. M., & Mello e Souza, T. (1998). Short- and long-term memory are differentially regulated by monoaminergic systems in the rat brain. *Neurobiology of Learning and Memory, 69,* 219–224.

Izquierdo, I., Quillfeldt, J. A., Zanatta, M. S., Quevedo, J., Schaeffer, E., Schmitz, P. K., & Medina, J. H. (1997). Sequential role of hippocampus and amygdala, entorhinal cortex and parietal cortex in formation and retrieval of memory for inhibitory avoidance in rats. *European Journal of Neuroscience, 9,* 786–793.

Izquierdo, I., Schröder, N., Netto, C. A., & Medina, J. H. (1999). Novelty causes time-dependent retrograde amnesia for one-trial avoidance in rats through NMDA receptor- and CaMKII-dependent mechanisms in the hippocampus. *European Journal of Neuroscience, 11,* 3323–3328.

Jacobsen, C. F. (1936). Studies of cerebral function in primates. *Comparative Psychology Monographs, 13,* 1–68.

James, W. (1890). *The principles of psychology.* New York: Holt.

Jerusalinsky, D., Ferreira, M. B. C., da Silva, R. C., Bianchin, M., Ruschel, A., Medina, J. H., & Izquierdo, I. (1992). Amnesia by infusion of glutamate receptor blockers into the amygdala, hippocampus and entorhinal cortex. *Behavioral and Neural Biology, 58,* 76–80.

Jerusalinsky, D., Quillfeldt, J. A., Walz, R., da Silva, R. C., Medina, J. H., & Izquierdo, I. (1993). Infusion of a protein kinase C inhibitor into the amygdala or entorhinal cortex causes retrograde amnesia in rats. *Comunicaciones Biologicas (Buenos Aires), 11,* 179–187.

Jerusalinsky, D., Quillfeldt, J. A., Walz, R., da Silva, R. C., Medina, J. H., & Izquierdo, I. (1994). Posttraining intrahippocampal infusion of protein kinase C inhibitors causes retrograde amnesia in rats. *Behavioral and Neural Biology, 61,* 107–109.

Kalivas, P. W., Sorg, B. A., & Pierce, C. P. (1998). Drug- and stress-induced psychotic behaviours implying multi-systems. In R. Beninger, T. Archer, & T. Palomo (Eds.), *Interactive monoaminergic basis of brain disorders* (pp. 217–231). Madrid: Complutense.

Kamin, L. J. (1963). The retention of an incompletely learned avoidance response. *Journal of Comparative and Physiological Psychology, 36,* 713–718.

Lüthi, A., Laurent, J.-P., Figurov, A., Muller, D., & Schachner, M. (1994). Hippocampal long-term potentiation and neural cell adhesion molecules L1 and NCAM. *Nature, 372,* 777–779.

Lynch, G. S., & Baudry, M. (1984). The biochemistry of memory: A new and specific hypothesis. *Science, 224,* 1057–1063.

Markowitsch, H. J. (1997). Varieties of memory systems, structures, mechanisms of disturbance. *Neurology, Psychiatry and Brain Research, 2,* 49–68.

Martin, K. C., & Kandel, E. R. (1996). Cell adhesion molecules, CREB, and the formation of new synaptic connections. *Neuron, 17,* 567–570.

Matthies, H. (1989). In search of the cellular mechanism of learning. *Progress in Neurobiology, 32,* 277–349.

Matthies, H., & Reymann, K. (1993). Protein kinase A inhibitors prevent the maintenance of long-term potentiation. *NeuroReport, 4,* 712–714.

Mayford, M., Bach, M. E., Huang Y.-Y., Wang, L., Hawkins, R. D., & Kandel, E. R. (1996). Control of memory formation through regulation of a CaMKII transgene. *Science, 274,* 1678–1683.

McGaugh, J. L. (1966). Time-dependent processes in memory storage. *Science, 153,* 1351–1359.

McGaugh, J. L. (1968). A multi-trace view of memory storage processes. *Accademia Nazionale dei Lincei, 109,* 13–24.

Menzel, R., & Müller, U. (1996). Learning and memory in honeybees: From behavior to neural substrates. *Annual Review of Neuroscience, 19,* 379–404.

Morris, R. G. M. (1998). Down with novelty. *Nature, 394,* 834–835.

Morris, R. G. M., Anderson, E., Lynch, G. S., & Baudry, M. (1986), Selective impairment of learning and blockade of long-term potentiation by an N-methyl-D-aspartate antagonist, Ap-5. *Nature, 319,* 774–776.

Moser, E., Krobert, K. A., Moser, M.-B., & Morris, R. G. M. (1998). Impaired spatial learning after saturation of long-term potentiation. *Science, 285,* 2038–2042.

Müller, G. E., & Pilzecker, A. (1900). Experimentelle Beitrage zur Lehre und Gedachtniss [Experimental contributions in learning and memory.] *Zeitschrift für Psychologie, 1,* 1–288.

Netto, C. A., Dias, R. D., & Izquierdo, I. (1985). Interaction between consecutive learnings: Inhibitory avoidance and habituation. *Behavioral and Neural Biology, 44,* 505–520.

Noguès, X., Micheau, J., & Jaffard, R. (1994). Protein kinase C activity in the hippocampus following spatial learning tasks in mice. *Hippocampus, 4,* 71–78.

O'Connell, C., O'Malley, A., & Regan, C. M. (1997). Transient learning-induced ultrastructural change in spatially-clustered dentate granule cells of the adult rat hippocampus. *Neuroscience, 76,* 55–62.

Riedel, G. (1996). Function of metabotropic receptors in learning and memory. *Trends in Neuroscience, 19,* 219–224.

Roesler, R., Vianna, M., Sant'Anna, M. K., Kuyven, C. R., Krueçl, A. V., Quevedo, J., & Ferreira, M. B. C. (1998). Intrahippocampal infusion of the NMDA receptor antagonist AP5 impairs retention of an inhibitory avoidance task: Protection from impairment by pretraining or preexposure to the task apparatus. *Neurobiology of Learning and Memory, 69,* 87–91.

Roullet, P., Mileusnic, R., Rose, S. P. R., & Sara, S. J. (1997). Neural cell adhesion molecules play a role in rat memory formation in appetitive as well as in aversive tasks. *NeuroReport, 8,* 1907–1911.

Salmon, E., van der Linden, M., Collette, F., Delfiore, G., Maquet, P., Degueldre, C.,

Luxen, A., & Franck, G. (1996). Regional brain activity during working memory tasks. *Brain, 119,* 1617–1625.

Sara, S. J. (1973). Recovery from hypoxia- and ECS-induced amnesia after a single exposure to training environment. *Physiology and Behavior, 10,* 85–89.

Sara, S. J. (1974). Delayed development of amnestic behavior after hypoxia. *Physiology and Behavior, 13,* 689–696.

Saucier, D., & Cain, D. P. (1995). Spatial learning without NMDA receptor-dependent long-term potentiation. *Nature, 378,* 186–189.

Scholey, A. N., Mileusnic, R., Schachner, M., & Rose, S. P. R. (1995). A role for a chicken homolog of the neural cell adhesion molecule L1 in consolidation of memory for a passive avoidance task in the chick. *Learning and Memory, 2,* 17–25.

Sergueeva, O. A., Fedorov, N. B., & Reymann, K. G. (1993). An antagonist of glutamate metabotropic receptors, (R)-methyl-carboxyphenyl glycine, prevents the LTP-related in postsynaptic AMPA sensitivity in hippocampal slices. *Neuropharmacology, 32,* 933–935.

Silva, A. J., Kogan, J. H., Frankland, P. W., & Lida, S. (1998). CREB and memory. *Annual Review of Neuroscience, 21,* 127–148.

Stevens, C. F. (1998). A million dollar question: Does LTP = memory? *Neuron, 20,* 1–2.

Tan, S. E., & Liang, K. C. (1996). Spatial learning alters calcium/calmodulin-dependent protein kinase II activity in rats. *Brain Research, 711,* 234–240.

Van der Zee, E. A., Douma, B. R. K., Bohus, B., & Luiten, G. M. (1994). Passive avoidance training induces enhanced levels of immunoreactivity for muscarinic acetylcholine receptor and coexpressed PKC and MAP-2 in rat cortical neurons. *Cerebral Cortex, 4,* 376–390.

Van Hoesen, G. W. (1985). Neural systems of the non-human primate forebrain implicated in memory. *Annals of the New York Academy of Sciences, 444,* 97–112.

Vianna, M. R. M., Izquierdo, L. A., Barros, D. M., Medina, J. H., & Izquierdo, I. (1999). Intrahippocampal infusion of an inhibitor of protein kinase A separates short- from long-term memory. *Behavioural Pharmacology, 10,* 223–227.

Walz, R., Roesler, R., Quevedo, J., Sant'Anna, M., Madruga, M., Rodrigues, C., Gottfried, C., Medina, J. H., & Izquierdo, I. (2000). Time-dependent impairment of inhibitory avoidance retention in rats by posttraining infusion of a mitogen-activated protein kinase kinase inhibitor into cortical and limbic structures. *Neurobiology of Learning and Memory, 73,* 1–11.

Willner, P., Bianchin, M., Walz, R., Bueno e Silva, M., Medina, J. H., & Izquierdo, I. (1993). Muscimol infused into the entorhinal cortex prior to training blocks the involvement of this area in post-training memory processing. *Behavioural Pharmacology, 4,* 95–100.

Wilson, M. A., & Tonegawa, S. (1997). Synaptic plasticity, place cells and spatial memory: Study with second-generation knockouts. *Trends in Neurosciences, 20,* 102–106.

Witter, M. P., Groenewegen, H. J., Lopes da Silva, F., & Lohman, A. H. M. (1989). Functional organization of the extrinsic and intrinsic circuitry of the rat parahippocampal region. *Progress in Neurobiology, 33,* 161–254.

Wolfman, C., Fin, C., Dias, M., da Silva, R. C., Schmitz, P. K., Medina, J. H., & Izquierdo, I. (1994). Intrahippocampal or intra-amygdala infusion of KN-62, a specific inhibitor of calcium/calmodulin dependent protein kinase II, causes retrograde amnesia in the rat. *Behavioral and Neural Biology, 61,* 203–205.

Xu, L., Anwyl, R., & Rowan, M. J. (1998). Spatial exploration induces a persistent reversal of long-term potentiation in rat hippocampus. *Nature, 394,* 891–894.

Yin, J. C. P., & Tully, T. (1996). CREB and the formation of long-term memory. *Current Opinion in Neurobiology, 6,* 264–268.

Zhuo, M., Hu, Y., Schultz, C., Kandel, E. R., & Hawkins, R. D. (1994). Role of guanylyl cyclase and cGMP-dependent protein kinase in long-term potentiation. *Nature, 368,* 635–639.

CHAPTER 6

Time-Dependent Processes in Memory Formation Revisited

Steven P. R. Rose

The four decades this festschrift celebrates have seen unrivaled progress in elucidating both the phenomenology of learning and memory consolidation and the molecular mechanisms that appear to underlie these processes. But there remain deep conceptual problems (Rose, 1997). Thus, despite the fact that cognitive psychology and molecular neurobiology are both ostensibly studying the same phenomenon, their protagonists rarely seem to communicate either their findings or the many apparent paradoxes they reveal. In fact, the neurobiology of memory formation rates not a mention in Baddeley's (1997) major monograph and scarcely more in Gallistel (1990) or the monumental *Handbook of Memory* (Tulving & Craik, 2000), and the dubious compliment is returned in much of the molecular neurobiological literature. Even when the same term is used, it does not have the same meaning for the two communities; therefore, *long-term memory* for cognitive psychology means memory that persists beyond a few minutes, as opposed to the transience of *working memory,* whereas for neurobiologists long-term memory occurs an hour or more after a training experience, following a series of intermediate "phases," christened *short-* and *intermediate-term memory*.

Psychologists have generally seen memory formation and retrieval as dynamic processes, not necessarily engaging the same brain regions—a view strengthened since the advent of position emission tomography (PET) studies showing clear hemispheric and anterior–posterior differences between cortical regions where activity increases during encoding and retrieval processes (e.g.,

I thank the many colleagues and visitors to the Brain and Behaviour Research Group, Open University Milton Keynes, whose work, much of which is referenced in this chapter, has formed the basis for this review, and also the funding agencies, notably the Medical Research Council (MRC), the Biotechnology and Biological Sciences Research Council (BBSRC), the Royal Society, the Wellcome Trust, and the European Science Foundation, whose support has sustained this research over many years.

Owen, 1997; Ungerleider, 1997). Some even doubt whether a permanent trace exists in the brain between learning and expression of memory—"ecphorising" (Tulving, 1991). By contrast, neurobiologists have tended to view memory consolidation as a serial process occurring within a given neuronal ensemble. Psychologists fractionate memory into multiple forms, yet because, for the most part, the experimental animals used by neurobiologists have to perform some task to demonstrate learning and subsequent recall, such differing forms are masked or confounded within the more molecular literature. Indeed, in contrast with the multiple forms of memory spoken of by psychologists, neurobiologists are demonstrating a remarkable convergence of molecular mechanisms in widely different species and tasks (Anokhin, 1997; Izquierdo & Medina, 1997).

How can such profound differences be reconciled? The linear neurobiological paradigm derives most clearly from Hebb's (1949) proposal that memory formation involved synaptic strengthening occurring as a result of the temporal and spatial convergence of neuronal inputs. This provided a cellular analog for association learning and a model within which to begin to explore such synaptic processes both physiologically and biochemically. The Hebbian model received empirical support from the discovery of long-term potentiation (LTP), first in the hippocampus and later as a more widely distributed neuronal property. LTP displays the properties of association, cooperation, and specificity that the Hebbian model requires and has become generally accepted as both a model and a mechanism for memory formation. A second major source of support for such a "cellular alphabet" model of memory formation came from the work of Kandel and his colleagues with aplysia, showing persisting changes in synaptic strength in defined neurons following both training protocols in the intact animal and analogous changes in a reduced preparation. Both the processes of induction and maintenance of LTP and the aplysia studies suggest a linear model in which learning involves the growth and stabilization of synapses, and the site of recall is the same as the site of learning. As Kandel (1995) put it with great clarity,

> explicit and implicit forms of memory storage proceed through stages and . . . the same synaptic sites that store the initial information relevant for short term memory, which lasts from minutes to hours, also store long term memory over a period of days and weeks. (p. 54)

It is clear, however, that whatever the validity of this linear model for aplysia, it cannot readily be squared with the more complex pattern observed in vertebrate learning. There has long been an alternative, "parallel processing" current in the neurobiology of memory, pioneered by James L. McGaugh and based on evidence of time-dependent processes in the form of both anterograde and retrograde amnesia, revealed by pharmacological dissection. As far back as 1966, McGaugh felt, there does seem to be increasing evidence that the temporary and longer term memory] systems are independent . . . *each* experience triggers activity in *each* memory system. . . . It seems clear that any search for *the* engram or *the* basis for memory is not going to be successful. . . . several independent processes may be involved at different stages of memory. (pp. 1357–1358)

The Chick Model

In what follows, I review recent evidence from my own lab supporting the view that the molecular and cellular processes involved in memory consolidation involve multiple forms, phases, cascades, and brain locations, results that bring neurobiology more closely into alignment with the more dynamic psychological view. My experimental model is the day-old chick, a precocial species that actively explores and learns about its environment from the moment the bird struggles out of its egg (and indeed even while in ovo). Chicks peck spontaneously at small objects in their field of view. If the object is distasteful, they peck once; evince a disgust response; and avoid objects of similar size, color, and shape thereafter. The merit of this task is that it is reliable, reproducible, and sharply timed, so that the concomitants of the training experience itself, which lasts no more than 30 seconds, can be separated from those of memory formation and consolidation that follow. Anterograde and retrograde pharmacological or behavioral interventions can be readily used, and the time of intervention relative to the training experience is also tightly controlled. In this version of the task, the chick is offered a small chrome bead dipped in the bitter-tasting methylanthranilate (MeA). If 100% MeA is used, avoidance persists for at least 24 hours subsequently. If a 10% solution of MeA is the aversive version, chicks will avoid the bead for only some 6 hours after the training experience. This then represents a behaviorally defined transition point between shorter and longer term memory (Sandi & Rose, 1994). Amnesia for the task is indicated by the chick pecking the bead on test.

Using the stronger version of the task, a biochemical cascade has been identified occurring over the minutes to hours following training which, beginning with transient changes in neurotransmitter release, culminates in the molecular and structural remodeling of synapses. The avian brain shows marked lateralization, and the cascade, studied in detail, occurs in a region of the left hemisphere homologous with striate cortex in mammals, the intermediate medial hyperstriatum ventrale (IMHV). Further biochemical and structural changes occur in a basal ganglion homologue, the lobus parolfactorius (LPO). This cascade has been reviewed (e.g., Rose, 1995; Rose & Stewart, 1999), and I merely summarize its salient features here. Early events in the first 10 minutes or so following training include enhanced potassium and N-methyl d-aspartate (NMDA)-stimulated calcium flux in synaptoneurosomes isolated from the IMHV

(Salinska, Chaudhury, Bourne, & Rose, 2000), and increased glutamate release detected either in vitro or by microdialysis in vivo (Daisley, Gruss, Rose, & Braun, 1998). Within 30 minutes there is an increase in NMDA-glutamate receptor binding, whereas NMDA receptor blockers such as MK801 or 7-chlorokynurenene, injected into the left IMHV, are amnestic. At this time, too, blockade of the synthesis of the putative retrograde messenger NO (nitric oxide) by injection of nitroarginine is also amnestic.

The assumption is that these synaptic events result in intracellular second messenger signals, probably both pre- and postsynaptically, which in due course activate transcription factors and switch on immediate early genes (IEGs). Enhanced message for *c-fos* and *c-jun* can be detected as early as 40 minutes posttraining, and increased fos and jun proteins are detectable 1–2 hours posttraining (Freeman & Rose, 1995a). Antisense to fos, injected 6 hours or more upstream of the training experience, prevents fos expression, and amnesia sets in within 3 hours (Mileusnic, Anokhin, & Rose, 1996). In turn, the IEGs trigger the enhanced synthesis of a family of cell adhesion molecules that, by some 6 hours downstream of training, are inserted into the synaptic membranes. These include the neural cell adhesion molecule (NCAM) and Ng-CAM/L1. Changes in the distribution of the NCAM molecules within the synaptic apposition zone and its dimensions (Skibo, Davies, Rusakov, Stewart, & Schachner, 1997), and in other synaptic morphological parameters within 12–24 hours posttraining (Rose & Stewart, 1999) are all in accord with a linear, Kandelian model of memory formation occurring in the left IMHV, and with a view of memory formation as requiring Hebbian-type modifications of synaptic connectivity. The sequence is summarized in Figure 6.1.

So where's the problem?

Temporal Complexities

One of the few universals in the study of the molecular mechanisms of memory formation is that protein synthesis inhibitors, injected at or around the time of training, result in amnesia that sets in an hour or so later (Davis & Squire, 1984). As it appears that memory can be blocked by injecting the inhibitors subsequent to that time, this protein-synthesis-insensitive phase was taken as the defining feature of long-term memory (e.g., Gibbs & Ng, 1977). Indeed, Gibbs and Ng proposed a rather mechanical stage model of memory formation in which there are sequential phases of short term, and two intermediate phases each characterized by distinct biochemical processes, which culminate in the protein-synthesis-insensitive long-term phase. The extensive subsequent research by this group, which has filled in many details of the biochemistry and pharmacology of these early posttraining periods (e.g., Zhao, Feng, Bennett, &

FIGURE 6.1

Molecular cascade of memory formation following one-trial passive avoidance training in the chick.

Pre/post Synaptic Parallel Processing

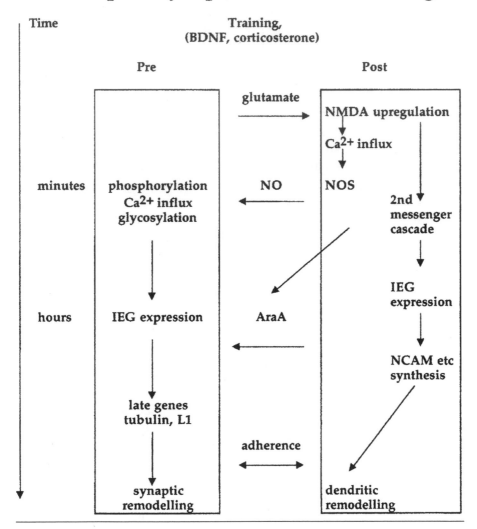

Ng, 1997), has continued to use versions of this linear model. Although useful heuristically, from evidence both in our chick model (which is similar to that used by Gibbs & Ng, 1977; see Burne & Rose, 1997) and in other systems, such as drosophila (deZazzo & Tully, 1995), it has become clear that such a formalism can no longer hold. Certainly inhibitors such as anisomycin are amnestic in the chick if injected within 30 minutes or so of the training experience, whereas if injected at 90, 120, or 180 minutes posttraining they are no longer amnestic. However, we found that if anisomycin is injected 4–5 hours post-training it once again results in chicks being amnestic on tests at 24 hours. Injections later than this time are without effect. Thus, there appeared (Freeman & Rose, 1995b) to be a second time window of sensitivity to protein synthesis blockers, downstream of the time when long-term memory was supposed to have been established. We argued that the first sensitive period was related to the blocking of expression of immediate early genes, whereas the second co-incided with the wave of expression of the structural genes coding for those proteins required for synaptic modulation.

This argument was strengthened when it came time to examine in more detail the protein species produced during this second wave. As mentioned above, among these species are the glycoprotein cell adhesion molecules (CAMS), NCAM and L1. Inhibitors of glycoprotein synthesis, such as the met-abolic competitor 2-deoxygalactose, are amnestic if injected either around the time of training or 5–7 hours posttraining. Antibodies to the external domains of NCAM or L1 are also amnestic during this later time window (Scholey, Rose, Zamani, Bock, & Schachner, 1993). The L1, but not the NCAM antibody, is also amnestic if injected just prior to training—that is, at both the earlier and the later time windows. To complete the picture, recombinant fragments that bind to the external domains of L1 are also amnestic. Fragments binding to the immunoglobulin domain block memory retention only at the early time point (injection 30 minutes prior to training), whereas those to the fibronectin do-main block at the later time point (injection 5.5 hours posttraining; Scholey, Mileusnic, Schachner, & Rose, 1995).

Let me offer an interpretation of these observations. The several roles of cell adhesion molecules are a matter of debate, but it is probable that they include at least two: signal transduction and intercellular adherence by both homphilic and heterophilic binding. I can argue that both roles are engaged during the cascade—signal transduction for L1 during the early phase, synaptic adherence at the second. Presumably it is the signal transduction function of the L1 that is being blocked by the recombinants to its immunoglobulin domain at this time. During the early posttraining period, there is no net synthesis of new adhesion molecules, but rather a posttranslational modification of existing glycoproteins, blocked by the 2-deoxygalactose. There is both net synthesis and redistribution (Skibo et al., 1997) during the second time window. However, if the role of the CAMs is to alter synaptic connectivity by restructuring existing synapses, two processes must be involved. In the initial phase the CAMs must de-adhere so that pre- and postsynaptic structures can move relative to each other, or expand in size. The second step requires re-adherence in the new configuration. The adherence state of NCAM is dependent on its degree of polysialylation, and the hypothesis, also developed in the context of a step-down avoidance task in the rat, which shows similar temporal dynamics (Doyle, Nolan, Bell, & Regan, 1992), is that during the period 5–8 hours posttraining both new NCAM molecules are being inserted into the pre- and postsynaptic membranes and existing ones are being sialylated so as to open the junction (Regan & Fox, 1995). It is at this stage that the exposed epitopes on the extracellular domains of the CAMs become available for antibody binding, hence preventing ordered re-adherence.

What might be the significance of this downstream time window? It is of interest that in chicks trained on the weak learning task (Sandi & Rose, 1994) memory persists only for about this time, and in this task there is no second time window of synthesis of cell adhesion molecules. The salience of the weak learning experience can be manipulated, for instance, by manipulating corticosterone levels (Sandi & Rose, 1997) or by mildly stressing the chicks posttraining (by placing them in separated pens; Johnston & Rose, 1998). Under such circumstances CAM synthesis occurs and memory persists until at least 24 hours.

It is attractive to speculate that there must be many relatively trivial experiences in an animal's life that can usefully be recalled for up to a few hours, if only to make later relevant associations. The so-called Garcia effect of taste aversion is an example, in which later sickness must be associated with tasting novel food or experiencing familiar food in a novel context some hours previously (e.g., Barber, Gilbert, & Rose, 1989). That we are here tapping into a more general mechanism at which the second time point around 6 hours downstream seems to be of importance is indicated by the fact that the same sensitivity to antibodies to NCAM injected at around this time has been found in both aversive (Doyle et al., 1992) and appetitive tasks in rats (Roullet, Mileusnic, Rose, & Sara, 1997). In these cases, although the time at which the antibodies must be injected is similar, amnesia is not apparent in animals tested at 24 hours, but it is at 48 hours. This implies that in the rat there must be a distinct CAM-independent memory holding system that persists for at least 24 hours posttraining before declining.

The demonstration of a second window of biochemical engagement downstream of the apparent formation of long-term memory is not in itself incompatible with the linear model of memory formation, although it significantly extends the time period over which it is supposed to occur, but this is only the start of the complexities. Using an alternative early learning task in the chick, a visual categorization procedure in which the bird learns to peck and distinguish edible crumbs from arrays of colored beads glued to the floor of its pen, we (Tiunova, Anokhin, & Rose, 1998) were not only able to replicate the time windows observed for the amnestic effect of antibodies to L1 in the passive avoidance task but also were able to observe a further period of vulnerability

15–18 hours downstream of the training experience. It may be relevant that this time point corresponds to one of a sequence of time windows of plasticity increasingly distant from the learning experience that Nottebohm and his colleagues have observed for song-learning zebra finches (Chew, Vicario, & Nottebohm, 1996). It is becoming clear that far from biochemical mechanisms somehow being permanently transduced into structural changes within hours of the training experience, there is a long period during which such processes are subtly involved, being revealed only when an animal is challenged in an appropriate manner.

The engagement of protein synthesis synthetic mechanisms is not the end of the story so far as the involvement of other synaptic processes is concerned. If one times the onset of amnesia following injecting putative blocking agents just prior to or just after training on the passive avoidance task, one can determine when the blocked process, or its downstream consequences, must become a necessary feature of the cascade. Although most such agents result in amnesia at times between 5 and 45 minutes posttraining—that is, before the effect of protein synthesis blockers like anisomycin—some induce amnesia only at later times. For example, nordihydroguaiaretic acid, which blocks the release of the putative retrograde messenger arachidonic acid, produces amnesia only by 75 minutes posttraining (Holscher & Rose, 1994) whereas indomethacin, which blocks cyclo-oxygenase, is amnestic only by 120 minutes (Holscher, 1995). Furthermore, although NMDA and not AMPA blockers such as CNQX are amnestic in the early phase (Burchuladze & Rose, 1992), CNQX is amnestic when injected 5 hours posttraining—that is, during the period of the second wave of protein synthesis (Steele & Stewart, 1995)—and at this time in the trained birds there is an increase in AMPA- but not NMDA-stimulated calcium flux (Salinska et al., 2000).

Remembering prior experiences and integrating them into a new context evidently involves some sort of a biochemical reprise. Thus, in a microdialysis experiment, Daisley et al. (1998) observed that simply presenting a dry bead to a previously trained chick evoked a surge in glutamate release. Anokhin and his colleagues have recently observed that if a chick is trained on the passive avoidance task and then 24 hours later given a reminder training, the evoked memory is once again sensitive to protein synthesis inhibitors or MK801 (Litvin & Anokhin, 1998; Radyushkin & Anokhin, 1998).

The Fluid Engram and the Fractionation of Memory

Thus the pharmacological approach to anterograde and retrograde amnesia pioneered by McGaugh and his colleagues is increasingly revealing the complexity of the temporal dynamics of any putative memory trace and that multiple processes, of varying posttraining onset and duration, are engaged. Although these observations can in themselves probably be accommodated within a simple Hebbian or connectionist framework, the evidence for trace mobility that comes from the imaging studies (e.g., Owen, 1997; Ungerleider, 1997) is harder to integrate. Here, too, studies in the chick have provided evidence for the fluidity of the engram.

The first indication of this fluidity came from electrophysiological recordings made with an extracellular electrode in the anaesthetized bird. In the hours following training on the task we detected a substantial increase in bursts of high-frequency neuronal firing in the IMHV of birds that had pecked a 100% methylanthranilate-coated bead and remembered the avoidance, compared with controls (Mason & Rose, 1988). When we examined the temporal dynamics of this bursting activity, it became apparent that it was unevenly distributed; there appeared to be two peaks of activity—the first some 3–4 hours posttraining, the second some 7–8 hours, the latter matching the "second wave" of cell adhesion molecule engagement (Gigg, Patterson, & Rose, 1993). Furthermore, although the first peak occurred in both the left and right IMHV, the second peak was largely confined to the right IMHV. There was also increased activity in the LPO (Gigg, Patterson, & Rose, 1994). Therefore, it appeared to be a sequential involvement of the two hemispheres in registering neurophysiological sequelae of memory formation.

It had been shown by Horn and his colleagues (Horn, 1985) that lesions to the left IMHV prior to exposing young chicks to an imprinting stimulus (a flashing light) prevented acquisition of the task. However, if the chick was imprinted and the lesion delayed for some hours, recall was unimpaired, suggesting to the authors that the trace had somehow migrated from the left IMHV to some other area, perhaps right hemisphere located. To explore the implications of this in more detail, we used a sequence of double dissociation lesions in the passive avoidance paradigm.

In the first experiment (Patterson, Gilbert, & Rose, 1990), we lesioned the IMHV bilaterally prior to training. Chicks so lesioned would peck at the bead and show a disgust response but did not avoid a similar bead when presented subsequently. A unilateral right IMHV lesion was without apparent effect on either acquisition or recall, whereas a unilateral left hemisphere lesion resulted in amnesia. Pretraining bilateral lesions of the LPO were also without effect on acquisition or recall. Repeating this experiment, but, instead, performing the lesions 3 hours posttraining gave very different results. Neither unilateral nor bilateral lesions of the IMHV were amnestic, whereas bilateral lesions of the LPO prevented recall of the task. Thus, chicks appeared to require their left IMHV to learn, but not to remember the avoidance, and their LPO to remember but not to learn the avoidance (Gilbert, Patterson, & Rose, 1991). The implication was that in some way the trace was transferred from the left IMHV to the LPO in the hours following training. Could this be via the right IMHV? If so, pretraining lesions of the LPO, which would not prevent acquisition, would result in the trace being somehow "blocked" in the IMHV and posttraining lesions of the IMHV would now be amnestic. So it proved—in chicks with pretraining LPO lesions, either bilateral or right IMHV posttraining lesions are amnestic. However, any "transport" of the trace to the LPO did not necessarily have to go via the right IMHV. If this were so, then pretraining right IMHV lesions (not amnestic) followed by posttraining left IMHV lesions should result in amnesia because the migration would be prevented. But chicks treated in this way still showed recall provided their LPOs were intact, so there had to be an independent conditional route from the left IMHV to the LPO (Rose, 1991). It turns out that this is via the archistriatum, an intermediate region monosynaptically connected to both the IMHV and LPO (Csillag, Szekely, & Davies, 1994; Csillag, Szekely, & Stewart, 1997). This is shown in Figure 6.2.

Could this be the full story? Do we simply have a moving trace, so that ultimately the connectionist memory for the avoidance is stored in some ensemble of cells in the LPO unless prevented by some prior lesion? One paradox persisted. If this were the case, and the IMHV is only transitorily involved, why should we be able to detect lasting structural and biochemical changes in the

FIGURE 6.2

Multiple representation model for memory of passive avoidance bead task in the chick.

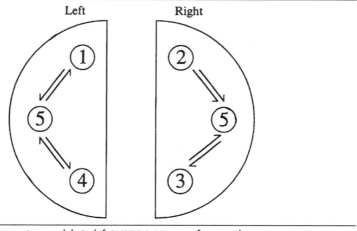

Multiple representation model. 1. left IMHV: Initiation of trace: short-term storage, longer term classification by color. 2. right IMHV: Intermediate processor: can be driven unilaterally. 3. left LPO: Initiation of long-term trace: long-term storage, classification by noncolor features. 4. right LPO: Long-term storage, classification by noncolor features. 5. archistriatum: Connections between IMHV and LPO.

left IMHV? The answer to this reveals yet more of the complexity of memory storage processes. Because we train the chick by presenting a chrome bead, we tend to regard this as a unitary experience. Yet, of course, the chick has no way of knowing just which of the features of the bead with which it has been presented are associated with the bitter taste. It is known that chicks can distinguish and classify items in terms of color, shape, size, and location (Vallortigara, Zanforlin, & Compostella, 1990). So in recalling and avoiding the bead the chick is able to remember many if not all of these features. Challenging the bird during the test simply by offering it a bead resembling that on which it has been trained does not require it to distinguish specific features of the bead. If chicks are trained on a chrome bead and later tested on both a chrome bead and one of another color, say red or white, they can discriminate and will continue to peck at the colored bead while avoiding the chrome. How would lesioned birds respond?

We trained birds to avoid a yellow bead and to discriminate between that and a blue bead, which they would continue to peck. Three hours posttraining, we lesioned either the LPO or the IMHV. Birds with lesions to the LPO pecked at both the blue bead and the yellow, as predicted from the previous lesion set. Birds that had posttraining lesions of the IMHV continued to avoid the yellow bead, also as predicted. However, they now avoided the blue bead, too (Patterson & Rose, 1992). That is, they could no longer discriminate between previously distasteful and neutral novel beads of different colors but the same shape and size and location. Thus, in some way memory for a color-based discrimination must reside in the left IMHV, whereas memory for other aspects of the bead-pecking experience depends on other brain regions, notably the LPO. Memory for even such a simple phenomenon as a distasteful bead is thus distributed across widely separated brain regions, showing fluidity in space as well as time. If we take the liberty of assuming that the chick, like ourselves, nonetheless perceives the bead as a coherent unitary experience, we must assume that avian brains, too, have discovered how to solve the famous binding problem.

References

Anokhin, K. V. (1997). Towards synthesis of systems and molecular genetics approaches to memory consolidation. *Journal of Higher Nervous Activity, 47,* 157–169.

Baddeley, A. (1997). *Human memory: Theory and practice* (rev. ed.). Boston: Allyn & Bacon.

Barber, A., Gilbert, D. B., & Rose, S. P. R. (1989). Glycoprotein synthesis is necessary for memory of sickness-induced learning in chicks. *European Journal of Neuroscience, 1,* 673–677.

Burchuladze, R., & Rose, S. P. R. (1992). Memory formation in day old chicks requires NMDA but not non-NMDA glutamate receptors. *European Journal of Neuroscience, 4,* 533–538.

Burne, T. H. J., & Rose, S. P. R. (1997). Effects of training procedure on memory formation using a weak passive avoidance learning paradigm. *Neurobiology of Learning and Memory, 68,* 133–139.

Chew, J. V., Vicario, D. S., & Nottebohm, F. (1996). Quantal duration of auditory memories. *Science, 274,* 1909–1914.

Csillag, A., Szekely, A. D., & Davies, D. C. (1994). Termination pattern of medial hyperstriatum ventrale efferents in the archistriatum of the domestic chick. *Journal of Comparative Neurology, 348,* 394–402.

Csillag, A., Szekely, A. D., & Stewart, M. G. (1997). Synaptic terminals immunolabelled against glutamate in the lobus parolfactorius of domestic chicks in relation to afferents from the archistriatum. *Brain Research, 750,* 171–179.

Daisley, J. N., Gruss, M., Rose, S. P. R., & Braun, K. (1998). Passive avoidance training and recall are associated with increased glutamate levels in the intermediate medial hyperstriatum ventrale of the day old chick. *Neural Plasticity, 6,* 53–61.

Davis, H. P., & Squire, L. R. (1984). Protein synthesis and memory: A review. *Psychological Bulletin, 96,* 518–559.

deZazzo, J., & Tully, T. (1995). Dissection of memory formation: From behavioral pharmacology to molecular genetics. *Trends in Neuroscience, 18,* 212–217.

Doyle, E., Nolan, P. M., Bell, R., & Regan, C. R. (1992). Intraventricular infusions of anti-neural cell adhesion molecules in a discrete posttraining period impair consolidation of a passive avoidance response in the rat. *Journal of Neurochemistry, 59,* 1570–1573.

Freeman, F. M., & Rose, S. P. R. (1995a). MK801 blockade of fos and jun expression following passive avoidance training in the chick. *European Journal of Neuroscience, 7,* 563–569.

Freeman, F. M., & Rose, S. P. R. (1995b). Two time windows of anisomycin-induced amnesia for passive avoidance training in the day old chick. *Neurobiology of Learning and Memory, 63,* 291–295.

Gallistel, C. R. (1990). *The organization of learning.* Cambridge, MA: MIT Press.

Gibbs, M. E., & Ng, K. T. (1977). Psychobiology of memory: Towards a model of memory formation. *Behavioral Review, 1,* 113–136.

Gigg, J., Patterson, T. A., & Rose, S. P. R. (1993). Training-induced increases in neuronal activity recorded from the forebrain of the chick are time-dependent. *Neuroscience, 56,* 771–776.

Gigg, J., Patterson, T. A., & Rose, S. P. R. (1994). Increases in neuronal bursting recorded from the chick lobus parolfactorius are both time-dependent and memory-specific. *European Journal of Neuroscience, 6,* 313–319.

Gilbert, D. B., Patterson, T. A., & Rose, S. P. R. (1991). Dissociation of brain sites necessary for registration and storage of memory for a one-trial passive avoidance task in the chick. *Behavioral Neuroscience, 195,* 553–561.

Hebb, D. O. (1949). *The organization of behavior.* New York: Wiley.

Holscher, C. (1995). Inhibitors of cyclooxygenases produce amnesia for a passive avoidance task in the chick. *European Journal of Neuroscience, 7,* 1360–1364.

Holscher, C., & Rose, S. P. R. (1994). Inhibitors of phospholipase A2 produce amnesia for a passive avoidance task in the chick. *Behavioral and Neural Biology, 61,* 225–232.

Horn, G. (1985). *Memory, imprinting, and the brain: An inquiry into mechanisms.* Oxford, England: Oxford University Press.

Izquierdo, I., & Medina, J. H. (1997). Memory formation: The sequence of biochemical events in the hippocampus and its connection to activity in other brain structures. *Neurobiology of Learning and Memory, 68,* 285–316.

Johnston, A. N. B., & Rose, S. P. R. (1998). Isolation-stress induced facilitation of passive avoidance memory in the day-old chick. *Behavioral Neuroscience, 112,* 1–8.

Kandel, E. R. (1995). *Neurosciences, memory and language.* Washington, DC: U.S. Library of Congress.

Litvin, O. O., & Anokhin, K. V. (1998). Transient amnestic effect of cycloheximide due to reminder treatment at various times after passive avoidance training in chicks. *Proceedings of the IV ERC Neural Mechanics of Learning and Memory,* A32.

Mason, R., & Rose, S. P. R. (1988). Passive avoidance learning produces focal elevation of bursting activity in the chick brain: Amnesia abolishes the increase. *Behavioral and Neural Biology, 49,* 280–292.

McGaugh, J. L. (1966). Time-dependent processes in memory storage *Science, 153,* 1351–1358.

Mileusnic, R., Anokhin, K., & Rose, S. P. R. (1996). Antisense oligodeoxynucleotides to c-fos are amnestic for passive avoidance in the chick. *Neurological Report, 7,* 1269–1272.

Owen, A. M. (1997). The functional organisation of working memory processes within human lateral frontal cortex: The contribution of functional imaging. *European Journal of Neuroscience, 9,* 1329–1339.

Patterson, T. A., Gilbert, D. B., & Rose, S. P. R. (1990). Pre- and post-training lesions of the IMHV and passive avoidance learning in the chick. *Experimental Brain Research, 80,* 189–195.

Patterson, T. A., & Rose, S. P. R. (1992). Memory in the chick: Multiple cues, distinct brain locations. *Behavioral Neuroscience, 106,* 465–470.

Radyushkin, K. A., & Anokhin, K. V. (1998). Reversibility of amnesia produced in chicks by NMDA-receptor antagonist MK-801: Effects of a reminder treatment. *Proceedings of the IV ERC Neural Mechanics of Learning and Memory,* A33.

Regan, C. M., & Fox, G. B. (1995). Polysialylation as a regulator of neural plasticity in rodent learning and ageing. *Neurochemistry Research, 20,* 521–526.

Rose, S. P. R. (1991). How chicks make memories: The cellular cascade from c-fos to dendritic remodelling. *Trends in Neuroscience, 14,* 390–397.

Rose, S. P. R. (1995). Cell adhesion molecules, glucocorticoids and memory. *Trends in Neuroscience, 18,* 502–506.

Rose, S. P. R. (1997). *Lifelines: Biology, freedom and determinism.* Harmondsworth, England: Allen Lane, Penguin Press.

Rose, S. P. R., & Stewart, M. G. (1999). Cellular correlates of memory formation in the chick following passive avoidance training. *Behavioral Brain Research, 98,* 237–243.

Roullet, P., Mileusnic, R., Rose, S. P. R., & Sara, S. J. (1997). Neural cell adhesion molecules play a role in rat memory formation in appetitive as well as aversive tasks. *NeuroReport, 8,* 1907–1911.

Salinska, E. J., Chaudhury, D., Bourne, R. C., & Rose, S. P. R. (2000). Passive avoidance training results in increased responsiveness of voltage and ligand-gated channels in chick brain synaptoneurosomes. *Neuroscience, 93,* 1507–1516.

Sandi, C., & Rose, S. P. R. (1994). Corticosterone enhances long-term retention in one day old chicks trained in a weak passive avoidance learning paradigm. *Brain Research, 647,* 106–112.

Sandi, C., & Rose, S. P. R. (1997). Training-dependent biphasic effects of corticosterone in memory formation for a passive avoidance tasks in chicks. *Psychopharmacology, 133,* 152–160.

Scholey, A. B., Mileusnic, R., Schachner, M., & Rose, S. P. R. (1995). A role for a chicken homolog of the neural cell adhesion molecule L1 in consolidation of memory for a passive avoidance task. *Learning and Memory, 2,* 17–25.

Scholey, A. B., Rose, S. P. R., Zamani, M. R., Bock, E., & Schachner, M. (1993). A role for the neural cell adhesion molecule in a late consolidating phase of glycoprotein synthesis 6 hr following passive avoidance training of the young chick. *Neuroscience, 55,* 499–509.

Skibo, G., Davies, H. A., Rusakov, D. A., Stewart, M. G., & Schachner, M. (1997). Increased immunogold labelling of neural cell adhesion molecule isoforms in synaptic active zones of the chick striatum 5–6 hr after one-trial passive avoidance training. *Neuroscience, 82,* 1–5.

Steele, R. J., & Stewart, M. G. (1995). Involvement of AMPA receptors in maintenance of memory for a passive avoidance task in day-old domestic chicks. *European Journal of Neuroscience, 7,* 1297–1304.

Tiunova, A., Anokhin, K. V., & Rose, S. P. R. (1998). Three time windows for amnestic effect of antibodies to cell adhesion molecule L1 in chicks. *NeuroReport, 9,* 1645–1648.

Tulving, E. (1991). Interview with Endel Tulving. *Journal of Cognitive Neuroscience, 3,* 89.

Tulving, E., & Craik, F. (2000). *Handbook of memory.* Oxford, England: Oxford University Press.

Ungerleider, L. G. (1997). Functional brain imaging studies of cortical representation for memory. *Science, 270,* 769–774.

Vallortigara, G., Zanforlin, M., & Compostella, S. (1990). Perceptual organisation in animal learning: Cues or objects? *Ethology, 85,* 89–102.

Zhao, W. Q., Feng, H., Bennett, P., & Ng, K. T. (1997). Inhibition of intermediate-term memory following passive avoidance training in neonate chicks by a presynaptic cholinergic blocker. *Neurobiology of Learning and Memory, 67,* 207–213.

CHAPTER 7

Neural Pathways Mediating the Modulation of Learning and Memory by Arousal

Robert A. Jensen

E arly work in James McGaugh's laboratory addressed the question of why some happenings or events are remembered so clearly whereas others are remembered only poorly or perhaps not at all. Dr. McGaugh's pioneering research clearly established in laboratory animals that retention can be either impaired or enhanced by experimental treatments given close to the time of a learning experience. He noted that these experimental treatments could take many forms, such as electrical brain stimulation; the administration of various pharmacological agents; or the administration of hormones, some of which are endogenously released during periods of arousal (McGaugh & Herz, 1972).

Emotional Arousal Causes Release of Hormones Associated With Modulation of Memory Storage Processes

Much of McGaugh's research was conducted using laboratory rodents as subjects and used simple Y-maze tasks or the inhibitory (passive) avoidance task. The latter task, which figures prominently in this chapter, involves the administration of punishment (usually mild electric footshock) so that the experimental animal learns to avoid a specific place, such as the darkened end of a runway where the punishment was previously administered. Electrical brain stimulation, pharmacological treatments, or hormone administration was typically given shortly after the time of training, and retention was typically tested one to several days after the learning experience. In experiments in which the treatment was given after the learning trial, findings were usually interpreted as indicating that memory storage processes in the brain were in some way modulated by the posttraining treatment. This is because learning occurred before the administration of an experimental treatment, and retention testing was given long after any residual effects of the treatment had disappeared. Therefore, it was reasoned that the only thing the posttraining treatment could have affected was the memory consolidation process. These studies provided many insights. Perhaps one of the most important findings arising from these experiments was strong support for the idea that the neural processes that underlie memory storage are regulated by the actions of neuromodulatory systems, such as hormone release triggered by the arousal associated with a training experience (Gold & McGaugh, 1975).

Epinephrine and norepinephrine are released from the adrenal medulla as a result of arousal or stress, such as the arousal produced by the delivery of shock in the inhibitory avoidance-learning situation. In 1975, working in the McGaugh laboratory, Gold and van Buskirk reported an enhancement of retention performance in an inhibitory avoidance task produced by peripheral injection of low doses of epinephrine given shortly after training. This finding was replicated and extended through a long series of experiments using active avoidance tasks, discrimination learning, and appetitive tasks (Gold, van Buskirk, & Haycock, 1977; Introini-Collison & McGaugh, 1986; Sternberg, Isaacs, Gold, & McGaugh, 1985).

Building on this foundation, Gold and McCarty (1981) showed that plasma epinephrine concentrations, measured after the administration of a memory-enhancing dose of epinephrine, are comparable to epinephrine levels seen in animals that received a footshock of sufficient intensity to produce good learning. This and other studies provided strong support for the idea that epinephrine and norepinephrine, released as the result of arousal in a learning experience, enhance memory storage processes. Other research performed in McGaugh's laboratory suggested that the pituitary hormones, such as adrenocorticotropic hormone (ACTH), vasopressin, and the opioid peptides, all hormonal substances associated with arousal, also modulate memory storage processes (see McGaugh, 1983, 1989).

Catecholamines Released From Adrenals Modulate Memory but Do Not Directly Affect Memory Processes in the CNS

It is unlikely that the memory modulatory effects produced by the release of endogenous catecholamines or pituitary peptides are the result of direct influences on the central nervous system (CNS). This is because epinephrine, norepinephrine, and the peptide hormones do not readily cross the blood–brain barrier. The idea that such substances might be acting through peripheral receptors received support from research performed in the late 1970s in the McGaugh lab. These studies showed that an amphetamine derivative, 4-OH-amphetamine, has much the same capacity (near equimolar doses) to enhance retention performance, when administered after training, as does d-amphetamine. However, 4-OH-amphetamine crosses the blood–brain barrier only very poorly, whereas d-amphetamine readily enters the CNS, so it was not at all clear how these two drugs could be having such similar effects on memory.

Sympathectomy with 6-hydroxydopamine (6-OHDA) administered intravenously caused the dose response curve of both 4-OH amphetamine and d-amphetamine to be shifted to the left. That is, lower doses of both drugs had a similar capacity to enhance retention, suggesting that some kind of peripheral denervation supersensitivity had likely developed (Martinez, Jensen, et al., 1980). Importantly, adrenal medullectomy attenuated the memory-enhancing effects of both 4-OH-amphetamine and d-amphetamine (Martinez, Vasquez, et al., 1980).

Taken together, these findings suggest that it is likely that both forms of amphetamine acted to modulate memory, not through direct actions on the brain but through drug-induced release of catecholamines from the adrenal medulla. These medullary catecholamines then acted on peripheral systems in some way to enhance the memory storage process. This hypothesis was later supported by a report that systemic injections of the beta-adrenergic antagonist, sotalol, another drug that does not freely cross the blood–brain barrier, attenuates the memory-enhancing effects of peripherally administered amphetamine (Introini-Collison, Saghafi, Novack, & McGaugh, 1992).

Severing the Vagus Nerve Attenuates Modulatory Effects on Memory Produced by Peripherally Administered Hormones

As a group, these and other studies suggested that the activation of peripheral receptors following arousal leads to the enhancement of memory storage processes. However, the mechanism by which this might occur was not known. One possible way that activation of peripheral receptors by arousal could lead to the modulation of memory storage processes might be that neural messages from these receptors are carried to the CNS by neural pathways such as the vagus nerve (cranial nerve X). To test this hypothesis, subdiaphragmic vagotomies were performed in rats. It was reasoned that if vagotomy attenuates the capacity of substances to modulate retention performance, then this finding would provide support for the hypothesis that neural messages carried by the vagus influence learning and memory (Williams & Jensen, 1991).

Vagotomies were performed by sectioning approximately 1 cm of the anterior, posterior, hepatic, and both celiac branches of the vagus just below the point where they pass through the diaphragm. After a 1-week recovery period, the rats were trained on an inhibitory avoidance task. Immediately after training, they were given intraperitoneal (ip) injections of saline or 2.0 or 4.0 mg/kg of 4-OH-amphetamine. In the sham-operated control animals, significant facilitation of performance, compared to saline-treated controls, was seen at the 2.0 mg/kg dose, but the 4.0 mg/kg dose produced impairment in retention performance. Such an inverted U-shaped function is characteristic of the effects of many substances that modulate memory (McGaugh & Herz, 1972; Yerkes & Dodson, 1908). In the vagotomized animals, in contrast, the dose–response curve for 4-OH-amphetamine was shifted to the right. That is, the 2.0 mg/kg dose had little effect, whereas the 4.0 mg/kg dose, which impaired retention performance in the control animals, now produced memory enhancement (Williams & Jensen, 1991). Subdiaphragmic vagotomy similarly attenuated the memory-impairing effects of leu-enkephalin, a peptide that has strong amnestic effects on memory but does not cross the blood–brain barrier (Williams & Jensen, 1993).

This hypothesis was supported by research from other laboratories demonstrating that subdiaphragmic vagotomy attenuates the memory modulation produced by substances such as cholecystokinin (Flood, Smith, & Morley, 1987) and substance P (Nogueira, Tomaz, & Williams, 1994). Additionally, reversible inactivation of the nucleus of the solitary tract, the primary relay site of vagal afferents in the brain stem, also attenuates the modulation of memory produced by peripherally administered epinephrine (Williams & McGaugh, 1993). Collectively these findings suggest that the vagus nerve may be an important pathway by which information about peripheral states, such as the presence of hormones that were released as a result of arousal, is carried to the brain to modulate memory storage processes.

However, in these experiments, subdiaphragmic vagotomy attenuated but did not entirely block the memory modulatory effects of the drugs. This may have been because a substantial portion of the vagus nerve, that is, all fibers above the level of the diaphragm, remained intact and were available to carry information to the CNS about hormone concentrations in the periphery. Alternatively, there might also be a sympathetic system component, such as the splanchnic nerve, that carries information to the CNS in parallel to the vagus to modulate memory. To test this hypothesis, bilateral splanchnicectomies were performed in the laboratory by sectioning 2–3 millimeters of nerve tissue above the celiac ganglion but below the adrenal branch of the splanchnic nerve. This produced a sympathetic denervation comparable in anatomical scope to the parasympathetic denervation produced by subdiaphragmic vagotomy. Splanchnicectomy had no effect on the capacity of 1.0 mg/kg 4-OH-amphetamine to enhance retention performance (Noyes, Murphy, & Jensen, 1995). Therefore, it appears likely that the vagus nerve serves as the primary neural pathway by which memory is modulated by substances released as a result of arousal or by the administration of pharmacological agents that do not cross the blood–brain barrier.

Increases in Circulating Glucose Concentrations in Blood Modulate Memory Storage Processes

The activation of peripheral receptors leading to neural messages that travel via the vagus nerve to the CNS is not the only mechanism by which peripheral events might modulate memory. Gold (1986) suggested that the effects of arousal might involve epinephrine-induced release of glucose from the liver. As a result of Gold's work, as well as that of his colleagues, there is a substantial literature indicating that posttraining injections of glucose produce effects on retention performance that are similar to those produced by the systemic administration of epinephrine (Gold, 1988, 1991). Further, as glucose readily enters the central nervous system (Lund-Anderson, 1979), it could easily serve as a humoral messenger to the CNS to signal peripheral arousal. Additionally, intracerebroventricular administration of glucose also enhances retention performance when given immediately after training in an inhibitory avoidance task (Lee, Graham, & Gold, 1988). Thus, it is likely that in addition to neural messages traveling to the CNS via the vagus nerve to activate memory, there is a parallel mechanism that involves glucose acting as a humoral messenger to carry information about peripheral arousal to the CNS and enhance the storage of memory.

Electrical Stimulation of Vagus Nerve at Moderate Intensities Can Enhance Memory Storage

Our research using vagotomy and splanchnicectomy procedures provided support for the idea that the vagus nerve is a major neural pathway by which peripherally acting substances modulate the memory storage process. Therefore, it seemed likely that electrical stimulation of the vagus nerve might also have the capacity to modulate memory storage by mimicking the effects of peripheral autonomic receptor activation. This hypothesis was tested by Clark, Krahl, Smith, and Jensen (1995), who implanted bipolar-stimulating electrodes on the left vagus nerve at the cervical level. Following recovery, animals were trained in an inhibitory avoidance task and vagus nerve stimulation (0.5 ms biphasic pulses; 20.0 Hz; 30.0-second duration) at one of three intensities (0.2, 0.4, or 0.8 mA) was given shortly after training. An inverted U-shaped pattern of retention performance was observed with the best retention performance seen in those animals that received vagus nerve stimulation at a moderate intensity (0.4 mA). Neither the low (0.2 mA) stimulation nor the high (0.8 mA) stimulation intensities affected retention performance compared to sham-stimulated control animals. As noted earlier, an inverted U-shaped function is seen in memory research using many experimental treatments and pharmacological agents suggesting that there may be some common substrate for their effects (see Jensen, 1996).

However, it was not clear in this study whether the observed improvement in memory was due to the activation of vagal afferents or efferents. It is possible that vagus nerve stimulation resulted in the activation of peripheral organs through stimulation of vagal efferents, which then caused some change that, by another route (e.g., the mobilization and transport of glucose), influenced memory storage (Gold, 1988). Alternatively, the enhancement of memory could have been the result of activation of brain structures known to directly or indirectly receive vagus nerve innervation or, possibly, some combination of both peripheral and central activation.

Therefore, an additional study was performed to explore these possibilities by reversibly inactivating vagus nerve fibers by the administration of lidocaine below the point of stimulation (Clark et al., 1998). Thus, with descending pathways blocked, vagus nerve stimulation could affect only ascending pathways to the brain and not cause peripheral effects that might indirectly influence the trajectory of memory storage. A cuff electrode/catheter system was devised to provide for bipolar stimulating electrodes, a recording electrode, and a small catheter by which saline or lidocaine could be administered. This catheter was positioned approximately 4 mm caudal to the point of stimulation and the recording electrode was positioned about 1 mm caudal to the catheter (Clark et al., 1998).

Both the lidocaine and saline-infused groups showed an intensity-dependent, inverted U-shaped pattern of retention performance with the greatest effect again observed at the 0.4 mA stimulation intensity. Additionally, animals that received lidocaine infusion, but no vagus nerve stimulation, showed impaired retention performance compared to saline-infused control rats. This latter finding suggests that the passage of information to the CNS about the degree of peripheral arousal induced by the shock, which would enhance memory, was blocked by lidocaine-induced inactivation of the vagus nerve. This study provided further support for the idea that vagal afferents carry messages about peripheral states of arousal that lead to the modulation of memory storage. In addition, the memory-enhancing effects of vagus nerve stimulation appear to be directly mediated by neural activation of brain structures and not by any peripheral changes caused by stimulation of vagal efferents.

Human Verbal Learning Is Facilitated by Vagus Nerve Stimulation

Research in our laboratory also assessed the applicability of these principles to the modulation of memory processes in humans. In the first of these studies, the effect on memory of a low level of arousal produced by squeezing a hand dynamometer was assessed. This technique had been shown (Nielson, Radtke, & Jensen, 1996) to produce a reliable enhancement of verbal recognition performance in young participants. The aim of this study was to determine whether antagonism of catecholamine receptors, specifically beta-adrenergic receptors, attenuates the memory-enhancing effects of muscle-tension-induced arousal. To accomplish this, the effect of muscle-tension-induced arousal on retention performance was tested using elderly human participants who were taking beta-adrenergic receptor antagonist drugs for the treatment of hypertension. The performance of these participants was compared to that of comparable unmedicated elderly participants or elderly participants taking other types of antihypertensive medication (Nielson & Jensen, 1995).

Fourteen narrative paragraphs were used as stimuli in this experiment, and each paragraph was approximately 200 words in length. Two versions of each paragraph were prepared. In one version, seven words in each paragraph were highlighted using a yellow marking pen, and the participants were told that a memory test of these words would follow. Words chosen for highlighting were all concrete imaginable nouns and were distributed equally throughout each paragraph. In the other set of paragraphs, no words were highlighted. In each block of seven paragraphs, the first paragraph was shorter and simpler than the subsequent paragraphs, and it served as a practice paragraph. There were six test paragraphs presented to the participants in each of two blocks. In each block, three paragraphs with highlighted words to be remembered were alternated with three paragraphs not containing highlighted words. Order of presentation of the paragraphs was counterbalanced across participants. In one of the two blocks of paragraphs, the muscle-tension-arousal manipulation (squeezing the hand dynamometer) was introduced. Thus, half the paragraphs with highlighted words were associated with muscle-tension-induced arousal, whereas half were not.

At the end of the experimental session, a recognition test of all highlighted words was given. In this test, the 42 target words that had been highlighted were randomly interspersed with 210 distractor words, which were also concrete, imaginable nouns. Participants were asked to mark all words that they recognized as having been previously presented as highlighted words in the paragraphs they had read earlier. Unmedicated elderly participants or those taking non-beta-blocker medications showed enhanced recognition performance of the 21 highlighted words that had been associated with muscle-tension-induced arousal. However, those participants chronically taking beta-receptor antagonist medications showed no comparable enhancement of memory (Nielson & Jensen, 1995). These findings are comparable to those of Cahil, Prins, Weber, and McGaugh (1994), who reported that beta-receptor antagonists impaired the retention of images depicting emotional events.

The behavioral methodology described above was then used to assess the possibility that recognition memory might be enhanced by vagus nerve stimulation in humans. This study was conducted ancillary to a double-blind clinical trial aimed at evaluating the effectiveness of vagus nerve stimulation as a therapy to control severe epilepsy (Penry & Dean, 1990). A vagus nerve stimulation device (Cyberonics, Inc., Houston, Texas) was surgically implanted in each patient (see Figure 7.1) and testing began 2 weeks later (Clark, Naritoku, Smith,

FIGURE 7.1

Illustration of the vagus nerve stimulation device.

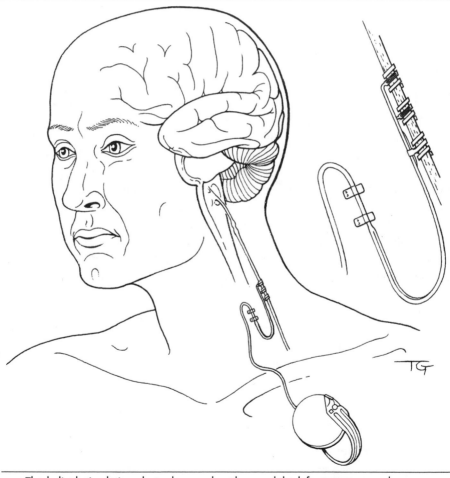

The helical stimulating electrode was placed around the left vagus nerve, whereas the case containing the stimulation power source and its regulatory circuitry were implanted in the pectoral region in much the same fashion as a cardiac pacemaker.

Browning, & Jensen, 1999). The time course of the study is shown in Figure 7.2. Both participants and experimenter were blind to stimulation parameter information, and the examiner did not know whether his actions delivered vagus nerve stimulation or sham stimulation. Data from Group A that received

FIGURE 7.2

Time course of the study.

	Group A (n=5)	Group B (n=5)
Visit 1 Week 0	Baseline test; subjects familiarized with testing procedure	
Week 1	Implantation of Vagus Nerve Stimulation Device	
Visit 2 Week 3	.50 mA VNS paired with reading paragraphs	Sham stimulation paired with reading paragraphs
Six-week period between test visits		
Visit 3 Week 9	.75–1.50 mA VNS paired with reading paragraphs	Sham stimulation paired with reading paragraphs
Eight-week period between test visits		
Visit 4 Week 17	.75–1.50 mA VNS paired with reading paragraphs	.50 mA VNS paired with reading paragraphs
Eight-week period between test visits		
Visit 5 Week 25	.75–1.50 mA VNS paired with reading paragraphs	.75–1.50 mA VNS paired with reading paragraphs

Participants were run in two groups of 5 each with 0.5 mA stimulation given either on Visit 2 (Group A) or Visit 4 (Group B) to control for the effects of novelty or time after surgery. Data looking at the effects of higher intensity stimulation were gathered on either Visit 3 or Visit 5.

0.5 mA vagus nerve stimulation paired with the reading of paragraphs during Visit 2 were combined with data obtained from Group B that received the same stimulation during Visit 4. Additionally, retention performance of subjects in Group A who received higher intensity stimulation during Visit 3 was combined with that from Group B that received the higher intensity stimulation on Visit 5.

Those participants that received 0.5-mA vagus nerve stimulation showed enhanced word recognition performance compared to the recognition of words from paragraphs that were paired with sham stimulation. Higher intensities of stimulation paired with highlighted words did not result in enhancement of retention performance (Clark et al., 1999). Importantly, the stimulation intensity that was most effective in this study using humans (0.5 mA) is similar to the stimulation that was most effective in rats (0.4 mA). In addition, as in the laboratory rats, higher levels of stimulation proved to be ineffective in modulating memory, suggesting the existence of an inverted U-shaped function here, as well as suggesting that vagal afferent fibers with low to moderate activation thresholds may mediate the observed effects.

Taken together the studies from both rats and humans suggest that memory is enhanced by a level of vagus nerve stimulation that is likely to recruit myelinated axons that transmit mechano-receptor signals from thoracic organs, such as the heart and lungs, to the brain (Cechetto, 1986). The demonstration that vagus nerve stimulation enhances shock-avoidance memory in laboratory rodents as well as verbal memory in humans emphasizes the idea that the processes involved in memory formation and memory modulation are likely to be similar, regardless of the nature of the memory itself or the particular mammalian species in which the learning occurs.

References

Cahil, L., Prins, B., Weber, M., & McGaugh, J. L. (1994). Beta-adrenergic activation and memory for emotional events. *Nature, 371,* 702–704.

Cechetto, D. F. (1986). Central representations of visceral function. *Federation Proceedings, 46,* 17–23.

Clark, K. B., Krahl, S. E., Smith, D. C., & Jensen, R. A. (1995). Post-training unilateral vagal stimulation enhances retention performance in the rat. *Neurobiology of Learning and Memory, 63,* 213–216.

Clark, K. B., Naritoku, D. K., Smith, D. C., Browning, R. A., & Jensen, R. A. (1999). Enhanced recognition memory following vagus nerve stimulation in human subjects. *Nature Neuroscience, 2,* 94–98.

Clark, K. B., Smith, D. C., Hassert, D. L., Browning, R. A., Naritoku, D. K., & Jensen, R. A. (1998). Post-training electrical stimulation of vagal afferents with concomitant vagal efferent inactivation enhances memory storage processes in the rat. *Neurobiology of Learning and Memory, 70,* 364–373.

Flood, J. F., Smith, G. E., & Morley, J. E. (1987). Modulation of memory storage processing by cholecystokinin: Dependence on the vagus nerve. *Science, 234,* 832–834.

Gold, P. E. (1986). Glucose modulation of memory storage processing. *Behavioral and Neural Biology, 45,* 342–349.

Gold, P. E. (1988). Plasma glucose regulation of memory storage processes. In C. D. Woody, D. L. Alkon, & J. L. McGaugh (Eds.), *Cellular mechanisms of conditioning and behavioral plasticity* (pp. 329–341). New York: Academic Press.

Gold, P. E. (1991). An integrated memory regulation system: From blood to brain. In R. C. A. Frederickson, J. L. McGaugh, & D. L. Felten (Eds.), *Peripheral signaling of the brain: Role in neural-immune interactions, learning and memory* (pp. 421–441). Lewiston, NY: Hogrefe & Huber.

Gold, P. E., & McCarty, R. (1981). Plasma catecholamines: Changes after footshock and seizure-producing frontal cortex stimulation. *Behavioral and Neural Biology, 31,* 247–260.

Gold, P. E., & McGaugh, J. L. (1975). A single-trace, two process view of memory storage processes. In D. Deutsch & J. A. Deutsch (Eds.), *Short-term memory* (pp. 355–378). New York: Academic Press.

Gold, P. E., van Buskirk, R. B., & Haycock, J. (1977). Effects of posttraining epinephrine injections on retention of avoidance training in mice. *Behavioral Biology, 20,* 197–204.

Introini-Collison, I. B., & McGaugh, J. L. (1986). Epinephrine modulates long-term retention of an aversively-motivated discrimination task. *Behavioral and Neural Biology, 45,* 358–365.

Introini-Collison, I. B., Saghafi, D., Novack, G., & McGaugh, J. L. (1992). Memory-enhancing effects of posttraining dipivefrin and epinephrine: Involvement of peripheral and central adrenergic receptors. *Brain Research, 572,* 81–86.

Jensen, R. A. (1996). The modulation of memory storage processes by peripherally acting pharmacological agents. *Proceedings of the Western Pharmacology Society, 39,* 85–89.

Lee, M., Graham, S., & Gold, P. E. (1988). Memory enhancement with posttraining intraventricular glucose injections in rats. *Behavioral Neuroscience, 102,* 591–595.

Lund-Anderson, H. (1979). Transport of glucose from blood to brain. *Physiology Reviews, 59,* 305–352.

Martinez, Jr., J. L., Jensen, R. A., Messing, R. B., Vasquez, B. J., Soumireu-Mourat, B., Geddes, D., Liang, K. C., & McGaugh, J. L. (1980). Central and peripheral actions of amphetamine on memory storage. *Brain Research, 182,* 157–166.

Martinez, Jr., J. L., Vasquez, B. J., Rigter, H., Messing, R. B., Jensen, R. A., Liang, K. C., & McGaugh, J. L. (1980). Attenuation of amphetamine-induced enhancement of learning by adrenal demedullation. *Brain Research, 195,* 433–443.

McGaugh, J. L. (1983). Hormonal influences on memory. *Annual Review of Psychology, 34,* 297–323.

McGaugh, J. L. (1989). Involvement of hormonal and neuromodulatory systems in the regulation of memory storage. *Annual Review of Neuroscience, 12,* 255–287.

McGaugh, J. L., & Herz, M. J. (1972). *Memory consolidation.* San Francisco: Albion.

Nielson, K. A., & Jensen, R. A. (1995). Beta-adrenergic receptor antagonist antihypertensive medications impair arousal-induced modulation of working memory in elderly humans. *Behavioral and Neural Biology, 62,* 190–200.

Nielson, K. A., Radtke, R. C., & Jensen, R. A. (1996). Arousal-induced modulation of memory storage processes in humans. *Neurobiology of Learning and Memory, 66,* 133–142.

Nogueira, P. J. C., Tomaz, C., & Williams, C. L. (1994). Contribution of the vagus nerve in mediating the memory-facilitating effects of substance P. *Behavioral Brain Research, 62,* 165–169.

Noyes, M., Murphy, L. L., & Jensen, R. A. (1995). Sympathetic afferents do not appear to participate in the modulation of memory storage processes. *Society for Neuroscience Abstracts, 21,* 1231.

Penry, J. K., & Dean, J. C. (1990). Prevention of intractable partial seizures by intermittent vagal stimulation in humans: Preliminary results. *Epilepsia, 31,* S40–S43.

Sternberg, D. B., Isaacs, K., Gold, P. E., & McGaugh, J. L. (1985). Epinephrine facilitation of appetitive learning: Attenuation with adrenergic receptor antagonists. *Behavioral and Neural Biology, 44,* 447–453.

Williams, C. L., & Jensen, R. A. (1991). Vagal afferents: A possible mechanism for the modulation of memory by peripherally acting agents. In R. C. A. Frederickson, J. L. McGaugh, & D. L. Felten (Eds.), *Peripheral signaling of the brain: Role in neural-immune interactions, learning and memory* (pp. 467–471). Lewiston, NY: Hogrefe & Huber.

Williams, C. L., & Jensen, R. A. (1993). Combined effects of vagotomy and atropine methyl bromide on Leu-enkephalin-induced changes in memory storage processes. *Physiology and Behavior, 54,* 659–663.

Williams, C. L., & McGaugh, J. L. (1993). Reversible lesions of the nucleus of the solitary tract attenuate the memory-modulating effects of posttraining epinephrine. *Behavioral Neuroscience, 107,* 955–962.

Yerkes, R. M., & Dodson, J. D. (1908). The relation of strength of stimulus to rapidity of habit-formation. *Journal of Comparative Neurology and Psychology, 18,* 459–482.

CHAPTER 8

Contribution of Brainstem Structures in Modulating Memory Storage Processes

Cedric L. Williams
Edwin C. Clayton

A consistent theme that has emerged from the laboratory of James McGaugh over the past three decades is that effective storage of memory involves both the secretion of peripheral hormones such as epinephrine (EPI) in response to arousing events and a subsequent release of norepinephrine (NE) in limbic structures that encode new experiences. Although the foundation for understanding how emotional arousal modulates the memory storage process had been firmly established by the findings from the McGaugh lab, several questions remained regarding the mechanisms that enabled peripherally secreted EPI to regulate NE release in the limbic system. An understanding of this process was hindered by the fact that EPI does not freely enter the brain and, therefore, cannot directly affect central noradrenergic activity. One focus of our research as graduate students (I, Williams, studied under Dr. Robert Jensen) was to contribute to the understanding of the memory modulation process laid down by the McGaugh laboratory by identifying the missing link that enabled these two systems to interact to modulate memory.

The research described in this chapter is a direct result of the efforts directed toward understanding this relationship. This research was guided by the premise that one putative mechanism by which hormones such as EPI influence the brain during emotional arousal involves activation of neurons in an area of the brainstem known as the nucleus of the solitary tract (NTS). The NTS receives input regarding fluctuations in autonomic and hormonal states following exposure to arousing experiences by ascending fibers of the vagus nerve. NTS neurons, in turn, convey this information to brain areas that process memory-related information. Recent findings indicate that activation of the NTS by pep-

Our research supported by the National Institute of Mental Health Grant MHO14505-01 to the first author.

tides, hormones, or noradrenergic agonists enhance retention in appetitive and aversive learning conditions. In contrast, the memory-enhancing effects of several compounds are attenuated by severing the connection between peripheral nerves and the NTS with vagotomy or by inactivating NTS neurons with reversible anesthetics. Currently, the mechanisms by which the NTS influences memory formation are not known. However, limbic structures that process memory such as the amygdala or hippocampus may utilize neural information provided by the NTS during the initial encoding and processing of new experiences.

This chapter is divided into four sections to provide an adequate illustration of the contribution of peripheral hormones in modulating memory and their interaction with specific brain systems during memory processing. The first section includes an overview of the anatomical connections among peripheral autonomic fibers, the NTS, and limbic structures involved in memory. The second part discusses the effects of manipulating neuronal activity in the NTS on retention of responses acquired in spatial and emotionally arousing learning tasks. This section is followed by the presentation of findings from in vivo microdialysis experiments demonstrating that amygdala norepinephrine activity is regulated, in part, by noradrenergic neurons originating in the NTS. The chapter concludes with a discussion of how memory processing in the hippocampus may be regulated by structures in the lower medulla that receive direct projections from the NTS.

Anatomy of the Vagal Modulating System: Bridging the Gap Between Peripheral Hormones and the Amygdala

Extensive evidence indicates that the enhancement in memory produced by peripheral hormones that are released by emotionally arousing experiences or administered directly to laboratory animals are mediated by influences on the amygdala NE system. For example, the memory deficits observed following adrenalectomy, a surgical procedure that severely depletes peripheral concentrations of EPI (Borrell, de Kloet, Versteeg, & Bohus, 1983; Liang, Juler, & McGaugh, 1986; Silva, 1974), can be reversed by direct infusion of NE into the amygdala (Liang et al., 1986). A relationship between EPI and the amygdala noradrenergic system is further supported by the finding that the enhancement in memory produced by systemic posttraining injection of epinephrine is completely abolished by either lesioning the amygdala (Cahill & McGaugh, 1991), blocking noradrenergic receptors in the amygdala (Liang et al., 1986), or by depleting amygdala NE concentrations with the selective neurotoxin DSP-4 (Liang, Chen, & Huang, 1995). Despite these findings, which clearly delineate a functional relationship between the amygdala and EPI in processing emotionally based memories, the pathway by which EPI exerts modulatory influences on the amygdala has not been well defined because peripherally released EPI does not freely enter the central nervous system (CNS; Weil-Malharbe, Axelrod, & Tomchick, 1959; see Figure 8.1). The experiments described in the remainder of this chapter were developed to address the hypothesis that EPI's effects on memory are mediated by vagal activation of brainstem nuclei in the NTS that project to the amygdala. Findings supporting this view are summarized in Figure 8.2.

The first investigation of a possible relationship between the adrenal gland, which releases EPI and the vagus nerve, was published by Kollmann (1860), who traced vagal fibers from an area below the diaphragm to the adrenals in humans. Using more sophisticated anatomical procedures, Teitelbaum (1933) and Coupland, Parker, Kesse, and Mohamed (1989) confirmed the finding that dorsal and ventral branches of the vagus nerve innervate the adrenal glands. Other studies have shown that electrical stimulation of the adrenal nerve evokes action potentials in the vagus nerve (Niijima, 1992). This finding can be interpreted to suggest that activated vagal fibers convey input regarding changes in hormonal release to the brain since ascending fibers of the vagus contain adrenergic receptors that bind beta-adrenergic agonists such as EPI in both rats (Schreurs, Seelig, & Schulman, 1986) and humans (Lawrence, Watkins, & Jarrott, 1995).

Vagal afferents terminate on a number of catecholamine and noncatecholaminergic neurons in the NTS. Following activation by vagal afferents, NTS neurons transmit information to brain areas that process memory-related information such as the amygdala (Ricardo & Koh, 1978; Zardetto-Smith & Gray, 1990). Recent findings using triple fluorescence labeling revealed that norepinephrine is the major neurotransmitter in projection neurons from the NTS to the amygdala. The cell bodies of these neurons were detected in the A2 catecholamine region of the NTS following injection of a retrograde tracer into the amygdala (Petrov, Krukoff, & Jhamandas, 1993). In addition, experiments using the expression of immediate early genes as a marker for activated neurons report that vagal nerve stimulation produces a statistically significant increase in the number of amygdala neurons that express c-fos (Naritoku, Terry, & Helfert, 1995). Other findings from electrophysiological studies show that the firing rates of amygdala neurons are increased following electrical stimulation of either the vagus nerve (Radna & MacLean, 1981) or the NTS (Rogers & Fryman, 1988).

This collection of experiments provides in a limited sense a description of some putative mechanisms involved in the processing of emotionally arousing events into memory storage. According to the available evidence, physiological arousal produced by stress or emotional learning experiences elicits the release

FIGURE 8.1

Schematic view of EPI effects on memory mediated via influences on amygdala noradrenergic systems.

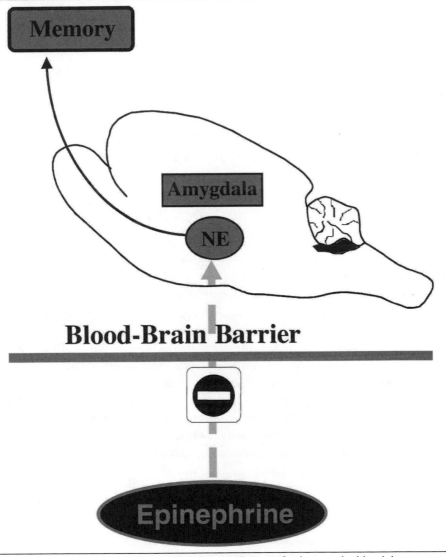

This view is complicated by the fact that EPI does not freely cross the blood–brain barrier to produce direct actions on central nervous system structures. EPI = epinephrine; NE = norepinephrine.

FIGURE 8.2

Schematic view of possible mechanisms by which EPI influences the
amygdala during memory formation.

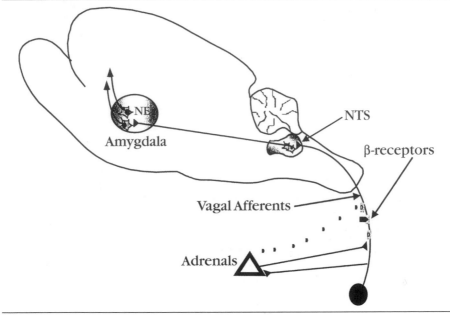

EPI binds to beta-adrenergic receptors on afferent fibers of the vagus nerve, which
terminate in the NTS. Stimulation of NE containing neurons in the NTS that have
terminal projections in the amygdala would subsequently result in increased
release of NE in this structure. EPI = epinephrine; NTS = nucleus of the solitary
tract; NE = norepinephrine.

of peripheral hormones from the adrenal medulla, which in turn bind to beta-adrenergic receptors on the vagus. Activation of these receptors influences the conduction properties of vagal afferent fibers that synapse on NE containing neurons in the NTS. Stimulation of NTS-A2 neurons that have terminal projections in the amygdala would subsequently result in increased release of NE in the amygdala during memory formation. However, until 1993, this scenario was only speculative because no experiment had examined whether or not EPI's effects on memory were influenced by manipulation of either the vagus nerve or the NTS.

Beyond Vagal Activation: Effects of Manipulating NTS Neuronal Activity on Memory Processing

One method of determining if the vagal–NTS pathway is involved in mediating EPI's effects is to examine whether this hormone improves memory for an arousing experience in the absence of the NTS. To address this issue, Williams and McGaugh (1993) assessed whether functional neural blockade of the NTS with the reversible local anesthetic lidocaine hydrochloride would alter the memory-enhancing effects of EPI. In this experiment, animals were trained for 5 days to consume 5 food pellets placed in the left alley and 10 pellets placed in the food cup of the right alley of a Y maze (Figure 8.3). On Day 6 of training, the cardboard inserts covering the metal footshock plates in the right alley were removed. After each animal consumed all of the pellets and reentered the right alley, a brief footshock (0.35 mA for 0.5 seconds) was administered. To determine if the vagal–NTS pathway mediates EPI's effects on memory for this type

FIGURE 8.3

Reversible lesions of the nucleus of the solitary tract (NTS) attenuate the memory-modulating effects of posttraining epinephrine.

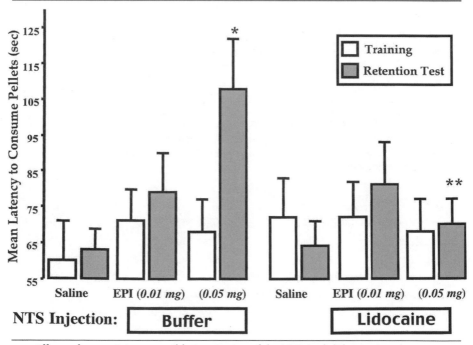

Effects of posttraining reversible inactivation of the NTS (with lidocaine) and peripheral injections of EPI (mg/kg) on the latencies to consume food pellets in the right alley where footshock was administered during training. *$p < .05$ as compared with buffer + saline or L + EPI 0.05 mg/kg; **$p < .01$, Fisher's post hoc test. NTS = nucleus of the solitary tract; EPI = epinephrine. From Figure 3 in "Reversible Lesions of the Nucleus of the Solitary Tract Attenuate the Memory-Modulatory Effects of Posttraining Epinephrine," by C. L. Williams and J. L. McGaugh, 1993, *Behavioral Neuroscience, 107*, p. 959. Copyright 1993 by the American Psychological Association. Adapted with permission of the publisher.

of arousing and perhaps unexpected experience, animals received an intra-NTS infusion of either phosphate buffered saline (PBS) or the local anesthetic lidocaine to produce a functional blockade of neural activity in the NTS. Two minutes after the brain injections, each animal received a systemic injection of saline, 0.01, or 0.05 mg/kg of EPI.

On a retention test given 24 hours later, the mean latency to enter the alley where footshock was received during training (data not shown) or to consume all of the food pellets in the right alley (Figure 8.3) was significantly longer in animals given a posttraining injection of 0.05 mg/kg of EPI than in saline-treated controls ($p < .05$). However, the enhancement in memory produced by the 0.05 mg/kg dose of EPI was attenuated by inactivation of the NTS. The retention latencies of animals given the effective dose of EPI immediately after a functional blockade of the NTS were significantly lower than those of animals given 0.05 mg/kg EPI and PBS, and their latencies did not differ from the saline controls. These findings confirm those of earlier studies (Gold & van Buskirk, 1978) and extend their conclusions by suggesting that activation of the NTS via vagal afferents may be one mechanism by which peripheral EPI exerts modulating influences on brain systems that regulate memory storage.

The findings from the Williams and McGaugh (1993) experiment also suggest that if inactivation of receptors in the NTS attenuates the mnemonic actions of EPI, then, by implication, activation of these receptors should produce effects on memory comparable to those observed following systemic injection of EPI. Although the results of the previous study suggest participation of the NTS in regulating hormone-induced changes in memory formation, the neurotransmitter systems involved in initiating this process in the NTS is currently not known. Electron microscopic studies have revealed that there is an abundance of noradrenergic terminals, cell bodies, and receptors in the NTS (Aoki & Pickel, 1992; Aoki, Zemcik, Strader, & Pickel, 1989; Smith, Egle, & Adams, 1982) and vagal afferents terminate on some noradrenergic neurons in this area (Sumal, Blessing, Joh, Reis, & Pickel, 1983). Furthermore, administration of drugs that increase sympathetic activity produce a significant elevation in NE levels in the NTS of normal rats (Dev & Philip, 1996). Given these findings, it is possible that NE may play an important role in influencing NTS activity during memory formation. To examine this hypothesis, a separate group of animals were trained in the Y-maze discrimination task using procedures identical to those described above (Williams, Men, & Clayton, 2000). After footshock training on Day 6, animals received an intra-NTS infusion of either PBS or the noradrenergic agonist clenbuterol (10, 50, or 100 ng/0.5 μl), which has been shown to facilitate the release of norepinephrine in several brain regions (Murugauah & O'Donnell, 1994, 1995). On a retention test given 24 and 48 hours later, groups receiving 100 ng/0.5 μl of clenbuterol took significantly longer to enter the right alley or consume food pellets in the alley where the original footshock was administered (Figure 8.4).

It is worth noting that the clenbuterol-treated animals exhibited good retention of the footshock experience even though the most prevailing cue associated with the shock (i.e., stainless steel footshock plates) was covered with the cardboard inserts on the 24-hour retention test. In addition, a similar pattern of memory enhancement was observed on the second retention test with the stainless steel plates uncovered 48 hours later. These findings were instrumental in demonstrating that memory processes can be substantially improved by posttraining activation of noradrenergic receptors in the NTS. The effects of clenbuterol may be mediated by facilitating NE output from terminals that innervate the NTS as opposed to any specific actions of this compound on the A2 catecholamine neurons in the NTS, because these cells are activated only by the binding of NE to postsynaptic $\alpha 1$ receptors (Feldman & Felder, 1989). This view is based on anatomical studies indicating that the $\beta 2$ receptors that bind clenbuterol are localized presynaptically on noradrenergic axons (Misu & Kubo, 1986) and function in a positive feedback loop to increase NE release from nerve terminals.

Given that clenbuterol does not directly stimulate the noradrenergic A2 neurons in the NTS, Clayton and Williams (2000a) examined whether or not memory storage processes are also influenced by catecholamine agonists that bind directly to postsynaptic NE receptors in the NTS. To answer this question, laboratory animals received injections of PBS or EPI, which has a high affinity for $\alpha 1$ receptors immediately after training with a 0.4 mA, 0.5 second footshock in an inhibitory avoidance task. On a retention test given 48 hours later, animals administered 125 ng/0.5 μl of EPI after training had retention latencies that were significantly longer than the PBS-injected controls (Figure 8.5A).

One-week after the retention test, the animals were placed on a weight maintenance schedule and then trained in an eight-arm radial arm maze task. During training, the animals learned to obtain one food pellet from each of four open arms. After a delay, the rats were returned to the maze for a retention test with all eight arms open, but food pellets were placed only in the four arms that were blocked during the initial training trial. Drug administration began on the day after each individual animal reached a criterion of 80% correct performance on 2 consecutive days. On this day, the animals were trained as before and PBS, 50, 125, or 250 ng/0.5 μl of EPI was infused into the NTS immediately after they obtained food pellets from the four open arms. On a retention test given 18 hours later, the percentage of correct responses in obtaining the pellets from the four new maze arms were recorded. As shown in Figure 8.5B, administration of a dose of EPI (125 ng/0.5 μl) that facilitated retention following footshock training also produced a significant enhancement in memory for the radial maze task. Animals given an intra-NTS infusion of

FIGURE 8.4

Effects of posttraining intra-NTS infusion of clenbuterol on retention in a Y-maze discrimination task.

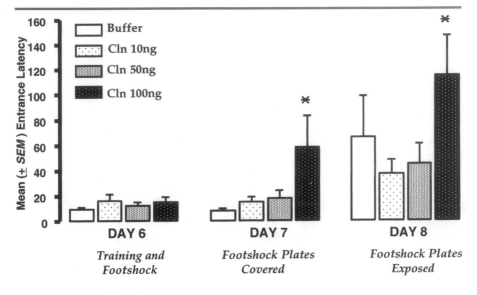

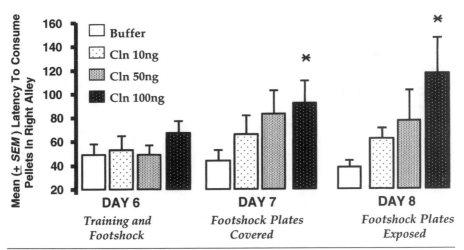

On the retention test given 24 and 48 hours after training, the latency to enter the maze or consume food pellets in the footshock alley was significantly longer in the group administered 100 ng/0.5 μl of clenbuterol relative to PBS-injected controls.*p <. 05. NTS = nucleus of the solitary tract; PBS = phosphate buffered saline; CLN = clenbuterol. From Figure 8 in "The Effects of Nonadrenergic Activation of the Nucleus Tractus Solitarius on Memory and in Potentiating Norepinephrine Release in the Amygdala," by C. L. Williams, D. Men, and E. C. Clayton, 2000, *Behavioral Neuroscience, 114*, p. 1140. Copyright 2000 by the American Psychological Association. Adapted with permission of the publisher.

FIGURE 8.5

Effects of intra-NTS infusion of EPI on retention in an inhibitory avoidance task.

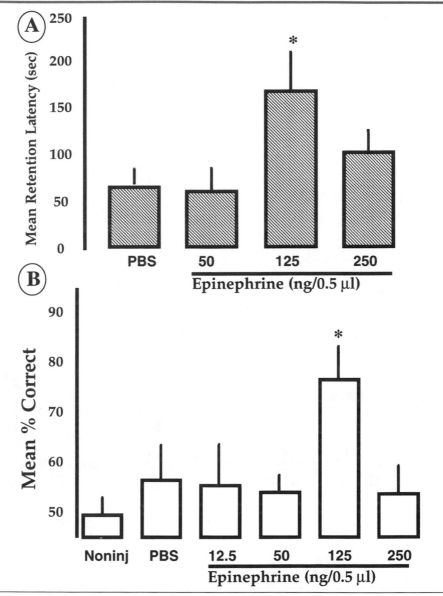

(A) Subjects receiving 125 ng of EPI took significantly longer to enter the dark compartment than did the PBS or 50 ng EPI group. *$p < .05$. (B) Effects of intra-NTS infusion of EPI on mean percentage of correct responses on a radial maze retention test. Rats receiving 125 ng EPI made a significantly higher percentage of correct responses than all other groups on a retention test administered 18 hours postinjection. *$p < .05$. NTS = nucleus of the solitary tract;

125 ng/0.5 μl of EPI made a significantly greater percentage of correct responses in locating food pellets in the arms that were not visited prior to the delay. Taken together, the findings from both the inhibitory avoidance and radial maze experiments provide additional evidence that activation of noradrenergic receptors in the NTS improves memory and also suggest that such effects are mediated by influences on NTS neurons that project to and release NE in the amygdala.

Evidence of a Functional Relationship Between the NTS and the Amygdala

The findings from anatomical, electrophysiological, and behavioral studies suggesting that EPI influences amygdala NE release by vagal activation of the NTS have been corroborated by the findings from a neurochemical experiment. Until recently, evidence indicating whether or not NE concentrations in the amygdala are actually modified by systemic administration of EPI was not available. Using in vivo microdialysis and high-performance liquid chromatography (HPLC), Williams, Men, Clayton, and Gold (1998) measured the changes in amygdala NE output following the administration of saline, EPI (0.1 or 0.3 mg/kg) and a single escapable footshock (0.8 mA, 1 second). As shown in Figure 8.6A, both doses of EPI produced a significant increase in extracellular concentrations of NE in the amygdala, which persisted for up to 60 minutes. After injection of 0.3 mg/kg of EPI, we observed a 79% increase in NE release relative to the baseline sample taken immediately before the injection. The concentrations of NE remained elevated to approximately 88% and 90% above baseline values when measured 40 and 60 minutes later. The 0.1 mg/kg dose of EPI caused a smaller, yet sustained increase in amygdala NE output, which was also significantly larger than the concentrations measured during the baseline period preceding the injection. These findings provide concrete evidence that elevations in peripheral concentrations of EPI lead to increased output of NE in the amygdala. The findings also strongly suggest that the EPI-induced memory enhancement reported in several behavioral studies may be mediated by noradrenergic activation of the amygdala.

In a second experiment, we were interested in determining whether the mnemonic effects of hormones such as EPI are conveyed to the amygdala by

---

EPI = epinephrine; PBS = phosphate buffered saline. From Figures 2 and 3 in "Adrenergic Activation of the Nucleus Tractus Solitarius Potentiates Amygdala Norepinephrine Release and Enhances Retention Performance in Emotionally-Arousing and Spatial Memory Tasks," by E. C. Clayton and C. L. Williams, 2000, *Behavioral Brain Research, 112,* p. 155. Copyright 2000 by Elsevier Science. Adapted with permission of the publisher.

FIGURE 8.6

Systematically administered EPI potentiates NE output in the amygdala.

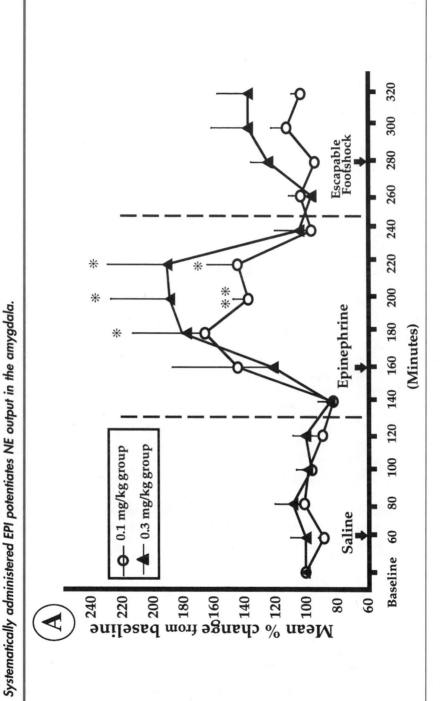

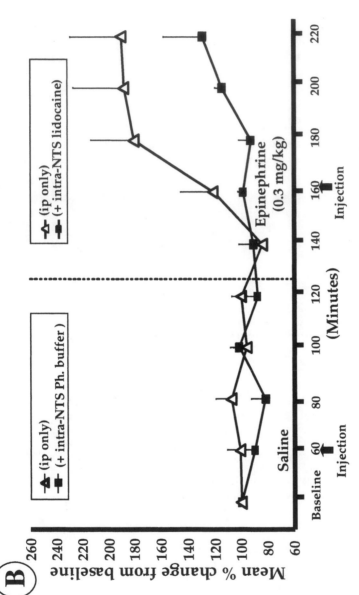

Note for caption appears on next page

activation of vagal fibers, which in turn influence the activity of NE containing NTS neurons that innervate the amygdala. If the vagal–NTS complex is involved in this process, then interruption of NTS transmission to the amygdala should alter the increased NE output produced by injection of EPI. During the control collection period, animals were infused with PBS into the NTS and then given a systemic injection of saline. One hundred minutes later, each rat was given an intra-NTS injection of lidocaine hydrochloride that was followed by the administration of 0.3 mg/kg of EPI. As shown in Figure 8.6B, inactivation of the NTS with lidocaine blocked the EPI-induced elevation in amgydala NE concentrations that were observed in the first experiment. After lidocaine infusion into the NTS and systemic injection of 0.3 mg/kg of EPI, NE output remained relatively unchanged until approximately 40 minutes after the combined treatments. It is interesting to note that the small 14% increase in amygdala NE release was not observed until 40 minutes postinjection, which corresponds to the time period in which lidocaine's effectiveness in blocking sodium channels begins to diminish (Randich & Aicher, 1988). Thus, the small elevation in NE observed 40 minutes after injection perhaps reflects a return of neural functioning in the NTS. Accordingly, restoration of neuronal activity would permit the transmission of neural input from peripheral vagal afferents

---

(A) Mean percentage change in extracellular concentrations of amygdala NE in response to systemic injection of saline, 0.1 mg/kg ($n = 7$) or 0.3 mg/kg of EPI ($n = 8$), and an escapable 0.8 mA, 1 second footshock. Each of the three sequential treatment phases are separated by the dashed vertical lines. The percentage increase in amygdala NE concentrations measured 20, 40, or 60 minutes after 0.3 mg/kg of EPI were all significantly greater than baseline values. *$p < .05$, repeated-measures analysis of variance. Administration of the 0.1 mg/kg dose also produced a significant elevation in extracellular concentrations of NE 40 (**$p < .01$) and 60 minutes (*$p < .05$) following the injection. There were no significant changes in NE output following the escapable footshock. (B) Mean percentage change in amygdala NE concentrations after intra-NTS infusion of PBS and systemic injection of saline, followed by intra-NTS microinjection of lidocaine (2%) and systemic EPI (0.3 mg/kg). The effects of the control vs. drug treatments are separated by the dashed vertical lines. For comparison, data from Experiment 2 are plotted against values obtained with the group from Experiment 1 that received an identical dose of EPI (open triangles). Inactivation of the NTS attenuated the elevation in NE release produced by injection of 0.3 mg/kg of EPI. Following this treatment, amygdala NE concentrations remained unchanged for approximately 40 minutes and did not differ from that observed following treatment with the control substances (i.e., saline and phosphate buffer). NE = norepinephrine; EPI = epinephrine; NTS = nucleus of the solitary tract; PBS = phosphate buffered saline. From Figures 2 and 3 in "Norepinephrine Release in the Amygdala Following Systemic Injection of Epinephrine or Escapable Footshock: Contribution of the Nucleus of the Solitary Tract," by C. L. Williams, D. Men, E. P. Clayton, and P. E. Gold, 1998, *Behavioral Neuroscience, 112*, pp. 1418, 1419. Copyright 1998 by the American Psychological Association. Adapted with permission of the publisher.

activated by EPI to be conveyed to the amygdala by these recovered neurons in the NTS. Taken together, the findings from both in vivo microdialysis experiments indicate that activation of visceral afferents projecting to the NTS provides one neural pathway by which peripheral EPI increases NE release in the amygdala to modulate memory formation.

Given these findings, our next objective was twofold. We wanted to first ascertain whether the clenbuterol-induced facilitation in memory observed in the Y-maze discrimination task was also mediated by NTS influences on amygdala NE release. Our second objective was to determine if amygdala NE concentrations are differentially affected by two separate treatments that enhance memory (i.e., systemic injection of EPI and intra-NTS infusion of clenbuterol). To address both of these objectives, amygdala NE concentrations were measured with in vivo microdialysis following three different treatments (Williams et al., 2000). In this experiment, the control animals first received an infusion of PBS into the NTS that was followed 120 minutes later by a sham footshock. Eighty minutes after this treatment, control animals received a systemic injection of saline. Animals in the remaining two groups received an intra-NTS injection of either 50 or 100 ng/0.5 μl of clenbuterol during the first treatment period, a 0.8 mA, 1 second escapable footshock during period two, and a systemic injection of 0.3 mg/kg of EPI during the final period. The results from this study are depicted in Figure 8.7. Administration of the 100 ng/0.5 μl dose of clenbuterol that facilitated memory on both retention tests in the Y-maze task also produced a significant elevation in amygdala NE concentrations that peaked at approximately 110% above baseline values. Administration of a lower dose of clenbuterol did not produce a marked change in amygdala output. As in the first microdialysis experiment, amygdala NE levels were also not responsive to the escapable footshock treatment. Consistent with the findings of Williams et al. (1998), amygdala NE concentrations were significantly elevated 20 minutes following injection of 0.3 mg/kg of EPI. The increase in NE release following this treatment ranged from 70% to 90% above baseline values. The results from this study demonstrate that activation of noradrenergic neurons in the NTS produce robust changes in NE output in the amygdala that are similar to those produced by a systemic injection of EPI. These findings also provide evidence to support the hypothesis that experimental treatments that stimulate the activity of noradrenergic neurons in the NTS may regulate memory formation by influencing NE release in the amygdala.

Role of Nuclei in the Lower Medulla in Regulating Memory Processing

A major focus of the experiments described in this chapter has been on elucidating the contribution of the noradrenergic projection between the NTS and

FIGURE 8.7

Changes in amygdala NE concentrations in response to activation of the NTS or systemic injection of EPI.

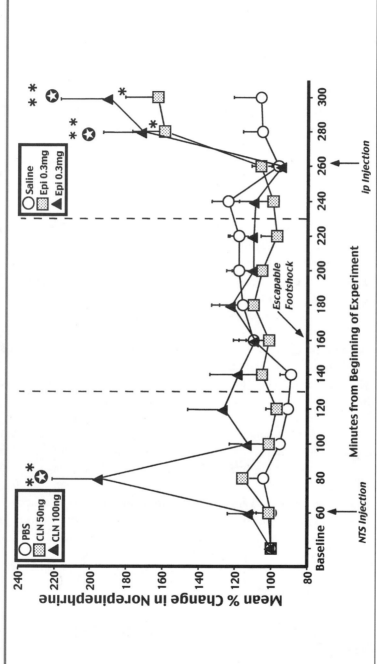

One-factor analysis of variance indicated that the elevation in amygdala NE levels 20 minutes following intra-NTS injection of clenbuterol (100 ng/0.5 μL) was significantly greater than baseline values. *p < .01. Peripheral EPI administration produced a significantly greater increase in NE concentrations relative to saline injection when assessed at 20 minutes (*p < .05) and 40 minutes (**p < .05) after the treatment. NE = norepinephrine; NTS = nucleus of the solitary tract; EPI = epinephrine; CLN = clenbuterol; PBS = phosphate buffered saline; IP = intraperitoneal. From "The Effects of Noradrenergic Activation of the Nucleus Tractus Solitarius on Memory and in Potentiating Norepinephrine Release in the Amygdala," by C. L. Williams, D. Men, and E. C. Clayton, 2000, *Behavioral Neuroscience, 114*, p. 1140. Copyright 2000 by the American Psychological Association. Adapted with permission of the authors.

FIGURE 8.8

Brainstem structures that influence NE release in the limbic system.

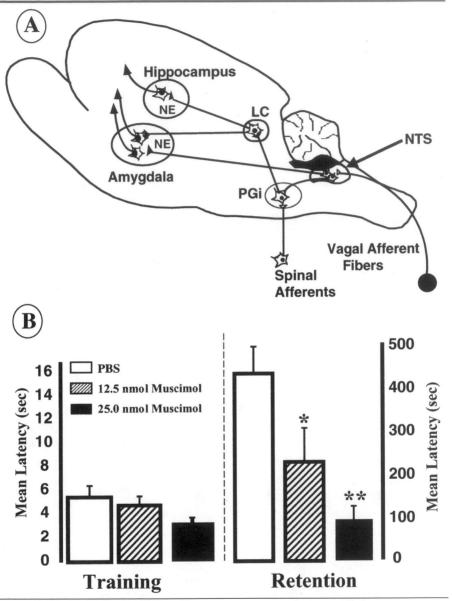

(A) Brain schematic depicting the flow of visceral information from the periphery through PGi and LC, and subsequently to higher cognitive areas such as the amygdala and hippocampus. (B) Effects of intra-PGi infusion of muscimol on latency to reenter the compartment where footshock was administered 48 hours earlier during training. No significant differences were observed between the separate groups during inhibitory avoidance training. Groups given posttraining amygdala in regulating memory storage. However, findings from a number of anatomical and behavioral experiments indicate that the mnemonic actions of centrally released NE are not limited solely to the amygdala but may also involve effects produced directly within the hippocampus. For example, infusion of noradrenergic agonists into the hippocampus also significantly enhances performance on memory tests if the compounds are administered immediately following learning (Lee & Ma, 1995). The finding indicating that intra-NTS infusion of EPI enhances retention in an eight-arm radial maze task (Clayton & Williams, 2000a) also suggests an involvement of the hippocampus, because spatial learning is considered to be hippocampally mediated.

These and other findings raise the question of whether the NTS may influence NE output in other brain regions that are involved in memory storage such as the hippocampus. Although there are no direct projections from the NTS to the hippocampus, several findings indicate that the NTS may influence hippocampal NE activity via its descending projections to cell groups in the lower medulla that send terminal projections to the locus coeruleus (LC; see Figure 8.8A). For example, the axons of NTS neurons that receive input from the vagus regarding changes in peripheral autonomic and neuroendocrine functioning descend into the lower medulla and innervate the lateral regions of a structure known as the nucleus paragigantocellularis (PGi; Van Bockstaele, Akaoka, & Aston-Jones, 1993; Van Bockstaele, Pieribone, & Aston-Jones, 1989). The lateral aspects of PGi that receive a dense supply of NTS axons contain the cell bodies of PGi neurons that provide the primary excitatory input to NE neurons in the dorsal region of the LC (Van Bockstaele, Colago, & Aicher, 1998). Axonal terminals from noradrenergic neurons in the dorsal regions of the LC have been shown to innervate several regions of the hippocampus including CA1, CA3, and the dentate gyrus (Mason & Fibiger, 1979). Given the finding that the dorsal LC provides the primary source of NE to the hippocampus (Loughlin, Foote, & Bloom, 1986), it is possible that structures such as the NTS and PGi may influence hippocampal NE activity via actions mediated on the LC. Other findings supporting this view are derived from studies demonstrating that stimulation of the vagus nerve, which directly activates NTS

---

injections of either 12.5 or 25 nmol of muscimol into PGi had significantly shorter latencies to reenter the dark compartment on the retention test relative to PBS-injected controls. *$p < .05$; **$p < .01$; PGi = paragigantocellularis; LC = locus coeruleus; PBS = phosphate buffered saline; NE = norepinephrine; NTS = nucleus of the solitary tract.

From Figure 3 in "Posttraining Inactivation of Excitatory Afferent Input to the Locus Coeruleus Impairs Retention in an Inhibitory Avoidance Learning Task," by E. C. Clayton and C. L. Williams, 2000, *Neurobiology of Learning and Memory*, *73*, p. 134. Copyright 2000 by Academic Press. Adapted with permission of the publisher.

FIGURE 8.9

Activation of excitatory input to the locus coeruleus facilitates mnemonic processes.

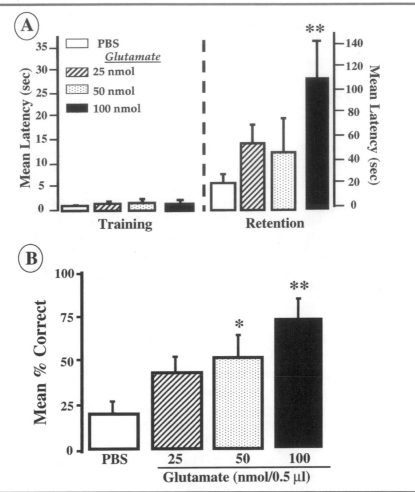

(A) Effects of intra-PGi infusion of glutamate on retention in an inhibitory avoidance task. On the 48-hour retention test, subjects receiving an immediate posttraining intra-PGi infusion of 100 nmol glutamate took significantly longer to reenter the dark compartment as compared to PBS injected controls. *p < .05. (B) Effects of intra-PGi infusion of glutamate on mean percentage of correct responses on a delayed matching to sample retention test. On an 18-hour retention test, subjects receiving either the 50 or 100 nmol intra-PGi glutamate infusion made a significantly higher percentage of correct responses than the PBS controls. *p < .05; **p < .01. PGi = paragigantocellularis; PBS = phosphate buffered saline.

From Figures 2 and 3 in "Glutamatergic Influences on the Nucleus Paragigantocellularis: Contribution to Performance in Avoidance and Spatial Memory Tasks," by E. C. Clayton and C. L. Williams, 2000, *Behavioral Neuroscience, 114,* p. 710. Copyright 2000 by the American Psychological Association. Adapted with permission of the publisher.

neurons, produces a significant increase in *c-fos* expression in the LC (Gieroba & Blessing, 1994; Naritoku et al., 1995) and also increases the firing rate of LC neurons (Krahl, Browning, Clark, & Smith, 1994). Taken together, these findings indicate that the conduction of neural input from the brainstem structures such as the NTS, PGi, and LC may play an important role in modulating NE activity in the hippocampus during memory storage.

Given the findings suggesting that neurons in PGi provide a major excitatory influence over LC neuronal activity, our next experiments examined whether memory storage processes are affected by treatments that either suppress or potentiate activity in PGi. Animals in this experiment (Clayton & Williams, 2000c) were trained with a 0.45 mA, 0.5 second footshock in an inhibitory avoidance task. Immediately after training, PBS, 12.5, or 25.0 nmol/0.5 μl of the GABA agonist muscimol was infused into PGi to interrupt the transmission of neural input from this nucleus to the LC. The findings from the retention test administered 48 hours later revealed that muscimol produced a dose-dependent impairment in memory for the footshock training (Figure 8.8B). Groups given posttraining injections of either 12.5 or 25.0 nmol/0.5 μl of muscimol entered the dark compartment where footshock was administered during training significantly faster than control groups on the retention test. In a follow-up experiment (Clayton & Williams, 2000b), a new group of animals received training in the same inhibitory avoidance task as well as in a radial maze task. Immediately after training, the animals were given an injection of PBS, 25, 50, or 100 nmol/0.5 μl of the excitatory amino acid agonist glutamate directly into PGi. Pharmacological activation of PGi neurons with glutamate produced a significant improvement in memory for animals trained in either the inhibitory avoidance or radial maze task (Figure 8.9). Taken together, the findings demonstrate that retention for responses acquired in emotionally arousing or spatially motivated learning tasks can be modulated by structures in the lower medulla such as PGi. Although the exact contribution of PGi in regulating memory has only recently been investigated, its involvement in memory may be related to the capacity for PGi neurons to activate LC noradrenergic neurons that release NE in a number of limbic and forebrain structures involved in mnemonic processing.

References

Aoki, C., & Pickel, V. (1992). C-terminal of β-adrenergic receptors: Immunocytochemical localization within astrocytes and their relation to catecholaminergic neurons in N. tractus solitarii and area postrema. *Brain Research, 571,* 35–49.

Aoki, C., Zemcik, B., Strader, C., & Pickel, V. (1989). Cytoplasmic loop of β-adrenergic receptors: Synaptic and intracellular localization and relation to catecholaminergic neurons in the nucleus of the solitary tracts. *Brain Research, 493,* 331–347.

Borrell, J., de Kloet, E. R., Versteeg, D. H. G., & Bohus, B. (1983). Inhibitory avoidance deficit following short-term adrenalectomy in the rat: The role of adrenal catecholamines. *Behavioral and Neural Biology, 39,* 241–258.

Cahill, L., & McGaugh, J. L. (1991). NMDA-induced lesions of the amygdaloid complex block the retention enhancing effect of posttraining epinephrine. *Psychobiology, 60,* 219–228.

Clayton, E. C., & Williams, C. L. (2000a). Adrenergic activation of the nucleus tractus solitarius potentiates amygdala norepinephrine release and enhances retention performance in emotionally-arousing and spatial memory tasks. *Behavioural Brain Research, 112,* 151–158.

Clayton, E. C., & Williams, C. L. (2000b). Glutamatergic influences on the nucleus paragigantocellularis: Contribution to performance in avoidance and spatial memory tasks. *Behavioral Neuroscience, 114,* 707–712.

Clayton, E. C., & Williams, C. L. (2000c). Posttraining inactivation of excitatory afferent input to the locus coeruleus impairs retention in an inhibitory avoidance learning task. *Neurobiology of Learning and Memory, 73,* 127–140.

Coupland, R. E., Parker, T. L., Kesse, W. K., & Mohamed, A. A. (1989). The innervation of the adrenal gland: III. Vagal innervation. *Journal of Anatomy, 163,* 173–181.

Dev, B., & Philip, L. (1996). Extracellular catechol and indole turnover in the nucleus of the solitary tract of spontaneously hypertensive and Wistar–Kyoto normotensive rats in response to drug-induced changes in arterial blood pressure. *Brain Research Bulletin, 40,* 111–116.

Feldman, P., & Felder, R. (1989). α_2-adrenergic modulation of synaptic excitability in the rat nucleus tractus solitarius. *Brain Research, 480,* 190–197.

Gieroba, Z., & Blessing, W. (1994). Fos-containing neurons in medulla and pons after unilateral stimulation of the afferent abdominal vagus in conscious rabbits. *Neuroscience, 59,* 851–858.

Gold, P. E., & van Buskirk, R. B. (1978). Posttraining brain norepinephrine concentrations: Correlation with retention performance of avoidance training with peripheral epinephrine modulation of memory processing. *Behavioral Biology, 23,* 509–520.

Kollmann, J. (1860). Ueber den Verlauf des Lungenmagennerven in der Bauchhohle. *Zeitschrift fur wissenschaftliche Zoologie, 10,* 413–448.

Krahl, S., Browning, R., Clark, K., & Smith, D. (1994). Possible mechanism of the seizure attenuating effects of vagus nerve stimulation. *Society for Neuroscience Abstracts, 20,* 1453.

Lawrence, A. J., Watkins, D., & Jarrott, B. (1995). Visualization of beta-adrenoceptor binding sites on human inferior vagal ganglia and their axonal transport along the rat vagus nerve. *Journal of Hypertension, 13,* 631–635.

Lee, E. H., & Ma, Y. L. (1995). Amphetamine enhances memory retention and facilitates norepinephrine release from the hippocampus in rats. *Brain Research Bulletin, 37,* 411–416.

Liang, K. C., Chen, L. L., & Huang, T. (1995). The role of amygdala norepinephrine in memory formation: Involvement in the memory enhancing effect of peripheral epinephrine. *Chinese Journal of Physiology, 38,* 81–91.

Liang, K. C., Juler, R., & McGaugh, J. L. (1986). Modulating effects of posttraining epinephrine on memory: Involvement of the amygdala noradrenergic system. *Brain Research, 368,* 125–133.

Loughlin, S., Foote, S., & Bloom, F. (1986). Efferent projections of nucleus locus coeruleus: Topographic organization of cells of origin demonstrated by three-dimensional reconstruction. *Neuroscience, 18,* 291–306.

Mason, S. T., & Fibiger, H. D. (1979). Regional topography within noradrenergic locus coeruleus as revealed by retrograde transport of horseradish peroxidase. *Journal of Comparative Neurology, 187,* 703–724.

Misu, Y., & Kubo, T. (1986). Presynaptic adrenoreceptors. *Medical Research Review, 6,* 197–225.

Murugauah, K., & O'Donnell, J. (1994). Clenbuterol increases norepinephrine release from rat brain slices by a calcium- and receptor-independent mechanism. *Research Communications in Molecular Pathology and Pharmacology, 86,* 311–323.

Murugauah, K., & O'Donnell, J. (1995). Beta adrenergic receptors facilitate norepinephrine release from hypothalamic and hippocampal slices. *Research Communications in Molecular Pathology and Pharmacology, 90,* 179–190.

Naritoku, D. K., Terry, W. J., & Helfert, R. H. (1995). Regional induction of *fos* immunoreactivity in the brain by anticonvulsant stimulation of the vagus nerve. *Epilepsy Research, 22,* 53–62.

Niijima, A. (1992). Electrophysiological study on the vagal innervation of the adrenal gland in the rat. *Journal of the Autonomic Nervous System, 41,* 87–92.

Petrov, T., Krukoff, T. L., & Jhamandas, J. H. (1993). Branching projections of catecholaminergic brainstem neurons to the paraventricular hypothalamic nucleus and the central nucleus of the amygdala in the rat. *Brain Research, 609,* 81–92.

Radna, R. J., & MacLean, P. D. (1981). Vagal elicitation of respiratory-type and other unit responses in basal limbic structures of squirrel monkeys. *Brain Research, 213,* 45–61.

Randich, A., & Aicher, S. A. (1988). Medullary substrates mediating antinociception produced by electrical stimulation of the vagus. *Brain Research, 445,* 68–76.

Ricardo, J. A., & Koh, E. T. (1978). Anatomical evidence of direct projections from the nucleus of the solitary tract to the hypothalamus, amygdala, and other forebrain structures in the rat. *Brain Research, 153,* 1–26.

Rogers, R. C., & Fryman, D. L. (1988). Direct connections between the central nucleus of the amygdala and the nucleus of the solitary tract: An electrophysiological study in the rat. *Journal of the Autonomic Nervous System, 22,* 83–87.

Schreurs, J., Seelig, T., & Schulman, H. (1986). Beta 2-adrenergic receptors on peripheral nerves. *Journal of Neurochemistry, 46,* 294–296.

Silva, M. T. A. (1974). Effects of adrenal demedullation and adrenalectomy on an active avoidance response of rats. *Physiological Psychology, 2,* 171–174.

Smith, W., Egle, J., & Adams, M. (1982). Adrenergic receptors in the nucleus tractus solitarii of the rat. *European Journal of Pharmacology, 81,* 11–19.

Sumal, K., Blessing, W., Joh, T., Reis, D., & Pickel, V. (1983). Synaptic interaction of vagal afferents and catecholaminergic neurons in the rat nucleus tractus solitarius. *Brain Research, 277,* 31–40.

Teitelbaum, H. (1933). The nature of the thoracic and abdominal distribution of the vagus. *Anatomical Record, 55,* 297–317.

Van Bockstaele, E., Akaoka, H., & Aston-Jones, G. (1993). Prominent exteroceptive sensory afferents to the rostral pole (juxtafacial portion) of the nucleus paragigantocellularis in the rat. *Brain Research, 603,* 1–8.

Van Bockstaele, E., Colago, E., & Aicher, S. (1998). Light and electron microscopic evidence for topographic and monosynaptic projections from neurons in the ventral medulla to noradrenergic dendrites in the rat locus coeruleus. *Brain Research, 784,* 123–138.

Van Bockstaele, E., Pieribone, V., & Aston-Jones, G. (1989). Diverse afferents converge on the nucleus paragigantocellularis in the rat ventrolateral medulla: Retrograde and anterograde tracing studies. *Journal of Comparative Neurology, 290,* 561–584.

Weil-Malharbe, H., Axelrod, H., & Tomchick, R. (1959). Blood–brain barrier for adrenaline. *Science, 129,* 1226–1228.

Williams, C. L., & McGaugh, J. L. (1993). Reversible lesions of the nucleus of the solitary tract attenuate the memory-modulatory effects of posttraining epinephrine. *Behavioral Neuroscience, 107,* 955–962.

Williams, C. L., Men, D., & Clayton, E. C. (2000). The effects of noradrenergic activation of the nucleus tractus solitarius on memory and in potentiating norepinephrine release in the amygdala. *Behavioral Neuroscience, 114,* 1131–1144.

Williams, C. L., Men, D., Clayton, E. P., & Gold, P. E. (1998). Norepinephrine release in the amygdala following systemic injection of epinephrine or escapable footshock: Contribution of the nucleus of the solitary tract. *Behavioral Neuroscience, 112,* 1414–1422.

Zardetto-Smith, A. M., & Gray, T. S. (1990). Organization of peptidergic and catecholaminergic efferents from the nucleus of the solitary tract to the rat amygdala. *Brain Research Bulletin, 25,* 875–887.

CHAPTER 9

Epinephrine Modulation of Memory:

Amygdala Activation and Regulation of Long-Term Memory Storage

Keng Chen Liang

I first met Dr. McGaugh in September 1977 as a new graduate student in the Department of Psychobiology at the University of California, Irvine (UCI). I was pretty naive about the field of neuroscience and had not even heard of long-term potentiation. I still remember vividly the stress, in terms of cultural shock and academic pressure, facing me in the first couple of quarters at UCI. Yet with Dr. McGaugh's continuous support and encouragement, as well as the assistance of others working in the laboratory, including Drs. Rob Jensen, Joe Martinez, Beatriz Vasquez, Rita Messing, and Bernard Soumireu-Mourat, I was able to survive the first quarter, then the first year, and finally complete my dissertation. From time to time as I ponder the days I spent in Dr. McGaugh's laboratory, I feel that I owe much to the epinephrine circulating in my blood stream and also the amygdala in my brain.

Epinephrine Enhancement of Memory

Hormonal modulation of memory and the effects of amygdala stimulation on retention of learned responses were two independent lines of research already initiated in Dr. McGaugh's laboratory when I arrived at UCI. At that time the team was studying the effects of amphetamine on memory. The results showed that peripheral injections of amphetamine enhanced retention in both inhibitory and active avoidance tasks; and the effect was mimicked by peripheral injection of 4-hydroxy-amphetamine, an amphetamine analog not able to enter the brain,

This work was supported by grants from National Science Council and Academia Sinica, Taiwan, Republic of China.

but not by intracerebroventricular infusion of amphetamine (Martinez, Jensen, et al., 1980). Attenuation of the amphetamine and 4-hydroxy-amphetamine effects by removal of the adrenal medulla, but not by sympathectomy via intravenous injections of 6-hydroxydopamine, suggested that adrenal epinephrine played a critical role in mediating the effect (Martinez, Vasquez, et al., 1980). These findings were consistent with previous ones from the laboratory showing that peripheral injections of epinephrine, which could not readily cross the blood–brain barrier, caused time-dependent and dose-dependent enhancement of memory (Gold & van Buskirk, 1975).

Through helping with these studies, I learned that various stress-related hormones might be released at training and work as endogenous memory modulators. Their effects are often biphasic: facilitating at low doses but impairing at high doses. Being aware of such facilitation eased my tension and brought my circulating level of epinephrine down from the descending limb of the inverted-U dose–response curve to a point optimal for learning. The memory modulatory effect of epinephrine has been replicated in various learning tasks since its initial demonstration (McGaugh, 1983). Here I would like to give an example observed in my own laboratory that epinephrine facilitates latent learning. In this study, rats were trained on a typical step-through inhibitory avoidance apparatus. On the first day, they were simply put into the apparatus and allowed to step from the lit compartment into the dark compartment. They received no foot shock in this preexposure trial. Immediately after the trial, various groups of rats received subcutaneous injections of saline or epinephrine at a dose of 0.001, 0.01, or 0.1 mg/kg. Rats were again put into the box on the next day. As shown in Figure 9.1, they all entered the dark site without hesitation, suggesting that the injection of epinephrine by itself had no punishing effect. This time rats received a mild inescapable shock (0.5 mA, 0.5 second) as soon as they stepped into the dark site. No treatment was given after the shock. All rats were tested for retention on the third day. As shown in Figure 9.1, the control group (after shock) showed poor memory that was typically observed in my laboratory under this intensity of shock. Injections of epinephrine immediately after the pre-exposure trial caused a dose-dependent effect on memory: Rats receiving 0.01 mg/kg epinephrine on the first day showed significantly better retention than the control group, but higher or lower doses had no effect. Thus, epinephrine given after the preexposure trial might enhance memory for contextual or spatial cues of the apparatus. The effect on performance became emergent only when the rat had to use such knowledge to avoid an aversive event. This enhancing effect of epinephrine on latent learning not only attests once again to the distinction between learning and performance but also confirms that epinephrine exerts its influence on memory formation processes per se.

FIGURE 9.1

Effects of epinephrine on latent learning.

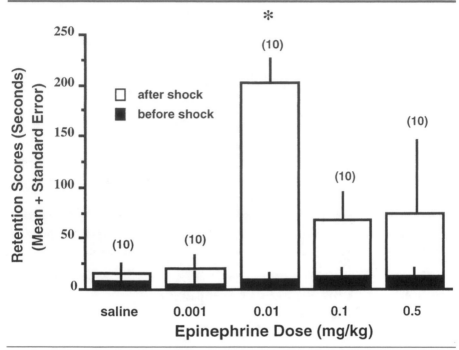

On the first day of training, rats explored the inhibitory avoidance apparatus without receiving shock, and immediately afterward they were injected with saline or various doses of epinephrine. Rats were placed again into the apparatus on the second day. They went into the dark side readily (filled bars) and received a 0.5 mA, 0.5 second shock. Retention was tested on the third day. Most rats remembered poorly, but those given 0.01 mg/kg epinephrine on the first day had enhanced retention (blank bars). *$p < .05$ in comparison with the saline group. Numbers in the parentheses denote the number of subjects in each group.

Involvement of Amygdala and Its Afferent–Efferent Pathways in Memory Modulation

From 1978 to 1980, I studied the effect of amygdala stimulation on memory. The McGaugh laboratory, among others, had demonstrated that posttraining stimulation of the amygdala with subseizure electrical currents impaired retention of an inhibitory avoidance task (Gold, Macri, & McGaugh, 1973). Based on the notion that the stimulation may activate output of the amygdala and affect memory storage processes elsewhere in the brain, Dr. McGaugh and I investigated whether severing the major amygdala afferent–efferent pathways, the stria terminalis (ST) or ventral amygdalofugal path (VAF), affected the amnesic effect of amygdala stimulation. The results showed that pretraining lesions of the ST, which had no effect on retention, blocked the amnesic effect of electrical stimulation of the amygdala administered after training in both inhibitory avoidance and active avoidance tasks. In contrast, transecting the VAF did not abolish the effect of amygdala stimulation on memory (Liang & McGaugh, 1983a).

Evidence available then indicated that fibers projecting from the amygdala to the bed nucleus of ST (BNST) contained met-enkephalin (Uhl, Kuhar, & Snyder, 1978). In view of the role of endogenous opioids in memory of aversively motivated behavior (Messing et al., 1979; Rigter et al., 1980), a follow-up study examined whether electrical stimulation of the amygdala induced amnesia by releasing met-enkephalin in the BNST (Liang, Messing, & McGaugh, 1983). The data showed that the amnesic effect of amygdala stimulation was mimicked by infusing an opiate agonist levorphanol into the BNST and attenuated by naloxone either injected peripherally or infused directly into the BNST. These results, taken together, suggested that amygdala influences on memory formation processing indeed rely on amygdaloid efferent fibers in the ST.

Involvement of Amygdala in Epinephrine Modulation of Memory

During the 1980s, a prevailing theme for amygdala function was to modulate endocrine and autonomic activities, and two targets of the ST—the hypothalamus and BNST—were implicated in such functions. Research in Dr. McGaugh's laboratory during the early 1980s was focused on the contribution of peripheral factors to memory formation. In such a context, the above findings naturally led to a hypothesis that in rats trained with an intense foot shock that released a substantial amount of epinephrine, stimulation of the amygdala might further elevate its level in circulation, and excessive epinephrine was detrimental to memory formation. This hypothesis predicted that the stimulation would not affect memory if release of epinephrine was blocked. That hexamethonium attenuated the effect of amygdala stimulation on retention of an inhibitory avoidance task appeared to be consistent with this notion (Martinez, Liang, & Oscos, 1983). To further address this issue, Kate Bennett, another of Dr. McGaugh's graduate students from whom I learned much, and I administered posttraining stimulation of the amygdala to rats with their adrenal medulla either removed or detached from the splanchnic nerve. The results were contradictory to our prediction. In both inhibitory and active avoidance tasks, pretraining adrenal demedullation or denervation impaired memory in sham-stimulated rats, which was expected in view of our previous results. However, demedullation or denervation of the adrenals failed to block the effect of posttraining amygdala stimulation. On the contrary, the stimulation enhanced retention in the adrenal demedullated or denervated rats in comparison with the poor control performance (Bennett, Liang, & McGaugh, 1985). More to our surprise, supplementing exogenous epinephrine to adrenal demedullated or denervated rats after training not only yielded normal retention in the sham-stimulated group but also reinstated the amnesic effect of posttraining amygdala stimulation if the stimulation was administered after, but not before, epinephrine injections (Liang, Bennett, & McGaugh, 1985). Thus, under the circumstance that circulating epinephrine was provided entirely from an exogenous source such that stimulated and control rats had the same amount of it, stimulation of the amygdala still influenced memory.

These puzzling results once again released lots of epinephrine in me at a time when our laboratory was about to move from Steinhaus Hall to the new Center for the Neurobiology of Learning and Memory. A possible impact of environmental changes on results of sensitive behavioral experiments could be the nightmare of any fifth-year graduate student. In a meeting during the Thanksgiving holiday of 1981, Dr. McGaugh and I discussed these data in his small office in Steinhaus Hall. These findings indicated to us that epinephrine might somehow be pivotal in the influence of the amygdala on memory. As usual, Dr. McGaugh encouraged me to write down all possible explanations and to think of the right experiment for the next step. In the following meeting, probably the last one held in Steinhaus Hall shortly after Christmas, I proposed to Dr. McGaugh that we examine the effect of epinephrine in animals with ST lesions. The rationale was that if peripheral epinephrine indeed affected memory through its influence on the amygdala, ST lesions, which blocked the effect of amygdala stimulation on memory (Liang & McGaugh, 1983a), should abolish this effect. Conversely, if epinephrine was a memory-modulating factor mediating the amygdala influence, ST lesions should not alter the effect of epinephrine given peripherally. This experiment was launched in the new laboratory and the results turned out to be clear: Epinephrine across a wide range of doses failed to affect memory in rats with pretraining ST lesions. These data suggested that integrity of the ST was essential for epinephrine to exert its influence on memory formation processes (Liang & McGaugh, 1983b). Subsequent studies have shown that intact ST fibers were needed for various peripheral or central treatments to affect memory (McGaugh, Introini-Collison, Juler, & Izquierdo, 1986).

Memory Modulatory Effects of Epinephrine Involved Central Norepinephrine

These findings shifted the focus of our research from the periphery back into the central nervous system. If epinephrine exerts its influence on memory through the amygdala, then what could be the mediator given that epinephrine does not readily enter the brain? Previous data had shown that peripheral epinephrine injections or foot shock training altered tissue levels of norepinephrine in brain (Gold & van Buskirk, 1978). The change was interpreted as an increase in release, which was later verified in the amygdala by a microdialysis study (Galvez, Mesches, & McGaugh, 1996). Thus, norepinephrine released in the amygdala may be a candidate for mediating the effect of peripheral epinephrine. Evidence available then did implicate amygdala noradrenergic activity in memory processing, but the direction of effects was somewhat in conflict among different studies (Ellis & Kesner, 1983; Gallagher, Kapp, Musty, & Driscoll, 1977). Dr. McGaugh ended his administrative duty as vice chancellor in 1982 and devoted himself to research in the new laboratory. He and I with the assistance of Ron Juler, one of the best undergraduate students at UCI, launched a systematic study on the role of amygdala norepinephrine in memory processing as well as the memory-enhancing effect of peripheral epinephrine. We infused norepinephrine into the amygdala immediately after training in an inhibitory avoidance task and found a strong dose-dependent memory-enhancing effect, which was due to activation of β adrenergic receptors, because it was blocked by propranolol (Liang, Juler, & McGaugh, 1986). Later it was also reported that the effect could be mimicked by the β agonist isoproterenol and 8-bromo-cAMP but not by the agonist phenylephrine infused into the amygdala after training (Liang, Chen, & Huang, 1995).

We went on to address the issue of whether amygdala noradrenergic activity was involved in the effect of peripheral epinephrine on memory. We found that intra-amygdala infusion of norepinephrine or 8-bromo-cAMP could compensate for a deficiency of peripheral epinephrine and hence attenuate the memory deficit in adrenal demedullated animals (Liang et al., 1986; Liang et al., 1995). In contrast, intra-amygdala infusion of propranolol abolished the memory-enhancing effect of epinephrine in normal rats (Liang et al., 1986) or in adrenal demedullated rats, but intra-amygdala infusion of prazosin had no such effect (Liang et al., 1995). These findings were consistent with the view that epinephrine given peripherally could lead to activation of amygdala β-noradrenergic receptors.

A potential interpretation for the above effect might be that epinephrine injected into the periphery increased blood pressure, which could weaken the blood–brain barrier and hence allow epinephrine to leak into the amygdala. This issue was later addressed in my own laboratory at the National Taiwan University, which receives continuous assistance from Dr. McGaugh—he shares with me from time to time his ideas and some laboratory supplies that I need urgently. Evidence indicated that pretraining intra-amygdala infusion of a neurotoxin N-(2-chloroethyl)-N-ethyl-2-bromobenzylamine (DSP-4) that depletes norepinephrine induced a dose-dependent amnesic effect, which could be ameliorated by posttraining intra-amygdala infusion of norepinephrine but not serotonin. Intra-amygdala infusion of DSP-4 also attenuated the memory-enhancing effect of epinephrine injected peripherally (Liang, 1998). This attenuation was not due to a summation of memory impairment and facilitation bearing no relevance in the underlying mechanisms, because intra-amygdala infusion of DSP-4 at a low dose could attenuate both impairing and enhancing effects of epinephrine at different doses as shown in Figure 9.2 (Liang et al., 1995). Because DSP-4 destroyed only the presynaptic terminals but left the

Depletion of amygdala norepinephrine attenuated memory-enhancing and impairing effects of peripheral epinephrine.

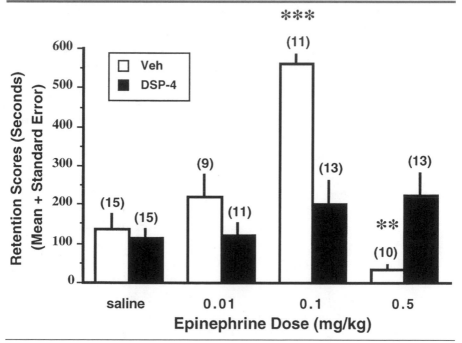

Two weeks before the inhibitory avoidance task, rats received intra-amygdala infusion of 3 μg N-(2-chloroethyl)-N-ethyl-2-bromobenzylamine (DSP-4) or vehicle (Veh). Immediately after training (1.0 mA/1 second foot shock) rats received injections of saline or epinephrine. In the 1-day test, epinephrine at 0.1 mg/kg enhanced but at 0.5 mg/kg impaired memory in the Veh groups (blankbars). In rats pretreated with DSP-4, epinephrine caused neither enhancing nor impairing effects (filled bars). ***$p < .001$, **$p < .01$ different from the corresponding DSP-4 group and saline group. From "The Role of Amygdala Norepinephrine in Memory Formation: Involvement in the Memory Enhancing Effect of Peripheral Epinephrine," by K. C. Liang, L. L. Chen, and T.-Z. Huang, 1995, *Chinese Journal of Physiology, 38*, p. 86. Copyright 1995 by the Chinese Physiological Society. Adapted with permission.

postsynaptic receptors undamaged, the lack of epinephrine enhancement in the DSP-4 treated rats rendered direct binding of epinephrine to amygdala receptors unlikely.

These findings pointed to an alternative hypothesis that peripheral epinephrine might affect amygdala functioning through neural input. In a series of experiments, we showed that transecting the VAF attenuated the effect of peripheral epinephrine but left the effect of norepinephrine infused into the amygdala intact, yet ST lesions abolished the latter effect (Liang, McGaugh, & Yao, 1990). Such findings, taken with the previous ones that ST lesions blocked the effects of peripheral epinephrine (Liang & McGaugh, 1983b), suggest that the VAF might convey influences of peripheral epinephrine into the amygdala to enhance release of norepinephrine, and ST output fibers in turn might mediate influences of norepinephrine on memory. This proposal was consistent with evidence that about 75% of noradrenergic fibers enter the amygdala via the VAF (Fallon & Ciofi, 1992). It should be noted that this may not be the only way by which peripheral epinephrine modulates memory, because epinephrine could increase plasma levels of glucose which also influence memory (Korol & Gold, 1998).

Other mechanisms might also be involved in release of norepinephrine in the amygdala. Many studies have shown that pre- or posttraining intra-amygdala infusion of an N-methyl-D-aspartate (NMDA) receptor antagonist, 2-amino-5-phosphonovaleric acid (APV), impaired retention in various learning tasks, and interpreting these data often invoked LTP-related neural plasticity to subserve information acquisition/storage processes (for review, see Izquierdo & Medina, 1995). However, evidence has shown that NMDA receptors mediated the glutamate-induced release of norepinephrine in various brain regions (Aliaga, Bustos, & Gysling, 1995; Lehman, Valentino, & Robine, 1992). Thus, APV may block norepinephrine release caused by glutamatergic inputs to the amygdala. To test this possibility, we examined whether infusion of norepinephrine into the amygdala would attenuate the effect of APV infused into the same locus. The results shown in Figure 9.3 indicate that in an inhibitory avoidance task, the amnesic effect of APV infused into the amygdala could be attenuated by norepinephrine in the 1-day retention test. This attenuation effect suggested that NMDA-mediated norepinephrine release was crucial for memory processing and contributed, at least in part, to the observed APV-induced amnesia. However, blocking norepinephrine release could not completely account for the amnesic effect of APV: Posttraining supplements of norepinephrine in the APV-treated rats yielded retention scores inferior to those of the controls or APV-treated rats receiving NMDA agonists, particularly in tests with extended retention intervals. Thus, intra-amygdala infusion of APV may also have other actions to impair memory formation processes.

FIGURE 9.3

Norepinephrine (NE) or N-methyl-D-aspartate (NMDA) attenuated the memory impairment induced by 2-amino-5-phosphonovaleric acid (APV).

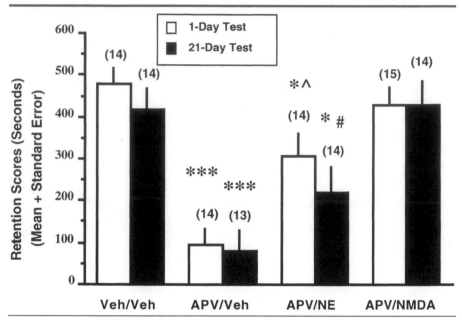

Rats were trained on an inhibitory avoidance task (1.7 mA, 1.2 second foot shock), and retention was tested 1 or 21 days later. In comparison with the vehicle (Veh) group, pretraining intra-amygdala infusion of APV (5.0 μg) induced a severe retention deficit, which was attenuated by norepinephrine (1.0 μg) or NMDA (0.5 μg). However, the attenuating effect of norepinephrine appeared to be less complete than that of NMDA, the difference was significant on the 21-day test. ***$p < .001$, *$p < .05$ different from the Veh/Veh group. ^$p < .05$ different from the APV/Veh group. #$p < .05$ different from the APV/Veh and the APV/NMDA group.

Involvement of Locus Coeruleus in Memory Modulation

Approximately 85% of noradrenergic fibers innervating the amygdala arise from the locus coeruleus (LC) and the remaining 15% from the more caudal noradrenergic cell groups (Fallon & Ciofi, 1992). In view of the above findings showing the importance of norepinephrine in memory-enhancing effects of peripheral epinephrine, my student T. C. Chiang explored the role of the LC in mediating the effect of epinephrine on memory. Cannulae were implanted bilaterally into the LC region through which clonidine, a drug suppressing LC activity by acting on the α2 adrenergic autoreceptors (Cederbaum & Aghajanian, 1977), was administered either before or after training. The results showed that pre- or posttraining infusion of clonidine into the LC region caused a dose-dependent retention deficit, the most effective dose was between 0.1 and 0.3 μg, higher or lower doses were ineffective, and the effect was time dependent. This effect could be ameliorated by either pretraining infusion of yohimbine— an α2 antagonist—into the LC region or posttraining infusion of norepinephrine into the lateral ventricle. Thus, the observed amnesia was indeed due to inhibition of norepinephrine release in the forebrain caused by activation of α2 autoreceptors in the LC. Clonidine infused into the cerebellum or adjacent areas did not produce a comparable effect, so the effect had some anatomical specificity (Liang & Chiang, 1994).

After establishing a role for the LC in memory formation, we pursued whether clonidine suppression of LC activity would attenuate the memory-enhancing effect of epinephrine. Rats were trained on the task and received posttraining infusion of clonidine into the LC region and a systemic injection of epinephrine at an enhancing dose. Clonidine infused into the LC region at an impairing or nonimpairing dose blocked the memory-enhancing effect of peripheral epinephrine as shown in Figure 9.4A. Thus, the LC appeared to play a role in mediating the effect of peripheral epinephrine on retention of aversive experience. How epinephrine activates peripheral inputs to reach the LC invites speculation. Epinephrine administered in the periphery could activate a constellation of responses. Vagal afferents may convey information of these peripheral actions back to the central nervous system. Work has shown the involvement of the vagus nerve in modulating memory in both rodents and humans (see Jensen, chapter 7, this volume). It was reported that the nucleus of the solitary tract, which receives profuse visceral input from the periphery, also played a critical role in the memory modulatory effect of epinephrine (Williams & McGaugh, 1993). This nucleus projects to the nucleus paragigantocellularis, which provides the major brain stem excitatory input to the LC. As indicated by Williams and Clayton (see chapter 8, this volume), suppression of activity in the nucleus paragigantocellularis shortly after training also impaired memory.

As noted in the previous section, the effect of peripheral epinephrine on memory involved amygdala noradrenergic activity. Data presented above showed an important role of LC activity in this effect. These two sets of findings suggest that the memory modulatory function of the LC may involve its projections to the amygdala. To evaluate this hypothesis, rats with cannulae implanted into the amygdala and LC were trained on an inhibitory avoidance task. Immediately after training, they received infusion of yohimbine or clonidine into the LC region followed by propranolol or norepinephrine, respectively, infused into the amygdala. In the first experiment, we found that infusion of yohimbine into the LC region enhanced retention, which was attenuated by intra-amygdala infusion of propranolol. Conversely, intra-amygdala infusion of norepinephrine also attenuated the memory-impairing effect of 0.1 μg clonidine infused into the LC region. Yet, as shown in Figure 9.4B, attenuation of

FIGURE 9.4

Involvement of the locus coeruleus (LC) in memory modulation.

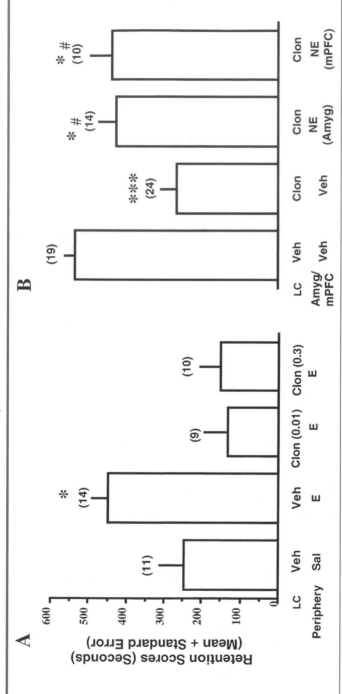

(A) Suppression of the LC attenuated the enhancing effect of epinephrine (E). Rats were trained with a 0.6 mA, 1 second foot shock. Epinephrine at a dose of 0.1 mg/kg given immediately after training enhanced 1-day retention in the vehicle (Veh) treated animals, but clonidine (Clon) at 0.3 or 0.01 µg which, respectively, did or did not impair retention by itself, infused into the LC region before training abolished the effect. *$p < .05$ different from all other groups. (B) Infusion of norepinephrine (NE) into the amygdala (Amyg) or medial prefrontal cortex (mPFC) partly attenuated the impairing effect of suppressing the LC. Rats were trained with a 1.2 mA, 1.2 second foot shock. In a 1-day test, pretraining infusion of clonidine (0.1 µg) or amygdala (0.2 µg). However, retention scores of the two norepinephrine-treated groups were still lower than those of the controls. ***$p < .001$, *$p < .05$ different from the controls. ***$p < .001$, *$p < .05$ different from the combined Veh/Veh group. #$p < .05$ different from combined Clon/Veh groups.

clonidine-induced amnesia by intra-amygdala infusion of norepinephrine was incomplete. A significant difference was detected between the Clon/NE group and Veh/Veh controls. Additional data (not shown here) indicated that if a higher dose (0.3 μg) of clonidine was infused to the LC region, then norepinephrine at a wide range of doses infused into the amygdala was only minimally effective in attenuating the amnesia. In contrast, intraventricular infusion of norepinephrine readily attenuated the amnesic effect, suggesting that structures other than the amygdala may also be involved (Liang & Chiang, 1994).

Previous studies have implicated the prefrontal cortex in memory processing. A study from our laboratory has shown that infusion of lidocaine into the medial prefrontal cortex within 1 hour after inhibitory avoidance training impaired retention (Liang & Hu, 1996). The LC projects profusely to the prefrontal cortex (Seguela, Watkins, Geffard, & Descarries, 1990) and stressful experience altered norepinephrine contents in the medial prefrontal cortex (Finlay, Zigmond, & Abercrombie, 1995). Infusion of clonidine into the LC to suppress its activity caused EEG synchronization in the cortex (Berridge, Page, Valentino, & Foote, 1993). These findings led us to investigate whether noradrenergic modulation of memory involved its projection to the medial prefrontal cortex. In an experiment, either norepinephrine or propranolol was infused into the medial prefrontal cortex after training on an inhibitory avoidance task, and results showed that posttraining infusion of norepinephrine into this region caused a time-dependent and dose-dependent memory enhancement. Posttraining infusion of propranolol into the medial prefrontal cortex caused an opposite effect and blocked the memory enhancement induced by norepinephrine (Liang & Hu, 1996). Given these results, we pursued whether prefrontal noradrenergic activity was involved in the amnesic effect of LC suppression. Rats received clonidine infused into the LC region shortly before training and norepinephrine infused into the medial prefrontal cortex right after training. The results showed that norepinephrine infused into the medial prefrontal cortex also ameliorated, but did not totally abolish, the memory-impairing effect of clonidine infused into the LC region (Figure 9.4B). Thus the memory modulatory influence ensuing from activation of the LC involves not only noradrenergic inputs to the amygdala but also those to the medial prefrontal cortex.

It is somewhat paradoxical that intra-amygdala infusion of norepinephrine fully counteracts the deleterious effect of adrenal demedullation (Liang et al., 1986) but only partially attenuates that of suppressing the LC, which is supposed to mediate the influence of peripheral epinephrine. A plausible explanation might be that peripheral epinephrine depletion deprives afferent input to only a subset of LC neurons that project preferentially to the amygdala. Yet local infusion of clonidine suppressed all LC neurons, which send widespread projections to all forebrain targets. Therefore, depressed norepinephrine release in structures other than the amygdala may contribute also to the amnesia induced by LC suppression. Whether such anatomical specificity indeed exists in LC input and output remains to be clarified.

Interaction Between Amygdala and Medial Prefrontal Cortex in Modulating Memory

Anatomical evidence has shown that the medial prefrontal cortex is reciprocally connected with the amygdala either directly or indirectly through relay of the mediodorsal thalamic nuclei (McDonald, 1987, 1998). An interesting question raised by the above findings is whether one of these two structures may serve to mediate the effect of the other. If there is a flow of memory modulatory influences, then the effect induced by altering the function of a downstream structure should block or override the effect induced by treatments applied to the upstream one. This issue was addressed by examining whether suppressing the amygdala or medial prefrontal cortex could block the memory-enhancing effect induced through the other structure (Liang & Hu, 1996). In the first experiment, we infused 6-cyano-7-nitroquinoxaline-2,3-dione (CNQX), an α-amino-3-hydroxyl-5-methyl-4-isoxazloe propionate (AMPA) receptor antagonist, into the medial prefrontal cortex before training and an enhancing dose of norepinephrine into the amygdala immediately after training. As indicated in Figure 9.5A, the memory-enhancing effect of norepinephrine infused into the amygdala could be completely attenuated by CNQX infused into the medial prefrontal cortex. These findings, considered alone, suggest that the medial prefrontal cortex may mediate influences of the amygdala on memory. Indeed, if this were the case, the memory-enhancing effect induced by posttraining infusion of norepinephrine into the medial prefrontal cortex should be resistant to the deleterious influence of suppressing the amygdala. This was proven untrue. Intra-amygdala infusion of CNQX also blocked the memory-enhancing effect of norepinephrine infused into the medial prefrontal cortex as shown in Figure 9.5A. These findings, considered together, imply that in modulating memory neither structure had a role overriding the other. Instead, integrity of both structures appeared to be necessary for normal or enhanced memory to occur.

Previous studies have shown that suppressing the amygdala or medial prefrontal cortex with posttraining local infusion of 2% lidocaine induced a marked retention deficit in an inhibitory avoidance task (Coleman-Mesches & McGaugh, 1995; Liang & Hu, 1996). To pursue further whether activating one of these two structures could surpass the effect of depressing the other structure, lidocaine was infused immediately after training into either the amygdala or medial prefrontal cortex, and glutamate was infused into the other region. Results shown in Figure 9.5B indicate that lidocaine infused into

FIGURE 9.5

Mutual dependence between the amygdala (Amyg) and medial prefrontal cortex (mPFC) in memory modulation.

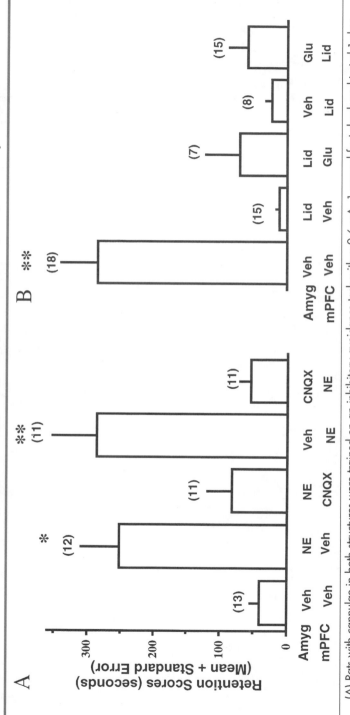

(A) Rats with cannulae in both structures were trained on an inhibitory avoidance task with a 0.6 mA, 1 second foot shock and tested 1 day later. They received pretraining infusion of vehicle (Veh) or 6-cyano-7-nitroquinoxaline-2,3-dione (CNQX, 0.3 μg) into one of the structures and posttraining infusion of Veh or norepinephrine (NE) into the other (0.2 and 0.01 μg for the amygdala and medial prefrontal cortex, respectively). Norepinephrine infused into either structure caused retention enhancement, which was abolished by CNQX infused into the other one. **$p < .01$, *$p < .05$ different from the Veh/Veh and the corresponding CNQX groups. (B) Rats were trained on the task with a 1.2 mA, 1.2 second foot shock, they received pretraining infusion of 2% lidocaine (Lid) into one of the two sites and posttraining infusion of glutamate (Glu) into the other (5.0 and 0.01 μg for the amygdala and medial prefrontal cortex, respectively). Lidocaine infused into either site impaired retention, and the deficits were not ameliorated by glutamate infused into the other structure. **$p < .01$ different from all other groups.

either the amygdala or medial prefrontal cortex caused marked amnesia in replicating the previous findings. However, such impairing effects were impervious to activating the other structure with glutamate at a dose that has been shown to facilitate memory (Izquierdo et al., 1992). These findings, taken together, are consistent with the suggestion that both structures are contained within a neural circuit influencing memory processing; consolidation of affective experience requires persistent activity in the circuit for a period of time after learning; disrupting functioning in either of the two structures, or any others contained in the circuit, may interrupt activity reverberation in it and thus impair long-term memory formation. In this regard, it would be very interesting to pursue whether there is lasting neurophysiological interaction between the amygdala and medial prefrontal cortex within a certain period of time after training.

Although both the amygdala and medial prefrontal cortex are involved in modulating memory, they by no means subserve identical roles in memory function. A recent study showed that some brain structures were differentially engaged in different temporal domains of memory processing (Izquierdo et al., 1997). In an attempt to explore the involvement of these two structures in expression of inhibitory avoidance memory, CNQX was infused into the amygdala or medial prefrontal cortex shortly before testing in a 1-day or 21-day retention test (Liang, Hu, & Chang, 1996). The results, as shown in Figure 9.6, indicate that pretest intra-amygdala infusion of CNQX suppressed performance in the 1-day test but had negligible effects in the 21-day test. In contrast, pretest infusion of CNQX into the medial prefrontal cortex suppressed performance in the 21-day test but had no effect in the 1-day test. Effects of pretrial treatments might be confounded by influences on performance. However, if this were in fact the case, CNQX infused into either area should have had similar effects in tests with different retention intervals. Thus, these data suggest that the amygdala and medial prefrontal cortex were involved in operating, respectively, recent and remote aversive memory, although they might not be the site of memory storage.

Conclusion

Since the modulatory effect of stress-related hormones on memory formation was reported, progress has been made in the past 20 years concerning the mechanisms and the generality of the effect. Dr. McGaugh has envisaged this progress and has made a significant contribution to it. He either participated in person in the work on this line of research, or inspired the incubation of some ideas that eventually led to critical findings, not only in my case but

FIGURE 9.6

Differential effects of suppressing the amygdala or medial prefrontal cortex during testing on 1-day and 21-day retention.

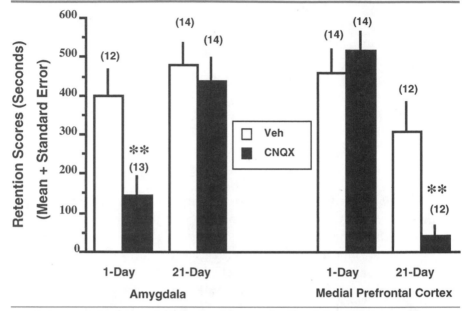

Rats were trained on an inhibitory avoidance task with a 1.7 mA, 1.2 second foot shock and tested for retention either 1 or 21 days later. They received infusion of vehicle (Veh) or 6-cyano-7-nitroquinoxaline-2,3-dione (CNQX, 0.3 μg) into either structure 5 minutes before testing. Suppressing the amygdala impaired retention performance in the 1-day test but had no effect in the 21-day test. In contrast, suppressing the medial prefrontal cortex impaired retention performance in the 21-day test but had no effect in the 1-day test. **$p < .01$ different from the corresponding Veh group. From "Formation and Retrieval of Inhibitory Avoidance Memory: Differential Roles of Glutamate Receptors in the Amygdala and Medial Prefrontal Cortex," by K. C. Liang, S.-J. Hu, and S. C. Chang, 1996, *Chinese Journal of Physiology, 39*, p. 161. Copyright 1996 by the Chinese Physiological Society. Adapted with permission.

also in many others, as attested by the content of this volume. Although much of how the brain represents, stores, and uses information acquired through various types of learning, either in the laboratory or in daily life, remains to be worked out, the dedication and accomplishment of Dr. McGaugh in the field of learning and memory would definitely encourage many more young scientists to devote themselves to solving these problems. This, in my opinion, is one of the greatest contributions of Dr. McGaugh to the neurobiological study of learning and memory, which may become more evident after another 40 years or even longer.

References

Aliaga, E., Bustos, G., & Gysling, K. (1995). Release of endogenous catecholamines from the striatum and bed nucleus of stria terminalis evoked by potassium and N-methyl-D-aspartate: In vitro microdialysis studies. *Journal of Neuroscience Research, 40*, 89–98.

Bennett, C., Liang, K. C., & McGaugh, J. L. (1985). Depletion of adrenal catecholamines alters the amnestic effect of amygdala stimulation. *Behavioural Brain Research, 15*, 83–91.

Berridge, C. W., Page, M. E., Valentino, R. J., & Foote, S. L. (1993). Effects of locus coeruleus inactivation on electroencephalographic activity in neocortex and hippocampus. *Neuroscience, 55*, 381–393.

Cederbaum, J. M., & Aghajanian, G. K. (1977). Catecholamine receptors on locus coeruleus neurons: Pharmacological characterization. *European Journal of Pharmacology, 44*, 375–385.

Coleman-Mesches, K., & McGaugh, J. L. (1995). Differential effects of pretraining inactivation of the right or left amygdala on retention of inhibitory avoidance training. *Behavioral Neuroscience, 109*, 642–647.

Ellis, M. E., & Kesner, R. P. (1983). The noradrenergic system of the amygdala and aversive memory processing. *Behavioral Neuroscience, 97*, 399–415.

Fallon, J. H., & Ciofi, P. (1992). Distribution of monoamines within the amygdala. In J. P. Aggleton (Ed.), *The amygdala: Neurobiological aspects of emotion, memory, and mental dysfunction* (pp. 97–114). New York: Wiley-Liss.

Finlay, J. M., Zigmond, M. J., & Abercrombie, E. D. (1995). Increased dopamine and norepinephrine release in medial prefrontal cortex induced by acute and chronic stress: Effects of diazepam. *Neuroscience, 64*, 619–628.

Gallagher, M., Kapp, B. S., Musty, R. E., & Driscoll, P. A. (1977). Memory formation: Evidence for a specific neurochemical system in the amygdala. *Science, 198*, 423–425.

Galvez, R., Mesches, M. H., & McGaugh, J. L. (1996). Norepinephrine release in the amygdala in response to footshock stimulation. *Neurobiology of Learning and Memory, 66*, 253–257.

Gold, P. E., Macri, J., & McGaugh, J. L. (1973). Retrograde amnesia produced by subseizure amygdala stimulation. *Behavioral Biology, 9*, 671–680.

Gold, P., & van Buskirk, R. (1975). Facilitation of time-dependent memory processes with posttrial epinephrine injections. *Behavioral Biology, 13*, 145–153.

Gold, P., & van Buskirk, R. (1978). Posttraining brain norepinephrine concentration: Correlation with retention performance of avoidance training and peripheral epinephrine modulation of memory processing. *Behavioral Biology, 23*, 509–520.

Izquierdo, I., Da Cunha, C., Rosat, R., Jerusalinsky, D., Ferreira, M. B. C., & Medina, J. H. (1992). Neurotransmitter receptors involved in post-training memory processing by the amygdala, medial septum, and hippocampus of the rat. *Behavioral and Neural Biology, 58,* 16–26.

Izquierdo, I., & Medina, J. H. (1995). Correlation between the pharmacology of LTP and the pharmacology of memory. *Neurobiology of Learning and Memory, 63,* 19–32.

Izquierdo, I., Quillfeldt, J. A., Zanatta, M. S., Quevedo, J., Schaeffer, E., Schmitz, P. K., & Medina, J. H. (1997). Sequential role of hippocampus and amygdala, entorhinal cortex and parietal cortex in formation and retrieval of memory for inhibitory avoidance in rats. *European Journal of Neuroscience, 9,* 786–793.

Korol, D. L., & Gold, P. E. (1998). Glucose, memory, and aging. *American Journal of Clinical Nutrition, 47,* 764–771.

Lehman, J., Valentino, R., & Robine, V. (1992). Cortical norepinephrine release elicited in situ by N-methyl-D-aspartate (NMDA) receptor stimulation: A microdialysis study. *Brain Research, 599,* 171–174.

Liang, K. C. (1998). Pretraining infusion of DSP-4 into the amygdala impaired retention in the inhibitory avoidance task: Involvement of norepinephrine but not serotonin in memory facilitation. *Chinese Journal of Physiology, 41,* 223–233.

Liang, K. C., Bennett, C., & McGaugh, J. L. (1985). Peripheral epinephrine modulates the effects of posttraining amygdala stimulation on memory. *Behavioural Brain Research, 15,* 93–100.

Liang, K. C., Chen, L. L., & Huang, T.-Z. (1995). The role of amygdala norepinephrine in memory formation: Involvement in the memory enhancing effect of peripheral epinephrine. *Chinese Journal of Physiology, 38,* 77–87.

Liang, K. C., & Chiang, T.-C. (1994). Locus coeruleus infusion of clonidine impaired retention and attenuated memory enhancing effects of epinephrine. *Neuroscience Abstracts, 20,* 153.

Liang, K. C., & Hu, S.-J. (1996). Posttraining or pretest infusion of glutamate antagonists into the medial prefrontal cortex impairs memory formation or retrieval in an inhibitory avoidance task. *Neuroscience Abstracts, 22,* 1382.

Liang, K. C., Hu, S.-J., & Chang, S. C. (1996). Formation and retrieval of inhibitory avoidance memory: Differential roles of glutamate receptors in the amygdala and medial prefrontal cortex. *Chinese Journal of Physiology, 39,* 155–166.

Liang, K. C., Juler, R. G., & McGaugh, J. L. (1986). Modulating effects of posttraining epinephrine on memory: Involvement of the amygdala noradrenergic system. *Brain Research, 368,* 125–133.

Liang, K. C., & McGaugh, J. L. (1983a). Lesions of the stria terminalis attenuate the amnestic effect of amygdaloid stimulation on avoidance responses. *Brain Research, 274,* 309–318.

Liang, K. C., & McGaugh, J. L. (1983b). Lesions of the stria terminalis attenuate the enhancing effect of posttraining epinephrine on retention of an inhibitory avoidance response. *Behavioural Brain Research, 9,* 49–58.

Liang, K. C., McGaugh, J. L., & Yao, H.-Y. (1990). Involvement of amygdala pathways in the influence of post-training intra-amygdala norepinephrine and peripheral epinephrine on memory storage. *Brain Research, 508,* 225–233.

Liang, K. C., Messing, R. B., & McGaugh, J. L. (1983). Naloxone attenuates amnesia caused by amygdaloid stimulation: The involvement of a central opioid system. *Brain Research, 271,* 41–49.

Martinez, J. L., Jr., Jensen, R. A., Messing, R. B., Vasquez, B. J., Liang, K. C., & McGaugh, J. L. (1980). Central and peripheral actions of amphetamine on memory storage. *Brain Research, 182,* 157–166.

Martinez, J. L., Jr., Liang, K. C., & Oscos, A. (1983). Amnesia induced by stimulation of the amygdala is attenuated by hexamethonium. *Psychopharmacology, 81,* 310–314.

Martinez, J. L., Jr., Vasquez, B. J., Rigter, H., Messing, R. B., Jensen, R. A., Liang, K. C., & McGaugh, J. L. (1980). Attenuation of amphetamine induced enhancement of learning by adrenal demedullation. *Brain Research, 195,* 433–443.

McDonald, A. J. (1987). Organization of amygdaloid projections to the mediodorsal thalamus and prefrontal cortex: A fluorescence retrograde transport study in the rat. *Journal of Comparative Neurology, 262,* 46–58.

McDonald, A. J. (1998). Cortical pathways to the mammalian amygdala. *Progress in Neurobiology, 55,* 257–332.

McGaugh, J. L. (1983). Hormonal influences on memory. *Annual Review of Psychology, 34,* 297–323.

McGaugh, J. L., Introini-Collison, I. B., Juler, R. G., & Izquierdo, I. (1986). Stria terminalis lesions attenuate the effects of posttraining naloxone and beta-endorphin on retention. *Behavioral Neuroscience, 100,* 839–844.

Messing, R. B., Jensen, R. A., Martinez, J. L., Jr., Spiehler, V. R., Vasquez, B. J., Soumireu-Mourat, B., Liang, K. C., & McGaugh, J. L. (1979). Naloxone enhancement of memory. *Behavioral and Neural Biology, 27,* 266–275.

Rigter, H., Jensen, R. A., Martinez, J. L., Jr., Messing, R. B., Vasquez, B. J., Liang, K. C., & McGaugh, J. L. (1980). Enkephalin and fear-motivated behavior. *Proceedings of the National Academy of Sciences, 77,* 3729–3732.

Seguela, P., Watkins, K. C., Geffard, M., & Descarries, L. (1990). Noradrenaline axon terminals in adult neocortex: An immunocytochemical analysis in serial thin sections. *Neuroscience, 35,* 249–264.

Uhl, G. R., Kuhar, M. J., & Snyder, S. H. (1978). Enkephalin-containing pathway: Amygdaloid efferents in the ST. *Brain Research, 149,* 223–228.

Williams, C. L., & McGaugh, J. L. (1993). Reversible lesions of the nucleus of the solitary tract attenuate the memory-modulating effects of posttraining epinephrine. *Behavioral Neuroscience, 107,* 955–962.

CHAPTER 10

Cortical Cholinergic Modulation in Memory Formation

Federico Bermúdez-Rattoni

María Isabel Miranda,

Humberto Gutiérrez González

The cerebral cortex has been considered as the ubiquitous place for the storage of long-term memory; in this regard we have found important data suggesting that the insular cortex (IC) is involved in associative learning. Additionally, a number of studies have demonstrated the importance of this neocortex region in the acquisition and long-term storage of visceral and aversively motivated learning (Bermúdez-Rattoni, Introini-Collison, & McGaugh, 1991; Bures, Bermúdez-Rattoni, & Yamamoto, 1998).

Jim McGaugh and his coworkers initiated several decades ago the search for the neuromodulation exerted by different neurotransmitters during the formation of aversively motivated memories (Cahill, Roozendaal, & McGaugh, 1997). In accord with this idea, we have investigated the in vivo and in vitro patterns of neurotransmission activity during the acquisition and performance of several learning tasks. Recently we have been investigating the influence that the ascending cholinergic pathways from the basal forebrain to the cortex have on the ability to learn aversively motivated tasks. In particular, we have used cortical models of associative learning, which depend on well-described underlying connections, allowing the study of the mechanisms involved.

The Role of Insular Cortex on Memory Formation

The IC in the rat is defined as an area spanning from the lateral frontal cortex to the perirhinal cortex in the rostrocaudal direction and from the ventral edge

This research was supported by Grant 3260P-N9608 from CONACyT (National Council for Science and Technology), Mexico, Districto Federal, Mexico. We appreciate the technical assistance of Oreste Carbajal and Federico Jandete and give thanks to Yolanda Díaz de Castro for preparing the chapter.

of the somatomotor cortex to the pyriform cortex in the dorsoventral direction (Saper, 1982). The IC (Krieg's areas 13 and 14 in rats) has been referred to as the visceral cortex, because it receives taste and visceral information from the thalamus and is known to be involved in visceral reactions and stress (Krushel & van der Kooy, 1988; van der Kooy, Koda, McGinty, Gerfen, & Bloom, 1984). Moreover, it has been postulated that the IC receives convergent limbic and primary sensory inputs that are not seen within any other area in the cortex (Krushel & van der Kooy, 1988). This defines the IC as a visceral cortex, but it is now clear that this cortex is involved in several aversive conditionings, which provides for a model of an associative cortex. Among the IC connections that may be important for mnemonic processing are those of the limbic system, the amygdala, the dorsomedial nucleus of the thalamus, and the prefrontal cortex. The IC and the amygdala are functionally and reciprocally interconnected (Pascoe & Kapp, 1987). The cortical projections to the amygdala, including those from the IC, have been suggested as conveyors of processed cognitive information that is then integrated with emotional and motivational processes (Pascoe & Kapp, 1987). In addition, recently the IC has been found to be involved in human cognitive processes (Kornhuber 1995; Scott, 1995), strengthening the idea that this is a cognitive associative cortex.

Experiments on the role of the IC in learning and memory processing started in the early 1970s. Those studies related the IC with the acquisition and retrieval of conditioned taste aversions (CTA). The CTA is a robust learning paradigm in which animals acquire aversions to a taste when it is followed by digestive malaise. In this regard, a number of experiments have demonstrated that IC lesions in animals made either before or after acquisition of the CTA disrupt this learning (Braun, Lasiter, & Kiefer, 1982). Because IC lesions do not produce obvious deficits in gustatory or gastrointestinal sensitivity, it has been suggested that IC lesions impair the mnemonic representation of tastes and their postgastrointestinal consequences (malaise; Braun et al., 1982; Kiefer & Brown, 1979). Several studies have confirmed that the IC is involved in mediation of the associative aspects of taste responses, but not in the hedonic responses to taste. Like normal rats, IC-lesioned animals prefer sucrose, as well as low concentrations of sodium chloride, to water and reject quinine and acid solutions. This is not surprising, because taste responsiveness remains intact even in decerebrated rats (Braun et al., 1982; Kiefer, 1985). Until recently, studies investigating the role of the IC in learning and memory processes focused primarily on taste–visceral memorial representation (García, Lasiter, Bermúdez-Rattoni, & Deems, 1985; Lasiter & Glanzman, 1985). However, we demonstrated that either permanent N-methyl-D-aspartate (NMDA)-induced lesions or reversible lesions, caused by microinjections of tetrodotoxin (TTX—a voltage-sensitive sodium channel blocker) into the IC of rats, produced severe impairments on retention of an inhibitory avoidance task and in a Morris water maze spatial task. These results clearly show that functional deactivation of the IC produces retrograde and anterograde amnesia in two aversively motivated cognitive tasks: (a) inhibitory avoidance and (b) water maze spatial learning (Bermúdez-Rattoni et al., 1991; Bermúdez-Rattoni & McGaugh, 1991). Therefore, the above-mentioned results lead us to think that the IC and the related structures could be used as a good model for the study of the neuromodulating effects exerted by acetylcholine (ACh) on memory formation.

Cholinergic Activity

For a long time, the cholinergic neurotransmitter system has been thought to be involved in learning and memory processes (Decker & McGaugh, 1991). Excitotoxic lesions of the cortical projecting cholinergic areas, pharmacological manipulations, aging of the central nervous system (CNS), and fetal cortical graft experiments have all strongly correlated the cortical cholinergic activity with associative functions in a wide variety of cognitive models. These studies have implied the involvement of the ascending basal–cortical cholinergic system in the regulation of learning and memory functions mediated by the cerebral cortex (for review, see Sinden, Hodges, & Gray, 1995). Moreover, recently there has been evidence that cholinergic neurons in the basal forebrain are involved in processes such as arousal and attention. A modulatory role for ACh in the activity of cortical neurons has been suggested by observations from electrophysiological and biochemical studies. Thus, a variety of behavioral and environmental conditions like motor activity or stress induced by restraining or handling produced significant ACh release in the rat neocortex. In addition to these findings, which demonstrate differences in ACh release related to different states of arousal, other evidence suggests that associative conditioning may also modify ACh release in the neocortex (Inglis, Day, & Fibiger, 1994; Sarter & Bruno, 1994). Thus, training for tactile discrimination causes a specific enhancement in ACh release in the somatosensory cortex that is related to discrimination performance (Butt, Testylier, & Dykes, 1997).

In our model, we have found through in vitro biochemical analyses that IC fetal grafts that released ACh in response to depolarization also induced recovery of learning deficits, whereas other cortical grafts that did not release ACh were ineffective in restoring these deficits, although both types of grafts released similar amounts of other neurotransmitters, such as γ amino-butyric-acid (GABA) and glutamate (López-García, Bermúdez-Rattoni, & Tapia, 1990). Recent experiments were designed to investigate the in vivo release of ACh in behavioral recovery by the fetal brain grafts. By using microdialysis in free-moving rats, we have demonstrated that homotopical, but not heterotopical, cortical brain grafts induce release of ACh similar to the control levels. Furthermore, homotopic grafts and lesioned groups showed significantly weaker specific receptor binding of [^{3}H]L-glutamate compared with controls. Altogether these results suggest that cortical ACh is specifically involved in the processes of recovery of the ability to acquire CTA induced by fetal brain grafts (Miranda & Bermúdez-Rattoni, 1998; Miranda, López-Colomé, & Bermúdez-Rattoni, 1997).

Recently, we have evaluated the effects of fetal brain grafts on the recovery of long-term memory of the CTA. With the use of fetal brain grafts as a "reversible lesion" model, it is possible to test whether the studied structure is a real storage site or is involved only in the exit of information stored somewhere else in the brain. In one study, we found that animals, which received either cholinergically rich or cholinergically poor grafts, were both able to recall a previously learned CTA (Ormsby, Ramírez-Amaya, & Bermúdez-Rattoni, 1998). However, only those animals receiving cholinergically rich tissue were able to learn a novel CTA. As mentioned, the cholinergic activity seen in fetal grafts seems to be very important to recover the ability to learn aversively motivated tasks. However, the role of cholinergic activity on the recovery of aversive memory seems less relevant than for recovery of learning abilities (Ormsby et al., 1998).

In several studies, it has been demonstrated that nerve growth factor (NGF) treatments induce recovery of the lesioned cholinergic neurons (Hefti, 1986), as well as ameliorate spatial impairments in aged rats and in animals with lesions of the nucleus basalis magnocelullaris (NBM; Gage, Björklund, Stenevi, Dunnet, & Kelly, 1984; Ogawa, Nabeshima, Kameyama, & Hayashi, 1993). Because our previous results suggest that cholinergic transmission may play a role in graft-mediated behavioral recovery, NGF could be involved. We have been able to demonstrate that supplementing IC fetal grafts with NGF not only induces recovery of cognitive function but also brings cholinergic activity back to normal unoperated control values, as measured by in vivo and in vitro biochemical analyses (Escobar, Jiménez, López-García, Tapia, & Bermúdez-Rattoni, 1993; Miranda & Bermúdez-Rattoni, 1998; Russell, Escobar, Booth, & Bermúdez-Rattoni, 1994).

Altogether these results showed that cholinergic activity coming from the brain grafts are important for recovery acquisition, but seems to be less important for the recovery of the retrieval phase of aversively motivated learning tasks. However, it is unknown to what extent the cholinergic input from basal forebrain is relevant for the functional recovery after brain grafts. Therefore, we decide to investigate the role of the ACh coming from the basal forebrain in memory formation.

Cholinergic Basal Forebrain Projections to the Cortex

The cholinergic basal forebrain (CBF) complex is a group of relatively large neurons located in the ventral region of the mammalian brain in the NBM, in the vertical and horizontal limbs of the diagonal band of Broca, and in the medial septal area, providing widespread cholinergic innervation throughout the brain, with projections to the hippocampus, amygdala, and neocortex, including the insular and pyriform cortices (Saper, 1982). This set of neurons has been considered to play an important role in learning and memory (Waite et al., 1995). As mentioned, cholinergic activity is suspected to be an important participant in the maintenance of normal cognitive functions, but it is not clear to what extent the deficits observed after CBF lesions can be attributable to the loss of cortical cholinergic neurotransmission. In this regard, it has been demonstrated that excitotoxic destruction of the NBM produced severe impairments in cognitive function (Dunnett, Everitt, & Robbins, 1991; Sinden, Hodges, & Gray, 1995). However, in a recent series of articles, Thal and coworkers (Connor, Langlais, & Thal, 1991) have demonstrated that there is a differential effect of NBM lesions on amygdala and cortical cholinergic markers, depending on the different excitotoxins used. That is, ibotenic acid lesions of the NBM produced greater impairments in the acquisition of a water maze learning task than quisqualic acid lesions, even though quisqualic acid produced a larger decrease in cortical ChAT activity. Further, Page and coworkers (Page, Everitt, Robbins, Marston, & Wilkinson, 1991) have reported that both acquisition and performance in the Morris water maze were unaffected by AMPA lesions, whereas significant impairments in this task were observed following ibotenic acid-induced lesions. Given the disparity between the degree of reduction of ChAT activity and the equivalent differences in behavioral effects, it is conceivable that there are subpopulations of cells differentially sensitive to excitotoxins, or that there is more than one neurotransmitter involved in cognitive-dependent CBF activity. Additionally, it is not clear whether the behavioral deficits observed after basal forebrain lesions reflect exclusively the basal-cortical component of the lesions, rather than nonspecific damage of its cholinergic projections to other important structures, i.e., the thalamus or amygdala. The lack of specific cholinergic excitotoxins has resulted in a search for alternative approaches. One promising example is to induce ACh depletion by chronic application of antibodies against NGF. It is known that neurons of the CBF seem to be the major population of cells in the CNS expressing receptors to NGF. When NGF is injected into the rat cortex, it is retrogradely transported to cell bodies of the NBM. Furthermore, it has been demonstrated from studies of fimbria fornix transection, and from nonlesioned-aged animals, that these neurons are able to respond to exogenously added NGF (Gage et al., 1984).

In a series of experiments, we investigated the regulatory involvement of the CBF in the learning and memory processes mediated by the cortex. To accomplish this we combined two main approaches: (a) functional inactivation of the CBF by specific retrograde deafferentation of the insular cortex and (b) analysis of the in vivo dynamics of extracellular ACh liberation in the IC during the formation of the gustatory association (acquisition) and during its recall (evocation).

As mentioned, the principal source of ACh to the cortex is the CBF, and it is well known that CBF lesions affect a number of learning tasks. Excitotoxic lesions of the NBM have been shown to impair acquisition of CTA and the inhibitory avoidance task (Etherington, Mittleman, & Robbins, 1987; López-García, Fernández-Ruiz, Escobar, Bermúdez-Rattoni, & Tapia, 1993). However, it should be pointed out that no effects on CTA conditioning after NBM lesions have also been reported (Kesner, Berman, & Tardif, 1992), although, as mentioned, different effects of NBM lesions on cortical cholinergic markers by different excitotoxins have been reported (Page et al., 1991). Therefore, to directly assess the role of CBF projecting neurons, we designed an experiment in which we obtained complete deafferentation of the IC by chronic application of anti-NGF antibodies into the IC. In accordance with the neurotrophic hypothesis, NGF is synthesized by target cells of CBF projections (i.e., neocortex, hippocampus, amygdala, and other brain structures), binds to the NGF receptor located on nerve terminals, and is retrogradely transported to cell bodies of the CBF (Cuello, Maysinger, & Garofalo, 1992).

Therefore, in a series of experiments we demonstrated that repeated application of antibodies against NGF into the IC produced a significant disruption in the acquisition of CTA in rats. However, the same animals were able to recall the task when the conditioning trial was established before the application of the antibodies. In vivo microdialysis revealed a dramatic lack of local extracellular levels of ACh in presence of K^+ stimulation. Furthermore, by using small injections of the neurotracer Fluorogold, we have found a corresponding disruption in the connectivity between the IC and the CBF (Gutiérrez, Miranda, & Bermúdez-Rattoni, 1997). Taken together, these results suggest that CBF input, as well as the physical connection between IC and basal forebrain, is actively dependent on cortically derived-NGF in the normal adult rat. Our behavioral results further support the notion that cholinergic activity from CBF is no longer necessary for recalling aversive memories, but it is necessary for the acquisition of aversively motivated conditionings (Gutiérrez et al., 1997).

After these results, we have postulated that cholinergic NBM cortical projection plays an important role during the early stages of learning (Gutiérrez et al., 1997; Miranda & Bermúdez-Rattoni, 1999). This view is in agreement with other authors, who have demonstrated that learning in a variety of tasks is a cholinergic-dependent process, as seen by lesions (Butt & Hodge, 1995) or measured activity of cortically projecting cholinergic neurons (Durkin & Toumane, 1992) or by postraining vulnerability to scopolamine-induced amnesia (Naor & Dudai, 1996; Toumane & Durkin, 1993).

To see the role of cholinergic activity during CTA acquisition, by means of microdialysis we are evaluating in vivo cortical ACh release during the consumption of novel, familiar taste stimuli, as well as taste in the process of becoming familiar in free-moving rats. Recent results showed a significant increment of ACh release in the IC when a novel taste, such as saccharin, was presented, as compared with the release induced by a familiar stimulus, such as water (see Figure 10.1). The ACh release decreased in a step-down fashion, when the taste became familiar during the 2nd, 3rd, and 4th saccharin presentation, reaching similar release levels as those induced by water (Miranda, Ramirez-Lugo, & Bermúdez-Rattoni, 2000). However, the preference for saccharin increased as the taste became familiar, as has been described elsewhere (Bures et al., 1998). These results suggested that the cholinergical system plays an important role in the identification and characterization of different kinds of stimuli. These results are in agreement with those published by Shimura and Yamamoto (Shimura, Suzuki, & Yamamoto, 1995), who found that intraoral

FIGURE 10.1

Release of ACh during consumption of novel and familiar taste.

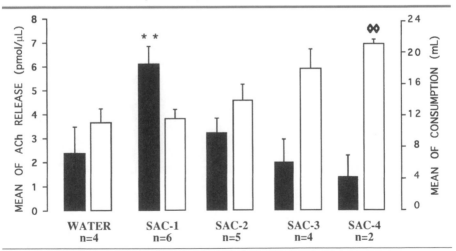

Consumption (in ml) of each group (light bars) and ACh release in the insular cortex (dark bars) during consumption of water, first presentation of saccharin as a novel taste (SAC-1), and after the taste became familiar (SAC-2, SAC-3, and SAC-4). The groups are independent. Values are M ± SEM. **p < .01 compared with ACh release during water consumption; ◊◊ p < .01 compared with water consumption.

infusions of a novel taste produced significant increments of ACh in the IC, when compared with those of the parietal cortex, during saccharin consumption.

In another series of experiments, we tried to establish the relationship between the cortical ACh activity and the CTA formation. In these experiments, the cholinergical release in the IC was measured during a reversible blockade of NBM by using bilateral microdialysis procedure in awake freely moving rats. The amounts of extracellular ACh in the IC were monitored in four groups of animals that were dialyzed, bilaterally into the NBM with either buffer or TTX, during both acquisition and retrieval. Two groups of animals received buffer during acquisition and TTX or buffer during taste test. The other two groups received TTX during acquisition and buffer or TTX during retrieval. The treatments were always given 1 hour before taste presentations in both acquisition and retrieval. The dialyzates of IC were obtained before, during, and after consumption of a novel taste (acquisition day) and before, during, and after aversively associated saccharin consumption (taste trial). The dialyzates were assayed for ACh content using HPLC (see Miranda & Bermúdez-Rattoni, 1998, 1999).

As can be seen in Figure 10.2, there is a significant cortical release of ACh just after consumption of a novel taste (BA group). However, a clear inhibition of that release was seen when the animals were perfused bilaterally with TTX into the NBM (TA; Figure 10.2B). In the test trial the group that received TTX during acquisition and buffer during the retrieval test (TA−B) had an increase of ACh release similar to that observed in the control group during the acquisition trial (see Figure 10.2B). These results suggest that blocking the NBM and, consequently, the cortical ACh release during acquisition interrupts information flow about the novelty of the stimulus and provokes, during the second presentation of that stimulus (test trial), a cortical ACh release similar to the first presentation during the acquisition. The TTX blockade of the NBM during acquisition (TA; see Figure 10.3) results in significant impairments of CTA in the animals that received buffer or TTX during the test trial (groups TA−B and TA−T). Conversely, when the animals received buffer during the acquisition, they showed normal taste aversions (BA−B and BA−T), although the group BA−T received TTX during the test (see Figure 10.3B; Miranda & Bermúdez-Rattoni, 1999).

The differential effects found indicate that only the inactivation of NBM during the acquisition phase had effects on the performance of CTA regardless of the status of the NBM during the evocation period of the behavior. Accordingly, the control group (BA), which received buffer in the NBM during acquisition, showed a significant saccharin aversion in the test trial regardless of the treatment received during the test (BA−B and BA−T). In other words, both the control group (BA−B) and the group that received TTX during the test (BA−T)

FIGURE 10.2

Cortical ACh release during reversible inactivation of the NBM.

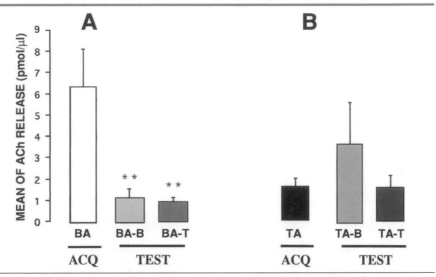

ACh release observed in the 7th dialysis fraction after the consumption of gustatory stimuli during acquisition and test of conditioned taste aversions. (A) The groups that received buffer in the nucleus basalis magnocelullaris (NBM) during acquisition (BA) and during the test recall (BA–B [buffer in test] and BA–T [TTX in test]) showed a significant decrement of ACh release regardless of the treatment received. (B) The ACh release observed in the groups that received TTX in the NBM during acquisition (TA) did not show any difference in ACh release during the test trial (TA–B and TA–T). **p < .01, paired t test.

showed strong taste aversions. Our results suggest that the release of cortical ACh during saccharin consumption in the acquisition trial could be related to recognition of the novelty of the gustatory stimulus. With this experiment we were able to directly assess the role of the ascending CBF fibers to the IC during learning of aversive memories, showing a significant disruption of CTA and a strong depletion of ACh release. In this regard Dudai and coworkers have suggested that cholinergic modulation participates in memory formation to aversive stimulus in the IC, either by encoding novelty at the cellular level or by instructing the neural circuits to store the novel taste representation (Naor & Dudai, 1996; Rosenblum, Berman, Hazvi, & Dudai, 1996).

Additionally, the involvement of ACh has been demonstrated in the acquisition of operant behavior (Orsetti, Casamenti, & Pepeu, 1996). In this experiment the authors found a significant increment of ACh release only when a steady rise in the number of lever pressings occurred, indicating that the rats began to associate lever operation with reward, and they did not find any

FIGURE 10.3

Aversion index during reversible inactivation of the NBM.

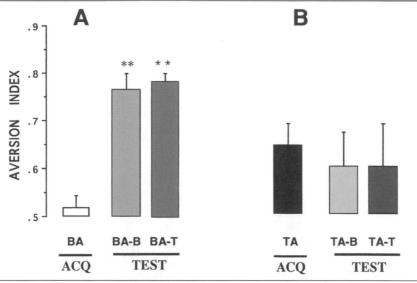

Means of aversion index defined as ml baseline consumption/(ml baseline consumption + ml test consumption) during acquisition and test of conditioned taste aversions (CTAs), e.g., 0.5 is chance level; >>0.5 is taste aversion. (A) The control group (BA) that received buffer in the nucleus basalis magnocelullaris (NBM) during acquisition showed a significant saccharin aversion regardless of the treatment received during the test trial. That is, both the control group (BA–B) and the group that received TTX (BA–T) during the CTA test showed strong taste aversion. (B) When TTX was perfused during the acquisition trial (TA), neither the buffer (TA–B) or TTX (TA–T) groups showed taste aversion. **$p < .01$, paired t test.

increase during performance after animals were well trained. This indicated that activation of the cholinergical pathways occurred during the acquisition of a rewarded operant response, whereas recall of the same behavior was not associated with the activation of the cholinergic system.

The above results suggest that the cholinergic system, as a neuromodulator, may facilitate cortical plasticity by signaling stimulus relevance during memory formation. In this regard, Bakin and Weinberger (1996) and Kilgard and Merzenich (1998) have demonstrated the role of the CBF in learning-induced plasticity. It has been shown that the convergence of acoustic information and the application of cortical ACh or electrical stimulation of the NBM induced receptive field plasticity similar to that produced by behavioral learning. Muscarinic antagonists (Bakin & Weinberger, 1996) blocked this plasticity. These results are consistent with the hypothesis that activation of the basal cholinergic system is highly involved in memory formation and are in agreement with our reports that the increase in ACh release seen during the acquisition of CTA reflects the involvement of this neurotransmitter during the early stages of memory formation.

Conclusion

Until recently, a number of studies using different experimental strategies like excitotoxic lesions of the CBF and in vivo monitoring of the release of ACh have shown that acetylcholine is involved in different aspects of memory formation. Thus, experiments using fetal brain grafts suggest that cholinergic transmission is important for the acquisition of aversively motivated learning tasks and that ACh may play a role in graft-mediated behavioral recovery. Furthermore, it was demonstrated that the release of ACh is related to the recovery of the ability to acquire CTA but seems to be less relevant to the recalling of an aversive stimulus. As mentioned, several authors (Kaneko & Thompson, 1997; Naor & Dudai, 1996; Toumane & Durkin, 1993) have found similar results by using different behavioral paradigms. For instance, acquisition, but not retrieval, of the conditioned responses is blocked with applications of scopolamine. Similarly, we observed that chronic deafferentation of the cortex by applications of anti-NGF antibodies produced a marked disruption of both ACh release, and acquisition of CTA, although the same treatment, did not affect the retrieval for aversive taste. Altogether these results strongly suggest that the role of ACh is during the acquisition phase of conditioning.

Many studies have shown that protein synthesis inhibitors produce impairments in the formation of long-term memories (Davis & Squire, 1984). In this regard, Dudai and coworkers found that application of anisomycin (a protein synthesis inhibitor) into the IC impaired CTA acquisition. However, if the same treatment was applied after the saccharin presentation or was located above the IC, it did not affect CTA (Rosenblum, Meiri, & Dudai, 1993). Furthermore, it has been demonstrated that when rats sample an unfamiliar taste either incidentally as well as during CTA training, NMDA receptor subunit NR2B undergoes tyrosine phosphorylation specifically into the IC (Rosenblum et al., 1995).

Microinjections of carbachol into the IC produced a significant enhancement of the levels of NMDA receptor subunit NR2B, similar to the effects of unfamiliar taste exposure (Rosenblum et al., 1996). In this regard, reversible blockade of NMDA receptors in the IC during training of CTA impaired acquisition and consolidation in two learning tasks, CTA and the Morris water spatial learning task (Gutiérrez, Hernández-Echeagaray, Ramírez-Amaya, & Bermúdez-Rattoni, 1999; Rosenblum et al., 1995). Therefore, in summary it seems plausible to believe that ACh activity is signaling the novelty of a given stimulus and that it induces a cellular cascade of events necessary for encoding the stimulus during the formation of long-term aversive memories.

References

Bakin, J. S., & Weinberger, N. M. (1996). Induction of a physiological memory in the cerebral cortex by stimulation of the nucleus basalis. *Proceedings of the National Academy of Sciences, 93,* 11219–11224.

Bermúdez-Rattoni, F., Introini-Collison, I. B., & McGaugh, J. L. (1991). Reversible inactivation of the insular cortex by tetrodotoxin produces retrograde and anterograde amnesia for inhibitory avoidance and spatial learning. *Proceedings of the National Academy of Sciences, 88,* 5379–5382.

Bermúdez-Rattoni, F., & McGaugh, J. L. (1991). Insular cortex and amygdala lesions differentially affect acquisition of inhibitory avoidance and conditioning taste aversion. *Brain Research, 49,* 165–170.

Braun, J. J., Lasiter, P. S., & Kiefer, S. W. (1982). The gustatory neocortex of the rat. *Physiological Psychology, 10,* 13–15.

Bures, J., Bermúdez-Rattoni, F., & Yamamoto, T. (1998). *Conditioned taste aversion* (Oxford Psychology Series, Vol. 31). London: Oxford University Press.

Butt, A. E., & Hodge, G. K. (1995). Acquisition, retention, and extinction of operant discrimination in rats with nucleus basalis magnocellularis lesions. *Behavioral Neuroscience, 109,* 699–713.

Butt, A. E., Testylier, G., & Dykes, R. (1997). Acetylcholine release in rat frontal and somatosensory cortex is enhanced during tactile discrimination learning. *Psychobiology, 25,* 18–33.

Cahill, L., Roozendaal, B., & McGaugh, J. L. (1997). The neurobiology of memory for aversive emotional events. In M. E. Bouton & M. S. Fanselow (Eds.), *Learning, motivation, and cognition: The functional behaviorism of Robert C. Bolles* (pp. 369–384). Washington, DC: American Psychological Association.

Connor, D. J., Langlais, P. J., & Thal, L. J. (1991). Behavioral impairments after lesions of the nucleus basalis by ibotenic acid and quisqualic acid. *Brain Research, 555,* 84–90.

Cuello, A. C., Maysinger, D., & Garofalo, L. (1992). Trophic factor effects on cholinergic innervation in the cerebral cortex of adult rat brain. *Molecular Neurobiology, 6,* 451–461.

Davis, H. P., & Squire, L. R. (1984). Protein synthesis and memory: A review. *Psychologica Bulletin, 96,* 518–559.

Decker, M. W., & McGaugh, J. L. (1991). The role of interactions between the cholinergic and other neuromodulatory system in learning and memory. *Synapse, 7,* 151–168.

Dunnett, S. B., Everitt, B. J., & Robbins, T. W. (1991). The basal forebrain cortical cholinergic system: Interpreting the functional consequences of excitotoxic lesions. *Trends in Neuroscience, 14,* 494–501.

Durkin, T. P., & Toumane, A. (1992). Septo-hippocampal and nBM-cortical cholinergic neurons exhibit differential time-courses of activation as a function of both type and duration of spatial memory testing in mice. *Behavioural Brain Research, 50,* 43–52.

Escobar, M. L., Jiménez, N., López-Garcia, J. C., Tapia, R., & Bermúdez-Rattoni, F. (1993). Nerve growth factor with insular cortical grafts induces recovery of learning and reestablishes graft choline acetyltransferase activity. *Journal of Neural Transplantation and Plasticity, 4,* 167–172.

Etherington, R. E., Mittleman, G., & Robbins, T. W. (1987). Comparative effects of nucleus basalis and fimbria fornix lesions on delay matching and alteration tests memory. *Neuroscience Research Communication, 22,* 441–469.

Gage, F. H., Björklund, A., Stenevi, U., Dunnet, S. B., & Kelly, O. P. (1984). Intrahippocampal grafts ameliorate learning impairments in aged rats. *Science, 225,* 533–536.

García, J., Lasiter, P. S., Bermúdez-Rattoni, F., & Deems, D. A. (1985). General theory of aversion learning. *Annals of the New York Academy of Sciences, 443,* 8–20.

Gutiérrez, H., Hernández-Echeagaray, E., Ramírez-Amaya, V., & Bermúdez-Rattoni, F. (1999). Blockade of NMDA receptors in the insular cortex disrupts taste aversion and spatial memory formation. *Neuroscience. 89,* 751–758.

Gutiérrez, H., Miranda, M. I., & Bermúdez-Rattoni, F. (1997). Learning impairments and cholinergic disjunction by direct infusion of anti-nerve growth factor antibodies into the insular cortex. *Journal of Neurosciences, 17,* 3796–3803.

Hefti, F. (1986). Nerve growth factor promotes survival of septal cholinergic neurons after fimbrial transections. *Journal of Neurosciences, 6,* 2155–2162.

Inglis, F. M., Day, J. C., & Fibiger, H. C. (1994). Enhanced acetylcholine release in hippocampus and cortex during the anticipation and consumption of a palatable meal. *Neuroscience, 62,* 1049–1056.

Kaneko, T., & Thompson, R. F. (1997). Disruption of trace conditioning of the nicitinating membrane response in rabbits by central cholinergic blockade. *Psychopharmacology, 131,* 161–166.

Kesner, R. P., Berman, R. F., & Tardif, R. (1992). Place and taste aversion learning: Role of basal forebrain, parietal cortex, and amygdala. *Brain Research Bulletin, 29,* 345–353.

Kiefer, S.W. (1985). Neural mediation of conditioned food aversions. *Annals of the New York Academy of Sciences, 443,* 100–109.

Kiefer, S. W., & Brown, J. J. (1979). Acquisition of taste avoidance habits in rats lacking gustatory neocortex. *Physiological and Psychology, 7,* 245–250.

Kilgard, M. P., & Merzenich, M. M. (1998). Cortical map reorganization enabled by nucleus basalis activity. *Science, 279,* 1714–1718.

Kornhuber, A. W. (1995). Unimanual motor learning impaired by frontomedial and insular lesions in man. *Journal of Neurology, 242,* 568–578.

Krushel, L. A., & van der Kooy, D. V. D. (1988). Visceral cortex: Integration of the mucosal senses with limbic information in the rat agranular insular cortex. *Journal of Comparative Neurology, 270,* 39–54.

Lasiter, P. S., & Glanzman, D. L. (1985). Cortical sustrates of taste aversion learning: Involvement of the dorsolateral amygdaloid nuclei and the temporal neocortex in taste aversion learning. *Behavioral Neuroscience, 99,* 257–276.

López-García, J. C., Bermúdez-Rattoni, F., & Tapia, R. (1990). Release of acetylcholine, g-aminobutyrate, dopamine and glutamate, and activity of some related enzymes, in rat gustatory neocortex. *Brain Research, 523,* 100–104.

López-García, J. C., Fernández-Ruiz, J., Escobar, M. L., Bermúdez-Rattoni, F., & Tapia, R. (1993). Effects of excitotoxic lesions of the nucleus basalis magnocellularis on conditioned taste aversion and inhibitory avoidance in the rat. *Pharmacology Biochemistry and Behavior, 45,* 147–152.

Miranda, M. I., & Bermúdez-Rattoni, F. (1998). Intracerebral dialysis of fetal brain grafts in freely moving rats during recovery of learning. *Brain Research Protocols, 2/3,* 215–222.

Miranda, M. I., & Bermúdez-Rattoni, F. (1999). Reversible inactivation of the nucleus basalis magnocellularis induces disruption of the cortical acetylcholine release and acquisition, but not retrieval, of aversive memories. *Proceedings of the National Academy of Sciences, 96,* 6478–6482.

Miranda, M. I., López-Colomé, A. M., & Bermúdez-Rattoni, F. (1997). Recovery of conditioned taste aversion induced by fetal neocortex graft: In vivo correlations of acetylcholine levels. *Brain Research, 759,* 141–148.

Miranda, M. I., Ramírez-Lugo, L., & Bermúdez-Rattoni, F. (2000). Cortical cholinergic activity is related to the novelty of the stimulus. *Brain Research, 882,* 230–235.

Naor, C., & Dudai, Y. (1996). Transient impairment of cholinergic function in the rat insular cortex disrupts the encoding of taste in conditioned taste aversion. *Brain Research, 79,* 61–67.

Ogawa, S., Nabeshima, T., Kameyama, T., & Hayashi, K. (1993). Effects of nerve growth factor (NGF) in rats with basal forebrain lesions. *Journal of Pharmacology, Japan, 61,* 141–144.

Ormsby, C., Ramírez-Amaya, V., & Bermúdez-Rattoni, F. (1998). Long-term memory retrieval deficits of learned taste aversions are ameliorated by cortical fetal brain implants. *Behavioral Neuroscience, 112,* 172–182.

Orsetti, M., Casamenti, F., & Pepeu, G. (1996). Enhanced acetylcholine release in the hippocampus and cortex during acquisition of an operant behavior. *Brain Research, 724,* 89–96.

Page, K. J., Everitt, B. J., Robbins, T. W., Marston, H. M., & Wilkinson, L. S. (1991). Dissociable effects on spatial maze and passive avoidance acquisition and retention following AMPA and ibotenic acid-induced excitotoxic lesions of the basal forebrain in rats: Differential dependence on cholinergic neuronal loss. *Neuroscience, 43,* 412–472.

Pascoe, J. P., & Kapp, B. S. (1987). Responses of amygdaloid central nucleus neurons to stimulation of the insular cortex in awake rabbits. *Neuroscience, 21,* 471–485.

Rosenblum, K., Berman, D. E., Hazvi, S., & Dudai, Y. (1996). Carbachol mimics effects of sensory input on tyrosine phosphorylation in cortex. *NeuroReport, 7,* 1401–1404.

Rosenblum, K., Meiri, N., & Dudai, Y. (1993). Taste memory: The role of protein synthesis in gustatory cortex. *Behavioral Neural Biology, 59,* 49–55.

Rosenblum, K., Shul, R., Meiri, N., Hadari, Y. R., Zick, Y., & Dudai, Y. (1995). Modulation of protein tyrosine phosphorylation in rat insular cortex after conditioned taste aversion training. *Proceedings of the National Academy of Sciences, 92,* 1157–1161.

Russell, R. W., Escobar, M. L., Booth, R. A., & Bermúdez-Rattoni, F. (1994). Accelerating behavior recovery after cortical lesions: II. In vivo evidence for cholinergic involvement. *Behavioral and Neural Biology, 61,* 81–92.

Saper, C. B. (1982). Convergence of autonomic and limbic projections in the insular cortex of the rat. *Journal of Comparative Neurology, 210,* 163–173.

Sarter, M. F., & Bruno, J. P. (1994). Cognitive functions of cortical ACh: Lessons from studies on trans-synaptic modulation of activated efflux. *Trends in Neuroscience, 17,* 217–221.

Scott, L. (1995). A positron emission tomographic study of simple phobic symptom provocation. *Archives of General Psychiatry, 52,* 20–28.

Shimura, T., Suzuki, M., & Yamamoto, T. (1995). Aversive taste stimuli facilitate extracellular acetylcholine release in the insular gustatory cortex of the rat: A microdialysis study. *Brain Research, 679,* 221–226.

Sinden, J. D., Hodges, H., & Gray, J. A., (1995). Neural transplantation and recovery of cognitive function. *Behavioral and Brain Science, 18,* 10–35.

Toumane, A., & Durkin, T. P. (1993). Time gradient for post-test vulnerability to scopolamina-induced amnesia following the initial acquisition session of a spatial reference memory task in mice. *Behavioral and Neural Biology, 60,* 139–151.

van der Kooy, D. L., Koda, L. Y., McGinty, C. R., Gerfen, C. R., & Bloom, F. E. (1984). The organization of projections from the cortex, amygdala and hypothalamus to the nucleus of the solitary tract in rat. *Journal of Comparative Neurology, 224,* 1–24.

Waite, J. J., Chen, A. D., Wardlow, M. L., Wiley, R. G., Lappi, D. A., & Thal, L. J. (1995). Immunoglobulin G-saporin produces graded behavioral and biochemical changes accompanying the loss of cholinergic neurons of the basal forebrain and cerebellar purkinje cells. *Neuroscience, 65,* 463–476.

CHAPTER 11

Amygdala Modulation of Multiple Memory Systems

Mark G. Packard

Jim McGaugh's ledger of research has resulted in seminal contributions to the understanding of the neurobiological bases of learning and memory. This chapter in part outlines an area of research that has been a focus of attention in McGaugh's laboratory, one that is designed to elucidate the neuromodulatory role of the amygdala in memory. Although early studies in the mid-1950s using lesion techniques suggested a role for the rodent amygdala in the acquisition of learned behavior (for a review, see Sarter & Markowitsch, 1985), some of the initial evidence indicating that the amygdaloid complex is involved in memory storage processes was provided by McGaugh and colleagues in studies revealing amnestic effects of posttraining electrical stimulation of the amygdala (for a review, see McGaugh & Gold, 1976). In ensuing years it has become increasingly clear that the neuromodulatory role of the amygdala in memory involves an interaction with peripheral hormonal systems activated by stress (Gold & McGaugh, 1975; for a review, see Packard, Williams, Cahill, & McGaugh, 1995). In addition, findings of studies using posttraining drug injections indicate that the amygdala mediates the memory modulatory influence of drugs affecting several neurotransmitter systems. However, for some learning tasks, the role of the amygdala in posttraining memory modulation does not appear to involve the storage of memory traces within the amygdala but rather appears to involve activation of efferent amygdala projections (e.g., stria terminalis pathway) that result in modulation of memory processes occurring in other brain structures.

In addition to examining the general neuromodulatory role of the amygdala in memory, data is reviewed that attempts to link this line of investigation with evidence indicating that the brain contains multiple memory systems (e.g.,

This research was supported by the National Institutes of Health Grants NRSA 1 F32 NS08973, RO3MH5307, and R2956973.

Packard, Hirsh, & White, 1989; Packard & McGaugh, 1992, 1996). Findings are reviewed supporting the hypothesis that the hippocampus and caudate-putamen are parts of independent memory systems, and evidence is presented suggesting that the basolateral nucleus of the amygdala exerts a modulatory influence on both hippocampal-dependent and caudate-dependent memory processes.

Amygdala Modulation of Memory

Extensive evidence indicates that the amygdala plays an important role in the modulatory effect of numerous posttraining drug treatments. Early studies suggested a role for opioid peptidergic neurotransmission in posttraining memory processes subserved by the amygdala (e.g., Gallagher & Kapp, 1978), and further research has indicated a role for the amygdala in the memory modulatory effects of noradrenergic (e.g., Introini-Collison, Miyasaki, & McGaugh, 1991), GABAergic (e.g., Brioni, Nagahara, & McGaugh, 1989; Tomaz, Anson-Dickinson, & McGaugh, 1991), glutamatergic (Izquierdo et al., 1992), and cholinergic (Introini-Collison, Arai, & McGaugh, 1989) drugs.

Although posttraining intra-amygdala administration of various agents influence memory storage processes, such treatments do not appear to store permanent memory traces within the amygdala. Rather, although the functional integrity of the amygdala is necessary to observe the memory modulatory effects of several posttraining drug treatments, this process, at least for some tasks, appears to ultimately involve an influence on memory storage in other brain structures (Packard, Cahill, & McGaugh, 1994; Packard & Teather, 1998; Packard et al., 1995). This hypothesis was originally derived in part from studies examining the effects of lesions of the stria terminalis (a major afferent–efferent pathway of the amygdala) on the memory modulatory effect of various posttraining treatments. Initial evidence indicated that lesions of the stria terminalis blocked the memory modulatory effects of both posttraining epinephrine injection (Liang & McGaugh, 1983a) and direct electrical stimulation of the amygdala (Liang & McGaugh, 1983b) on inhibitory avoidance training. Additional studies revealed that attenuation of the memory modulatory effects of posttraining treatments by stria terminalis lesions is observed for a wide range of neurochemical systems, including opioid (McGaugh, Introini-Collison, Juler, & Izquierdo, 1986), noradrenergic (Introini-Collison et al., 1991), cholinergic (Introini-Collison et al., 1989), and glucocorticoid (Roozendaal & McGaugh, 1996) systems.

Interestingly, stria terminalis lesions do not themselves impair learning or retention (Introini-Collison et al., 1989, 1991; Liang & McGaugh, 1983a, 1983b; McGaugh et al., 1986), suggesting, at least indirectly, that activation of efferent amygdala projections may serve to modulate memory storage processes occurring in other brain structures. More direct evidence is provided by findings indicating that lesions of the stria terminalis block the memory-enhancing effects of posttraining intracaudate-putamen injection of the cholinergic receptor antagonist oxotremorine on inhibitory avoidance training (Packard, Introini-Collison, & McGaugh, 1996). Taken together with anatomical evidence indicating that amygdalo–striatal projections are nonreciprocal in nature (e.g., Kita & Kitai, 1990), these behavioral findings strongly implicate efferent projections as an important component of the memory modulatory role of the amygdala.

The hypothesis that activation of efferent amygdala projections plays a general modulatory role in memory processes occurring in other brain structures has also recently been examined in the context of a multiple systems approach to memory organization in the brain, and findings of this line of research are considered below. First, evidence supporting the multiple memory systems hypothesis is briefly reviewed, focusing on the differential roles of the hippocampal system and caudate-putamen in memory. The hypothesis that the basolateral amygdala exerts a memory modulatory influence on hippocampal-dependent and caudate-dependent memory processes is then examined.

Neuroanatomical Bases of Multiple Memory Systems: Hippocampus and Caudate-Putamen

Over the past two decades, it has become increasingly evident that the mammalian brain does not contain a single memory "center" or brain structure that mediates the acquisition, consolidation, and retrieval of all types of learned information. Although it may be suggested that such a conclusion was inescapable following Karl Lashley's (1950) exhaustive and failed "search for the engram," it is also the case that Lashley's conclusion that memory functions cannot be localized in specific brain regions was, in part, incorrect. Thus, consistent with Lashley's theorizing, extensive evidence from studies employing a variety of mammalian species, including humans, monkeys, and rats, indicates that memory is organized in multiple brain systems (for a review, see Squire, Knowlton, & Musen, 1993). At the same time, however, localization of mnemonic function is also present, as these multiple brain systems differ in terms of the "type" of memory they mediate.

In rats, evidence for the multiple memory systems hypothesis is found in experiments comparing the effects of manipulations of the hippocampal system and caudate-putamen. In several studies using pairs of tasks with similar motivational, sensory, and motoric processes, lesions of the rat hippocampal system and caudate-putamen result in a double dissociation of task acquisition (Kesner, Bolland, & Dakis, 1993; McDonald & White, 1993; Packard & McGaugh,

1992; Packard et al., 1989). For example, lesions of the fimbria fornix impair acquisition of "win–shift" behavior in the radial maze, a learning task that requires rats to remember which maze arms have been visited within a daily training session (Packard et al., 1989). In contrast, fornix lesions facilitate acquisition of a simultaneous visual discrimination "win–stay" radial maze task, in which food-baited maze arms are signaled by a light cue (Packard et al., 1989). Lesions of the caudate-putamen produce the opposite pattern of effects; such lesions impair acquisition of the win–stay task but have no effect on acquisition of win–shift behavior (McDonald & White, 1993; Packard et al., 1989). A double dissociation between the mnemonic functions of the hippocampal system and caudate-putamen can also be observed using two versions of a two-platform water maze task. In this task two rubber balls, protruding above the water surface, serve as cues. One ball (correct) is on a rectangular platform that can be mounted to escape the water, and the other ball (incorrect) is mounted on a thin rod and thus does not provide escape. The two balls also differ in visual appearance (i.e., vertical vs. horizontal black-and-white stripes). In a spatial version of the task, the correct platform is located in the same location on every trial, but the visual appearance of the ball varies. Thus, this version of the task requires rats to learn to approach the correct ball on the basis of spatial location and not visual pattern. In the cued version of the task, the correct platform is located in different spatial locations across trials, but the visual pattern is consistent. Thus, this task can be acquired by learning an approach response to the visual cue (i.e., pattern discrimination). Lesions of the fornix, but not the caudate-putamen, impair acquisition of the spatial task, whereas lesions of the caudate, and not the hippocampus, impair acquisition of the cued task (Packard & McGaugh, 1992).

Evidence that the brain contains multiple memory systems has led to the proposal of several "dual-memory" theories designed to define the psychological operating principles that distinguish different forms of memory (for a review, see Kesner, 1998). Each of these theories was derived essentially from a comparison of the pattern of spared and impaired learning and memory functions observed following damage to the hippocampal system. In addition, the operating principles described in many dual-memory theories, particularly those derived from the animal literature, are heavily influenced by the historical debate between "cognitive" (e.g., Tolman, 1932) and "stimulus–response" (e.g., Hull, 1943; Thorndike, 1933) animal learning theorists. For example, the memory functions of the mammalian hippocampus have been described as essentially neo-Tolmanian in nature, whereas the types of learning spared following hippocampal system damage are often readily interpreted by stimulus–response learning theories.

In a series of experiments in the late 1940s–early 1950s (for review, see Restle, 1957), one task that served as a "battleground" for the debate between cognitive and stimulus–response learning theorists involved the use of a cross maze, an apparatus that is essentially two T mazes arranged so that a goal box (e.g., east or west) can be approached from one of two start boxes (e.g., north or south). In one version of the task, rats are trained over trials to obtain food from a consistently baited goal box (e.g., west), starting from the same start box (e.g., south). According to cognitive learning theory, rats in this task learn the spatial location of the reinforcer, and this knowledge can be used to guide an approach response to the baited goal box. In contrast, according to stimulus–response learning theory, rats can learn to approach the baited goal box by acquiring a response tendency (i.e., a specific body turn at the choice point). Although both of these theories can explain the acquisition of this task, a probe trial in which trained rats are given a trial starting from the opposite start box (e.g., north) can be used to assess the type of learning acquired. Thus, rats with knowledge of the spatial location of the reinforcer should continue to approach the baited goal box on the probe trial (i.e., place learning), whereas rats that have learned a specific body turn should choose the opposite goal box on the probe trial (i.e., response learning).

Although intact rats can use both types of learning in performing the task (depending in part on intra- and extramaze environmental conditions; for a review, see Restle, 1957), the multiple memory systems hypothesis raises the possibility that these two type of learning may have distinct neural substrates. This hypothesis was addressed in a cross-maze study designed to differentiate the role of the hippocampus and caudate-putamen in memory (Packard & McGaugh, 1996). Adult male Long–Evans rats were trained in a daily session of six trials to obtain food from a consistently baited goal box and were allowed to approach this maze arm from the same start box on each trial. Following 7 days of training (i.e., on Day 8), rats were given a probe trial to determine whether they had acquired the task using place information, or had learned a specific body turn response tendency. Prior to the probe trial, rats received intrahippocampal or intracaudate injections of either saline or the local anesthetic lidocaine, to produce neural inactivation and examine the role of these two structures in expression of the learned behavior.

As illustrated in Figure 11.1 (left), on the Day 8, probe trial rats receiving saline injections into the hippocampus or caudate-putamen were predominantly place learners. Lidocaine injection into the hippocampus blocked expression of place learning, whereas similar injections into the caudate-putamen did not. Thus, the functional integrity of the hippocampus, but not caudate-putamen, is necessary for expression of place learning.

Previous research suggests that with extended training in the cross maze, intact rats switch from the use of place learning to a response learning tendency (Restle, 1957). Therefore, the rats were trained for an additional 7 days, given a second probe trial on Day 16, and again received intracerebral injections of lidocaine or saline prior to the probe trial. As shown in Figure 11.1 (right), rats receiving saline injections into either the hippocampus or caudate-putamen were predominantly response learners on the Day 16 probe trial, confirming previous reports of a shift from the use of place information to response learning with extended training. Intrahippocampal injections of lidocaine did not block expression of response learning. However, rats receiving intracaudate injections of lidocaine exhibited place learning, demonstrating a blockade of the expression of response learning observed in control rats. These findings provide further evidence of the differential roles of the hippocampus and caudate-putamen

FIGURE 11.1

Place and response learning.

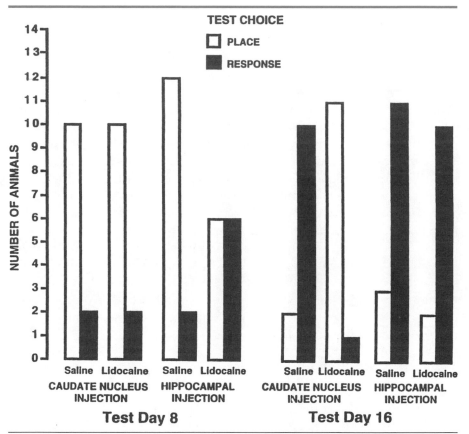

Number of rats in each treatment group that exhibited place or response learning on the Day 8 and Day 16 test trials. From "Inactivation of the Hippocampus or Caudate Nucleus with Lidocaine Differentially Affects Expression of Place and Response Learning," by M. G. Packard and J. L. McGaugh, 1996, *Neurobiology of Learning and Memory, 65,* p. 69. Copyright 1996 by Academic Press. Printed with permission.

in memory. Moreover, although hippocampal-dependent place learning is acquired quicker than caudate-dependent response learning, there is a shift in the control of learned behavior from the hippocampus to the caudate-putamen in well-trained animals. Finally, the results suggest that when this shift in strategy is made, the hippocampal-based place representation is not extinguished or "forgotten." Rather, the place representation, although not being accessed in intact rats with extended training, can be called into use by blockade of the caudate response learning system.

In addition to lesion studies, double dissociations between the roles of the hippocampus and caudate-putamen in memory have also been observed following posttraining intracerebral drug injections (Packard & Teather, 1997, 1998; Packard & White, 1991; Packard et al., 1994). For example, posttraining intrahippocampal injections of dopaminergic agonists selectively enhance memory in a win–shift radial maze task, whereas similar injections into the caudate-putamen selectively enhance memory in a win–stay radial maze task (Packard & White, 1991). Moreover, posttraining intrahippocampal injections of the glutamatergic N-methyl d-aspartate (NMDA) receptor antagonist AP5 selectively impair memory in a hidden platform water maze task, whereas similar injections into the caudate-putamen selectively impair memory in a visible platform water maze task (Packard & Teather, 1997). In both the hippocampus and caudate-putamen, the effects of the posttraining treatments are time dependent; injections delayed 2 hours posttraining have no effect on memory. The time-dependent nature of these posttraining injections strongly implicates these brain regions in modulation of memory processes (McGaugh, 1966), and the task-dependent nature of the treatments indicates a role for the hippocampus and caudate-putamen in different types of memory.

Amygdala Modulation of Hippocampal and Caudate-Putamen Memory Systems

As reviewed earlier, extensive evidence suggests that the amygdala plays a neuromodulatory role in memory, and it has been suggested that activation of efferent amygdala projections (e.g., stria terminalis) modulates memory storage processes occurring in other brain structures. Although the rodent amygdaloid complex projects to widespread regions of the brain, it is of particular interest that both the hippocampal system and caudate-putamen receive efferent amygdala projections originating in basolateral and lateral nuclei (for a review, see Alheid, de Olmos, & Beltramino, 1995). In addition to anatomical evidence of amygdala connectivity with the hippocampal system and caudate-putamen, data from electrophysiological and molecular studies suggest a functional interaction between the amygdala and these two structures. For example, injection of

NMDA into the basolateral nucleus induces *c-fos* expression in both the hippocampus (dentate gyrus) and caudate-putamen (Packard et al., 1995). Furthermore, electrical stimulation of the basolateral amygdala evokes field potentials in the dentate gyrus, and synaptic plasticity in the hippocampus (e.g., long-term potentiation) is attenuated by lesions of the basolateral amygdala (Ikegaya, Saito, & Abe, 1995).

In view of evidence indicating that the hippocampus and caudate-putamen are parts of independent memory systems, one test of the hypothesis that the amygdala plays a general modulatory role in memory is to examine the effects of amygdala manipulations on hippocampal-dependent and caudate-dependent tasks. In experiments examining this implication (Packard & Teather, 1998; Packard et al., 1994), adult male Long–Evans rats received a single eight-trial training session in either a hidden or visible platform water maze task. In the hippocampal-dependent hidden platform water maze task, a submerged escape platform is located in the same spatial location on all trials, and acquisition of this task may require rats to learn the spatial location of the hidden escape platform relative to the topographical relationship among extramaze cues. In the caudate-dependent visible platform task, a visibly cued escape platform is moved to a new spatial location on each trial (i.e., one of four maze quadrants). Acquisition of this task may involve the formation of a stimulus (platform)– response (approach) habit. In both water maze tasks, rats learn to approach the platform from different start positions around the perimeter of the maze. On escape, rats were allowed to stay on the platform for 20 seconds and then were removed from the maze for a 30-second intertrial interval. Twenty-four hours after training, rats were returned to the maze for a retention test, and latency to escape to the platform was used as a measure of memory in both tasks. In each of the studies described here, there were no group differences in rate of task acquisition of naïve rats (i.e., prior to the posttraining treatments), indicating that any differences observed in retention are not due to differential rates of task acquisition among groups. Under the training parameters used, in a typical acquisition curve over the eight-trial training session, rats improve from a group mean escape latency of approximately 60 seconds on Trial 1 (i.e., maximum swim time allowed) to group means of approximately 10–15 seconds on Trial 8.

The experiments were designed to address three primary questions: (a) Are the effects of intrahippocampal, intracaudate, and intra-amygdala injections of amphetamine task-dependent? (b) Do intracerebral injections of amphetamine enhance memory via a "storage" process in the structure in which amphetamine was injected, or a "modulatory" influence on other brain sites? (c) Do intra-amygdala injections of amphetamine enhance memory via an efferent modulatory influence on the hippocampus and caudate-putamen?

In the first set of experiments (Packard & Teather, 1998; Packard et al.,

1994), immediately following training in either water maze task, unilaterally (left side) cannulated rats received a posttraining injection of the indirect catecholamine agonist amphetamine or saline into the dorsal hippocampus, posteroventral caudate nucleus, or basolateral amygdala (0.5 μl injection volume). As shown in Figure 11.2, the effects of intrahippocampal injections of amphetamine are task dependent; the injections enhanced memory in the hidden platform task and had no effect in the visible platform task. Intracaudate injections of amphetamine were also task dependent; the injections enhanced memory in the visible platform task, but had no effect on memory in the hidden platform task (Figure 11.3). These findings provide further evidence of a double dissociation of the mnemonic functions of the hippocampus and caudate-putamen. In both tasks and brain structures, the effects of the injections were

FIGURE 11.2

Effects of posttraining hippocampal amphetamine.

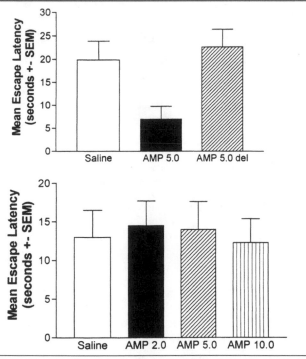

Effects of posttraining intrahippocampal injection of amphetamine on memory in hidden platform (top) and visible platform (bottom) water maze tasks. Doses are expressed in micrograms. AMP = amphetamine; del = injection delayed 2 hours posttraining. Adapted from Figure 4 in "Amygdala Modulation of Multiple Memory Systems: Hippocampus and Caudate-Putamen," by M. G. Packard and L. A. Teather, 1998, *Neurobiology of Learning and Memory, 69*, p. 174. Copyright 1998 by Academic Press. Adapted with permission.

FIGURE 11.3

Effects of posttraining intracaudate amphetamine.

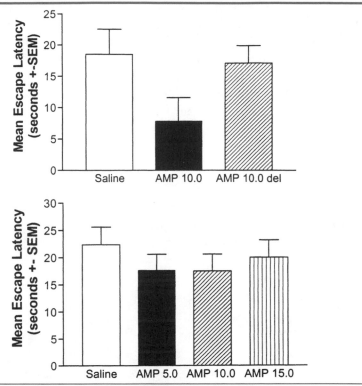

Effects of posttraining intracaudate injection of amphetamine on memory in visible
platform (top) and hidden platform (bottom) water maze tasks. Doses are
expressed in micrograms. AMP = amphetamine; del = injection delayed 2 hours
posttraining. Adapted from Figure 6 in "Amygdala Modulation of Multiple
Memory Systems: Hippocampus and Caudate-Putamen," by M. G. Packard and
L. A. Teather, 1998, *Neurobiology of Learning and Memory, 69,* p. 176.
Copyright 1998 by Academic Press. Adapted with permission.

time dependent; injections that were delayed 2 hours posttraining did not affect
memory. The time-dependent nature of the posttraining injections is consistent
with the hypothesis that the treatments influence a memory consolidation process and also rule out the possibility that the effects of the immediate injections
on retention are due to a proactive, nonmnemonic drug effect (McGaugh,
1966).

In contrast to the task-dependent effect of the intrahippocampal and intracaudate injections, intrabasolateral amygdala injections of amphetamine enhanced memory in both water maze tasks in a time-dependent manner (Figure
11.4). The nontask-dependent nature of the intra-amygdala injections is con-

FIGURE 11.4

Effects of posttraining intraamygdala amphetamine.

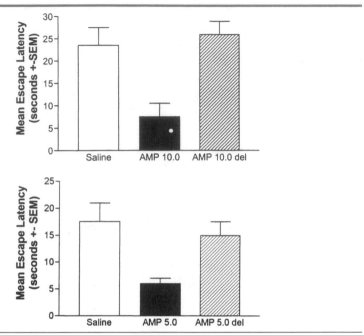

Effects of posttraining intrabasolateral nucleus injection of amphetamine on memory in hidden platform (top) and visible platform (bottom) water maze tasks. Doses are expressed in micrograms. AMP = amphetamine; del = injection delayed 2 hours posttraining. Adapted from Figures 5 and 7 in "Amygdala Modulation of Multiple Memory Systems: Hippocampus and Caudate-Putamen," by M. G. Packard and L. A. Teather, 1998, *Neurobiology of Learning and Memory, 69,* pp. 175, 177. Copyright 1998 by Academic Press. Adapted with permission.

sistent with the hypothesis that the amygdala may exert a modulatory influence on the hippocampus and caudate nucleus; however, it is also possible that the injections enhanced memory in both tasks via a storage process within the amygdala. To examine this hypothesis, rats trained in either water maze task received posttraining intracerebral injections of amphetamine or saline and a preretention test injection of the local anesthetic lidocaine (2% solution/10 μg/ 0.5 μl) or saline (0.5 μl). If the memory-enhancing effects of amphetamine are mediated by storage within the structure in which amphetamine is injected, then preretention test lidocaine should block expression of this enhancement. Preretention intrahippocampal lidocaine injections block expression of the memory-enhancing effects of intrahippocampal amphetamine in the hidden platform task, and a similar pattern of results is observed using caudate injections in the visible platform task. These findings are consistent with the hypothesis that posttraining amphetamine injections into these two structures may act to enhance memory storage within these brain sites. In contrast, preretention test intra-amygdala injections of lidocaine do not block the memory-enhancing effects of posttraining intra-amygdala amphetamine in either water maze task (Figure 11.5). This finding indicates that intra-amygdala amphetamine is acting to enhance memory via a modulatory influence in other brain regions, although the findings do not directly identify these sites.

In an additional set of experiments (Packard & Teather, 1998), the hypothesis that the amygdala exerts a memory modulatory influence on the hippocampus and caudate-putamen was examined. In these studies, rats were unilaterally cannulated in two brain structures (basolateral amygdala–caudate or basolateral amygdala–hippocampus). Immediately following training in either water maze task, rats received concurrent posttraining injections of ampheta-

FIGURE 11.5

Amygdala modulation, not storage, of memory.

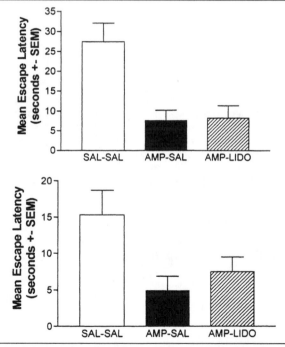

Effects of posttraining intrabasolateral amygdala injections of amphetamine and preretention intra-amygdala injections of lidocaine on retention in hidden platform (top; 10 μg AMP) and visible platform (bottom; 5 μg AMP) water maze tasks. SAL = saline; AMP = amphetamine; LIDO = lidocaine. Adapted from Figures 10 and 11 in "Amygdala Modulation of Multiple Memory Systems: Hippocampus and Caudate-Putamen," by M. G. Packard and L. A. Teather, 1998, *Neurobiology of Learning and Memory, 69*, pp. 181, 182. Copyright 1998 by Academic Press. Adapted with permission.

mine or saline into the amygdala, and lidocaine or saline into the hippocampus or caudate-putamen. In the hidden platform task intrahippocampal, but not intracaudate, lidocaine injections blocked the memory-enhancing effects of intra-amygdala amphetamine (Figure 11.6). In the visible platform task intracaudate, but not intrahippocampal, lidocaine injections blocked the memory-enhancing effects of intra-amygdala amphetamine (Figure 11.7). Thus, a memory system that includes the hippocampus receives a modulatory influence from the amygdala in the hidden platform task, whereas a memory system that includes the caudate-putamen receives a modulatory influence from the amygdala in the visible platform task.

It is important to note that the ability of intra-amygdala injections of am-

FIGURE 11.6
Amygdala modulation of the hippocampus.

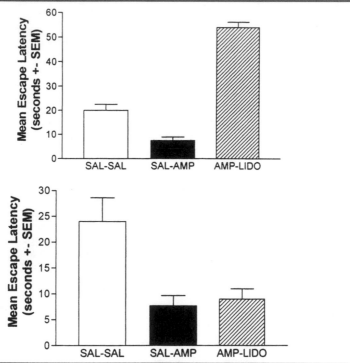

Effects of concurrent posttraining intrabasolateral amygdala injections of amphetamine (10 μg) and intrahippocampal injections of lidocaine on memory in a hidden platform (top) and visible platform (bottom) water maze tasks. SAL = saline; AMP = amphetamine; LIDO = lidocaine. Adapted from Figure 13 in "Amygdala Modulation of Multiple Memory Systems: Hippocampus and Caudate-Putamen," by M. G. Packard and L. A. Teather, 1998, *Neurobiology of Learning and Memory, 69*, p. 187. Copyright 1998 by Academic Press. Adapted with permission.

FIGURE 11.7

Amygdala modulation of caudate-putamen.

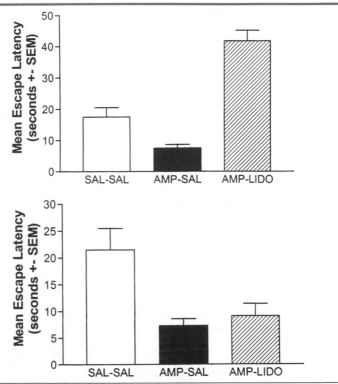

Effects of concurrent posttraining intrabasolateral amygdala injections of amphetamine (5 μg) and intracaudate injections of lidocaine on memory in a visible platform (top) and hidden platform (bottom) water maze tasks. SAL = saline; AMP = amphetamine; LIDO = lidocaine. Adapted from Figure 13 in "Amygdala Modulation of Multiple Memory Systems: Hippocampus and Caudate-Putamen," by M. G. Packard and L. A. Teather, 1998, *Neurobiology of Learning and Memory, 69,* p. 187. Copyright 1998 by Academic Press. Adapted with permission.

phetamine to enhance memory in both water maze tasks is not simply due to the aversive motivational nature of the tasks. The rationale for the hypothesis that the aversive nature of the tasks may be an important factor derives from extensive evidence indicating that lesions of the amygdala impair the acquisition and retention of various Pavlovian fear-conditioning tasks (for reviews, see Davis, 1992; LeDoux, 1998). However, lesions of the amygdaloid complex do not impair the acquisition of either the hidden (Sutherland & McDonald, 1990) or visible (Cahill, Packard, & McGaugh, unpublished data, 1994) platform water maze tasks. These findings mirror the lack of effect of stria terminalis lesions on tasks in which posttraining treatments nonetheless exert a robust memory modulatory effect. Furthermore, when rats are tested differently in the water maze task than that in which they were trained (i.e., trained in the visible platform task and tested in the hidden platform task or vice versa), intra-amygdala injections of amphetamine do not enhance memory (Packard & Teather, unpublished data, 1998). If the memory-enhancing effects of amphetamine were due to an influence on a common underlying "fear" process, then such enhancement might be observed regardless of the type of training received, because the two tasks share the same motivational properties. In addition, amygdala modulation of hippocampal-dependent memory processes is not restricted to aversively motivated tasks; posttraining intra-amygdala injections of amphetamine also enhance memory in an appetitively motivated win–shift radial maze task (Schroeder & Packard, 1998).

The modulation view of amygdala function in memory is distinct from that proposed by investigators examining the role of the amygdala in Pavlovian fear conditioning (e.g., Davis, 1992; LeDoux, 1998) and stimulus–reward learning tasks (e.g., Everitt, Morris, O'Brien, & Robbins, 1991; Hiroi & White, 1991), in which evidence suggests that the amygdala plays a memory storage role. However, although the modulatory and storage theories of amygdala function in memory may be construed as competing ideas, there is no a priori reason to assume that they are mutually exclusive. This is particularly true in view of the anatomical complexity of the amygdaloid complex, the use of different learning tasks to elucidate these two hypotheses, and the differential reliance on pre- versus posttraining amygdala manipulations in studying fear conditioning, stimulus–reward learning, and memory modulation, respectively (for a discussion, see Packard & Teather, 1998). Clearly, further research examining these two hypotheses across similar experimental settings and parameters is necessary to determine whether the role of the amygdala in memory is best described as involving modulation of memory in other brain structures, storage of learned associations underlying fear or reward, or both.

Conclusion

The evidence reviewed suggests that the basolateral amygdala exerts a robust neuromodulatory influence on memory storage processes. This influence involves an interaction with peripheral stress hormone systems and several neurotransmitters within the amygdala, including norepinephrine, opioid peptides, GABA, and acetylcholine. Lesions of the stria terminalis block the memory modulatory effects of numerous posttraining treatments, without themselves affecting memory in untreated animals, suggesting that activation of efferent amygdala pathways may modulate memory processes occurring in other brain structures.

Findings of studies using a systems approach to understanding the organization of memory in the brain support the hypothesis that the brain contains multiple systems that differ in terms of the type of memory they mediate. Findings of double dissociation experiments using both irreversible and reversible lesion techniques, as well as intracerebral posttraining drug injections, indicate that the hippocampal system and caudate-putamen are parts of independent memory systems.

The general memory modulatory influence of the basolateral amygdala can be observed in studies in which intra-amygdala injections of amphetamine enhance memory in both hippocampal-dependent and caudate-dependent memory tasks. Moreover, this effect does not involve storage of memory traces within the amygdala in these tasks, but rather activation of efferent amygdala projections to separate memory systems that include the hippocampus and caudate-putamen.

References

Alheid, G. F., de Olmos, J. S., & Beltramino, C. A. (1995). Amygdala and extended amygdala. In G. Paxinos (Ed.), *The rat nervous system* (pp. 495–572). New York: Academic Press.

Brioni, J. D., Nagahara, A. H., & McGaugh, J. L. (1989). Involvement of the amygdala GABAergic system in the modulation of memory storage. *Brain Research, 487,* 105–112.

Davis, M. (1992). The role of the amygdala in conditioned fear. In J. P. Aggleton (Ed.), *The amygdala: Neurobiological aspects of emotion, memory, and mental dysfunction* (pp. 255–306). New York: Wiley-Liss.

Everitt, B. J., Morris, K. A., O'Brien, A., & Robbins, T. W. (1991). The basolateral amygdala–ventral striatal system and conditioned place preference: Further evidence of limbic–striatal interactions underlying reward-related processes. *Neuroscience, 42,* 1–18.

Gallagher, M., & Kapp, B. S. (1978). Manipulation of opiate activity in the amygdala alters memory processes. *Life Sciences, 23,* 1973–1978.

Gold, P. E., & McGaugh, J. L. (1975). A single-trace, two process view of memory storage processes. In D. Deutsch & J. A. Deutsch (Eds.), *Short term memory* (pp. 355–378). New York: Academic Press.

Hiroi, N., & White, N. M. (1991). The lateral nucleus of the amygdala mediates expression of the amphetamine conditioned place preference. *Journal of Neuroscience, 11,* 2107–2116.

Hull, C. L. (1943). *Principles of behavior.* New York: Appleton-Century-Crofts.

Ikegaya, Y., Saito, H., & Abe, K. (1995). Requirement of basolateral amygdala neuron activity for the induction of long-term potentiation in the dentate gyrus in vivo. *Brain Research, 671,* 351–354.

Introini-Collison, I. B., Arai, Y., & McGaugh, J. L. (1989). Stria terminalis lesions attenuate the effects of post-training oxotremorine and atropine on retention. *Psychobiology, 17,* 397–401.

Introini-Collison, I. B., Miyasaki, B., & McGaugh, J. L. (1991). Involvement of the amygdala in the memory enhancing effects of clenbuterol. *Psychopharmacology, 104,* 541–544.

Izquierdo, I., da Chuna, C., Rosat, R., Jerusalinsky, D., Ferreira, M. C. B., & Medina, J. H. (1992). Neurotransmitter receptors involved in post-training memory processing by the amygdala, medial septum, and hippocampus of the rat. *Behavioral and Neural Biology, 58,* 16–26.

Kesner, R. P. (1998). Neurobiological views of memory. In J. L. Martinez & R. P. Kesner (Eds.), *The neurobiology of learning and memory* (pp. 361–416). San Diego: Academic Press.

Kesner, R. P., Bolland, B. L., & Dakis, M. (1993). Memory for spatial locations, motor responses, and objects: Triple dissociation among the hippocampus, caudate nucleus, and extrastriate visual cortex. *Experimental Brain Research, 93,* 462–470.

Kita, H., & Kitai, S. T. (1990). Amygdaloid projections to the frontal cortex and striatum in the rat. *Journal of Comparative Neurology, 298,* 40–49.

Lashley, K. (1950). In search of the engram. *Symposia of the Society for Experimental Biology, 4,* 454–482.

LeDoux, J. E. (1998). Fear and the brain: Where have we been and where are we going? *Biological Psychiatry, 44,* 1229–1238.

Liang, K. C., & McGaugh, J. L. (1983a). Lesions of the stria terminalis attenuate the amnestic effect of amygdaloid stimulation on avoidance responses. *Brain Research, 274,* 309–318.

Liang, K. C., & McGaugh, J. L. (1983b). Lesions of the stria terminalis attenuate the enhancing effect of post-training epinephrine on retention of an inhibitory avoidance response. *Behavioral Brain Research, 9,* 49–58.

McDonald, R. J., & White, N. M. (1993). A triple dissociation of memory systems: Hippocampus, amygdala, and dorsal striatum. *Behavioral Neuroscience, 107,* 3–22.

McGaugh, J. L. (1966). Time-dependent processes in memory storage. *Science, 153,* 1351–1358.

McGaugh, J. L., & Gold, P. E. (1976). Modulation of memory by electrical stimulation of the brain. In M. R. Rosenzweig & E. L. Bennett (Eds.), *Neural mechanisms of learning and memory* (pp. 549–560). Cambridge, MA: MIT Press.

McGaugh, J. L., Introini-Collison, I. B., Juler, R. G., & Izquierdo, I. (1986). Stria terminalis lesions attenuate the effects of post-training naloxone and beta-endorphin on retention. *Behavioral Neuroscience, 100,* 839–844.

Packard, M. G., Cahill, L., & McGaugh, J. L. (1994). Amygdala modulation of hippocampal-dependent and caudate nucleus-dependent memory processes. *Proceedings of the National Academy of Sciences, 91,* 8477–8481.

Packard, M. G., Hirsh, R., & White, N. M. (1989). Differential effects of fornix and caudate nucleus lesions on two radial maze tasks: Evidence for multiple memory systems. *Journal of Neuroscience, 9,* 1465–1472.

Packard, M. G., Introini-Collison, I. B., & McGaugh, J. L. (1996). Stria terminalis lesions attenuate memory enhancement produced by intra-caudate nucleus injections of oxotremorine. *Neurobiology of Learning and Memory, 65,* 278–282.

Packard, M. G., & McGaugh, J. L. (1992). Double dissociation of fornix and caudate nucleus lesions on acquisition of two water maze tasks: Further evidence for multiple memory systems. *Behavioral Neuroscience, 106,* 439–446.

Packard, M. G., & McGaugh, J. L. (1996). Inactivation of the hippocampus or caudate nucleus with lidocaine differentially affects expression of place and response learning. *Neurobiology of Learning and Memory, 65,* 65–72.

Packard, M. G., & Teather, L. A. (1997). Double dissociation of hippocampal and dorsal striatal memory systems by post-training intracerebral injections of 2-amino-phosphonopentanoic acid. *Behavioral Neuroscience, 111,* 543–551.

Packard, M. G., & Teather, L. A. (1998). Amygdala modulation of multiple memory systems: Hippocampus and caudate-putamen. *Neurobiology of Learning and Memory, 69,* 163–203.

Packard, M. G., & White, N. M. (1991). Dissociation of hippocampus and caudate nucleus memory systems by posttraining intracerebral injection of dopamine agonists. *Behavioral Neuroscience, 105,* 295–306.

Packard, M. G., Williams, C. L., Cahill, L., & McGaugh, J. L. (1995). The anatomy of a memory modulatory system: From periphery to brain. In N. E. Spear, L. P. Spear, & M. L. Woodruff (Eds.), *Neurobehavioral plasticity: Learning, development, and response to brain insults* (pp. 149–183). Hillsdale, NJ: Erlbaum.

Restle, F. (1957). Discrimination of cues in mazes: A resolution of the place vs. response controversy. *Psychological Review, 64,* 217–228.

Roozendaal, B., & McGaugh, J. L. (1996). The memory modulatory effects of glucocorticoids depend on an intact stria terminalis. *Brain Research, 709,* 243–250.

Sarter, M. A., & Markowitsch, H. J. (1985). Involvement of the amygdala in learning and memory: A critical review, with emphasis on anatomical relations. *Behavioral Neuroscience, 99,* 342–380.

Schroeder, J. P., & Packard, M. G. (1998). Amygdala modulation of appetitively motivated hippocampal-dependent memory. *Society for Neuroscience Abstracts, 24,* 1900.

Squire, L. R., Knowlton, B. J., & Musen, G. (1993). The structure and organization of memory. *Annual Review of Psychology, 44,* 453–495.

Sutherland, R. J., & McDonald, R. J. (1990). Hippocampus, amygdala, and memory deficits in rats. *Behavioral Brain Research, 37,* 57–79.

Thorndike, E. L. (1933). A proof of the law of effect. *Science, 77,* 173–175.

Tolman, E. C. (1932). *Purposive behavior in animals and men.* New York: Appleton-Century Crofts.

Tomaz, C., Dickinson-Anson, H., & McGaugh, J. L. (1991). Amygdala lesions block the amnestic effects of diazepam. *Brain Research, 568,* 85–91.

CHAPTER 12

Neurochemical Referees of Dueling Memory Systems

Paul E. Gold, Christa McIntyre, Ewan McNay, Mark Stefani, and Donna L. Korol

I began my postdoctoral work in Jim McGaugh's lab in 1970 at an interesting juncture between two eras of memory consolidation research, the transition from one to the other motivated largely by Jim's work. By the early 1970s, Jim had documented carefully a range of treatments and conditions under which retrograde amnesia and retrograde enhancement were clearly seen. On the horizon, however, was the fact that the temporal gradients of retrograde effects on memory were not a basic property of memory formation *per se*, but were a property of the efficacy of different treatments and doses. There was a morning in 1973 when Jim came to my desk and announced, "I feel the need for a new theory." Perhaps by coincidence (but, in retrospect, I think Jim knew what was coming), I had just finished analyzing data showing that multiple retrograde amnesia gradients could be produced by different intensities of supraseizure electrical stimulation of the neocortex (Gold, Macri, & McGaugh, 1973).The implication was that a single time course for memory consolidation might not be forthcoming from studies of retrograde effects on memory. Jim encouraged me to formalize the new thinking about temporal gradients, rejecting each attempt at a new theory by counterexplanation, until the product emerged in which we began to use the term *modulation* instead of *consolidation* of memory. That revision of how we thought about memory guides my research to this day, and a current version is presented in this chapter.—Paul E. Gold

This chapter has two main goals. The first is to describe the transition from hormonal modulation of memory to more recent work on glucose and memory, including ideas about cellular mechanisms by which glucose might act

The research described in this chapter was supported by research grants from the National Institute on Aging (AG 07648), the National Institute of Neurological Diseases and Stroke (NS 32914), and the National Science Foundation (IBN-0081061).

in the brain. The second is to describe the way in which modulation of memory, when applied to multiple memory systems, may represent the mode of regulation through which multiple memory systems interact and compete for memory processing. We propose that modulators of memory might determine not only the strength or quantity of memory formation for an experience, but also the character or quality of memory for that experience.

Neuroendocrine Modulation of Memory

Before describing the evidence that release or administration of hormones can modulate memory formation, it is perhaps instructive to consider the initial rationale for testing the role of hormones in regulating memory. When Jim McGaugh began his work on memory consolidation in the late 1950s, there was only a bit of information showing retrograde amnesia gradients that suggested that memory formation was sensitive to impairing treatments. By the end of the 1960s, largely because of Jim's research, there was overwhelming evidence that a host of treatments administered after an experience could enhance or impair memory in a time-dependent retrograde manner. One goal of this research, a goal embedded in the name of the topic, "memory consolidation," was that the temporal properties of memory formation would be revealed by the time-dependent nature of the retrograde effects on memory (McGaugh, 1966; McGaugh & Dawson, 1971). The temporal properties of memory formation, that is, how long short-term memory lasted, how long it took for intermediate- or long-term memory to be formed, would provide an important, even critical, bit of information that would reveal the possible biological bases of memory formation.

But, the intended time-constant never emerged. Instead, there were multiple temporal gradients across laboratories, treatments, and intensities or doses of a particular treatment. For example, some retrograde amnesia gradients were quite short, on the order of seconds, whereas others were as long as hours and even days (cf. McGaugh & Herz, 1972). Now, *memory consolidation* is a term sometimes used to refer to long retrograde amnesia gradients (cf. Nadel & Moskowitch, 1997), such as those that last across weeks in rats (e.g., Cho & Kesner, 1996; Knowlton & Fanselow, 1998; Winocur, 1990), months in non-human primates (Zola-Morgan & Squire, 1990), and years in humans (Reed & Squire, 1998; Squire & Alvarez, 1995). Evidently, there is no single temporal gradient but a plethora of temporal gradients. Any one gradient, therefore, does not likely reveal a temporal property of memory formation *per se*. Instead, the general principle of retrograde amnesia gradients is that they demonstrate decreasing susceptibility to modification over time after training (Gold & McGaugh, 1975). In contemporary terms, these findings might reflect many biological processes, including anatomical reorganization (see Greenough, chapter 4, this volume), switching synapses from silent to active (Swain et al., 1995), and initiation of biochemical cascades that can include gene expression (Abel, Martin, Bartsch, & Kandel, 1998; Izquierdo & Medina, 1997; Rose, 1995). Some of these processes must occur in series and others in parallel, with consolidation in its original form being a reasonable term to describe gradual accrual of neural reorganizations representing memory formation.

From the perspective of the 1970s, and from our perspective now, why do the neurobiological mechanisms of memory formation proceed through a set of processes that can be modified, with decreasing efficiency, after an experience has ended? Instead, why does the biological plan for memory not proceed in a rapid and relatively irrevocable manner? Thoughts like these led to the view that experiences might elicit physiological responses that regulate the formation of memory for that experience. In this light, stress and arousal reactions to an experience would serve well as regulators of memory (Gold & McGaugh, 1975). Likely components of these physiological events, such as hormonal responses, would often outlast the experience. A reasonable biological plan for memory formation might well make use of these responses to select and to modulate which memories should be stored. In this regard, components of high arousal such as hormonal responses might identify times when memories—memories of the principal event as well as ancillary events—would be stored more readily and efficiently than at times of low arousal (Cahill & McGaugh, 1998; Gold, 1992; Reisberg & Heuer, 1995; Winograd & Neisser, 1992).

Although there are several hormones and neurotransmitter systems that contribute to modulation of memory, the best-characterized example of hormonal regulation of memory is that by epinephrine. Epinephrine is released into the circulation in a graded manner from the adrenal medulla in response to stress or novelty (Gold & McCarty, 1995; Mabry, McCarty, Gold, & Foster, 1996; McCarty & Gold, 1996). Posttraining administration of epinephrine is well established as a treatment that enhances memory for many tasks in rodents (Gold, 1992, 1995; McGaugh, 1983). Figure 12.1 shows an early demonstration of enhancement of memory by peripheral injections of epinephrine administered to rats shortly after training in an inhibitory avoidance task (Gold & van Buskirk, 1975). This figure illustrates the inverted-U dose–response curve and the time-dependent enhancement of memory that are characteristic of the effects on memory of many drugs.

Glucose Regulation of Memory

These findings have led to questions of the mechanisms by which epinephrine enhances memory. There are several ideas about possible mechanisms, with

FIGURE 12.1

Epinephrine enhancement of memory for inhibitory avoidance training in rats.

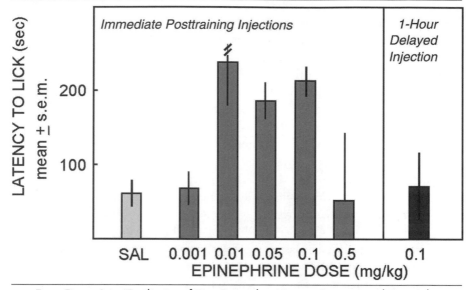

From Figure 1 in "Facilitation of Time Dependent Memory Processes with Posttrial Epinephrine Injections," by P. E. Gold and R. B. van Buskirk, 1975, *Behavioral Biology, 13*, p. 148. Copyright 1975 by Academic Press. Adapted with permission of the publisher.

continuing research likely to provide evidence that several mechanisms contribute in parallel to epinephrine effects on memory. One possibility involves actions of epinephrine on vagal afferents terminating in the nucleus of the solitary tract (for a review, see Williams and Clayton, chapter 8, this volume). In our laboratory, we have focused on glucose as an intermediary step between circulating epinephrine and memory enhancement. Epinephrine has limited access to the central nervous system (CNS) but acts peripherally to increase circulating glucose levels, largely by liberating hepatic glucose stores (Ellis, Kennedy, Eusebi, & Vincent, 1967).

As shown by many investigators (Gold, 1986; Messier & White, 1984; for reviews, see Gold, 1991, 1995; White, 1991), glucose administration enhances memory for many tasks (Gold, 1995), making glucose a likely contributor to epinephrine effects on memory. Like epinephrine, glucose administration enhances memory in a dose- and time-dependent manner (Figure 12.2).

Thus, there is substantial evidence showing that increases in circulating glucose contribute to epinephrine's effects on memory. Largely because of the safety of glucose as a treatment, a considerable literature has developed showing

FIGURE 12.2

Enhancement of memory for inhibitory avoidance training with posttraining injections of glucose.

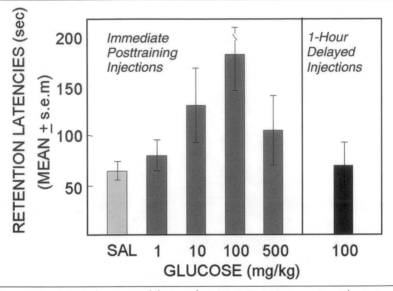

From Figure 1 in "Glucose Modulation of Memory Storage Processing," by P. E. Gold, 1986, *Behavioral and Neural Biology, 45*, p. 345. Copyright 1986 by Academic Press. Used with permission of the publisher.

that glucose enhances cognitive functions in humans, particularly on measures of verbal declarative memory (cf. Benton, Parker, & Donohoe, 1996; Korol & Gold, 1998; Messier & Gagnon, 1996). These demonstrations have been made in a wide range of populations, first in healthy elderly humans (Craft, Murphy, & Wemstrom, 1994; Hall, Gonder-Frederick, Chewning, Silveira, & Gold, 1989; Manning, Hall, & Gold, 1990; Manning, Parsons, Cotter, & Gold, 1997; Manning, Parsons, & Gold, 1992; Manning, Stone, Korol, & Gold, 1998), later in people with Alzheimer's disease and Down's syndrome (Craft, Zallen & Baker, 1992; Craft et al., 1993; Manning, Honn, Stone, Jane, & Gold, 1998; Manning, Ragozzino, & Gold, 1993), and then in college students (Korol et al., 1995; Owens, Parker, & Benton, 1997). In Alzheimer's patients, glucose enhances performance on several cognitive functions, including a marked increase in memory for a narrative passage (Figure 12.3). In humans as in rodents, glucose is effective if administered within a posttraining design (Manning et al., 1992) and the dose–response relationship for the effects of glucose on memory follow !n inverted-U function (Parsons & Gold, 1992).

FIGURE 12.3

Glucose enhancement of cognitive functions in patients with Alzheimer's disease.

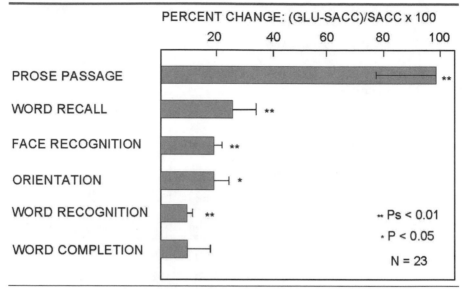

From "Glucose Enhancement of Memory in Patients with Alzheimer's Disease," by C. A. Manning, M. Ragozzino, and P. E. Gold, 1993, *Neurobiology of Aging, 14*, p. 526. Copyright 1993 by Elsevier Science. Adapted with permission of the publisher.

Neurobiological Bases for Glucose Effects on Memory

Studies on rodents have provided substantial information about the neurobiological bases for the effects of glucose on memory. Three main sets of findings are reviewed here:

1. decreases in extracellular glucose levels while rats are engaged in cognitive tasks and replenishment of those levels with memory-enhancing doses of glucose

2. regulation of K^+-ATP channels, a mechanism by which glucose may regulate neurotransmitter release and cell excitability

3. regulation of acetylcholine output during learning.

Fluctuations in Brain Extracellular Glucose Levels During Learning

Although it is generally presumed that available brain glucose saturates uptake processes (Lund-Andersen, 1979), more recent findings indicate that extracellular glucose levels in the brain are lower than previously thought and, especially important to understanding how glucose administration might influence brain functions, that the extracellular levels decrease in response to cognitive demand. Early models of glucose transport suggested that brain extracellular glucose levels were only a bit lower than the 5 mM seen in blood. Later evidence suggested that the concentration might be as low as 2 mM (Lund-Andersen, 1979).

More recent evidence suggests values even lower than that. The measurement of glucose in awake, freely moving rats, poses special problems, because most methods used to measure glucose, for example, *in vivo* microdialysis, require removal of the substance at the time of testing, with subsequent dynamic changes in glucose delivery to the site of measurement. We as well as others have coupled *in vivo* microdialysis with zero-net-flux procedures in which the glucose infused into the dialysis probe is varied to determine the concentration at which the glucose concentration in equals the glucose concentration out. The value at which there is no net transfer of glucose in or out of the brain is taken as the extracellular concentration of glucose. Using such methods, the glucose concentration of the striatum of freely moving rats appears to be between 0.35 and 0.5 mM (Fellows, Boutelle, & Fillenz, 1992; Forsyth et al., 1996; Fray, Boutelle, & Fillenz, 1997). Results of such an experiment measuring glucose in the hippocampus are shown in Figure 12.3. Note that the point of zero net flux corresponds to an extracellular glucose concentration of approximately 1 mM in the hippocampus (McNay & Gold, 1999).

In itself, the low extracellular glucose concentrations in the brain suggest that relatively small fluctuations in circulating glucose, within a physiological range, might be more important to brain functions than thought previously. Nonetheless, it remains possible that even the 1-mM glucose concentration is stable and insensitive to behavioral manipulations. However, our recent evidence (McNay, Fries, & Gold, 2000) suggests that hippocampal glucose is indeed sensitive to behavioral testing and to systemic injections of glucose at doses that enhance learning and memory. Rats were tested for spontaneous alternation on a four-arm radial maze. Consistent with previous findings (Ragozzino, Unick, & Gold, 1996), alternation performance was enhanced by a systemic injection of glucose (Figure 12.4). The extracellular glucose levels in the hippocampus of these rats obtained during testing are shown in Figure 12.5. Note that in the saline and uninjected control rats, extracellular glucose concentrations in the hippocampus decreased by about 30% during testing. Administration of glucose in the animals with enhanced performance, shown in Figure 12.4, fully blocked the decrease in hippocampal glucose.

Several important control conditions suggest that these findings are related to brain activity associated with alternation performance (McNay, McCarty, & Gold, in press). First, the results cannot be explained as indirect reflections of

FIGURE 12.4

Enhancement of spontaneous alternation performance by intraperitoneal glucose injections.

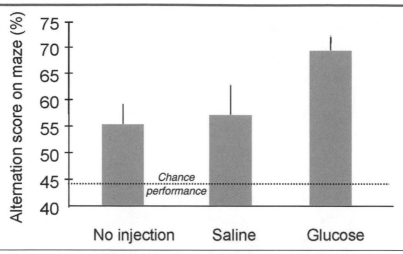

From Figure 1 in "Decreases in Rat Extracellular Hippocampal Glucose Concentration Associated with Cognitive Demand During a Spatial Task," by E. C. McNay, T. M. Fries, and P. E. Gold, 2000, *Proceedings of the National Academy of Sciences, 97,* p. 2883. Copyright 2000 by the National Academy of Sciences, USA. Adapted with permission of the publisher.

changes in blood glucose levels. When fluctuations in blood and brain glucose levels are monitored together, it is clear that changes in blood glucose levels do not occur in parallel with the brain changes. Moreover, if hippocampal extracellular glucose levels passively followed changes in blood glucose, similar effects would be expected throughout the brain. However, excluding this possibility, glucose depletion is not evident in the striatum. These latter results also address a second point that the effects appear to be specific to brain regions important for cognitive performance. In this case, decreases in glucose are seen in the hippocampus but not the striatum when rats are tested on a task that is hippocampus, but not striatum, dependent. Third, and especially interesting, glucose depletion is not seen when rats are tested in a three-arm maze in the same room with the same extramaze cues available. This task is one in which glucose does not enhance performance. The three-arm maze is presumably less challenging and yet requires about the same amount of locomotor activity as does the four-arm maze.

These results suggest that, under high cognitive demand, glucose reserves are drained from brain areas activated by that demand. Thus, "normal" learning and memory may be functioning at a deficit relative to optimal conditions.

FIGURE 12.5

Extracellular glucose concentrations in the hippocampus of rats before,
during, and after testing for spontaneous alternation performance.

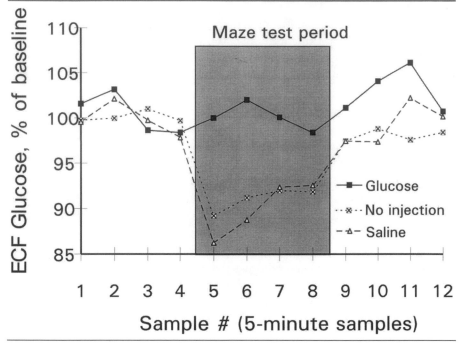

Alternation testing resulted in depletion of extracellular glucose, and the depletion
was blocked by pretreatment with intraperitoneal injections of glucose. From Figure
2 in "Decreases in Rat Extracellular Hippocampal Glucose Concentration
Associated with Cognitive Demand During a Spatial Task," by E. C. McNay, T. M.
Fries, and P. E. Gold, 2000, *Proceedings of the National Academy of Sciences,*
97, p. 2885. Copyright 2000 by the National Academy of Sciences, USA.
Adapted with permission of the publisher.

Role of K⁺-ATP Channels

The evidence above suggests that extracellular glucose levels fluctuate with cognitive demand. The next issue is, What might be the mechanism by which such
fluctuations influence neural activity to regulate the formation of memory? Our
findings suggest that glucose metabolism beyond pyruvate is necessary for the
effects on memory (Ragozzino, Hellems, Lennartz, & Gold, 1995; Stefani et al.,
1994). Recently, we investigated the possibility that glucose influences neural
functions by regulating central K^+-ATP channels. At pancreatic β cells, fluctuations in blood glucose levels control insulin release by opening and closing
K^+-ATP channels (Ashcroft, 1988; Panten, Schwanstecher, & Schwanstecher,
1996). ATP generated by glucose metabolism in β cells closes the channels so

that at high circulating glucose levels, the cells are depolarized and insulin release is increased. Conversely, at low glucose levels, the ATP block is removed, increasing K^+-ATP channel conductance and hyperpolarizing the cell, making the cell less sensitive to stimulus-evoked secretion of insulin.

In principle, the mechanism by which glucose regulates K^+-ATP channels to control insulin release might apply to other neurosecretory cells, including neurons. It is important to note that, in addition to their presence in peripheral tissues, K^+-ATP channels are also prevalent on neurons throughout the CNS (Mourre, Widmann, & Lazdunski, 1990; Zini, Tremblay, Pollard, Moreau, & Ben-Ari, 1993). Glucose might then modulate release of many neurotransmitters by closing the channels to increase release of some neurotransmitters (Amoroso, Schmid-Antomarchi, Fosset, & Lazdunski, 1990). Some support for this view comes from studies showing that drugs that act on the K^+-ATP channel influence neurotransmitter release both *in vitro* and *in vivo* (Amoroso et al., 1990; During, Leone, Davis, Kerr, & Sherwin, 1995; Fellows & Boutelle, 1993; Lee, Dixon, Rowe, Ashford, & Richardson, 1996; Tanaka, Yoshida, Yokoo, Mizoguchi, & Tanaka, 1995).

The findings of a series of experiments examining the effects on memory of direct brain injections of several drugs that act at the K^+-ATP channel support the view that glucose actions via central K^+-ATP channels may modulate learning and memory processes. In particular, the results suggest that glucose may modulate learning and memory by providing ATP to close this channel. One set of experiments tested the effects on memory of glibenclamide, a sulfonylurea agent that closes K^+-ATP channels. Injections of glibenclamide into either the medial septum or the hippocampus result in significantly higher spontaneous alternation scores on a four-arm plus maze (Stefani & Gold, 2001; Stefani, Nicholson, & Gold, 1999). Conversely, injections of lemakalim or galanin, drugs that open the K^+-ATP channel, impair alternation performance; these impairments can be reversed by concomitant glucose administration (Stefani & Gold, 2001; see Figure 12.6). These results support earlier suggestions that drugs directed at K^+-ATP channels in the brain may be effective as therapeutic treatments for cognitive pathologies like Alzheimer's disease (Lavretsky & Jarvik, 1992; Wiseman & Jarvik, 1991).

Acetylcholine Output and Glucose Regulation of Memory

Actions at the K^+-ATP channels may represent a proximal action of glucose, with increased activation of neurons underlying effects on memory. A subsequent question is whether there is a pharmacological basis beyond the K^+-ATP channel for glucose effects on learning and memory that implicates actions through particular neurotransmitters. One neurotransmitter of particular inter-

FIGURE 12.6

Effects of intraseptal injections of lemakalim or glibenclamide, drugs that open and close the K^+-ATP channel, alone and in conjunction with glucose injections, on alternation performance.

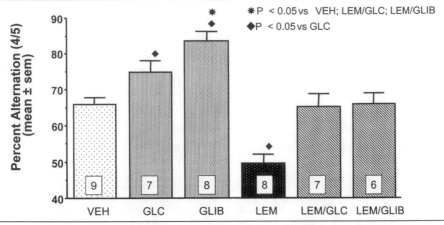

The channel openers impaired alternation performance, and the impairments were reversed by concomitant glucose administration. VEH = vehicle; GLC = glucose; GLIB = glibenclamide; LEM = lemakalim. From Figure 2 in "Intra-Hippocampal Infusions of K-ATP Channel Modulators Influence Spontaneous Alteration Performance: Relationships to Acetylcholine Release in the Hippocampus," by M. R. Stefani and P. E. Gold, 2001, *Journal of Neuroscience, 21*, p. 613. Copyright 2001 by the Society for Neuroscience. Adapted with permission of the publisher.

est was acetylcholine (ACh). Extensive evidence indicates that glucose interacts readily with a variety of cholinergic agents on learning and memory, as well as many other measures of brain function (Durkin, Messier, de Boer, & Westerink, 1992; Kopf & Baratti, 1994, 1996; Messier, Durkin, Mrabet, & Destrade, 1990, 1991; Stone, Cottrill, Walker, & Gold, 1988; Stone, Walser, Gold, & Gold, 1991).

We approached the question of whether ACh might contribute to the effects of glucose on memory by examining ACh release during training in combination with glucose and other drugs that modulate memory. In these experiments, rats are prepared with guide cannulae directed at the hippocampus. Microdialysis probes are then inserted prior to testing for collection of samples every 12 or 15 minutes (in different experiments). The results of one experiment are shown in Figure 12.7 (Ragozzino et al., 1996). The left panel of Figure 12.7 shows an inverted-U dose–response curve for enhancement of alternation scores by systemic (intraperitoneal) glucose injections. The right panel of Figure 12.7 shows the effects of alternation testing and of glucose injections on release

FIGURE 12.7

Glucose effects on alternation performance and on release of ACh in the hippocampus.

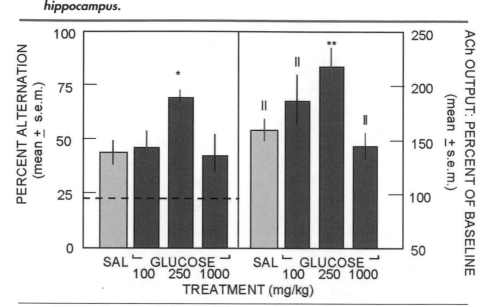

Left panel: Effects of glucose on spontaneous alternation performance in a four-arm maze. Right panel: Effects of alternation testing and of glucose on release of ACh in the hippocampus. Note the parallel inverted-U dose-response curves for the effects of glucose on performance and on ACh release. ACh = acetylcholine. From Figure 2 in "Hippocampal Acetylcholine Release During Memory Testing in Rats: Augmentation by Glucose," by M. E. Ragozzino, K. E. Unick, and P. E. Gold, 1996, *Proceedings of the National Academy of Sciences, 93,* p. 4695. Copyright 1996 by the National Academy of Sciences, USA. Adapted with permission of the publisher.

of ACh in the hippocampus. Note first that alternation testing itself resulted in a substantial increase in ACh output. Glucose augmented that output in a dose–response manner that mirrored that seen for alternation performance. Remarkably, glucose injections release ACh in the hippocampus only during behavioral testing; glucose had no effect on ACh release when injected in rats that remained in a holding cage (Figure 12.8). Thus, there is an interaction between maze testing and glucose injections that enables the effects on ACh release. Moreover, on the basis of additional evidence described below, it appears that ACh output in different neural systems for memory may be a marker of activation, and of relative activation, of those systems. As shown in Figure 12.9, although alternation testing resulted in increased norepinephrine release in the hippocampus, glucose administration did not modify that release, revealing some specificity to the effects of glucose on neurotransmitter release (Men, McCarty, & Gold, 1999).

FIGURE 12.8

Absence of glucose effect on ACh release in the hippocampus in rats kept in a holding cage and not tested behaviorally.

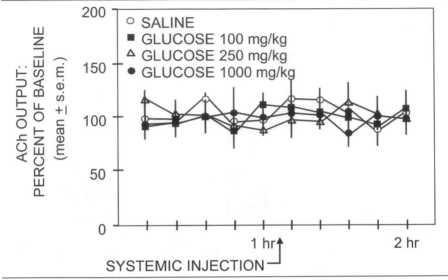

ACh = acetylcholine. From Figure 4 in "Hippocampal Acetylcholine Release During Memory Testing in Rats: Augmentation by Glucose," by M. E. Ragozzino, K. E. Unick, and P. E. Gold, 1996, *Proceedings of the National Academy of Sciences, 93*, p. 4697. Copyright 1996 by the National Academy of Sciences, USA. Adapted with permission of the publisher.

Memory Modulation: Glucose and Acetylcholine as Referees of Competition Between Memory Systems

Typically, discussion of modulation of learning and memory centers on pharmacological mechanisms by which hormones and neurotransmitters strengthen and weaken recent memories. However, the suggestions that changes in extracellular brain glucose concentrations and in ACh output may both be regionally specific according to the task demands suggests that, by differentially influencing neural systems responsible for forming memories of different attributes of an experience, modulators of learning and memory might be important not only in regulating the strength of memory formation generally, but also in regulating what an animal learns.

When systemic treatments, for example, epinephrine or glucose, are administered, similar effects are evident on many different measures of cognition. These include enhancement in tasks ranging from habituation to avoidance learning to shock learning to verbal learning to attention to retrieval of old information (cf. Gold, 1995). It is these broad effects that must be compared

FIGURE 12.9

NE and ACh release in the hippocampus during alternation testing with and without injections of glucose.

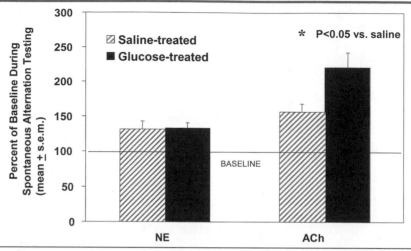

Release increased during behavior testing. However, glucose injections did not alter the magnitude of NE release in the hippocampus as measured in rats during alternation testing or at rest. NE = norepinephrine; ACh = acetylcholine. From "Enhanced Release of Norepinephrine in Rat Hippocampus During Spontaneous Alternation Tasks," by D. Men, R. McCarty, and P. E. Gold, 1999, *Neurobiology of Learning and Memory, 71.* Copyright 1999 by Academic Press. Adapted with permission of the authors/publisher.

with those seen in studies of multiple memory systems. Although memory consolidation has its roots in manipulations of the whole brain and even the whole organism, with treatments like electroconvulsive shock, protein synthesis inhibitors, and the like, studies of multiple memory systems have their roots in studies of the neuropsychology of human memory. Simply put, damage to different brain regions—mostly cortical in humans—impairs different kinds of cognitive functions with sometimes extraordinary specificity. Recent studies of memory in rats have revealed differential involvement of different neural systems for different kinds of memory. Of particular relevance here are recent triple dissociations for tasks that seem in many ways similar—motivational demands, motor demands, and so forth—but for which specific damage to different neural systems results in apparently different and precise deficits in cognition (Kesner, Bolland, & Dakis, 1993; McDonald & White, 1993). The McDonald and White (1993) findings provided a good example for this chapter. These investigators found that damage to the hippocampal formation, striatum, and amygdala impaired learning on three variants of food-motivated maze learning—win–shift, win–stay, and conditioned-cue preference, respectively.

These are cleverly conceived tasks designed to require one or another memory system. Of course, most tasks and most experiences are not as specifically linked to independent memory systems but must instead involve interplay of these systems. If different memory systems acquire different classes of information, it becomes easy to imagine that cooperation across systems will be important to the quality of learned information. Conversely, if the systems compete with each other for access to information, participation of one system may interfere with learning by another system. There are concrete examples of such competition in which lesions to one system can enhance learning dependent on another system. Learning in the conditioned-cue preference task, an amygdala-dependent task, can at times be enhanced by damage to the septo-hippocampal system. Prior maze experience during habituation trials, probably including acquisition of spatial information, retards the acquisition of conditioned-cue preference learning. Important here, rats with fornix lesions made prior to the habituation trials are better at learning the conditioned-cue preference task than are intact rats (McDonald & White, 1995; White & McDonald, 1993).

These findings suggest that management by the hippocampus of the acquisition of place information, providing information that is not critical to the conditioned-cue preference task, competes with the amygdala for control of the information. With impaired hippocampal function, the amygdala has more control over what is learned and acquisition proceeds more quickly. Similar results have been reported by others (e.g., Matthews & Best, 1995).

What referees the competition between neural systems that process information for relatively independent attributes of memory? Recall that depletion of extracellular glucose and release of ACh appear to differ by brain region and task demands, perhaps on the basis of the neural system activated by specific tasks. If there is regional specificity for these neurochemical responses to experience, similar results are likely for other neurotransmitters and neurochemical responses as well. This view leads to the suggestion that modulators of memory formation are ideal candidates for regulating the relative contributions and participation of discrete memory systems during learning.

Combining features of independent memory systems with our findings that ACh release was associated with glucose modulation of memory and also was released in the hippocampus while rats performed on hippocampus-dependent spontaneous alternation tasks, we have examined ACh release in different brain areas while rats were trained in different tasks. One issue was whether ACh release in different brain areas during training would be associated with the extent to which that brain area participated in learning and memory. At least across conditions, ACh release in the hippocampus is correlated with alternation performance (Figure 12.10; Ragozzino, Wenk, & Gold, 1994). As noted above, McDonald and White (1995) showed that an intact septohippocampal system

FIGURE 12.10

Positive correlation, across drug conditions, between ACh release in the hippocampus and performance on the hippocampus-dependent alternation task.

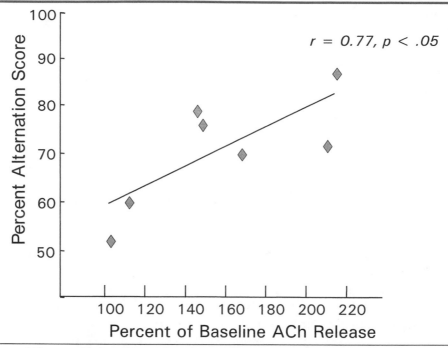

ACh = acetylcholine. Adapted from data in "Glucose Attenuates Morphine-Induced Decrease in Hippocampal Acetylcholine Output: An In Vivo Microdialysis Study in Rats," by M. E. Ragozzino, G. L. Wenk, and P. E. Gold, 1994, *Brain Research, 655,* pp. 77–82. Copyright 1994 by Elsevier Science. Adapted with permission of the publisher.

impaired acquisition of a conditioned-cue preference task. Using a task much like theirs, we examined the relationship between release of ACh in the hippocampus and acquisition of the conditioned-cue preference task (McIntyre, Pal, Marriott, & Gold, 2001a). The results, shown in Figure 12.11, reveal a striking inverse correlation between ACh release in the hippocampus and acquisition of the conditioned-cue preference response. We interpret these findings to indicate that, whereas the extent to which the septohippocampal system is activated or engaged by learning—as marked here by ACh release—can be beneficial for hippocampus-dependent tasks, the same level of activation can be detrimental for acquisition of a task dependent on the amygdala.

These results imply that, by controlling the efficacy of memory formation in different neural systems, the consequence will be not only to enhance or impair memory in the manner usually considered but also to control what is

FIGURE 12.11

Inverse correlation between release of ACh in the hippocampus and acquisition of an amygdala-dependent conditioned-cue preference task.

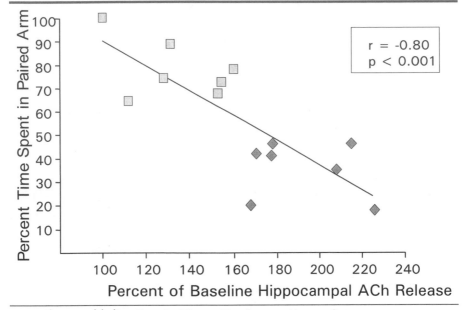

ACh = acetylcholine. From in "Competition Between Memory Systems: Acetylcholine Release in the Hippocampus Correlates Negatively with Good Performance on an Amygdala-Dependent Task," by C. K. McIntyre, S. N. Pal, L. K. Marriott, and P. E. Gold, 2001, manuscript submitted for publication.

learned. The findings that fornix lesions can enhance conditioned-cue preference learning and that ACh release in the hippocampus is inversely related to conditioned-cue preference learning both suggest that when hippocampal functions including spatial processing are engaged, acquisition of the amygdala-dependent conditioned-cue preference task is poor.

An important remaining issue is to determine whether multiple memory systems act in parallel as equals or whether there is a hierarchical organization to these interactions. For example, in the present case, the description of results makes it appear that the extent of hippocampus activation may control what is learned. But, the findings of the converse experiments are needed before one can make statements about which neural system is or is not dominant. For example, if one were to measure release of ACh (or other modulator) in the amygdala during spatial training, would there be a similarly inverse relationship between amygdala activation and acquisition of a place-learning task? Another way to approach this issue is to examine whether one can pharmacologically bias memory systems to determine which system is in control of learning.

Certainly it must be the case that when a rat learns anything in the real world (or almost anything in the laboratory world), the rat must simultaneously engage multiple memory systems. Competition between these systems will determine what will be learned. Experiments such as these will be important in determining the manner in which processing in multiple memory systems is coordinated during most experiences, that is, experiences that require integration of information across memory "modalities."

Modulators of Memory as Selectors of Learning Strategy

If the up and down regulation of processing in different memory systems precedes an experience, the result might be a shift in the learning strategy selected by an animal. Several recent findings support this view. One task used is an ambiguous T maze (Barnes, 1988; Barnes, Nadel, & Honig, 1980; Packard & McGaugh, 1996; Restle, 1957). In this task, a rat is trained to approach a single goal arm. This response can be learned equally well using response (turn right, egocentric) strategies or place (go to the arm on a particular side of the room, allocentric) strategies. Which strategy a rat has used for learning is assessed on probe trials after training. On these trials, a rat is tested on the T maze with the start arm rotated 180°. The rat then displays what it learned by returning either to the arm located in the same place in the room or to the arm reached by making the same turn on the maze. The response versus place strategies are likely to be caudate versus hippocampal dependent (Cook & Kesner, 1988; Kesner et al., 1993; Mitchell & Hall, 1988; Packard & McGaugh, 1996). Korol, Couper, McIntyre, and Gold (1996) found that female rats learned this task differently depending on the stage of the estrous cycle at the time of training (Figure 12.12). At proestrus (high estrogen), most rats learned using a place strategy. At estrus (low estrogen), most rats learned using a response strategy. At diestrus (intermediate estrogen), rats learned with either strategy in about equal proportions.

In another experiment (Korol, Clark, & Gold, 1998; Figure 12.13), ovariectomized rats with or without estrogen replacement were trained on either place or response versions of a four-arm maze. In the place version of the task, rats begin a trial from any of three randomly ordered arms; a single arm is the goal arm. In the response version of the task, rats start a trial randomly from any arm and the goal is always in a fixed location (right or left turn) from the start arm. When trained on the place task, estrogen-treated rats learned the task to a 9/10 correct criterion more quickly than did ovariectomized controls. Conversely, when trained on the response task, estrogen-treatment rats learned more slowly than did their ovariectomized controls. These results may explain apparent discrepancies across experiments in assessing gender differences and dif-

FIGURE 12.12

Selection of different learning strategy at different stages of the estrous cycle.

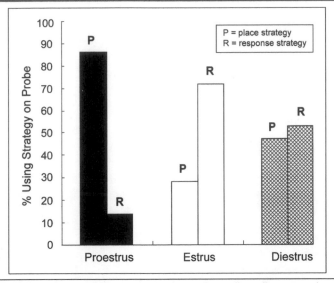

Rats were trained on a task that could be learned equally well using a place or response strategy. On a probe test that revealed which strategy had been selected, most rats trained at high estrogen (proestrus) used a place strategy whereas those trained at low estrogen (estrus) used a response strategy. Rats with intermediate estrogen levels showed no bias. From "Strategies for Learning Across the Estrous Cycle in Female Rats" by D. L. Korol, J. M. Couper, C. K. McIntyre, & P. E. Gold, 1996. Used with permission of the authors.

ferences based on estrogen status in learning ability. Depending on task, estrogen might either enhance or impair learning. But, given the results obtained with training on the ambiguous T maze, it may be more accurate to form an interpretation based on estrogen regulation of what will be learned in a given situation.

Generalizing from these findings, it might be the case that when one merges traditional ideas of modulation of memory—that is, enhancement or impairment of memory processes—with multiple memory systems, modulatory influences acting differentially on memory systems can determine what is learned by virtue of amplifying and damping the contributions of different memory systems. We have recently begun to examine this possibility (McIntyre et al., 2001b). On an ambiguous T maze, male rats are divided about evenly in terms of using response or place strategies during learning. Using *in vivo* microdialysis, we collected samples from the hippocampus and from the striatum in the same rats before, during, and after training on the maze. During training, ACh release increased in the hippocampus and striatum regardless of the strategy each rat

FIGURE 12.13

Estrogen enhancement of place learning and impairment of response learning in ovariectomized rats.

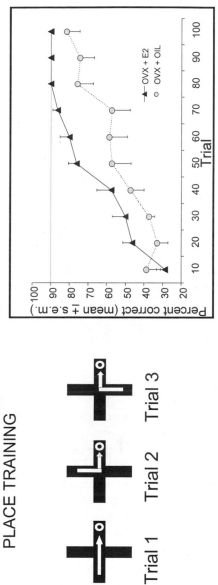

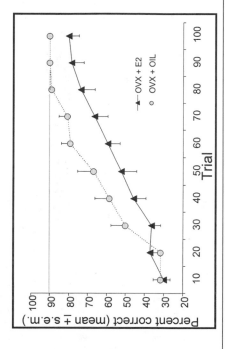

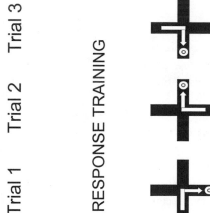

OVX = ovariectomy; E2 = estrogen; OIL = vehicle.

used. However, the ratio of the increases in hippocampus and striatum were very different depending on what each rat learned, that is, the strategy revealed on a probe trial. Those rats that showed place learning had significantly higher ratios of hippocampus/striatum ACh release than did the rats that showed response learning. Even more remarkable were the findings obtained when ACh release was measured before learning. During the hour prior to training, those rats that would later adopt a place strategy for learning had higher ratios of hippocampus/striatum ACh release than did the rats that would use a response strategy. The difference in ACh ratios was then maintained during training. These results suggest that extracellular ACh levels in the hippocampus and striatum reveal individual differences across memory systems that predict what will be learned by different animals facing a single problem with multiple successful solutions. Unknown is what produces the predisposition in individual rats to use one or another learning strategy. One possibility is that past experience might produce the bias. According to this view, the memory system that has provided the most success in past challenges will be tried first by a rat facing a new challenge. Perhaps this might be characterized as a version of metaplasticity (Abraham & Bear, 1996; Fisher, Blazis, Priver, & Carew, 1997) coupled to metamodulation.

This view has implications not only for memory in healthy adult animals but also for studies of aging and age-related memory pathologies. The usual assumption is that aging, for example, brings with it a loss of memory abilities. In rodents and many other animals, there is excellent evidence that aging is accompanied by more rapid forgetting, compared to young animals, of many tasks (e.g., Barnes, 1990; Barnes & McNaughton, 1985; Gold & Stone, 1988; Mabry et al., 1996; Winocur, 1988; Zornetzer, Thompson, & Rogers, 1982). But, in some circumstances, it is possible that aging may bring a change in the preferred memory system with resultant memory differences that are qualitative, not quantitative, in nature. This is a view with recent support in positron emission tomography (PET) studies in elderly humans (Hazlett et al., 1998).

Therefore, in some experimental conditions, apparent age-related memory loss may involve age-related changes in the strategy selected to deal with a new problem rather than memory loss per se. For example, in a T maze like the ambiguous task described above, aged rats might be biased to learn response rather than place cues. These are precisely the findings found by Barnes et al. (1980). Another example in which similar factors might be important is in the swim task used so often in studies of aging. There are large age-related differences in the neuroendocrine stress responses in this task. Compared to young rats, aged rats show substantially greater plasma epinephrine and norepinephrine increases after immersion in water (Mabry, Gold, & McCarty, 1995a, 1995b, 1995c; Mabry et al., 1996). Moreover, prior adaptation of the stress response ameliorates much of the age-related "memory" loss. The significance of possible age-related differences in strategy selection to this issue is that thigmotaxis increases with stress and might then reveal a strategy that is incompatible with optimal acquisition of finding a platform hidden away from the wall. In contrast, finding an elevated platform might be a reasonable alternative for a rat that would otherwise stay near the outer wall.

The findings obtained with estrogen suggest that, at menopause, one might see cognitive problems not because of loss of function but because of shift to strategies used less often before menopause. It seems important to explore such concerns in all avenues of pathology, much as one would with comparative psychology across species. For example, in aging or in genetic models of Alzheimer's disease or Down's syndrome, one important issue is to determine whether the deficits seen reflect changes in modulation of memory or changes in preferences for particular learning strategies, rather than deficits in the mechanisms of plasticity *per se*.

Conclusion

This chapter gains its basis in the findings that there are drugs, such as strychnine (McGaugh & Petrinovich, 1959), that enhance memory. There is now extensive evidence supporting the view that there are natural, endogenous modulators of memory that enhance memory. More recent evidence suggests the possibility that modulators may regulate the extent to which different memory systems are engaged when an animal is faced with a new problem. Some peripheral factors, perhaps including epinephrine and glucose, appear to enhance memory for a broad class of tasks (Gold, 1995), whereas other peripheral factors, perhaps gonadal steroids, may bias the relative participation of different memory systems so that one or another strategy is tried until learning and memory for a particular task are accomplished successfully.

We appear to be moving to an era in which we can consider the consequences of modulation of memory in different neural systems responsible for processing different attributes of memory. These studies address the possibility that glucose and other modulators of learning and memory may, by virtue of their ability to regulate learning and memory in different neural systems, regulate the relative participation of different neural systems during learning. In this manner, modulators might bias rats to adopt different learning strategies and to learn about different features of an experience, thereby regulating what an individual rat learns in these situations. According to this view, modulators of learning and memory may at times reconcile and at times exaggerate tensions across relatively independent memory systems for control over what is learned. In this way, modulators of memory not only serve a quantitative function of regulating the strength of memory formation for many classes of tasks but also serve a qualitative function of regulating what is learned in those tasks.

References

Abel, T., Martin, K. C., Bartsch, D., & Kandel, E. R. (1998). Memory suppressor genes: Inhibitory constraints on the storage of long-term memory. *Science, 279,* 338–341.

Abraham, W. C., & Bear, M. F. (1996). Metaplasticity: The plasticity of synaptic plasticity. *Trends in Neuroscience, 19,* 126–130.

Amoroso, S., Schmid-Antomarchi, H., Fosset, M., & Lazdunski, M. (1990). Glucose, sulfonylureas, and neurotransmitter release: Role of ATP-sensitive K^+ channels. *Science, 247,* 852–854.

Ashcroft, F. M. (1988). Adenosine 5-triphosphate-sensitive potassium channels. *Annual Review of Neuroscience, 11,* 97–118.

Barnes, C. A. (1988). Aging and the physiology of spatial memory. *Neurobiology of Aging, 9,* 563–568.

Barnes, C. A. (1990). Effects of aging on the dynamics of information processing and synaptic weight changes in the mammalian hippocampus. *Progress in Brain Research, 86,* 89–104.

Barnes, C. A., & McNaughton, B. L. (1985). An age comparison of the rates of acquisition and forgetting of spatial information in relation to long-term enhancement of hippocampal synapses. *Behavioral Neuroscience, 99,* 1040–1048.

Barnes, C. A., Nadel, L., & Honig, W. K. (1980). Spatial memory deficit in senescent rats. *Canadian Journal of Psychology, 34,* 29–39.

Benton, D., Parker, P. Y., & Donohoe, R. T. (1996). The supply of glucose to the brain and cognitive functioning. *Journal of Biosocial Science, 28,* 463–479.

Cahill, L., & McGaugh, J. L. (1998). Mechanisms of emotional arousal and lasting declarative memory. *Trends in Neuroscience, 21,* 294–299.

Cho, Y. H., & Kesner, R. P. (1996). Involvement of entorhinal cortex or parietal cortex in long-term spatial discrimination memory in rats: Retrograde amnesia. *Behavioral Neuroscience, 110,* 436–442.

Cook, D., & Kesner, R. P. (1988). Caudate nucleus and memory for egocentric localization. *Behavioral and Neural Biology, 49,* 332–343.

Craft, S., Dagogo-Jack, S. E., Wiethop, B. V., Murphy, C., Nevins, R. T., Fleischman, S., Rice, V., Newcomer, J. W., & Cryer, P. E. (1993). Effects of hyperglycemia on memory and hormone levels in dementia of the Alzheimer type: A longitudinal study. *Behavioral Neuroscience, 107,* 926–940.

Craft, S., Murphy, C. G., & Wemstrom, J. (1994). Glucose effects on complex memory and nonmemory tasks: The influence of age, sex, and glucoregulatory response. *Psychobiology, 22,* 95–105.

Craft, S., Zallen, G., & Baker, L. D. (1992). Glucose and memory in mild senile dementia of the Alzheimer type. *Journal of Clinical and Experimental Neuropsychology, 14,* 253–267.

During, M. J., Leone, P., Davis, K. E., Kerr, D., & Sherwin, R. S. (1995). Glucose modulates rat substantia nigra GABA release in vivo via ATP-sensitive potassium channels. *Journal of Clinical Investigations, 95,* 2403–2408.

Durkin, T. P., Messier, C., de Boer, P., & Westerink, B. H. (1992). Raised glucose levels enhance scopolamine-induced acetylcholine overflow from the hippocampus: An in vivo microdialysis study in the rat. *Behavioural Brain Research, 49,* 181–188.

Ellis, S., Kennedy, B. L., Eusebi, A. J., & Vincent, N. H. (1967). Utonomic control of metabolism. *Annals of the New York Academy of Sciences, 139,* 826–832.

Fellows, L. K., & Boutelle, M. G. (1993). Rapid changes in extracellular glucose levels and blood flow in the striatum of the freely moving rat. *Brain Research, 604,* 225–231.

Fellows, L. K., Boutelle, M. G., & Fillenz, M. (1992). Extracellular brain glucose levels reflect local neuronal activity: A microdialysis study in awake, freely moving rats. *Journal of Neurochemistry, 59,* 2141–2147.

Fisher, T. M., Blazis, D. E., Priver, N. M. A., & Carew, T. J. (1997). Metaplasticity at identified inhibitory synapses in aplysia. *Nature, 389,* 860–865.

Forsyth, R., Fray, A., Boutelle, M., Fillenz, M., Middleditch, C., & Burchell, A. (1996). A role for astrocytes in glucose delivery to neurons? *Developmental Neuroscience, 18,* 360–370.

Fray, A. E., Boutelle, M., & Fillenz, M. (1997). Extracellular glucose turnover in the striatum of unanaesthetized rats measured by quantitative microdialysis. *Journal of Physiology (London), 504,* 721–726.

Gold, P. E. (1986). Glucose modulation of memory storage processing. *Behavioral and Neural Biology, 45,* 342–349.

Gold, P. E. (1991). An integrated memory regulation system: From blood to brain. In R. C. A. Frederickson, J. L. McGaugh, & D. L. Felten (Eds.), *Peripheral signaling of the brain: Role in neural-immune interactions, learning and memory* (pp. 391–419). Toronto, Ontario, Canada: Hogrefe & Huber.

Gold, P. E. (1992). A proposed neurobiological basis for regulating memory storage for significant events. In E. Winograd & U. Neisser (Eds.), *Affect and accuracy in recall: Studies of "flashbulb" memories* (pp. 141–161). New York: Cambridge University Press.

Gold, P. E. (1995). Modulation of emotional and non-emotional memories: Same pharmacological systems, different neuroanatomical systems. In J. L. McGaugh, N. M. Weinberger, & G. S. Lynch (Eds.), *Brain and memory: Modulation and mediation of neural plasticity* (pp. 41–74). New York: Oxford University Press.

Gold, P. E., Macri, J., & McGaugh, J. L. (1973). Retrograde amnesia gradients: Effects of direct cortical stimulation. *Science, 197,* 1343–1345.

Gold, P. E., & McCarty, R. (1995). Stress regulation of memory processes: Role of peripheral catecholamines and glucose. In M. J. Friedman, D. S. Charney, & A. Y. Deutch (Eds.), *Neurobiological and clinical consequences of stress: From normal adaptation to PTSD* (pp. 151–162). Philadelphia: Lippincott-Raven.

Gold, P. E., & McGaugh, J. L. (1975). A single trace, two process view of memory storage processes. In D. Deutsch & J. A. Deutsch (Eds.), *Short term memory* (pp. 355–378). New York: Academic Press.

Gold, P. E., & Stone, W. S. (1988). Neuroendocrine factors in age-related memory dysfunctions: Studies in animals and humans. *Neurobiology of Aging, 9,* 709–717.

Gold, P. E., & van Buskirk, R. B. (1975). Facilitation of time dependent memory processes with posttrial epinephrine injections. *Behavioral Biology, 13,* 145–153.

Hall, J. L., Gonder-Frederick, L. A., Chewning, W. W., Silveira, J., & Gold, P. E. (1989). Glucose enhancement of performance on memory tests in young and aged humans. *Neuropsychologia, 27,* 1129–1138.

Hazlett, E. A., Buchsbaum, M. S., Mohs, R. C., Spiegel-Cohen, J., Wei, T. C., Azueta, R., Haznedar, M. M., Singer, M. B., Shihabuddin, L., Luu-Hsia, C., & Harvey, P. D. (1998). Age-related shift in brain region activity during successful memory performance. *Neurobiology of Aging, 19,* 437–445.

Izquierdo, I., & Medina, J. H. (1997). Memory formation: The sequence of biochemical events in the hippocampus and its connection to activity in other brain structures. *Neurobiology of Learning and Memory, 68,* 285–316.

Kesner, R. P., Bolland, B. L., & Dakis, M. (1993). Memory for spatial locations, motor responses and objects: Triple dissociation among the hippocampus, caudate nucleus, and extrastriate visual cortex. *Experimental Brain Research, 93,* 462–470.

Knowlton, B. J., & Fanselow, M. S. (1998). The hippocampus, consolidation and on-line memory. *Current Opinions in Neurobiology, 8,* 293–296.

Kopf, S. R., & Baratti, C. M. (1994). Memory-improving actions of glucose: Involvement of a central cholinergic muscarinic mechanism. *Behavioral and Neural Biology, 62,* 237–243.

Kopf, S. R., & Baratti, C. M. (1996). Effects of posttraining administration of glucose on retention of a habituation response in mice: Participation of a central cholinergic mechanism. *Neurobiology of Learning and Memory, 65,* 253–260.

Korol, D. L., Clark, L. L., & Gold, P. E. (1998). *Presence of estradiol predicts learning strategy in female rats.* Paper presented at the 28th annual meeting of the Society for Neuroscience, Los Angeles.

Korol, D. L., Couper, J. M., McIntyre, C. K., & Gold, P. E. (1996). *Strategies for learning across the estrous cycle in female rats.* Paper presented at the 26th annual meeting of the Society for Neuroscience, Washington, DC.

Korol, D. L., & Gold, P. E. (1998). Glucose, memory and aging. *American Journal of Clinical Nutrition, 67,* 764S–771S.

Korol, D. L., Lexcen, F. J., Parent, M. B., Ragozzino, M. E., Manning, C. A., & Gold, P. E. (1995). *Glucose enhancement of cognitive performance in college students.* Paper presented at the 25th annual meeting of the Society for Neuroscience, San Diego.

Lavretsky, E. P., & Jarvik, L. F. (1992). A group of potassium-channel blockers—acetylcholine releasers: New potentials for Alzheimer disease? A review. *Journal of Clinical Psychopharmacology, 12,* 110–118.

Lee, K., Dixon, A. K., Rowe, I. C. M., Ashford, M. L. J., & Richardson, P. J. (1996). The high-affinity sulphonylurea receptor regulates KATP channels in nerve terminals of the rat motor cortex. *Journal of Neurochemistry, 66,* 2562–2571.

Lund-Andersen, H. (1979). Transport of glucose from blood to brain. *Physiology Review, 59,* 305–352.

Mabry, T. R., Gold, P. E., & McCarty, R. (1995a). Age-related changes in plasma catecholamine and glucose responses of F-344 rats to footshock as in inhibitory avoidance training. *Neurobiology of Learning and Memory, 64,* 146–155.

Mabry, T. R., Gold, P. E., & McCarty, R. (1995b). Age-related changes in plasma catecholamine responses to acute swim stress. *Neurobiology of Learning and Memory, 63,* 260–268.

Mabry, T. R., Gold, P. E., & McCarty, R. (1995c). Age-related changes in plasma catecholamine responses to chronic intermittent stress. *Physiology and Behavior, 58,* 49–56.

Mabry, T. R., McCarty, R., Gold, P. E., & Foster, T. C. (1996). Age and stress-history effects on spatial performance in a swim task in Fischer-344 rats. *Neurobiology of Learning and Memory, 66,* 1–10.

Manning, C. A., Hall, J. L., & Gold, P. E. (1990). Glucose effects on memory and other neuropsychological tests in elderly humans. *Psychological Science, 1,* 307–311.

Manning, C. A., Honn, V. S., Stone, W. S., Jane, J. S., & Gold, P. E. (1998). Glucose effects on cognition in adults with Down's syndrome. *Neuropsychology, 12,* 479–484.

Manning, C. A., Parsons, M. W., Cotter, E. M., & Gold, P. E. (1997). Glucose effects on declarative and nondeclarative memory in healthy elderly and young adults. *Psychobiology, 25,* 103–108.

Manning, C. A., Parsons, M. W., & Gold, P. E. (1992). Anterograde and retrograde enhancement of 24-hour memory by glucose in elderly humans. *Behavioral and Neural Biology, 58,* 125–130.

Manning, C. A., Ragozzino, M., & Gold, P. E. (1993). Glucose enhancement of memory in patients with Alzheimer's disease. *Neurobiology of Aging, 14,* 523–528.

Manning, C. A., Stone, W. S., Korol, D. L., & Gold, P. E. (1998). Glucose enhancement of 24-hour memory retrieval in healthy elderly humans. *Behavioural Brain Research, 93,* 71–76.

Matthews, D. B., & Best, P. J. (1995). Fimbria/fornix lesions facilitate the learning of a nonspatial response task. *Psychonomic Bulletin and Review, 2,* 113–116.

McCarty, R., & Gold, P. E. (1996). Catecholamines, stress and disease: A psychobiological perspective. *Psychosomatic Medicine, 58,* 590–597.

McDonald, R. J., & White, N. M. (1993). A triple dissociation of memory systems: Hippocampus, amygdala and dorsal striatum. *Behavioral Neuroscience, 107,* 3–22.

McDonald, R. J., & White, N. M. (1995). Information acquired by the hippocampus interferes with acquisition of the amygdala-based conditioned-cue preference in the rat. *Hippocampus, 5,* 189–197.

McGaugh, J. L. (1966). Time-dependent processes in memory storage. *Science, 153,* 1351–1358.

McGaugh, J. L. (1983). Hormonal influences on memory. *Annual Review of Psychology, 34,* 297–323.

McGaugh, J. L., & Dawson, R. G. (1971). Modification of memory storage processes. *Behavioral Science, 16,* 45–63.

McGaugh, J. L., & Herz, M. J. (1972). *Memory consolidation.* San Francisco, CA: Albion.

McGaugh, J. L., & Petrinovich, L. (1959). The effect of strychnine sulphate on maze-learning. *American Journal of Psychology, 72,* 99–102.

McIntyre, C. K., Pal, S. N., Marriott, L. K., & Gold, P. E. (2001a). Competition between memory systems: Acetylcholine release in the hippocampus correlates negatively with good performance on an amygdala-dependent task. Submitted.

McIntyre, C. K., Pal, S. N., Marriott, L. K., & Gold, P. E. (2001b). Individual differences in learning strategy predicted by brain acetylcholine. Submitted.

McNay, E. C., Fries, T. M., & Gold, P. E. (2000). Decreases in rat extracellular hippocampal glucose concentration associated with cognitive demand during a spatial task. *Proceedings of the National Academy of Sciences, 97,* 2881–2885.

McNay, E. C., & Gold, P. E. (1999). Extracellular glucose concentrations in the rat hippocampus measured by zero-net-flux: Effects of microdialysis flow rate, strain and age. *Journal of Neurochemistry, 72,* 785–790.

McNay, E. C., McCarty, R., & Gold, P. E. (in press). Fluctuations in glucose concentration during behavioral testing: Dissociations both between brain areas and between brain and blood. *Neurobiology of Learning and Memory.*

Men, D., McCarty, R., & Gold, P. E. (1999). Enhanced release of norepinephrine in rat hippocampus during spontaneous alternation tests. *Neurobiology of Learning and Memory, 71,* 289–300.

Messier, C., Durkin, T., Mrabet, O., & Destrade, C. (1990). Memory-improving action of glucose: Indirect evidence for a facilitation of hippocampal acetylcholine synthesis. *Behavioural Brain Research, 39,* 135–143.

Messier, C., Durkin, T., Mrabet, O., & Destrade, C. (1991). Contribution of hippocampal acetylcholine synthesis to the memory-improving action of glucose. In R. C. A. Frederickson, J. L. McGaugh, & D. L. Felten (Eds.), *Peripheral signaling of the brain: Role in neural–immune interactions, learning and memory* (pp. 473–477). Toronto, Ontario, Canada: Hogrefe & Huber.

Messier, C., & Gagnon, M. (1996). Glucose regulation and cognitive functions: Relation to Alzheimer's disease and diabetes. *Behavioural Brain Research, 75,* 1–11.

Messier, C., & White, N. M. (1984). Contingent and non-contingent actions of sucrose and saccharin reinforcers: Effects on taste preference and memory. *Physiology and Behavior, 32,* 195–203.

Mitchell, J. A., & Hall, G. (1988). Caudate-putamen lesions in the rat may impair or potentiate maze learning depending upon availability of stimulus cues and relevance of response cues. *Quarterly Journal of Experimental Psychology: B, Comparative and Physiological Psychology, 40,* 243–258.

Mourre, C., Widmann, C., & Lazdunski, M. (1990). Sulfonylurea binding sites associated with ATP-regulated K⁺ channels in the central nervous system: Autoradiographic analysis of their distribution and ontogenesis, and of their localization in mutant mice cerebellum. *Brain Research, 519,* 29–43.

Nadel, L., & Moskowitch, M. (1997). Memory consolidation, retrograde amnesia and the hippocampal complex. *Current Opinions in Neurobiology, 7,* 217–227.

Owens, D. S., Parker, P. Y., & Benton, D. (1997). Blood glucose and subjective energy following cognitive demand. *Physiology and Behavior, 62,* 471–478.

Packard, M. G., & McGaugh, J. L. (1996). Inactivation of hippocampus or caudate nucleus with lidocaine differentially affects expression of place and response learning. *Neurobiology of Learning and Memory, 65,* 65–72.

Panten, U., Schwanstecher, M., & Schwanstecher, C. (1996). Sulfonylurea receptors and mechanism of sulfonylurea action. *Experimental and Clinical Endocrinology, 104,* 1–9.

Parsons, M., & Gold, P. E. (1992). Glucose enhancement of memory in elderly humans: An inverted-U dose-response curve. *Neurobiology of Aging, 13,* 401–404.

Ragozzino, M. E., Hellems, K., Lennartz, R. C., & Gold, P. E. (1995). Pyruvate infusions into the septal area attenuate spontaneous alternation impairments induced by intraseptal morphine injections. *Behavioral Neuroscience, 109,* 1074–1080.

Ragozzino, M. E., Unick, K. E., & Gold, P. E. (1996). Hippocampal acetylcholine release during memory testing in rats: Augmentation by glucose. *Proceedings of the National Academy of Sciences, 93,* 4693–4698.

Ragozzino, M. E., Wenk, G. L., & Gold, P. E. (1994). Glucose attenuates morphine-induced decrease in hippocampal acetylcholine output: An in vivo microdialysis study in rats. *Brain Research, 655,* 77–82.

Reed, J. M., & Squire, L. R. (1998). Retrograde amnesia of facts and events: Findings from four new cases. *Journal of Neuroscience, 18,* 3943–3954.

Reisberg, D., & Heuer, F. (1995). Emotion's multiple effects on memory. In J. L. McGaugh, N. M. Weinberger, & G. S. Lynch (Eds.), *Brain and memory: Modulation and mediation of neural plasticity* (pp. 84–92). New York: Oxford University Press.

Restle, F. (1957). Discrimination of cues in mazes: A resolution of the "place-vs.-response" question. *Psychological Review, 64,* 217–228.

Rose, S. P. R. (1995). Time-dependent biochemical and cellular processes in memory formation. In J. L. McGaugh & F. Bermudez-Rattoni (Eds.), *Plasticity in the central nervous system: Learning and memory* (pp. 171–184). Mahwah, NJ: Erlbaum.

Squire, L. R., & Alvarez, P. (1995). Retrograde amnesia and memory consolidation: A neurobiological perspective. *Current Opinions in Neurobiology, 5,* 178–183.

Stefani, M. R., & Gold, P. E. (1998). Intra-septal injections of glucose and glibenclamide attenuate galanin-induced spontaneous alternation performance deficits in the rat. *Brain Research, 813,* 50–56.

Stefani, M. R., & Gold, P. E. (2001). Intra-hippocampal infusions of K-ATP channel modulators influence spontaneous alternation performance: Relationships to acetylcholine release in the hippocampus. *Journal of Neuroscience, 21*, 609–614.

Stefani, M. R., Nicholson, G. M., & Gold, P. (1999). ATP-sensitive potassium channel blockade enhances spontaneous alternation performance in the rat: A potential mechanism for glucose-mediated memory enhancement. *Neuroscience, 93*, 557–563.

Stefani, M. R., Ragozzino, M. E., Thompson, P. K., Hellems, K., Lennartz, R. C., & Gold, P. E. (1994). *Regulation of spontaneous alternation in the rat by glucose: A role for glycolysis.* Paper presented at the 24th annual meeting of the Society for Neuroscience, Miami.

Stone, W. S., Cottrill, K., Walker, D., & Gold, P. E. (1988). Blood glucose and brain function: Interactions with CNS cholinergic systems. *Behavioral and Neural Biology, 50*, 325–334.

Stone, W. S., Walser, B., Gold, S. D., & Gold, P. E. (1991). Scopolamine- and morphine-induced impairments of spontaneous alternation behavior in mice: Reversal with glucose and with cholinergic and adrenergic agonists. *Behavioral Neuroscience, 105*, 264–271.

Swain, R. A., Armstrong, K. E., Comery, T. A., Humphreys, A. G., Jones, T. A., Kleim, J. A., & Greenough, W. T. (1995). In D. L. Schacter (Ed.), *Memory distortions: How minds, brains and societies reconstruct the past* (pp. 274–297). Cambridge, MA: Harvard University Press.

Tanaka, T., Yoshida, M., Yokoo, H., Mizoguchi, K., & Tanaka, M. (1995). The role of ATP-sensitive potassium channels in striatal dopamine release: An in vivo microdialysis study. *Pharmacology Biochemistry and Behavior, 52*, 831–835.

White, N. (1991). Peripheral and central memory-enhancing actions of glucose. In R. C. A. Frederickson, J. L. McGaugh, & D. L. Felten (Eds.), *Peripheral signaling of the brain: Role in neural–immune interactions and learning and memory* (pp. 421–441). Toronto, Ontario, Canada: Hogrefe & Huber.

White, N. M., & McDonald, R. J. (1993). Acquisition of a spatial conditioned place preferences impaired by amygdala lesions and improved by fornix lesions. *Behavioural Brain Research, 55*, 269–281.

Winocur, G. (1988). A neuropsychological analysis of memory loss with age. *Neurobiology of Aging, 9*, 487–494.

Winocur, G. (1990). Anterograde and retrograde amnesia in rats with dorsal hippocampal or dorsomedial thalamic lesions. *Behavioural Brain Research, 38*, 145–154.

Winograd, E., & Neisser, U. (Eds.). (1992). *Affect and accuracy in recall: Studies of "flashbulb" memories.* New York: Cambridge University Press.

Wiseman, E. J., & Jarvik, E. F. (1991). Potassium channel blockers: Could they work in Alzheimer disease? *Alzheimer Disease and Associated Disorders, 5*, 25–30.

Zini, S., Tremblay, E., Pollard, H., Moreau, J., & Ben-Ari, Y. (1993). Regional distribution of sulfonylurea receptors in the brain of rodent and primate. *Neuroscience, 55,* 1085–1091.

Zola-Morgan, S. M., & Squire, L. R. (1990). The primate hippocampal formation: Evidence for a time-limited role in memory storage. *Science, 250,* 288–290.

Zornetzer, S. F., Thompson, R., & Rogers, J. (1982). Rapid forgetting in aged rats. *Behavioral and Neural Biology, 36,* 49–60.

CHAPTER 13

Process-Oriented View of Amygdala and Hippocampus

Mediation of Reward Value and Spatial Location Information

Raymond P. Kesner
Paul E. Gilbert

In 1966 Jim McGaugh formulated a theory of memory addressing the role of the central nervous system in the control of consolidation processes. The operation of a consolidation process was inferred from a paradigm in which a specific treatment (e.g., electroconvulsive shock, ECS, or electrical brain stimulation, EBS) was capable of producing a time-dependent disruption or facilitation in long-term retention of newly acquired experiences. In other words, these treatments were capable of disrupting or facilitating long-term retention when applied immediately after a training experience, but became less effective when delayed a few minutes or a few hours.

The pattern of results obtained with this paradigm led to the proposal that memory traces of new experiences initially reside in a labile short-term memory (STM), which decays within hours. This STM serves as the basis for retention of recent experiences and promotes the transfer of information to long-term memory (LTM) by initiating consolidation processes (McGaugh, 1966). This sequential dual-trace hypothesis is similar to that proposed by Hebb (1949).

Subsequent theoretical formulations (McGaugh & Dawson, 1971) assume that both STM and consolidation processes within LTM are initiated by new experiences but, in addition, information can also be transferred from STM to LTM. Furthermore, it is assumed that even though the duration of the STM

This research was supported by National Science Foundation Grant BNS 892-1532 and Human Frontier Science Program Grant RG0110/1998B.

trace is limited (information decays within hours), it determines the rate of growth of the trace in LTM.

One assumption usually made in interpreting results obtained from the consolidation paradigm is that the structure of memory consists of a monolithic trace, the strength of which can be represented by a one-dimensional measure. An alternative view (Kesner, 1998; Kesner & DiMattia, 1987) assumes that LTM consists of a set or bundle of traces, each representing some attribute or feature of the learning experience, requiring a multidimensional scaling of memory traces (see also Spear, 1976; Tulving, 1983). Within this multidimensional memory framework, it should be the case that an EBS-induced retention deficit is the result of altered storage of some of the necessary attributes, rendering the memory trace as weak, incomplete, and qualitatively different.

Thus, it becomes an important task for the researcher to identify the salient attributes of a specific experience and to select the essential neural brain regions that might subserve these attributes. For example, in a typical inhibitory avoidance training situation, the encoded memory might be composed of attributes associated with pain, environmental context (e.g., odor, illumination, location of painful shock), motivational state, affective reaction to pain (e.g., fear), and feedback from jumping and subsequent freezing responses.

Consolidation Research

To test whether different neuronal systems might contribute to the consolidation of specific attributes within an inhibitory avoidance learning situation, the amygdala and hippocampus were selected for study (Baker, Kesner, & Michal, 1981).

Rats with electrodes implanted in the amygdala or hippocampus were trained to enter a goal box to lick a tube containing water. After reaching a predetermined latency criterion, rats were given a 3 mA, 3-second foot shock followed 1 minute later by EBS. A subset of rats with electrodes implanted in the amygdala or hippocampus and nonoperated animals did not receive any stimulation. Retention was evaluated 24 hours later as an increase in latency to enter the goal box and lick the water tube at least 10 times. One hour after the retention test, all animals received a reminder cue (3 mA, 3-second foot shock) in a different apparatus (reminder cue apparatus) located in a different room. Twenty-three hours later they were tested for the second time in the original apparatus for retention of the foot shock experiences. It is important to note that a 3-mA, 3-second foot shock in the reminder cue apparatus does not increase latency to lick in the original apparatus. Also, placing the animal in the reminder cue apparatus without presentation of a foot shock results in a decrease in latency (less retention) on the second compared to the first retention test. Results are shown in Figure 13.1 and indicate that the nonoperated and operated but nonstimulated controls showed excellent retention, which was potentiated by a subsequent foot shock reminder cue. In contrast, stimulation of amygdala or hippocampus resulted in a retention deficit, which was reversed by presentation of the foot shock reminder cue for the hippocampus-stimulated group. The foot shock reminder cue was ineffective in reinstating the memory for the amygdala-stimulated group. These data suggest that amygdala stimulation might have disrupted attributes associated with emotional consequences of a foot shock, rendering a subsequent foot shock ineffective, whereas hippocampal stimulation affected different attributes, making it possible for a foot shock reminder to interact with the existing memory and thus increase subsequent retention.

In an additional experiment, rats with electrodes implanted in the amygdala or hippocampus and unoperated animals were trained to enter a goal box to lick a tube containing water. After reaching a predetermined latency criterion, all rats were given a 3 mA, 3-second foot shock. Retention was evaluated 24 hours later as an increase in latency to enter the goal box and lick the water

FIGURE 13.1

Group means of 10-lick latency scores (in seconds) for rats with electrical brain stimulation (EBS) of the amygdala or hippocampus or no EBS controls on Test 1 and Test 2 for reminder and nonreminder conditions.

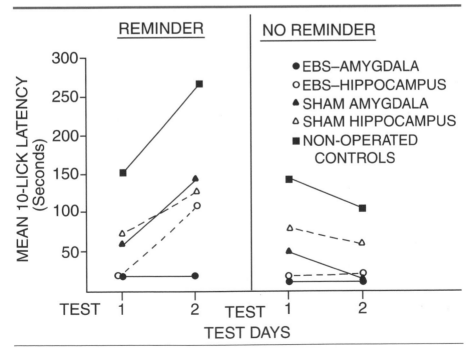

tube at least 10 times. One hour after the retention test, four groups of animals received a reminder cue (3 mA, 3-second foot shock) in a different apparatus (reminder cue apparatus) located in a different room followed immediately by hippocampal or amygdala stimulation or no stimulation (implanted and non-operated animals). The latter two groups of animals served as controls. They were placed in the reminder cue apparatus, but did not receive a foot shock reminder. Twenty-three hours later, all animals were tested for the second time in the original apparatus for retention of the foot shock experiences.

Nonoperated and amygdala- or hippocampus-implanted control animals that received a reminder foot shock, but no brain stimulation, showed a marked increase in latency on the second (Test 2) compared to the first (Test 1) retention test, suggesting that the foot shock reminder was effective in enhancing retention of the aversive experiences. In contrast, the absence of a foot shock reminder in nonoperated and implanted control animals resulted in a decrease in latency on Test 2 as compared to Test 1, suggesting that some extinction had occurred as a result of exposure to the original apparatus during Test 1. Animals that received a reminder foot shock followed by amygdala stimulation showed a decrease latency on Test 2 compared to Test 1, similar to the groups that never received a foot shock. In contrast, animals that received a reminder foot shock followed by hippocampal stimulation showed an increase in latency, albeit somewhat reduced. These data suggest that the amygdala, but not the hippocampus, is involved in processing of intense reinforcement contingencies utilizing affect or reward value mediated attributes.

A double dissociation effect can be obtained if one manipulates the distinctiveness of the inhibitory avoidance training apparatus rather than the reinforcement contingency. Rats were given inhibitory avoidance training using the same apparatus and training procedure as described by Baker et al. (1981), but in this case treatments were given within a phosphorescent environment. The animals were then tested for retention of the aversive experience using a partial cue (subset of the original training environment) and a complete cue (the original training environment). The results are shown in Figure 13.2 and indicate that posttrial hippocampus stimulation produced a retention deficit in both the partial and complete cueing conditions, whereas posttrial amygdala stimulation produced an intermediate retention deficit in the partial but no deficit in the complete cueing condition (Kesner & Hardy, 1983). These data suggest that the hippocampus, but not the amygdala, is involved in processing of the environmental context utilizing spatial–temporal attributes. In contrast the amygdala, but not the hippocampus, is involved in processing of intense reinforcement contingencies utilizing affect or reward value attributes.

Further support for the presumed differential contribution of the amygdala and hippocampus to memories for specific events using the consolidation paradigm comes both from between- and within-task analyses. Using a variety of

FIGURE 13.2

Group means of 10-lick latency (in seconds) for rats with electrical brain stimulation (EBS) of the amygdala or hippocampus or no EBS controls on Test 1 (partial cue) and Test 2 (complete cue) conditions.

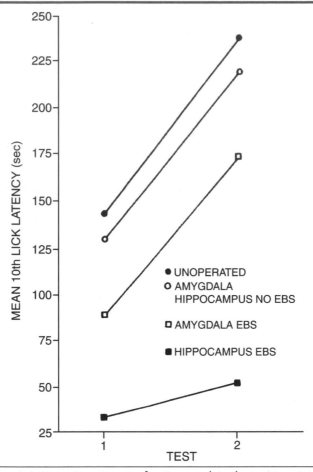

From Figure 3 in "Long-Term Memory for Contextual Attributes: Dissociation of Amygdala and Hippocampus," by R. P. Kesner & J. D. Hardy, 1983, *Behavioral Brain Research, 8*, p. 146. Reprinted with permission from Elsevier Science.

tasks in which reinforcement contingencies of sufficiently high magnitude were employed, it has been shown that pre- or posttraining electrical or chemical stimulation of the amygdala will result in impaired retention of inhibitory and active avoidance learning, shock-motivated visual discrimination learning, and taste-aversion learning (Baker et al., 1981; Gold, Hankins, Edwards, Chester, & McGaugh, 1975; Gold, Rose, Hankins, & Spanis, 1976; Handwerker, Gold, & McGaugh, 1975; Kesner, Berman, Burton, & Hankins, 1975; Kesner & Conner, 1974; Liang, McGaugh, Martinez, Jensen, & Vasquez, 1979; McDonough & Kesner, 1971; Todd & Kesner, 1978). In contrast, using relatively weak reinforcement contingencies similar treatments of the amygdala have no effect on retention of inhibitory avoidance learning, one-trial appetitive learning, and recovery from neophobia (Berman & Kesner, 1976; Gold et al., 1975; Kesner et al., 1975). Using a variety of tasks with distinctive environmental contexts and long-term retention tests, it has been shown that pre- or posttraining electrical stimulation of the hippocampus disrupts memory for one-trial appetitive learning and inhibitory avoidance learning (Berman & Kesner, 1976; Kesner & Conner, 1974). In contrast, using tasks that do not have distinctive environmental contextual components, similar treatments of the hippocampus have no effect on memory for taste-aversion learning or recovery from neophobia (Kesner & Berman, 1977).

Additional data that are not based on the consolidation paradigm but involve new learning implying the need to consolidate new information include a series of experiments with monkeys demonstrating that fornix lesions disrupt new learning involving associations between spatial information and discrete stimuli, whereas new learning of visual–visual associations remains intact (Gaffan, 1994). Furthermore, it has been reported that hippocampal lesions impair the acquisition of a spatial location navigation task using the Morris water maze or visual–place associations (Sutherland & McDonald, 1990; Sutherland, McDonald, Hill, & Rudy, 1989). whereas odor–odor associations remain intact (Bunsey & Eichenbaum, 1996). In addition, a series of experiments with monkeys demonstrated that bilateral lesions of the amygdala disrupt new learning that involves the association of the intrinsic value of food reward value with discrete stimuli, whereas new learning of visual–visual associations remains intact (Gaffan, 1992). Also, rats with amygdala lesions are impaired in the acquisition of a food–reward-dependent cue preference task as well as fear conditioning (Everitt, Morris, O'Brien, & Robbins, 1991; Killcross, Robbins, & Everitt, 1997; McDonald & White, 1993), but the acquisition of a spatial location navigation task using the Morris water maze remains intact (Sutherland & McDonald, 1990).

Theoretical Models

How is one to account for the double dissociation between the amygdala and hippocampus in influencing the consolidation of reward value versus spatial and environmental contextual attributes.

One model assumes that there are two memory systems, declarative and nondeclarative, with each characterized by a specific set of operations within or between tasks (Squire, 1983). The declarative memory system is based on explicit information that is easily accessible and is concerned with specific facts or data. It includes episodic and semantic representations of propositions and images. The hippocampus and interconnected neural regions, such as the entorhinal cortex, parahippocampal gyrus, and perirhinal cortex, mediate declarative, but not nondeclarative, memory. On the other hand, the nondeclarative memory system is based on implicit information that is not easily accessible and includes unaware representations of motor, perceptual, and cognitive skills as well as priming, simple classical conditioning, and nonassociative learning. It is assumed that skills and habits are mediated by the striatum, priming by the neocortex, simple classical conditioning of emotional responses by the amygdala, simple classical conditioning of skeletal musculature by the cerebellum, and nonassociative learning by reflex pathways (Squire, 1995). Furthermore, it is assumed that the two memory systems are independent of each other. Thus, the hippocampus is part of the declarative memory system and the amygdala is part of the nondeclarative memory system, and the two systems can operate independently of each other. One problem with the model is that it is not clear how the spatial component of a memory is exclusively mediated by the declarative memory system and how the affect component of a memory is exclusively mediated by the nondeclarative implicit memory system.

A different model assumes that the amygdala modulates memory by promoting the consolidation of other memory attributes (McGaugh, Introini-Collison, Cahill, Kim, & Liang, 1992). This is likely to be accomplished by direct amygdala activation of neural circuits that mediate attention and arousal processes (Kapp, Whalen, Supple, & Pascoe, 1992). The best evidence in support of amygdala modulation of the consolidation of other forms of memory representations comes from a study by Packard and Teather (1998). They showed that posttraining intrahippocampal injections of d-amphetamine facilitated retention of a spatial task, but had no facilitatory effect on a cued task. In contrast, posttraining intracaudate injections of d-amphetamine facilitated retention of the cued task, but had no facilitatory effect on the spatial task. Posttraining intra-amygdala injections of d-amphetamine enhanced retention of both tasks, even though amygdala lesions did not affect performance in the spatial and cued tasks. These results suggest that the amygdala might indeed modulate consolidation of attribute information that is dependent on mediation by other neural regions. Again, it is not clear how this model can account for double dissociation of function between the hippocampus and amygdala, because manipulation of the amygdala should produce comparable changes in the function of the hippocampus.

Another model, the attribute model, assumes that any specific memory is organized into a data-based memory system and a knowledge-based memory system (Kesner, 1998; Kesner & DiMattia, 1987). The data-based memory system is biased in providing for temporary representations of incoming data concerning the present, with an emphasis on facts, data, and events that are usually personal or egocentric and that occur within specific external and internal contexts. The data-based memory system is composed of different independently operating forms or attributes of memory. Even though there could be many attributes, the most important attributes include space, time, response, sensory perception, and affect. In humans a language attribute is also added.

The knowledge-based memory system is biased in providing more permanent representations of previously stored information in LTM and can be thought of as one's general knowledge of the world. It can operate in the abstract in the absence of incoming data. The knowledge-based memory system is composed of the same set of different independently operating forms or attributes of memory. These attributes include space, time, response, sensory perception, affect, and language. The data-based versus knowledge-based memory model recognizes different forms or attributes of memory within each system supported by different operating neural substrates. For example, within the data-based memory system, the hippocampus and interconnected neural regions subserve spatial, temporal, and linguistic attribute information; the caudate and interconnected neural regions subserve response and stimulus–response attribute information; the amygdala and interconnected neural regions subserve affect and stimulus–reward attribute information; and perirhinal visual cortex and interconnected neural regions subserve visual object information as an example of sensory–perceptual attribute information. Within the knowledge-based memory system, the parietal cortex and interconnected neural regions subserve spatial attribute information; the prefrontal cortex and interconnected neural regions subserve temporal and response attribute information; the orbital frontal cortex and interconnected neural regions subserve the affect attribute, and the inferotemporal cortex and interconnected neural regions subserve object information as an example of the sensory–perceptual attribute; and temporal, parietal, and frontal neural regions subserve linguistic attribute information. Furthermore, these substrates can operate independently of each other as indexed by empirical observations of double dissociations between neural regions and between attributes.

In the context of the two experiments presented above, the model suggests that the hippocampus promotes the consolidation of spatial attribute information into LTM or the knowledge-based memory system, and the amygdala promotes the consolidation of reward value or reinforcement as constituents of affect attribute information into LTM or the knowledge-based memory system. Thus, both the hippocampus and amygdala are part of the same data-based memory system, but each is different in processing different attributes. To test this idea further, it should be the case that the same operating processes that characterize the data-based memory system should apply to both the amygdala and hippocampus, but specified only for spatial versus affect attributes. Elsewhere (Kesner, 1998) it has been suggested that the data-based memory system can be characterized by a set of unique operating processes, including (a) consolidation or elaborative rehearsal of new attribute information and associations with other attributes, (b) STM or working memory of new attribute information and associations with other attributes, (c) pattern separation based on selective filtering or attenuation of interference associated with temporary memory representations of new attribute information, and (d) retrieval of attribute information based on flexibility and pattern completion.

Short-Term or Working Memory

One can measure the operation of STM or working-memory processes independently of consolidation by pretraining on a delayed matching-to-sample or delayed conditional discrimination task prior to a lesion manipulation (in this case, hippocampus vs. amygdala) followed by subsequent retests. It has been shown that hippocampus or fimbria fornix, but not amygdala, lesions disrupt STM or working memory in a spatial delayed nonmatching-to-sample task using a T maze or 8-arm maze (Becker, Walker, & Olton, 1980; Wan, Pang, & Olton, 1994). We examined this question in a slightly different fashion by using a spatial delayed matching-to-sample task and a list length of five spatial locations on an 8-arm maze (Kesner, 1988). In this experiment each rat was allowed to visit a sequence of five arms on each trial (one per day), which was selected on a pseudorandom basis. This constituted the study phase. Immediately after the rat had received reinforcement from the last of the five arms, the test phase began. Only one test was given for each trial and consisted of opening two doors simultaneously, with one door representing a novel arm for that trial. The rule to be learned leading to an additional reinforcement was to choose the arm that had been previously visited during the study phase of the trial. After training and reaching criterion performance the rats received lesions of the dorsal hippocampus, control lesions dorsal to the dorsal hippocampus, or basolateral amygdala lesions followed after a 1-week recovery by a new set of trials. The results for postoperative performance for each lesion group as a function of serial position are shown in Figure 13.3 and indicate that the dorsal hippocampal-lesioned group was impaired relative to the controls, but the basolateral amygdala-lesioned group performed as well as the controls. These data are consistent with the previous findings from the Olton laboratory. Thus, STM or working memory for spatial location information is mediated by the hippocampus, but not the amygdala.

To examine whether there is double dissociation in function of the amygdala and hippocampus, we selected an STM task that measured reward value. In this case rats were trained on a successive delayed conditional discrimination

FIGURE 13.3

Mean percentage correct postoperative performance for dorsal hippocampus, basolateral amygdala, and controls on item recognition for spatial locations across serial positions.

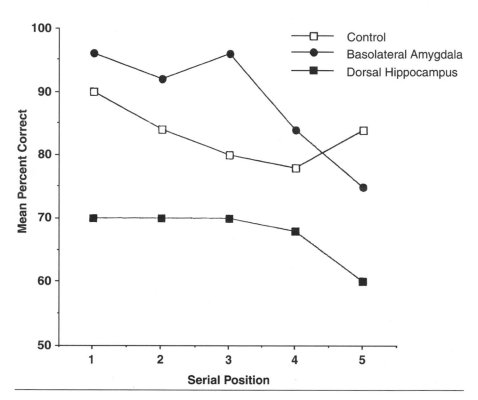

task measuring memory for magnitude of reinforcement (Kesner & Williams, 1995). In the study phase of the task, the rats were given one of two cereals. One cereal contained 25% sugar; the other 50% sugar. One of the two cereals was always designated the positive stimulus and the other the negative stimulus. This study phase was followed by the test phase in which the rat was shown an object which covered a food well. If the rat was given the negative stimulus in the study phase of the trial, no food reward was placed beneath the object. Whenever the positive stimulus was presented a food reward was available beneath the object. Performance was measured as the latency to uncover the food well. After reaching criterion level, the rats were given amygdala, hippocampal, or control lesions. The results are shown in Figure 13.4 and indicate that amygdala-lesioned rats showed significant deficits in performance, whereas

FIGURE 13.4

Pre- and postoperative mean latency (in seconds) for positive and negative trials for control (A), amygdala- (B), and hippocampus-lesioned (C) animals.

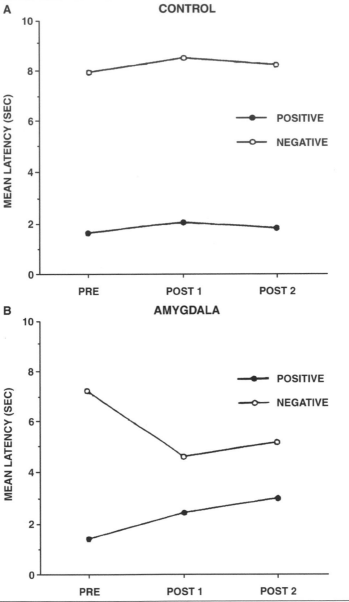

FIGURE 13.4

Continued

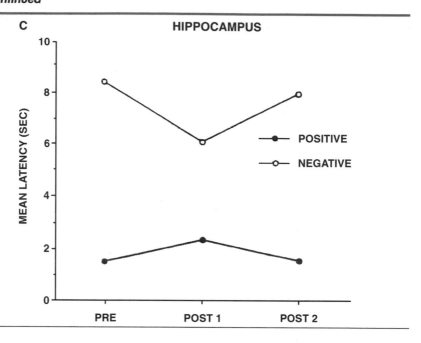

no deficits were observed for the hippocampal-lesioned groups even at longer retention delays. In additional experiments, it was shown that amygdala-lesioned rats, like normal rats, had similar taste preferences. Finally, normal and hippocampal-, but not amygdala-, lesioned rats transferred readily to different cereals containing 25% or 50% sugar. Thus, it appears that the amygdala, but not the hippocampus, plays a significant role in STM or working memory for affect information based on magnitude of reinforcement.

It is possible to combine spatial location and magnitude of reinforcement or reward value in an STM experiment to test whether both the amygdala and hippocampus play a role. In this experiment (Kesner, Walser, & Winzenried, 1989, and unpublished observations from our laboratory), rats received in the study phase one or seven pieces of sugar-coated cereal on different arms of an 8-arm maze. After the study phase, the rats were delayed for 10 seconds or 5 or 15 minutes. After the delay during the test phase, the rats were allowed to choose between the two arms presented in the study phase. The correct response leading to an additional cereal reinforcement was to select the arm in which the rat received the seven pieces of food. After training, lesions were made in the central or basolateral amygdala or the hippocampus. The results indicated that there was a deficit at all delays for the hippocampal-lesioned rats, but a deficit only for the 5- and 15-minute delays for the central amygdala-lesioned rats, and no deficits for the basolateral-lesioned rats. The data suggest that for STM of reward value the central amygdala might be more important than the basolateral amygdala. However, at present the central amygdala function can be dissociated from the basolateral amygdala on many dimensions and thus the meaning of this finding is not clear. Thus, in this experiment both lesions of the amygdala and hippocampus subserve STM for spatial location– reward value associations.

In general the overall data provide further support for the idea that the hippocampus and the amygdala can operate independently of each other and that they may be part of the same data-based memory system.

Pattern Separation

With respect to pattern separation, it is assumed that the function of the hippocampus is to use sensory information to mark the boundaries for spatial information, so that the hippocampus would temporarily store (STM) one spatial location as separate from another spatial location (spatial pattern separation) and promote the association between spatial information and other types of information (pattern association) for subsequent learning (consolidation), as well as retrieval (pattern completion) of new information. Support for this idea is based on the following observations: (a) that single cells within the hippocampus are activated by most sensory inputs, including vestibular, olfactory, visual, auditory, and somatosensory, as well as by higher order integration of sensory stimuli (Cohen & Eichenbaum, 1993); (b) that STM or working memory for spatial information is markedly disrupted following hippocampal lesions (Kesner, 1998); and (c) that STM or working memory for sensory (e.g., odor or visual object) information is not altered by lesions of the hippocampus (Aggleton, Hunt, & Rawlins, 1986; Jackson-Smith, Kesner, & Chiba, 1993; Kesner, Bolland, & Dakis, 1993; Mumby, Wood, & Pinel, 1992; Otto & Eichenbaum, 1992).

To examine the role of the hippocampus in separating patterns of spatial information, Gilbert, Kesner, and DeCoteau (1998) developed a paradigm based on measuring STM memory for spatial location information as a function of spatial similarity between two spatial locations. Specifically, the study was designed to examine the role of the hippocampus in separating spatial events when rats were required to remember a spatial location dependent on environmental cues and differentiate between the to-be-remembered location and a different location with different degrees of similarity or overlap among the cues. Animals were tested using a dry land version of the Morris water maze on a delayed match-to-sample for spatial location task. Animals were trained to displace an object that was randomly positioned to cover a baited food well in 1 of 15 locations along a row of food wells positioned perpendicular to a start box. Following a short delay, the animals were required to choose between two objects identical to the sample phase object. One object was in the same lo- cation as the sample phase object and the second object was in a different location along the row of food wells. An animal was rewarded for displacing the object in the same position as the sample phase object (correct choice) but received no reward for displacing the foil object (incorrect choice). Five spatial distances, from 15 cm to 105 cm, were used to separate the correct object from the foil object on the choice phase. The data are shown in Figure 13.5 and indicate that animals with cortical control lesions matched their preoperative performance across all spatial separations. In contrast, animals with hippocam- pal lesions were significantly impaired across all spatial separations with the exception of the largest (105 cm) separation. There was also a linearly increasing improvement in performance as a function of distance of the spatial separation. Transfer tasks have demonstrated that animals tend to use environmental cues to solve this task rather than other possible strategies. Based on these results, it is concluded that lesions of the hippocampus decrease efficiency in spatial pattern separation that resulted in impairments on trials with increased spatial similarity among working-memory representations. In additional studies we have demonstrated that colchicine lesions of the dorsal dentate gyrus parallel the same deficit pattern for spatial pattern separation observed following com- plete dorsal and ventral hippocampal lesions. In contrast, ibotenic acid lesions of dorsal CA1 have no effect on spatial pattern separation, whereas ibotenic acid lesions of CA3 produce a total deficit for all distances. The CA3 results reflect the presumed operation of STM or working memory.

Enhanced spatial similarity between environmental cues and decreased efficiency in pattern separation could represent a key process deficiency in hippocampal-lesioned rats on spatial memory tasks, such as the Morris water maze and the 8-arm radial maze. Support for this idea comes from Eichenbaum, Stewart, and Morris (1990), who reported that when rats with fimbria-fornix lesions were trained on a water maze from a constant starting position they learned the task as well as controls. However, if the starting point varied on each trial, fornix-lesioned rats displayed deficits in acquisition of the task. In a similar study, Hunt, Kesner, and Evans (1994) demonstrated that rats with hippocampal lesions learned to enter a designated arm on an 8-arm radial maze when the arm remained constant. However, when the reward arm varied on each trial, hippocampal-lesioned animals were impaired relative to controls. Hippocampal-lesioned rats were significantly impaired on these tasks when there was increased overlap or similarity among distal cues, but performed the task well when the similarity was decreased. Thus, if lesions in the hippocampus or disruptions of hippocampal function result in inefficient pattern separation, then this may result in deficits on spatial tasks when there is increased overlap

FIGURE 13.5

Pre- and postoperative mean percentage correct performance for cortical control (A) and hippocampus-lesioned (B) groups as a function of distance (in cm).

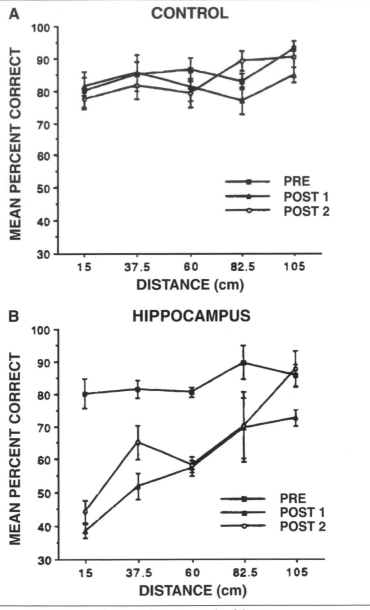

From Figure 2 in "Memory for Spatial Location: Role of the Hippocampus in Mediating Spatial Pattern Separation," by P. E. Gilbert, R. P. Kesner, & W. E. DeCoteau, 1998, *Journal of Neuroscience, 18,* p. 807. Reprinted with permission of the Society for Neuroscience.

or similarity among distal cues and presumably increased similarity among representations. Unfortunately, we have not yet tested amygdala-lesioned rats in this task, but we would predict that there would not be any deficits.

With respect to pattern separation, it is assumed that the function of the amygdala is to use sensory information to mark the content of reward value information, so that the amygdala would temporarily store (STM) one reward value as separate from another reward value (reward value pattern separation) and promote the association between reward value information and other types of information (pattern association) for subsequent learning (consolidation) as well as retrieval (pattern completion) of new information.

To examine the role of the amygdala in separating patterns of reward value information, Gilbert, Kesner, and DeCoteau (1998) developed a paradigm to measure drinking behavior based on anticipatory differential discrimination of reward value as a function of magnitude of similarity between two reward values. Rats with either quinolinic-acid-induced lesions of the amygdala, electrolytic lesions of the amygdala, electrolytic lesions of the hippocampus, or control lesions were tested using a modified version of Flaherty's (1996) anticipatory contrast paradigm. Prior to testing, all rats were water deprived for 15 minutes. In the home cage, each rat was given 1 trial per day consisting of a sample phase followed by a test phase. During the sample phase, each rat was allowed to drink a water solution containing 2% sucrose for 3 minutes. On the ensuing test phase, each animal was then allowed to drink a water solution containing 32% sucrose for 3 minutes. The phases of testing were separated by a 15-second delay. The amount of each solution consumed was then recorded. Across 10 days of testing, control-lesioned animals demonstrated a small reduction in the intake of the 2% solution and a large increase in the intake of the 32% solution that is referred to as an anticipatory differential discrimination effect. The performance of the hippocampal- and the amygdala-lesioned group matched the performance of the control group, similarly to that described by Flaherty, Coppotelli, Hsu, and Otto (1997). Therefore, it appears that neither the amygdala nor the hippocampus are involved in the acquisition of anticipatory discrimination between different values of reward.

To assess the operation of a pattern separation mechanism, all animals were then tested using the same procedure; however, the 2% sample phase solution was followed by a test phase solution consisting of water containing 16% sucrose for 10 days and then by an 8% sucrose solution for 10 days. Thus, on each consecutive 10-day block of testing, the relative difference between the sucrose concentration of the sample phase and test phase was reduced. The results are shown in Figure 13.6 and indicate that control- and hippocampal-lesioned animals continued to show an anticipatory discrimination effect as evidenced by a significant increase in the intake of the 16% and 8% solution and no increase in the 2% solution intake. In contrast, the amygdala-lesioned

FIGURE 13.6

Mean fluid consumption (in ml) in a 3-minute period for control (A), hippocampus- (B), and amygdala-lesioned (C) animals as a function of different test phase sucrose concentration.

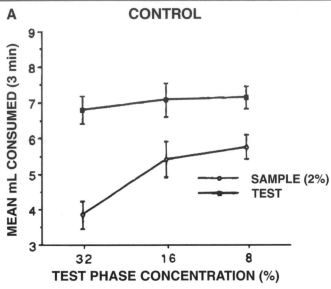

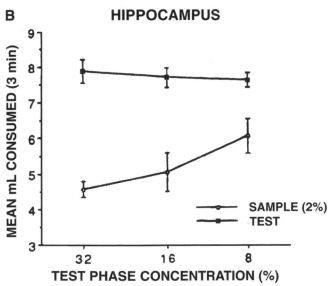

FIGURE 13.6

Continued

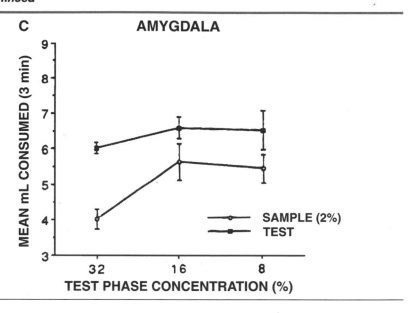

group did not display a significant anticipatory discrimination effect (no significant difference in the amount of each solution consumed) when the 2% preceded either the 16% or 8% sucrose solution.

It was important to demonstrate that the increase in the amount of the 32% sucrose solution consumed and the small decrease in the amount of 2% solution consumed were the result of the less preferred 2% solution preceding the preferred 32% solution. Therefore, prior to testing, half of a group of control animals was given only the 2% sucrose solution for 3 minutes and the other half was given only 32% sucrose solution for 3 minutes. This procedure was followed once daily for 10 days. Therefore, it was possible to compare how much of each solution was consumed when each solution was presented separately (no discrimination condition) with how much was consumed when the 2% solution preceded the 32% solution (discrimination condition). In the no contrast condition, there were no significant differences in the amount of the solutions consumed between the group given only the 2% solution and the group given only the 32% solution. This can be compared with the differential discrimination condition, when the 2% solution precedes the 32% solution, where control animals drink significantly more of the 32% sucrose solution than the 2% sucrose solution.

Following all testing, each animal was then tested on a preference test to demonstrate that any deficits observed were not due to disinhibition or a sensory deficit. During the preference test, each animal was again given 1 trial per day across 5 days in the home cage. However, both a 2% sucrose and 32% sucrose solution were presented simultaneously and the animal was allowed to drink from either or both of the solutions for 15 minutes. The amount of each solution consumed was then recorded. The same procedure was then followed; however, the 2% solution was presented simultaneously with a 16% sucrose solution and then with a 8% sucrose solution. The position of each solution varied each day such that one solution was not always on the same side of the cage on each trial. Animals in the control, hippocampal, amygdala, and lesion groups showed a significant preference for the 32%, 16%, and 8% solutions when compared to the 2% sucrose solution. The results indicate that the deficit in the amygdala-lesioned group did not appear to be due to an inability to inhibit responding or due to a sensory deficit. Thus, if lesions in the amygdala or disruptions of amygdala function result in inefficient pattern separation, then this may result in deficits on differential discrimination of magnitude of reinforcement (reward) when there is increased overlap or similarity among reward value cues and presumably increased similarity among representations.

In general, it appears that the hippocampus is involved in spatial location pattern separation, whereas the amygdala is involved in reward value pattern separation.

Retrieval

Even though it has been proposed that the hippocampus also plays an important role in retrieval of new information (Hirsh, 1980), there is only a limited database for an important retrieval function for the hippocampus. Eichenbaum and colleagues have devised a series of transitivity tasks demonstrating that rats with hippocampal lesions are impaired in retrieving novel information, suggesting an inflexibility in solving new problems (Eichenbaum, 1994, 1996). However, other studies that have tested hippocampal-lesioned rats have shown normal transfer to novel tasks, suggesting flexible use of information to solve new problems (Cho & Kesner, 1995; DeCoteau, Kesner, & Williams, 1997; Jackson-Smith & Kesner, 1989; Walker & Olton, 1984).

A different approach to measure the operation of a retrieval process is based on measuring retention following lesions applied after learning a specific task. Furthermore, one can then compare the results with the effects of lesions prior to acquisition of the task, so that comparisons can be made between the operation of consolidation and retrieval processes. It should be noted that the operation of a retrieval process or consolidation process does not imply that the hippocampus stores information in LTM. It is more likely that the hippocampus participates in the promotion of consolidation elsewhere (e.g., entorhinal and parietal cortex) and is involved in retrieval of spatial information from elsewhere (e.g., entorhinal and parietal cortex). There is a vast and often contradictory literature using these types of paradigms. We illustrate its utility using retention of the Morris water maze or dry land version of the water maze spatial navigation task. It can be shown that compared to controls lesions of the hippocampus disrupt not only acquisition but also subsequent retention using either the water maze or dry land version of the water maze (DiMattia & Kesner, 1998; Kesner, Farnsworth, & Kametani, 1992; Morris, Schenk, Tweedie, & Jarrard, 1990). In terms of regional specificity, Moser, Moser, & Anderson (1993) and Moser and Moser (1998) have shown that ibotenic acid lesions of the dorsal, but not ventral, hippocampus impaired acquisition, whereas dorsal and some ventral hippocampus lesions were necessary to impair retention. These results suggest that the hippocampus is both involved in consolidation and retrieval processes. Also, it is of interest that AP5 (an N-methyl d-aspartate, NMDA, antagonist) injections into the hippocampus disrupted acquisition, but not retention, suggesting that the NMDA receptors within the hippocampus may play a critical role in consolidation, but not in retrieval of spatial information (Morris, Anderson, Lynch, & Baundry, 1986).Thus, there is some, albeit limited, support for a hippocampus-mediated retrieval function.

With respect to the role of the amygdala in retrieving reward value information, the same paradigm described for examining hippocampus function in consolidation versus retrieval has been employed, but in this case fear-conditioning tasks have been used extensively.

It should be noted that the operation of a retrieval process or consolidation process does not imply that the amygdala stores information in LTM. It is more likely that the amygdala participates in the promotion of consolidation elsewhere (e.g., orbital frontal and agranular insular cortex) and is involved in retrieval of spatial information from elsewhere (e.g., orbital frontal and agranular insular cortex). It has been shown that excitotoxic lesions of the basolateral amygdala 6 or 30 days after training completely blocked the expression or retrievability of fear-potentiated startle (Lee, Walker, & Davis, 1996). Similar lesions of the basolateral amygdala 1, 14, or 28 days after Pavlovian fear conditioning abolished conditional freezing to both the acoustical and contextual stimuli at all retention delays, suggesting that this neural region plays an important role in retrieval of conditioned fear information (Maren, Aharonov, & Fanselow, 1996). Also, it is of interest that AP5 (an NMDA antagonist) injections into the amygdala disrupted acquisition but not retention of fear-potentiated startle (Campeau, Miserendino, & Davis, 1992), suggesting that the NMDA receptors within the amygdala may play a critical role in consolidation but not in retrieval of affect (fear) information. The amygdala parallels the results observed for the hippocampus in mediating spatial information in that both consolidation and retrieval of fear conditioning is mediated by the amygdala. Some additional support for an amygdala mediation of action perhaps subserved by retrieval processes comes from a study demonstrating that lesions of the basolateral, but not central, amygdala disrupts classical conditioning of fear responses, whereas central, but not basolateral, amygdala disrupt instrumental conditioning of fear, suggesting that different subregions within the amygdala contribute based on different response requirements resulting in different actions. Clearly, more research is needed to understand the contribution of both the amygdala and hippocampus in supporting the retrieval process.

Conclusion

In summary, it appears that there is excellent support for parallel processing for the amygdala and hippocampus with respect to reward value and spatial location information not only for supporting consolidation processes but also for pattern separation, STM, and retrieval as well. The two brain regions appear to be part of the same operating system. The attribute model can account for these results rather well and continues to serve as a model to guide future research.

References

Aggleton, J. P., Hunt, P. R., & Rawlins, J. N. P. (1986). The effects of hippocampal lesions upon spatial and non-spatial tests of working memory. *Behavioral Brain Research, 19,* 133–146.

Baker, L. J., Kesner, R. P., & Michal, R. E. (1981). Differential effects of a reminder cue on amnesia induced by stimulation of amygdala and hippocampus. *Journal of Comparative and Physiological Psychology, 95,* 312–321.

Becker, J. T., Walker, J. A., & Olton, D. S. (1980). Neuroanatomical bases of spatial memory. *Brain Research, 200,* 307–320.

Berman, R. F., & Kesner, R. P. (1976). Posttrial hippocampal, amygdaloid and lateral hypothalamic electrical stimulation: Effects upon memory of an appetitive experience. *Journal of Comparative and Physiological Psychology, 90,* 260–267.

Bunsey, M., & Eichenbaum, H. (1996). Conservation of hippocampal memory function in rats and humans. *Nature, 379,* 255–257.

Campeau, S., Miserendino, M. J. D., & Davis, M. (1992). Intra-amygdala infusion of the N-methyl-D-aspartate receptor antagonist AP5 blocks acquisition but not expression of fear-potentiated startle to an auditory conditioned stimulus. *Behavioral Neuroscience, 106,* 569–574.

Cho, Y. H., & Kesner, R. P. (1995). Relational object association learning in rats with hippocampal lesions. *Behavioral Brain Research, 67,* 91–98.

Cohen, N. J., & Eichenbaum, H. B. (1993). *Memory, amnesia, and hippocampal function.* Cambridge, MA: MIT Press.

DeCoteau, W. E., Kesner, R. P., & Williams, J. M. (1997). Short-term memory for food reward magnitude: The role of the prefrontal cortex. *Behavioural Brain Research, 88,* 239–249.

DiMattia, B. V., & Kesner, R. P. (1998). Spatial cognitive maps: Differential role of parietal cortex and hippocampal formation. *Behavioral Neuroscience, 102,* 471–480.

Eichenbaum, H. (1994). The hippocampal system and declarative memory in humans and animals: Experimental analysis and historical origins. In D. L. Schacter & E. Tulving (Eds.), *Memory systems 1994* (pp. 147–201). Cambridge, MA: MIT Press.

Eichenbaum, H. (1996). Is the rodent hippocampus just for "place"? *Current Opinion in Neurobiology, 6,* 187–195.

Eichenbaum, H., Stewart, C., & Morris, R. G. M. (1990). Hippocampal representation in spatial learning. *Journal of Neuroscience, 10,* 331–339.

Everitt, B. J., Morris, K. A., O'Brien, A., & Robbins, T. W. (1991). The basolateral amygdala-ventral striatal system and conditioned place preference: Further evidence of limbic-striatal interactions underlying reward-related processes. *Neuroscience, 42,* 1–18.

Flaherty, C. F. (1996). *Incentive relativity.* New York: Cambridge University Press.

Flaherty, C. F., Coppotelli, C., Hsu, D., & Otto, T. (1997). Excitotoxic lesions of the hippocampus disrupt runway but not consummatory contrast. *Behavioural Brain Research, 93,* 1–9.

Gaffan, D. (1992). Amygdala and the memory of reward. In J. P. Aggleton (Ed.), *The amygdala: Neurobiological apsects of emotion, memory, and mental dysfunction* (pp. 471–484). New York: Wiley-Liss.

Gaffan, D. (1994). Disassociated effects of perirhinal cortex ablation, fornix transaction, and amygdalectomy: Evidence for multiple memory systems in the primate temporal lobe. *Experimental Brain Research, 99,* 411–422.

Gilbert, P. E., Kesner, R. P., & DeCoteau, W. E. (1998). Memory for spatial location: Role of the hippocampus in mediating spatial pattern separation. *Journal of Neuroscience, 18,* 804–810.

Gold, P. E., Hankins, L., Edwards, R. M., Chester, J., & McGaugh, J. L. (1975). Memory interference and facilitation with posttrial amygdala stimulation: Effect on memory varies with footshock level. *Brain Research, 86,* 509–513.

Gold, P. E., Rose, R. P., Hankins, L. L., & Spanis, C. (1976). Impaired retention of visual discriminated escape training produced by subseizure amygdala stimulation. *Brain Research, 118,* 73–85.

Handwerker, M. J., Gold, P. E., & McGaugh, J. L. (1974). Impairment of active avoidance learning with posttraining amygdala stimulation. *Brain Research, 75,* 324–327.

Hebb, D. O. (1949). *The organization of behavior.* New York: Wiley.

Hirsh, R. (1980). The hippocampus, conditional operations, and cognition. *Physiological Psychology, 8,* 175–182.

Hunt, M. E., Kesner, R. P., & Evans, R. B. (1994). Memory for spatial location: Functional dissociation of entorhinal cortex and hippocampus. *Psychobiology, 22,* 186–194.

Jackson-Smith, P., & Kesner, R. P. (1989). Does the hippocampus play a role in mediating spatial and temporal configurations? *Society for Neuroscience Abstracts, 15,* 608.

Jackson-Smith, P., Kesner, R. P., & Chiba, A. A. (1993). Continuous recognition of spatial and nonspatial stimuli in hippocampal lesioned rats. *Behavioral and Neural Biology, 59,* 107–119.

Kapp, B. S., Whalen, P. J., Supple, W. F., & Pascoe, J. P. (1992). Amygdaloid contributions to conditioned arousal and sensory information processing. In J. P. Aggleton (Ed.), *The amygdala: Neurobiological aspects of emotion, memory, and mental dysfunction* (pp. 229–254). New York: Wiley-Liss.

Kesner, R. P. (1988). Reevaluation of the contribution of the basal forebrain cholinergic system to memory. *Neurobiology of Aging, 9,* 609–616.

Kesner, R. P. (1998). Neurobiological views of memory. In J. L. Martinez, Jr., & R. P. Kesner (Eds.), *Neurobiology of learning and memory* (pp. 361–416). New York: Academic Press.

Kesner, R. P., & Berman, R. F. (1977). Effects of midbrain reticular formation, hippocampal and lateral hypothalamic stimulation upon recovery from neophobia and taste aversion learning. *Physiology and Behavior, 18,* 763–768.

Kesner, R. P., Berman, R. F., Burton, B., & Hankins, W. G. (1975). Effects of electrical stimulation of amygdala upon neophobia and taste aversion. *Behavioral Biology, 13,* 349–358.

Kesner, R. P., Bolland, B. L., & Dakis, M. (1993). Memory for spatial locations, motor responses, and objects: Triple dissociation among the hippocampus, caudate nucleus, and extrastriate visual cortex. *Experimental Brain Research, 93,* 462–470.

Kesner, R. P., & Conner, H. S. (1974). Effects of electrical stimulation of limbic system and midbrain reticular formation upon short- and long-term memory. *Physiology and Behavior, 12,* 5–12.

Kesner, R. P., & DiMattia, B. V. (1987). Neurobiology of an attribute model of memory. In A. N. Epstein & A. R. Morrison (Eds.), *Progress in psychobiology and physiological psychology* (Vol. 12, pp. 207–277). New York: Academic Press.

Kesner, R. P., Farnsworth, G., & Kametani, H. (1992). Role of parietal cortex and hippocampus in representing spatial information. *Cerebral Cortex, 1,* 367–373.

Kesner, R. P., & Hardy, J. D. (1983). Long-term memory for contextual attributes: Dissociation of amygdala and hippocampus. *Behavioral Brain Research, 8,* 139–149.

Kesner, R. P., Walser, R. D., & Winzenried, G. (1989). Central but not basolateral amygdala mediates memory for positive affective experiences. *Behavioural Brain Research, 33,* 189–195.

Kesner, R. P., & Williams, J. M. (1995). Memory for magnitude of reinforcement: Dissociation between the amygdala and hippocampus. *Neurobiology of Learning and Memory, 64,* 237–244.

Killcross, S., Robbins, T. W., & Everitt, B. J. (1997). Different types of fear-conditioned behavior mediated by separate nuclei within amygdala. *Nature, 388,* 377–380.

Lee, Y., Walker, D., & Davis, M. (1996). Lack of a temporal gradient of retrograde amnesia following NMDA-induced lesions of the basolateral amygdala assessed with the fear-potentiated startle paradigm. *Behavioral Neuroscience, 110,* 836–839.

Liang, K. C., McGaugh, J. L., Martinez, J. L., Jr., Jensen, R. A., & Vasquez, B. J. (1979). Time dependent effect of posttrial amygdaloid lesions on retention of an inhibitory avoidance response. *Society for Neuroscience, 5,* 319.

Maren, S., Aharonov, G., & Fanselow, M. S. (1996). Retrograde abolition of conditional fear after excitotoxic lesions in the basolateral amygdala of rats: Absence of a temporal gradient. *Behavioral Neuroscience, 110,* 718–726.

McDonald, R. J., & White, N. M. (1993). A triple dissociation of systems: Hippocampus, amygdala, and dorsal striatum. *Behavioral Neuroscience, 107,* 3–22.

McDonough, J. R., Jr., & Kesner, R. P. (1971). Amnesia produced by brief electrical stimulation of the amygdala or dorsal hippocampus in cats. *Journal of Comparative and Physiological Psychology, 77,* 171–178.

McGaugh, J. L. (1966). Time-dependent processes in memory storage. *Science, 153,* 1351–1358.

McGaugh, J. L., & Dawson, R. G. (1971). Modification of memory storage processes. *Behavioral Science, 16,* 45–63.

McGaugh, J. L., Introini-Collison, I. B., Cahill, L., Kim, M., & Liang, K. C. (1992). Involvement of the amygdala in neuromodulatory influences on memory storage. In J. Aggleton (Ed.), *The amygdala* (pp. 431–451). New York: Wiley-Liss.

Morris, R. G., Anderson, E., Lynch, G. S., & Baundry, M. (1986). Selective impairment of learning and blockade of long-term potentiation by an N-methyl-D-aspartate receptor antagonist, AP5. *Nature, 319,* 774–776.

Morris, R. G., Schenk, F., Tweedie, F., & Jarrard, L. E. (1990). Ibotenate lesions of hippocampus and/or subiculum: Dissociating components of allocentric spatial learning. *European Journal of Neursocience, 2,* 1016–1028.

Moser, E. I., Moser, M. B., & Anderson, P. (1993). Spatial learning impairment parallels the magnitude of dorsal hippocampal lesions, but is hardly present following ventral lesions. *Journal of Neuroscience, 13,* 3916–3925.

Moser, M. B., & Moser, E. I. (1998). Distributed encoding and retrieval of spatial memory in the hippocampus. *Journal of Neuroscience, 18,* 7535–7542.

Mumby, D. G., Wood, E. R., & Pinel, J. P. J. (1992). Object recognition memory is only mildly impaired in rats with lesions of the hippocampus and amygdala. *Psychobiology, 20,* 18–27.

Otto, T., & Eichenbaum, H. (1992). Complementary roles of the orbital prefrontal cortex and the perirhinal-entorhinal cortices in an odor-guided delayed-nonmatching-to-sample task. *Behavioral Neuroscience, 106,* 762–775.

Packard, M. G., & Teather, L. A. (1998). Amygdala modulation of multiple memory systems: Hippocampus and caudate-putamen. *Neurobiology of Learning and Memory, 69,* 163–203.

Spear, N. E. (1976). Retrieval of memories: A psychobiological approach. In W. K. Estes (Ed.), *Handbook of learning and cognitive processes: Vol. 4. Attention and memory* (pp. 17–90). Hillsdale, NJ: Erlbaum.

Squire, L. R. (1983). The hippocampus and the neuropsychology of memory. In W. Seifert (Ed.), *Neurobiology of the hippocampus* (pp. 491–511). New York: Academic Press.

Squire, L. R. (1995). Biological foundation of accuracy and inaccuracy in memory. In D. L. Schacter (Ed.), *Memory distortion* (pp. 197–225). Cambridge, MA: Harvard University Press.

Sutherland, R. J., & McDonald, R. J. (1990). Hippocampus, amygdala, memory deficits in rats. *Behavioural Brain Research, 37,* 57–79.

Sutherland, R. J., McDonald, R. J., Hill, C. R., & Rudy, J. W. (1989). Damage to the hippocampal formation in rats selectively impairs the ability to learn cue relationships. *Behavioral and Neural Biology, 52,* 331–356.

Todd, J. W., & Kesner, R. P. (1978). Effects of posttraining injection of cholinergic agonists and antagonists into the amygdala on retention of passive avoidance training in rats. *Journal of Comparative and Physiological Psychology, 92,* 958–968.

Tulving, E. (1983). *Elements of episodic memory.* Oxford, England: Clarendon Press.

Walker, J. A., & Olton, D. S. (1984). Fimbria-fornix lesions impair spatial working memory but not cognitive mapping. *Behavioral Neuroscience, 98,* 226–242.

Wan, R.-Q., Pang, K., & Olton, D. S. (1994). Hippocampal and amygdaloid involvement in nonspatial and spatial working memory in rats: Effects of delay and interference. *Behavioral Neuroscience, 108,* 866–882.

CHAPTER 14

Learning and Neural Plasticity Over the Life Span

Mark R. Rosenzweig

A s one who has enjoyed many personal, academic, and professional contacts with Jim McGaugh since the 1950s, including being the chair of his doctoral dissertation committee, it gives me great pleasure to take part in this fest-schrift and celebrate his productive and distinguished career.

Part of Jim's strength is that he takes comprehensive views of learning and memory, putting specific research into a larger framework. This chapter deals with two areas with which Jim has long been concerned: The first, and shorter, part deals with the stages of memory formation. A recent article challenges the widely held conclusion that formation of long-term memory depends on earlier stages of memory formation, but that research may have its own flaws. The second, and main part, deals with learning, memory, and neural plasticity over the life span. This topic has yielded surprising findings recently, and there is still much to learn about it.

Are the Stages of Memory Formation Sequentially Dependent?

In 1967 at a meeting in Italy, I enjoyed hearing Jim present a paper in which he hypothesized an intermediate-term stage of memory formation (ITM; McGaugh, 1968). He saw the necessity for such a stage to bridge the gap between short-term memory (STM) and long-term memory (LTM), because research of the late 1950s showed STM to last less than 1 minute, if rehearsal was prevented (Brown, 1958; Peterson & Peterson, 1959), whereas LTM forms only an hour or more after training. In the same year, Halstead and Rucker (1968) also concluded that a two-stage model of memory formation was too simple, and they proposed a three-phase model with an intermediate phase arising soon after learning and lasting about 3 hours. Jim also raised the question whether the successive stages of memory formation occur independently or are sequentially dependent (McGaugh, 1968). This question has continued to stimulate research and comment. Although many investigators have concluded that the stages are sequentially dependent, a recent article by Ivan Izquierdo, Barros, Mello e Souza, de Souza, and Izquierdo (1998) claimed that LTM is independent of STM, and I consider some of the issues raised by their investigation.

Izquierdo et al. (1998) gave rats inhibitory avoidance training in a step-down apparatus, then injected certain amnestic agents into the hippocampus immediately posttraining, and tested each animal at two or three posttraining intervals. With some agents, the rats showed impaired performance at what the investigators called the "short-term" training–testing interval of 1.5 hours but showed evidence of strong memory at the long-term interval of 24 hours. Although further work on the relations among stages of memory formation is welcome, I believe the Izquierdo et al. study does not prove the independence of LTM from STM, as I have pointed out to Ivan (Izquierdo) in detailed email correspondence and discuss briefly here.

The paper by Izquierdo et al. (1998) raised several issues: (a) Is this the first assertion of independence of successive memory stages from each other? (The authors stated that their report "shows, for the first time, to our knowledge, that short-term and long-term memory mechanisms are separated" [p. 635].) (b) Is it correct to designate the earlier memory they tested at 1.5 hours posttraining as STM? (c) Do their data require us to accept their conclusion of independence of LTM from the earlier memory stages, or are there other possible interpretations?

Prior Claims of Independence of LTM From Earlier Memory Stages

In regard to the first question, other investigators have already presented evidence for the independence of LTM from either STM or other stages that precede LTM. For example, Kesner and Conner (1972) published an article entitled "Independence of Short- and Long-Term Memory: A Neural System Analysis." They reported that rats that received electrical stimulation to the midbrain reticular formation 4 seconds after training showed amnesia at the 64-second test but memory at the 24-hour test; in contrast, rats that received stimulation to the hippocampus showed memory at the 64-second test but amnesia at the 24-hour test. Warrington and Shallice (1969) and Baddeley, Papagano, and Vallar (1988) investigated patients with brain damage who had severely deficient verbal STM but appeared to have normal LTM. Squire, Knowlton, and Musen (1993) pointed out, however, that further testing of these and similar patients revealed that the deficit was for one component of STM and that a corresponding deficit was found in a comparable kind of LTM. The later work supported what Squire et al. (1993) called "the traditional view that STM grades into LTM and is essential for its formation" (p. 457).

Other investigators have reported evidence of the independence of LTM from stages after STM. For example, Frieder and Allweis (1978) reported that hypoxia immediately after training of rats did not prevent complete retention for about 12 minutes, but then memory decayed to the naive level over the next 75 minutes, only to reappear about 100 minutes later. Their interpretation was that hypoxia prevented the transcription of memory from the short-term to the medium-term holding mechanism, but did not prevent the formation of LTM. Further evidence of independence among some stages of memory comes from research on *Drosophila* (Dubnau & Tully, 1998; Tully et al., 1996). Tully and colleagues reported that memory in *Drosophila* is consolidated in four stages, each of which can be prevented by deficiencies in one or more genes specific to that stage. In their report, STM lasts less than 1 hour; medium-term memory (MTM) lasts a few hours; anesthesia-resistant memory (ARM) begins close to the time of training and lasts more than 24 hours; LTM starts about 5 hours after training and lasts for days. Tully and his colleagues found that the pathway of stages is sequential through MTM but then branches into two independent paths—one leading to ARM and the other to LTM. This brief review shows that several investigators have claimed independence of LTM from earlier stages of memory.

It is well known that, without any pharmacological or other treatment, many experiments show a decline in memory strength about from 1 through 6 hours after aversive training, with a gradual rise thereafter; this is often referred to as the Kamin effect (Kamin, 1957, 1963). Halstead and Rucker (1968) proposed that the Kamin effect might reflect the decline of ITM before LTM became fully established. Others have accounted for the Kamin effect in terms of both an inhibitory process and an incubation of LTM, without suggesting that the Kamin effect indicates independence of LTM from earlier stages of memory. The timing, duration, and depth of the Kamin effect are affected by several variables (Kamin, 1963).

Differing Definitions of Memory Stages

What stage of memory appeared to be independent of LTM in Izquierdo et al. (1998)? These investigators stated that they "tested animals twice . . . once at 1.5 hours after training, to measure short-term memory, and once at 24 hours after training, to measure long-term memory" (p. 635). Because the earliest tests of memory in their study were made 1.5 hours after training, the usage of most investigators indicates that they were studying ITM rather than STM. It was noted above that early users of the term STM used it to designate memory that lasts for only seconds, unless the memory is rehearsed (Brown, 1958; Peterson

& Peterson, 1959). Many investigators using animals or human subjects continue to use STM in the sense that the originators of this term meant and in the sense that McGaugh (1968) employed. For example, Craik (1992) stated, "The phrase *short-term retention* is used here to refer to situations in which subjects retain a small amount of material over several seconds" (p. 12).

When I wrote to Izquierdo about this and related questions, he replied that the designation "short-term memory" properly applies to memory tested about 1–3 hours after training and that memory tested earlier should be called "immediate memory." This is an example of the lack of consensus about the terms used to describe stages of memory, a situation that my colleagues and I have pointed out as an impediment to research and understanding (e.g., Rosenzweig, 1996, pp. 15–16, 1998a, p. 7, 1998b, p. 7; Rosenzweig, Bennett, Colombo, Lee, & Serrano, 1993; Rosenzweig, Leiman, & Breedlove, 1996, 1999, pp. 474–475).

Alternative Interpretations of the Results

Regardless of the name assigned to the earlier stage of memory tested by Izquierdo et al. (1998), can their observations be interpreted in a way that does not conflict with the widely held conclusion that LTM depends on formation of earlier stages of memory—especially because the latter conclusion is supported by voluminous data from humans, rats, mice, chicks, honeybees, and *Drosophila*? Two alternative interpretations involve (a) the Kamin effect and (b) the reactivation or reminder effect.

The Kamin effect could account for a dip in memory anywhere from 1 hour to 6 hours after training, the exact timing and strength of the effect depending on the details of the experiment. The drug injections may have altered the timing and strength of the effect to produce declines at the 1.5–3-hour times measured by Izquierdo and his colleagues for STM. Investigating this possibility would require determining the retention curve at closely spaced time intervals.

Reminder effects (reactivation of memory) might account for the observations of Izquierdo et al. because their experimental design involved testing the same subjects at successive time intervals. Experiments from the 1970s to the present have investigated reminder effects or have used them as part of the experimental designs (e.g., Cherkin, 1972; Davis, Rosenzweig, Bennett, & Orme, 1978; Deweer & Sara, 1984; Lewis & Bregman, 1973; Przybslawski, Roullet, & Sara, 1999; Przybslawski & Sara, 1997; Rosas & Bouton, 1998). Thus, my colleagues and I (Davis et al., 1978) studied memory for a step-through task, rather similar to the step-down task of Izquierdo et al. (1998). We found that when memory had been weakened either by use of an amnestic agent or by passage of time, exposure of mice to the apparatus, without delivery of a foot shock, significantly enhanced avoidance on a subsequent trial. In the experiments of Izquierdo et al., the appearance of strong memory at the long-term interval, after poor memory at the so-called short-term interval, may have reflected the reminder effect of the first test trial. Testing different subjects at the different time intervals would have obviated this ambiguity. It is true, as Izquierdo pointed out, that repeated testing had no effect on the performance of the control (saline-injected) animals, but the saline controls showed high performance, and reminder effects are seen only when initially poor performance is improved after one or more earlier trials.

Plasticity Over the Life Span

Now let us turn to plasticity of the brain and behavior over the life span. Currently, much attention is being given to changes in the brain during early development and the importance of early experience for children's later development. This is certainly important, but exclusive focus on early learning and plasticity should be resisted, it seems to me, both for research and also for discussions of public policy. Here are two examples of the current emphasis on early experience: the journal *Science,* noting a research report by Knudsen (1998) describing a kind of brain plasticity in the barn owl that occurs readily during early development but only under special circumstances in the adult, commented that this finding "reinforces what Hillary Clinton and the news magazines have been telling us: that exposing our kids to more experiences at a young age may make them smarter adults" (Baringara, 1998, p. 1452). Some have pushed this line even farther. Thus, the California Superintendent of Public Instruction stated, "There is extraordinary research coming out that shows the brain is being wired before the age of 6. If you haven't done a good job of wiring, the system won't work properly" (Minton, 1998). I am concerned that overemphasis on early learning and plasticity may lead to neglect of learning and neural plasticity later in the life span. After all, most of us continue to learn well beyond childhood, and many people continue to learn as elders. Since the 1960s I have tried to counter the popular belief that brain plasticity is largely restricted to infancy. Thus, when I gave an invited address to the American Psychological Association's Division of Developmental Psychology in 1965 (Rosenzweig, 1966), the aspect of our research that raised the most interest, surprise, and skepticism among my developmental colleagues was that the brains of adult rats changed anatomically and biochemically in response to environmental experience and that these changes were associated with better learning ability. Bruer (1999) referred to this 1966 article and the response to it even though it occurred before his date for the origin of the "myth of the first three years." Concern with overemphasis on the early years has also been expressed by others, including Bill Greenough, as noted in *Science* (Holden, 1997, p. 1570).

Overemphasis on plasticity during the first few years has complicated attempts to apply research on environmental enrichment to improve the cognitive status of children raised in inadequate environments. Some proponents have overestimated the potential effects of relatively short periods of enrichment and then have been disappointed that the effects were not larger or longer lasting. This has been one of the problems confronting the Head Start program that began in 1963 in the United States (Zigler & Muenchow, 1992). Although this and related programs have proved to be beneficial and cost-effective, they were unable to bring most participating children up to the scholastic levels of children living in better environments. A combination of early and later enriched training can be effective. I saw this firsthand beginning in 1964 when I became cochair of the new Special Opportunity Scholarship program inaugurated by members of the faculty at the University of California at Berkeley. This program gave supplementary training to students of local high schools, coming from impoverished or otherwise deprived backgrounds, who were promising but who were unlikely to be able to qualify for entrance to the university. The additional training and guidance during the high school years enabled many of the participants to enter the University of California or other universities and to pursue successful studies.

Rather than expand further on this point, let us examine some of the different ways in which certain kinds of learning and neural plasticity occur over the life span.

There Are Two Major Models of Neural Plasticity

Two major models of neural plasticity were discovered in the 1960s: First, investigators at Berkeley (Bennett, Diamond, Krech, & Rosenzweig, 1964; Krech, Rosenzweig, & Bennett, 1960; Rosenzweig, Krech, & Bennett, 1961; Rosenzweig, Krech, Bennett, & Diamond, 1962) found that enriched experience, versus either standard colony experience or isolation, alters neurochemistry and neuroanatomy of the cortex of rats. Successive extensions of the initial work showed that such effects could be induced not only in young rats but also in juveniles (Zolman & Morimoto, 1962), in young adults (Bennett et al., 1964; Rosenzweig, Bennett, & Krech, 1964), and in old rats (Riege, 1971), although the size of the effects was greatest in the young animals (Figure 14.1b). Further work showed that enriched experience or formal training of adult rats altered neuronal anatomy in several ways, including increased dendritic branching (Greenough & Volkmar, 1973; Holloway, 1966), increased size of neuronal cell bodies and nuclei (Diamond, 1967), increased area of synaptic contacts

(West & Greenough, 1972), and increased numbers of dendritic spines (Globus, Rosenzweig, Bennett, & Diamond, 1973). Second, the work of Hubel and Wiesel (1965; Wiesel & Hubel, 1963) showed that occluding one eye of a kitten during a critical period reduced the number of cortical cells that respond to that eye (Figure 14.1a). After a few months of age, depriving an eye of light did not affect its cortical representation, so this kind of plasticity occurs only during an early critical period.

Recently it has been reported that not only can existing neurons be altered by experience throughout the life span but formation and survival of new neurons can also be enhanced by enriched experience. Neurogenesis seems to decrease markedly with age, and its function in adults is not yet clear. Gage, van Praag, and Kempermann (2000) review nearly 40 years of research on neural consequences of enriched environment, including reports on neurogenesis.

The research reviewed in the last paragraphs clearly demonstrates neural plasticity throughout the life span. Further experimental demonstrations of life-long plasticity include remapping the somesthetic cortex of adult animals as a function of experience (Kaas, 1991), remapping auditory receptive fields (Weinberger, 1998), and adaptation and reorganization of the adult visual cortex (Singer, 1992). Singer concluded, "behavioral, electrophysiological, and morphological evidence confirms the persistence of use-dependent plasticity in the striate cortex of adult mammals and humans" (p. 453).

Another example is the recent surprising finding that sexual behavior can alter the structure of the nervous system, even in adulthood (Breedlove, 1997). Thus, it is possible that some structural differences between the sexes (or between people of differing sexual orientation) are the result of the behavioral differences rather than the cause. Although these examples give clear evidence of neural plasticity throughout the life span, it must be emphasized that there has been relatively little work so far to measure how the degree of most kinds of plasticity varies over the life span.

Many examples of neural plasticity are not limited to these two contrasting models of plasticity, either limited to an early critical period or maintained well over the life span. Several different models are needed to encompass all the findings. Furthermore, even kinds of learning and neural plasticity that seem similar may follow different time courses over the life span. For example, one study reported that long-term potentiation (LTP) can be evoked in the supragranular visual cortex of rats only to Day 30, whereas it can be evoked in the infragranular layers into adulthood (Perkins & Teyler, 1988). More generally, we should remember that a person who can no longer form certain kinds of memory, because of brain damage or disease, can still form other kinds of memory perfectly well. The next sections show some examples of different models of plasticity.

FIGURE 14.1

Some patterns of behavioral and neural plasticity across the life span.

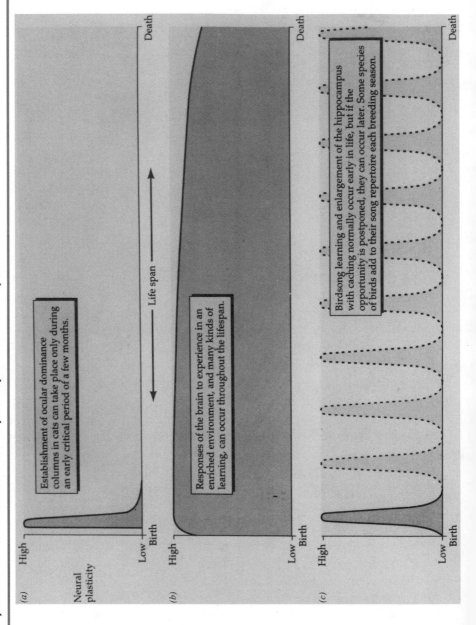

(a)

Establishment of ocular dominance columns in cats can take place only during an early critical period of a few months.

(b)

Responses of the brain to experience in an enriched environment, and many kinds of learning, can occur throughout the lifespan.

(c)

Birdsong learning and enlargement of the hippocampus with caching normally occur early in life, but if the opportunity is postponed, they can occur later. Some species of birds add to their song repertoire each breeding season.

Neural plasticity

High

Low

Birth

Life span

Death

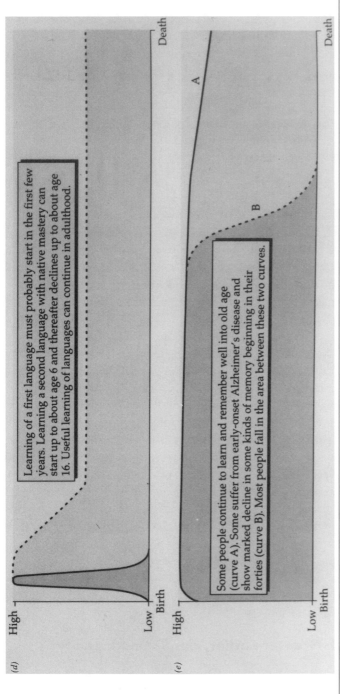

High

Low

Birth

Death

(d)

Learning of a first language must probably start in the first few years. Learning a second language with native mastery can start up to about age 6 and thereafter declines up to about age 16. Useful learning of languages can continue in adulthood.

High

Low

Birth

Death

(e)

A

B

Some people continue to learn and remember well into old age (curve A). Some suffer from early-onset Alzheimer's disease and show marked decline in some kinds of memory beginning in their forties (curve B). Most people fall in the area between these two curves.

2nd ed., From Figure 1 of *Biological Psychology: An Introduction to Behavioral, Cognitive, and Clinical Neuroscience* (p. 558), by M. R. Rosenzweig, A. L. Leiman, and S. M. Breedlove, 1999. Sunderland, MA: Sinauer Associates. Copyright 1999 by Sinauer Associates. Reprinted with permission of the publisher.

Some Kinds of Plasticity Occur at the First Opportunity

Some kinds of plasticity occur as soon as the opportunity occurs. The limit is not a matter of age or maturity but of opportunity. Ocular dominance columns in cats normally form early and do not change later (Hubel & Wiesel, 1965).

> In cats, plasticity appears to be maximal at about 1 month of age and then declines over the next 3 months, after which time the visual pathways are virtually immutable. During this plastic period, every major response property of cortical cells (ocular dominance, orientation selectivity, direction selectivity, disparity sensitivity) can be modified by manipulation of the visual environment. (Mower, Christen, & Caplan, 1983, p. 178)

It is not clear what normally terminates plasticity in these aspects of the visual system. Baer and Singer (1986) suggested one possibility: They reported that they could restore plasticity in the visual cortex of adult cats by perfusing the area with acetylcholine and noradrenaline, so perhaps localized developmental decreases in synthesis of these transmitters are responsible for the decline in plasticity. The critical period for plasticity of the visual system can be extended if cats are reared in the dark, but a 6-hour period of exposure to light triggers the developmental process, and once triggered, it runs to completion in the absence of further input (Mower et al., 1983).

Birdsong learning provides another example in which learning occurs at the first opportunity. Normally a male bird learns its song from its father. If a bird is kept from hearing birdsong at the usual age, it can learn later, provided it is given an accurate model (Eales, 1987). Eales concluded that the sensitive phase for song learning remains open-ended until the bird hears suitable material. For some time it was thought not to be possible to acquire birdsong after the normal age. That conclusion was based on experiments with a taped tutor, but later acquisition was shown to be possible from a live tutor or from a taped tutor if the tape was very accurate. Some species of songbird, such as canaries, add to their repertoire during each breeding season, so there is periodic plasticity (Figure 14.1c).

In species of birds that cache food, the hippocampus grows larger than in related species that do not cache. If the bird does not have the opportunity to cache, the hippocampus does not enlarge. The opportunity can be postponed well beyond the usual age in laboratory-raised birds. Once they have the opportunity to cache, they do so promptly, and the hippocampus reflects this experience by enlarging (Clayton, 1995).

Plasticity Is Much Greater Earlier, but Some Plasticity Remains Later

Two examples in which plasticity is greater earlier but some plasticity remains later come from the visual system and from neurogenesis.

Plasticity Over the Life Span in the Visual System

Speculation and investigation of plasticity in the adult visual system has a long and varied history. Some of it deals with human recovery from congenital blindness. This question goes back at least to John Locke (1690). He supposed that a man, born blind but then given sight, would not be able initially to identify a sphere or a cube by sight but would then learn, guided by touch, to perceive them visually. Studies of human recovery from congenital blindness include both examples of rather successful recovery and of failure, according to a review by Gregory (1987). It has been studied in people born with dense cataracts that were removed in adulthood. Gregory noted "often the eye takes a long time to settle down after a cataract operation" (p. 95), which may partially explain why many of the historical cases show slow development of vision. A patient studied by Gregory and Wallace (1963) received corneal grafts that provided good retinal images immediately, and the patient could recognize almost immediately objects he already knew by touch, but his vision never became fully normal. Learning to see is slow in adults, as it is in infants, but it appears to be possible to learn to see as an adult. The question is complicated by the fact that a person who has not seen until adulthood has learned other ways to adjust to the environment, and it may be difficult to abandon these.

Aligning the two eyes, preventing amblyopia, is usually thought to be limited to the first 5–6 years, but considerable improvement can be shown, even by adults, if the amblyopia is not too severe and if they exercise the weak eye sufficiently. One study reported considerable recovery from long-standing amblyopia after the good eye was lost or severely damaged (Romero-Apis et al., 1982).

In an important animal experiment on acquisition of vision in adults, Chow and Stewart (1972) deprived kittens of pattern vision in one eye for about 20 months after birth. When such kittens were tested for pattern perception with the previously deprived eye, they showed almost no discrimination on formal tests and were not able to guide locomotion with the previously deprived eye, although they performed well with the other eye. The investigators then undertook an intensive program of rehabilitation with some of the kittens. Over time, the kittens developed some pattern discrimination in the previously deprived eye, and they could use it to guide their locomotion. Furthermore, recovery of vision was accompanied by morphological changes in the lateral geniculate nucleus, and electrical recording showed increased numbers of binocular cells in the visual cortex. Here again, learning to see and plasticity of the visual system can occur after the usual developmental period.

Neurogenesis Over the Life Span

Neurogenesis has recently been recognized to occur in the hippocampus throughout the life span, not only in rodents (Altman & Das, 1967; Kempermann, Kuhn, & Gage, 1997; York, Breedlove, Diamond, & Greer, 1989) but also in monkeys (Gould, Tanapat, McEwen, Flugge, & Fuchs, 1998) and in humans (Erikson et al., 1998). Until recently most neuroscientists believed that, with a few exceptions such as olfactory receptor neurons, most mammals have at birth all the nerve cells they will ever have. Some evidence had been reported for postnatal neurogenesis in rodents, including guinea pigs that are born with almost completely developed brains (Altman & Das, 1967), but at the time this aroused little interest. In an influential article Rakic (1985) reported inability to find neurogenesis in adult rhesus monkeys. Rakic argued that perhaps neurogenesis could not be permitted in adult primates because a stable population of neurons may be important for the continuity of learning and memory over a lifetime.

In the recent research, the subjects were injected with the thymidine analog bromodeoxyuridine (BrdU), which labels dividing cells, and also with an agent that marks neurons and an agent that marks glial cells. The rate of production of neurons in the hippocampus has been found to decline with age in rodents, but the rate is increased by exposure to a complex environment, and this increase is relatively larger in aged than in young adults (Kempermann, Kuhn, & Gage, 1998). Formal training in tasks in which acquisition requires the hippocampus appears to enhance the survival of recently generated neurons (Gould, Beylin, Tanapat, Reeves, & Shors, 1999). The interpretation of enhanced survival is supported by two recent findings: (a) There is an increased number of BrdU-labeled neurons in the dentate gyrus of animals injected before training but not in animals injected during training. (b) Learning these tasks decreases the number of pyknotic (dying) cells found in the dentate gyrus. Another test would provide further evidence on whether training and enriched experience enhance survival of recently generated neurons. This would be to sacrifice animals at various intervals after BrdU injections, given to some animals before training and to others during training, and to study the changes in numbers of labeled neurons at successive time intervals.

In Some Cases, Later Plasticity Depends on Early Training

Knudsen (1998) found that auditory–visual neurons in the optic tectum of the owl can be trained over a wide range of adjustments in a young owl equipped with prismatic lenses; it learns to adapt and locate objects accurately. The range of adjustment is normally quite restricted in adults. But if an owl learns an abnormal auditory–visual adjustment as a juvenile and is then returned to the normal condition, it can reacquire the abnormal adjustment again as an adult.

It appears that the early learning leaves a neural trace that, even if not used for an extended period, can be reestablished later, when needed.

The ability to learn a second language with native mastery is possible if the learner starts the second language by the age of 6 or 7 years (Johnson & Newport, 1989), provided the first language was begun during the first few years (Figure 14.1d). Investigators are not in complete agreement about the age limits for first language learning, but this appears to be possible up to about 3 years of age, with a gradual falloff thereafter (Morford & Mayberry, 2000). Fortunately, very few children with normal hearing are deprived of the possibility of acquiring speech in their first years, so most of the research in this area is based on acquisition of sign language by deaf children.

Mastery of the second language is reported to show increasing departures from full native skill as the starting age increases from 7 to 16 years (Johnson & Newport, 1989). Other investigators (e.g., Bates, 1999), using different measures of language ability, doubt that there is any single period for language learning. People who start learning their second language in their teenage years form a second Broca's area adjacent to the Broca's area for their first language (Kim, Relkin, Lee, & Hirsh, 1997). Nevertheless, even people who start to learn a second (or third, or fourth) language as adults can gain conversational fluency, provided they work hard enough at it. Formation of a second Broca's area as a result of language learning in the teens provides a striking example of neural plasticity beyond the early part of the life span.

Varied Decline Occurs in Plasticity in the Latter Part of Life

Abilities to learn and remember decline on the average in the latter part of the life span, although some older people and animals perform as well as younger conspecifics (Figure 14.1e, Curve A). In contrast to long-term maintenance of learning and neural plasticity, some individuals suffer from early onset Alzheimer's disease and show a marked decline in formation of declarative memories in their 40s (Curve B). Most people fall into the area between these two curves as they age. In those older individuals who show declines in ability with age, some studies show changes in neuroanatomy (such as shrinkage of the hippocampus) or in neurochemistry that may explain the decline. The *ApoE4* gene, which intensifies the effects of conditions that impair the brain, also shows its effects mainly in older individuals. Thus, the observed declines in ability may be pathological rather than normal, and it may become possible to counteract or prevent them. It has been proposed that the decline of abilities to learn and remember in the latter part of the life span occurs because there has been no evolutionary pressure to maintain these abilities or even to repair worn structures after the reproductive period (Baltes, 1997), which may indicate why special efforts are needed to prevent such declines. Enriched experience early in life and continued throughout the life span helps to reduce the risk of cognitive decline in old age. At an international symposium on cognitive decline in old age, I summarized the research in this way (Rosenzweig & Bennett, 1996, p. 63):

> It's a fortunate person whose brain
> Is trained early, again and again,
> And who continues to use it
> To be sure not to lose it,
> So the brain, in old age, may not wane.

Mechanisms That Enable and Limit Plasticity

To the extent that certain types of neural plasticity are limited to parts of the life span, it will be important to find the mechanisms that enable plasticity and that limit it. One factor that may limit plasticity was mentioned in regard to the visual system—decline in production of synaptic transmitters (Baer & Singer, 1986). Another is shrinkage of the hippocampus (Golomb et al., 1994). Other neurobiological changes with aging that may bear on neural plasticity have been reviewed by Gallagher and Rapp (1997). Formation of memory has been shown to require a cascade of several neurochemical processes (e.g., Rosenzweig, 1996, pp. 14–17), and so does induction of LTP (e.g., Rosenzweig et al., 1999, pp. 505–508). Interfering with any step in the cascade impairs formation of memory, but little has been done so far to study the steps in the cascade as a function of age. Investigating such mechanisms and their age dependencies may, in the future, allow us to find both behavioral and biological treatments to improve learning and memory and to extend some kinds of learning farther over the life span.

Modulatory factors that affect learning and memory storage also vary with age. For example, nerve growth factor (NGF) is important both in the development of the nervous system and in the maintenance and plasticity of the nervous system later in life, but the production of NGF declines with age. In an attempt to counter this decline, investigators grafted CNS-derived stem cells, genetically engineered to secrete NGF, into the basal forebrain of aged rats (Martinez-Serrano, Fischer, Soderstrom, Ebendal, & Bjorklund, 1996). Testing in the Morris water maze showed that the treated rats recovered their cognitive ability. The mechanism by which NGF restores cognitive ability is not clear, but a recent study reports that when the decline of cortical innervation by cholinergic systems in aged monkeys was reversed by placing NGF-secreting cells in the basal forebrain, this also reversed the age-related decline in number and complexity of cholinergic axon terminals in the cortex (Conner, Darracq, Roberts, & Tuszynski, 2001). Even without genetic intervention, giving rats enriched experience increases significantly the cerebral levels of NGF and other neurotrophins (Ickes et al., 2000), and it improves their problem-solving behavior. Giving rats a combination of genetically engineered cells to increase NGF and experience in complex mazes led to major increases in the size of cells in the basal forebrain and also superior problem solving (Brooks, Cory-Slechta, & Federoff, 2000). In clinical tests derived from such research, investigators have begun transplanting into the brains of Alzheimer's disease patients cells taken from the patients' skin and modified to produce NGF, hoping to slow and perhaps even reverse the decline of memory. So, study of modulatory as well as direct factors may help to improve learning and memory over the life span.

References

Altman, J., & Das, G. D. (1967). Postnatal neurogenesis in the guinea pig. Nature, 214, 1098–1101.

Baddeley, A. D., Papagano, C., & Vallar, G. J. (1988). When long-term learning depends on short-term storage. Journal of Memory and Language, 27, 586–595.

Baer, M. F., & Singer, W. (1986). Modulation of visual cortical plasticity by acetylcholine and noradrenaline. Nature, 320, 172–176.

Baltes, P. B. (1997). On the incomplete architecture of human ontogeny: Selection, optimization, and compensation as foundation of developmental theory. American Psychologist, 52, 366–380.

Baringara, M. (1998). Owl study sheds light on how young brains learn. Science, 279, 1451–1452.

Bates, E. (1999). Plasticity, localization, and language development. In S. E. Broman & J. M. Fletcher (Eds.), The changing nervous system: Neurobehavioral consequences of early brain disorders (pp. 214–253). New York: Oxford University Press.

Bennett, E. L., Diamond, M. C., Krech, D., & Rosenzweig, M. R. (1964). Chemical and anatomical plasticity of brain. Science, 146, 610–619.

Breedlove, S. M. (1997). Sex on the brain. Nature, 389, 801.

Brooks, A. I., Cory-Slechta, D. A., & Federoff, H. J. (2000). Gene-experience interaction alters the cholinergic septohippocampal pathway of mice. Proceedings of the National Academy of Sciences, 97, 13378–13383.

Brown, J. (1958). Some tests of the decay theory of immediate memory. Quarterly Journal of Experimental Psychology. 10, 12–21.

Bruer, J. T. (1999). The myth of the first three years: A new understanding of early brain development and lifelong learning. New York: Free Press.

Cherkin, A. (1972). Retrograde amnesia in the chick: Resistance to the reminder effect. Physiology and Behavior, 8, 949–955.

Chow, K. L., & Stewart, D. L. (1972). Reversal of structural and functional effects of long-term visual deprivation in cats. *Experimental Neurology, 34,* 409–433.

Clayton, N. S. (1995). The neuroethological development of food-storing memory: A case of use it, or lose it. *Behavioural Brain Research, 70,* 95–102.

Conner, J. M., Darracq, M. A., Roberts, J., & Tuszynski, M. H. (2001). Nontropic actions of neurotrophins: Subcortical nerve growth factor gene delivery reverses age-related degeneration of primate cortical cholinergic innervation. *Proceedings of the National Academy of Sciences, 98,* 1941–1946.

Craik, F. I. M. (1992). Aging and memory in humans. In L. R. Squire (Ed.), *Encyclopedia of learning and memory* (pp. 12–16). New York: Macmillan.

Davis, H. P., Rosenzweig, M. R., Bennett, E. L., & Orme, A. (1978). Recovery as a function of the degree of amnesia due to protein synthesis inhibition. *Pharmacology Biochemistry and Behavior, 8,* 701–710.

Deweer, B., & Sara, S. J. (1984). Background stimuli after spontaneous forgetting: Role of duration of cueing and cueing-test interval. *Animal Learning and Behavior, 12,* 238–247.

Diamond, M. C. (1967). Extensive cortical depth measurements and neuron size increases in the cortex of environmentally enriched rats. *Journal of Comparative Neurology, 131,* 357–364.

Dubnau, J., & Tully, T. (1998). Gene discovery in *Drosophila*: New insights for learning and memory. *Annual Review of Neuroscience, 21,* 407–444.

Eales, L. A. (1987). Song learning in female-raised zebra finches: Another look at the sensitive phase. *Animal Behaviour, 35,* 1356–1365.

Erikson, P. S., Perfilieva, E., Bjork-Eriksson, T., Alborn, A. M., Nordberg, C., Peterson, D. A., & Gage, F. H. (1998). Neurogenesis in the adult human hippocampus. *Nature Medicine, 4,* 1313–1317.

Frieder, B., & Allweis, C. (1978). Transient hypoxic-amnesia: Evidence for a triphasic memory consolidating mechanism with parallel processing. *Behavioral and Neural Biology, 22,* 178–189.

Gage, F. H., van Praag, H., & Kempermann, G. (2000). Neural consequences of environmental enrichment. *Nature Reviews Neuroscience, 1*(3), 191–198.

Gallagher, M., & Rapp, P. R. (1997). The use of animal models to study the effects of aging on cognition. *Annual Review of Psychology, 48,* 339–370.

Globus, A., Rosenzweig, M. R., Bennett, E. L., & Diamond, M. C. (1973). Effects of differential experience on dendritic spine counts in rat cerebral cortex. *Journal of Comparative and Physiological Psychology, 82,* 175–181.

Golomb, J., de Leon, M. J., George, A. E., Klufer, A., Convit, A., Rusinek, H., de Santi, S., Litt, A., Foo, S. H., & Ferris, S. H. (1994). Hippocampal atrophy correlates with severe cognitive impairment in elderly patients with suspected normal hydrocephalus. *Journal of Neurology, Neurosurgery and Psychiatry, 57,* 590–593.

Gould, E., Beylin, A., Tanapat, P., Reeves, A. J., & Shors, T. J. (1999). Learning enhances adult neurogenesis in the hippocampal formation. *Nature Neuroscience, 2,* 260–265.

Gould, E., Tanapat, P., McEwen, B. S., Flugge, G., & Fuchs, E. (1998). Proliferation of granule cell precursors in the dentate gyrus of adult monkeys is diminished by stress. *Proceedings of the National Academy of Sciences (USA), 95,* 3168–3171.

Greenough, W. T., & Volkmar, F. R. (1973). Pattern of dendritic branching in occipital cortex of rats reared in complex environments. *Experimental Neurology, 40,* 491–504.

Gregory, R. L. (1987). Blindness, recovery from. In R. L. Gregory (Ed.), *The Oxford companion to the mind* (pp. 94–96). Oxford, England: Oxford University Press.

Gregory, R. L., & Wallace, J. G. (1963). *Recovery from early blindness: A case study.* Cambridge, England: Cambridge University Press.

Halstead, W. C., & Rucker, W. B. (1968). Memory: A molecular maze. *Psychology Today, 2,* 38–41, 66–67.

Holden, C. (1997). Overstimulated by early brain research? *Science, 278,* 1569–1570.

Holloway, R. L. (1966). Dendritic branching: Some preliminary results of training and complexity in rat visual cortex. *Brain Research, 2,* 393–396.

Hubel, D. H., & Wiesel, T. N. (1965). Binocular interaction in striate cortex of kittens reared with artificial squint. *Journal of Neurophysiology, 28,* 1041–1059.

Ickes, B. R., Pham, T. M., Sanders, L. A., Albeck, D. S., Mohammed, A. H., & Granholm, A. C. (2000). Long-term environmental enrichment leads to regional increase in neurotrophin levels in rat brain. *Experimental Neurology, 164*(1), 45–52.

Izquierdo, I., Barros, D. M., Mello e Souza, T., de Souza, M. M., & Izquierdo, L. A. (1998). Mechanisms for memory types differ. *Nature, 393,* 635.

Johnson, J. S., & Newport, E. L. (1989). Critical period effects in second language learning: The influence of maturational state on the acquisition of English as a second language. *Cognitive Psychology, 21,* 60–99.

Kaas, J. H. (1991). Plasticity of sensory and motor maps in adult animals. *Annual Review of Neuroscience, 14,* 137–167.

Kamin, L. J. (1957). The retention of an incompletely learned avoidance response. *Journal of Comparative and Physiological Psychology, 50,* 457–460.

Kamin, L. J. (1963). Retention of an incompletely learned avoidance response: Some further analyses. *Journal of Comparative and Physiological Psychology, 56,* 713–718.

Kempermann, G., Kuhn, H. G., & Gage, F. H. (1997). More hippocampal neurons in adult mice living in an enriched environment. *Nature, 386,* 493–495.

Kempermann, G., Kuhn, H. G., & Gage, F. H. (1998). Experience-induced neurogenesis in the senescent dentate gyrus. *Journal of Neuroscience, 18,* 3206–3212.

Kesner, R. P., & Conner, H. S. (1972). Independence of short- and long-term memory: A neural system analysis. *Science, 176,* 432–434.

Kim, K. H. S., Relkin, N., Lee, K.-M., & Hirsh, J. (1997). Distinct cortical areas associated with native and second languages. *Nature, 388,* 171–174.

Knudsen, E. I. (1998). Capacity for plasticity in the adult owl auditory system expanded by juvenile experience. *Science, 279,* 1531–1533.

Krech, D., Rosenzweig, M. R., & Bennett, E. L. (1960). Effects of environmental complexity and training on brain chemistry. *Journal of Comparative and Physiological Psychology, 53,* 509–519.

Lewis, D. J., & Bregman, N. J. (1973). Source of cues for cue-dependent amnesia in rats. *Journal of Comparative and Physiological Psychology, 85,* 421–426.

Locke, J. (1690). *An essay concerning human understanding.* London: T. Basset.

Martinez-Serrano, A., Fischer, W., Soderstrom, S., Ebendal, T., & Bjorklund, A. (1996). Long-term functional recovery from age-induced spatial memory impairments by nerve growth factor gene transfer to the rat basal forebrain. *Proceedings of the National Academy of Sciences, 93*(13), 6355–6360.

McGaugh, J. L. (1968). A multi-trace view of memory storage processes. In D. Bovet, F. Bovet-Nitti, & A. Oliverio (Eds.), *Attuali orientamenti della ricerca sull'apprendimento e la memoria* [Current directions of research on learning and memory] (pp. 13–24). Rome: National Academy of Lincei.

Morford, J. P., & Mayberry, R. I. (2000). A reexamination of "early exposure" and its implications for language acquisition by eye. In C. Chamberlain, J. P. Morford, & R. I. Mayberry (Eds.), *Language acquisition by eye* (pp. 111–127). Mahwah, NJ: Erlbaum.

Mower, G. D., Christen, W. G., & Caplan, C. J. (1983). Very brief visual experience eliminates plasticity in the cat visual cortex. *Science, 221,* 178–180.

Perkins, A. T., & Teyler, T. J. (1988). A critical period for long-term potentiation in the developing rat visual cortex. *Brain Research, 39,* 222–229.

Peterson, L. R., & Peterson, M. J. (1959). Short-term retention of individual verbal items. *Journal of Experimental Psychology, 58,* 193–198.

Przybslawski, J., Roullet, P., & Sara, S. J. (1999). Attenuation of emotional and nonemotional memories after their reactivation: Role of betaadrenergic receptors. *Journal of Neuroscience, 19,* 6623–6628.

Przybslawski, J., & Sara, S. J. (1997). Reconsolidation of memory after its reactivation. *Behavioural Brain Research, 84,* 241–246.

Rakic, P. (1985). Limits of neurogenesis in primates. *Science, 227,* 1054–1056.

Riege, W. H. (1971). Environmental influences on brain and behavior in old rats. *Developmental Psychobiology, 4,* 157–167.

Romero-Apis, D., Babayan-Mena, J. I., Fonte-Vazquez, A., Gutierrez-Perez, D., Martinez-Oropeza, S., & Murillo-Murillo, L. (1982). Perdida del ojo en adulto con ambliopia estrabica [Loss of an eye in adults with amblyopia]. *Annals of the Mexican Society of Ophthalmology, 56,* 445–452.

Rosas, J. M., & Bouton, M. E. (1998). Context change and retention interval can have additive, rather than interactive, effects after taste aversion extinction. *Psychonomic Bulletin and Review, 5,* 79–83.

Rosenzweig, M. R. (1966). Environmental complexity, cerebral change, and behavior. *American Psychologist, 21,* 321–332.

Rosenzweig, M. R. (1996). Aspects of the search for neural mechanisms of memory. *Annual Review of Psychology, 47,* 1–32.

Rosenzweig, M. R. (1998a). Historical perspectives on the development of the biology of learning and memory. In J. Martinez & R. Kesner (Eds.), *Neurobiology of learning and memory* (pp. 1–53). San Diego, CA: Academic Press.

Rosenzweig, M. R. (1998b). Some historical background of topics in this conference. *Neurobiology of Learning and Memory, 70,* 3–13.

Rosenzweig, M. R., & Bennett, E. L. (1996). Psychobiology of plasticity: Effects of training and experience on brain and behavior. *Behavioural Brain Research, 78,* 57–65.

Rosenzweig, M. R., Bennett, E. L., Colombo, P. J., Lee, D. W., & Serrano, P. A. (1993). Short-term, intermediate-term, and long-term memories. *Behavioural Brain Research, 57,* 193–198.

Rosenzweig, M. R., Bennett, E. L., & Krech, D. (1964). Cerebral effects of environmental complexity and training among adult rats. *Journal of Comparative and Physiological Psychology, 57,* 438–439.

Rosenzweig, M. R., Krech, D., & Bennett, E. L. (1961). Heredity, environment, brain biochemistry, and learning. In D. Wayne (Ed.), *Current trends in psychological theory* (pp. 87–110). Pittsburgh, PA: University of Pittsburgh Press.

Rosenzweig, M. R., Krech, D., Bennett, E. L., & Diamond, M. C. (1962). Effects of environmental complexity and training on brain chemistry and anatomy: A replication and extension. *Journal of Comparative and Physiological Psychology, 55,* 429–437.

Rosenzweig, M. R., Leiman, A. L., & Breedlove, S. M. (1996). *Biological psychology.* Sunderland, MA: Sinauer Associates.

Rosenzweig, M. R., Leiman, A. L., & Breedlove, S. M. (1999). *Biological psychology: An introduction to behavioral, cognitive, and clinical neuroscience* (2nd ed.). Sunderland, MA: Sinauer Associates.

Minton, T. (1988, March 13). State plan for public preschools proposal to pay for every California child. *San Francisco Chronicle,* p. A1.

Singer, W. (1992). Adult visual cortex—Adaptation and reorganization. In L. R. Squire (Ed.), *Encyclopedia of learning and memory* (pp. 453–454). New York: Macmillan.

Squire, L. R., Knowlton, B., & Musen, G. (1993). The structure and organization of memory. *Annual Review of Psychology, 44,* 453–495.

Tully, T., Bolwig, G., Christensen, T., Connolly, J., DelVecchio, M., DeZazzo, J., Dubnau, J., Jones, C., Pinto, S., Regulski, M., Svedberg, B., & Velinzon, K. (1996). A return to genetic dissection of memory in *Drosophila:* Function and dysfunction in the nervous system. *Cold Spring Harbor Symposia on Quantitative Biology, 61,* 207–218.

Warrington, E. R., & Shallice, T. (1969). The selective impairment of auditory verbal short-term memory. *Brain, 92,* 885–896.

Weinberger, N. L. (1998). Physiological memory in primary auditory cortex: Characteristics and mechanisms. *Neurobiology of Learning and Memory, 70,* 226–251.

West, R. W., & Greenough, W. T. (1972). Effects of environmental complexity on cortical synapses of rats: Preliminary results. *Behavioral Biology, 7,* 279–284.

Wiesel, T. N., & Hubel, D. H. (1963). Single-cell responses in striate cortex of kittens deprived of vision in one eye. *Journal of Neurophysiology, 26,* 1003–1017.

York, A. D., Breedlove, S. M., Diamond, M. C., & Greer, E. R. (1989). Housing adult male rats in enriched conditions increases neurogenesis in the dentate gyrus. *Society for Neuroscience Abstracts, 15,* 962.

Zigler, E., & Muenchow, S. (1992). *Head Start: The inside story of America's most successful educational experiment.* New York: Basic Books.

Zolman, J. F., & Morimoto, H. (1962). Effects of age of training on cholinesterase activity in the brains of maze-bright rats. *Journal of Comparative and Physiological Psychology, 55,* 794–800.

CHAPTER 15

A Neuroholographic Model of Memory:

Theta Rhythms, Facilitation, and Calcium Channels

Philip W. Landfield

Olivier Thibault

It has been more than 20 years since it was initially proposed that synchronous electroencephalographic (EEG) rhythms such as the hippocampal theta rhythm (HTR) might function in memory deposition, consolidation, and retrieval somewhat analogously to the way in which a coherent light source (laser) functions in the formation and retrieval of holograms, that is, by generating neuronal "interference fringe patterns" (see Figure 15.1; Landfield, 1976). This model in part grew out of work on theta rhythms and memory consolidation begun in the laboratory of James L. McGaugh some time earlier (Landfield, McGaugh, & Tusa, 1972). However, the original neuronal interference–holographic model depicted in Figure 15.1 was somewhat limited in scope and left several important operational questions unanswered. In addition, there has been explosive development in the study of brain function during the years since it was proposed, and a number of findings in this period appear to be directly relevant to or consistent with the model's predictions. Together, these factors suggest that revisiting and extending the model within a more recent context might be worthwhile. There seems to be no more appropriate place to do so than in a volume honoring the eminent scientist in whose lab this work was begun.

At the time of that initial work on theta in McGaugh's lab, the posttraining, or posttrial, period had been shown to be a critical phase for the study of memory consolidation processes (McGaugh, 1966). We therefore used a posttraining paradigm to seek EEG correlates of memory consolidation. Those studies found that the duration of time occupied by EEG theta rhythm activity

We thank Kelley Secrest for excellent assistance with the manuscript. Aspects of this work were supported by National Institute on Aging Grants AG04542 and AG10836.

FIGURE 15.1

Hypothetical model of the manner in which the hippocampal theta rhythm might function in memory storage analogously to the way in which a laser beam (coherent wave) functions in making a hologram.

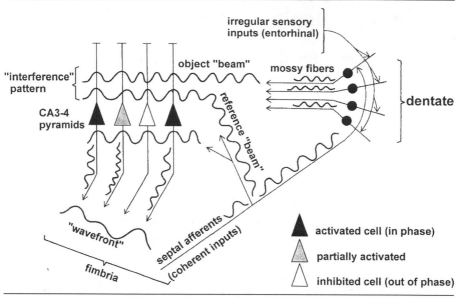

From Figure 7 in "Synchronous EEG Rhythms: Their Nature and Their Possible Functions in Memory, Information Transmission and Behavior," by P. W. Landfield, 1976, in W. H. Gispen (Ed.), *Molecular and Functional Neurobiology,* p. 390, Amsterdam, Elsevier. Reprinted with permission of the author.

during a 30-minute posttraining period correlated quantitatively across individual rats with the apparent degree of concurrent memory consolidation, as evaluated on a subsequent (48-hour) retention test (Landfield et al., 1972; see also Figure 15.2A). In addition to these correlational results, subsequent posttraining intervention studies found that experimental induction of hippocampal theta by 7.7 Hz medial septal stimulation (low-frequency stimulation, or LFS) during the posttrial period enhanced apparent memory consolidation of both active and inhibitory avoidance tasks. LFS also facilitated retrieval when given during a later retention test. In contrast, posttrial high-frequency (77 Hz) septal stimulation, which blocks theta, resulted in reduced apparent memory storage (Landfield, 1976, 1977; Figure 15.3). Several other posttrial theta-driving studies (Destrade, 1982; Wetzel, Ott, & Matthies, 1977), as well as septal lesion or pharmacological application studies (Markowska, Olton, & Givens, 1995; Mitchell, Rawlins, Steward, & Olton, 1982; Winson, 1978) subsequently obtained highly similar results regarding the effects of altering theta rhythms on memory and learning. Thus, substantial data were consistent with our working hypothesis that synchronous EEG rhythms might reflect a neurobiological state that favored the consolidation of memory (Landfield et al., 1972).

Development of the initial interference pattern–holographic model described below was stimulated by several factors, including the above findings on theta and memory, the apparent similarities between optical interference patterns and graded neural summation processes (cf. section immediately following), and what seemed to be an intriguing analogy between the relative coherence (single primary frequency) of synchronous EEG theta rhythms and the coherence (monochromatic frequency) of the lasers used in holography (Landfield, 1976).

Optics Analogy and Original Interference Pattern–Holographic Model of Theta Rhythms

Memory Formation

In optics, interference "fringes" or patterns are formed when two relatively monochromatic (coherent) beams of similar frequency are projected to overlap on a detector screen. The interference patterns consist of "stripes" of light, where the waves of the two beams are in phase, and stripes of darkness, where the two waves are out of phase and cancel one another. In holography, a highly coherent laser beam is split and divided into two beams, one of which is directed at and reflected back from an object of interest (the "object beam") and one of which does not contain any information about the object ("reference beam") but is projected to overlap and interact (interfere) with the reflected object beam. The hologram is formed where the two beams overlap.

The essential discovery that gave rise to holography was that a reflected monochromatic object beam contained not only conventional intensity information, but also the information on the phase relationships among the countless smaller beams reflected from different regions of the object (Gabor, 1972). These phase relationships encode a great deal more information on spatial relationships in detectable form than the intensity information generally obtained from wide-spectrum light waves (thus, the term *holo* from the Greek word *holos* for "whole"). The use of a second beam (reference beam) of the same coherent frequency provided a means to create interference patterns between two beams and thereby "capture" and record the spatial phase information in the object beam at a point in space (Gabor, 1972). A photographic plate in a plane at some arbitrary distance from the object and reference beams is "etched" where the maxima of the two interfering waves are fully in phase and is left unaffected where they are out of phase. Thereafter, the hologram can be recreated by directing only the reference beam at the plate, because transmission of light at

FIGURE 15.2

Three levels of correlation of electrophysiology with memory.

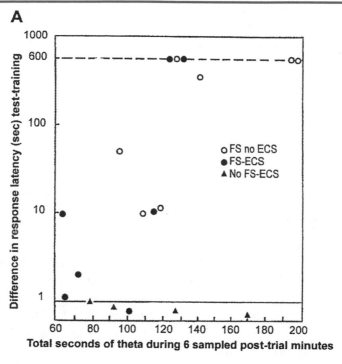

A

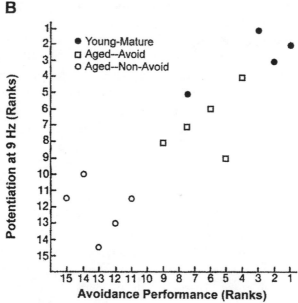

B

C

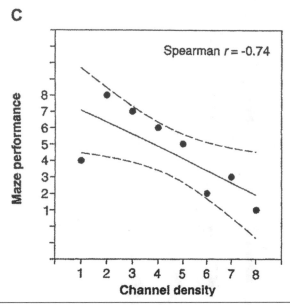

Spearman $r = -0.74$

(A) Relationship in individual subjects between amount of posttrial EEG activity in the 4–9 Hz range (theta) and degree of retention of a one-trial inhibitory avoidance 2 days after training. Elevated latency reflects good retention. FS = foot shock training; ECS = electroconvulsive shock after training. From Figure 1 in "Theta Rhythm: A Temporal Correlate of Memory Storage Processes in the Rat," by P. W. Landfield, J. L. McGaugh, and R. J. Tusa, 1972, *Science, 175*, p. 87. Copyright 1972 by the American Association for the Advancement of Science. Reprinted with permission. (B) Correlation data for individual aged and young animals for which both behavioral (active avoidance) and neurophysiological (frequency facilitation) data were available (Spearman rank correlation; r_s = +0.85). Good performance on the active avoidance (lowest numbers) is reflected by low latencies. Aged animals that were able to learn to avoid in this task exhibited stronger facilitation, which was more similar to that in young rats. From Figure 2 in "Hippocampal Neurobiological Mechanisms of Age-Related Memory Dysfunction, by P. W. Landfield, 1988, *Neurobiology of Aging, 9*, p. 571. Reprinted with permission from Elsevier Science. (C) Rank order scores of L-type calcium channel membrane density (8 is highest) and Morris water-maze performance (8 is best) for aged animals for which scores on both variables were available. The task depends significantly on hippocampal function and is impaired with aging in F344 rats. A significant negative correlation (Spearman's nonparametric test) was found between maze performance and increasing channel density, indicating that channel density was highest in neurons from the most impaired animals. Dotted lines represent 95% confidence intervals. From Figure 4 in "Increase in Single L-Type Calcium Channels in Hippocampal Neurons During Aging, by O. Thibault and P. W. Landfield, 1996, *Science, 272*, p. 1017. Copyright 1996 by the American Association for the Advancement of Science. Reprinted with permission of the publisher.

FIGURE 15.3
Theta-driving enhances consolidation.

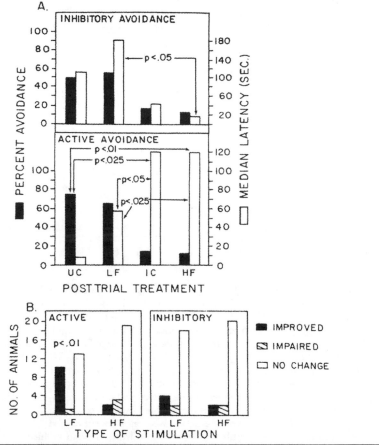

(A) Effects of posttraining theta-driving septal stimulation on retention performance measured 48 hours after the stimulation. In the active avoidance task good retention is indicated by low latencies to avoid, whereas in the inhibitory avoidance, good retention is indicated by long latencies. Theta-driving stimulation enhanced apparent consolidation in both tasks, relative to theta blocking. Posttrial treatments: LF = low-frequency (7 Hz, theta-driving) posttraining stimulation; HF = high-frequency (77 Hz, theta-blocking) posttraining stimulation; IC = implanted controls; UC = unoperated controls. (B) Effects on retention performance of septal stimulation during testing. Shown is the number of animals exhibiting a latency change (improved or impaired) greater than 15 seconds during stimulation, in comparison to latencies obtained during the prior no-stimulation retention tests. The effects of low-frequency stimulation in the active task produced a significant difference in performance compared to the no-stimulation tests. LF = low-frequency; HF = high-frequency. From Figure 1 in "Different Effects of Posttrial Driving or Blocking of the Theta Rhythm on Avoidance Learning in Rats," by P. W. Landfield, 1977, *Physiology & Behavior, 18*, p. 439. Reprinted with permission from Elsevier Science.

the wave maxima of the reference beam also recreates the wave maxima pattern of the object beam.

As envisioned in the initial neural "holographic" hippocampal model, the role of theta in memory formation was highly analogous to that of the laser beam (Figure 15.1). The excitatory peaks of EEG theta waves and the high-frequency bursts of action potentials that are synchronized to those peaks (see below, Nature and Role in Memory of Electrophysiological Processes, and review in Landfield, 1976) were viewed as similar to the maxima of the coherent waves in holography. The theta wave maxima in dentate gyrus (DG) were proposed to summate (interfere) in specific granule cells with a continuous stream of irregular, nonsynchronized activity arriving over inputs from entorhinal cortex. These irregular inputs were viewed as analogous to the "object" in that they represented sensory or other information. Only those DG neurons in which the entorhinal irregular inputs induced strong excitatory responses that coincided with an excitatory peak of the theta wave would be able to generate sufficient postsynaptic summation to fire action potentials and project activity outward over the mossy fibers to the next set of relay neurons in CA3. Therefore, some DG neurons would project intense activity during the EEG wave peak, whereas others would be silent. These gradations of output activity would be proportional to the preceding variations in activity across the different entorhinal inputs. However, the varied inputs would now be time locked together and projected out as a simultaneous wavefront. In this way, nonsynchronized entorhinal input activity would be encoded as time-slices of information in the coherent temporally spaced wavefronts being projected rhythmically out of the DG. The theta waves projected from the DG would each contain an encoded representation of the input information ("object") at a point in time and therefore be analogous to the "reflected object beam."

In holography, the object beam must then interfere with a reference beam to form a permanent hologram and, in the model, the projected information-containing "object beam" theta waves were proposed to form "neuroholograms" in the CA3/CA1 hippocampal regions by summating (interfering) with other theta waves arriving over a separate pathway from the septum. The septal pathway theta waves were proposed to contain no information and to function analogously to a holographic "reference beam." The "object" and "reference" theta rhythms were proposed to interact in CA3 or CA1, which receive both DG and septal inputs. Because both inputs would be at similar frequencies (i.e., theta) a form of neural hologram would be formed. That is, excitatory postsynaptic potential (EPSP) summation and sufficient postsynaptic excitation to generate spikes would occur only in those CA3/CA1 relay neurons in which the excitatory maxima of both rhythmic waves (object and reference beams) were in phase. Those relay neurons activated sufficiently to fire by the simultaneous excitation (summation) patterns would form the actual interference pattern or neurohologram. Thus, only selected neurons (analogous to the limited slits on a photographic plate where two laser beams are in phase) would be activated sufficiently to form lasting traces ("engrams"; Lashley 1952) as well as to project activity to other neurons in CA1 or elsewhere (Figure 15.1).

Memory Consolidation and Retrieval in the Original Model

The original model also proposed a theta rhythm–dependent cellular mechanism for the process of memory consolidation, a phenomenon critical to neural memory (McGaugh, 1966, 2000) that shares no obvious optical counterpart. This mechanism was based on the high-frequency bursts of spikes that accompany a wave peak. In holography, a non-information-containing reference beam of the same frequency can be subsequently directed at the trace and can recreate the hologram. Similarly, in the model non-information-containing (reference) theta waves were proposed to be able to preferentially reactivate the recently established interference patterns. However, as long as theta rhythms continued to be activated by the arousal of the learning event (i.e., during the posttraining period; McGaugh, 2000), the circulating theta waves would repeatedly reactivate the memory traces. By virtue of the high-frequency bursts of spikes that "ride" on the peaks of rhythmic waves, theta waves were suggested to thereby provide a means of intensely activating and "engraving" (consolidating) long-term neuronal changes in the recently acquired trace. In some ways, this HTR consolidation hypothesis might be viewed as an extended version of the much earlier proposal by Hebb (1949), in which it was suggested that "reverberating circuits" in newly established cell assemblies could induce some growth or metabolic process that subsequently made the firing of a cell in the reverberating circuit more probable. However, the theta model also differed from the Hebbian model in that the theta model did not attribute the reverberation to restricted activity generated in a newly established selective assembly. Instead, the consolidating activity was viewed as a normal ongoing and widespread rhythmic activity process that was induced to preferentially activate recently established patterns. The theta model also did not depend on continuous reverberating activity but rather on periodic reactivation.

To account for retrieval in the model, the holographic analogy was again invoked with the suggestion that, in a manner similar to the way in which the reference waves consolidated memory traces, non-information-containing coherent theta waves of a similar frequency (e.g., the reference beam) could circulate through the brain to preferentially reactivate and thereby retrieve the previously formed traces (Landfield, 1976). Thus, in the model, hippocampal theta was necessary for storage, consolidation, and retrieval. Interestingly, those are behavioral periods during which theta is intensely activated (e.g., Landfield, 1976).

Nature and Role in Memory of Electrophysiological Processes

Early Studies on Cellular Mechanisms of the EEG

In the 1960s and early 1970s, several other investigators had suggested either a role for rhythmic EEG patterns (e.g., HTRs) in processing and memory recall (Adey, 1966) or a role for neural holograms in several aspects of memory (Pribram, 1971). However, neither of those hypotheses specifically linked the two concepts to one another nor drew an analogy between rhythmic EEG waves and the coherent light waves used in holograms. Those early views also did not attempt to directly specify how either rhythmic EEG patterns or brain holograms might modulate or interact with brain mechanisms of memory at the cellular level.

Nevertheless, much was being learned about the underlying cellular mechanisms of the EEG in that period. It had become evident, for example, that slow (e.g., synaptic) potentials are the source of most EEG waves. In addition, it was being documented that as the EEG becomes more synchronous, underlying neurons increasingly fire in brief, high-frequency bursts of action potentials (spikes) that are phase locked to the excitatory peaks of each slow wave. Moreover, these waves or bursts were found to circulate repeatedly in multiple directions throughout local networks (cf. reviews in Andersen & Andersson, 1968; Verzeano, 1970). The alternating patterns of excitatory and inhibitory postsynaptic potentials in linked cell assemblies were proposed to provide a basis for the generation of biphasic rhythmic EEG waves (Andersen & Andersson, 1968; see also Bal, von Krosigk, & McCormick, 1994, and Steriade, 1994, for more recent treatments). Several studies also showed that the phase of a neuronal excitatory (EPSP)–inhibitory postsynaptic potential (IPSP) cycle determined whether new spike inputs summated (with the EPSP) and were projected outward as additional spikes or were canceled (by the IPSP) and lost (e.g., Andersen & Andersson, 1968). This growing understanding of EEG rhythms provided a basis for a variety of hypotheses by multiple investigators on the functions of EEG rhythms in cognitive processes (for reviews, see Andersen & Andersson, 1968; Landfield, 1976; see also Buszaki & Chrobak, 1995; Gray & Singer, 1989; McNaughton, 1998; and Shadlen & Newsome, 1998, for more recent views on the roles of neuronal oscillations in cognition).

Findings on Theta Rhythms and Long-Term Potentiation Relevant to the Model

An important index of any model's potential usefulness is its ability to generate testable predictions. As noted, the initial model was based on evidence that theta rhythms were correlated with consolidation (Figure 15.2A) and that posttrial driving of theta could enhance consolidation and possibly retrieval (Figure 15.3). However, in the intervening years, new lines of investigation have provided apparent additional support for the model. For example, the study of hippocampal long-term potentiation (LTP) has expanded dramatically in recent years, based on LTP's putative role as a neuronal substrate of memory. If this role is in part valid, then results of studies in the 1980s and 1990s linking the HTR to LTP seem highly consistent with implicit or explicit predictions of the original model. Synaptic stimulation at theta frequencies has been found to be particularly effective in directly inducing monosynaptic LTP (Larson & Lynch, 1986; Rose & Dunwiddie, 1986) or polysynaptic LTP (Yeckel & Berger, 1998). Further, stimulation at theta frequency has been found to induce a burst pattern (complex spikes) of postsynaptic firing that, even with only a single burst, selectively favors LTP generation (Thomas, Watabe, Moody, Makhinson, & O'Dell, 1998). Moreover, it has become apparent that spike bursts are critical signals for memory storage processes (Lisman, 1997). Thus, if LTP is a neuronal reflection of consolidated memory (e.g., Guzowski et al., 2000), the finding that theta frequency stimulation favors LTP generation clearly fits well with the model's proposition that recirculating theta waves (by virtue of their associated high-frequency spike bursts) drive memory consolidation (e.g., induce LTP).

Moreover, an observation that seems particularly consistent with the interference pattern component of the model has been that activation of neurons during the excitatory peak of a local theta wave provides maximal induction of LTP (Holscher, Anwyl, & Rowan, 1997; Huerta & Lisman, 1995). Conversely, stimulation during the inhibitory phase of a paired-pulse facilitation protocol (Doyere, Errington, Laroche, & Bliss, 1996; Thiels, Barrionuevo, & Berger, 1995) or during the negative phase of theta (Holscher et al., 1997) does not induce LTP and can actually induce depotentiation. Under physiological conditions as well, hippocampal neurons often fire high-frequency bursts that are phase locked to the excitatory phase of the theta wave (Buzsaki & Chrobak, 1995; Mizumori, Barnes, & McNaughton, 1990; Stewart & Fox, 1990) and do so during behavioral conditions that induce LTP (Otto, Eichenbaum, Wiener, & Wible, 1991).

Clearly, many of these findings could also be consistent with alternative models. However, if LTP somehow reflects a cellular manifestation of memory, or at least, a consequence of the intense activity needed to establish a memory trace, the observations that theta rhythms may both preferentially induce and "gate" LTP seem directly consistent with predictions of the model.

Frequency Facilitation Relevance to Memory in Aging Animals

Some forms of short-term hippocampal synaptic plasticity (STP) have also been found to correlate with memory processes, although STP would clearly fulfill different functions from LTP. The form of STP termed *frequency facilitation* (FF; also *frequency potentiation,* the growth of excitatory synaptic potentials during repetitive synaptic stimulation, generally at 5–15 Hz) was first identified as a powerful hippocampal mechanism of synaptic plasticity even before LTP was discovered in the same laboratories (Andersen & Lomo, 1970; Bliss & Lomo, 1973). The rapid increase in EPSP amplitude and spike activity that occurs during FF seems to make it a strong candidate for a dynamic cellular mechanism of initial memory deposition, and several studies in aged animals have supported this possibility (cf. review in Landfield, 1988).

In a renewed collaboration with McGaugh, whose laboratory had begun to investigate memory in aging animals (Gold & McGaugh, 1975), we found that FF, even more than LTP, was impaired consistently in "memory-deficient" aged animals (Landfield & Lynch, 1977; Landfield, McGaugh, & Lynch, 1978). Further studies yielded additional results consistent with the hypothesis that FF is critical to the initial stages of memory deposition. That is, magnitude of FF was found to correlate with learning capacity in aged animals (Landfield, 1980; Figure 15.2B) and a treatment that selectively strengthened FF (elevated extracellular Mg^{2+}) also improved learning in aged animals (Landfield & Morgan, 1984; Landfield, Pitler, & Applegate, 1986; see review in Landfield, 1988). Other groups have also found impaired facilitation with aging (Ouanounou, Zhang, Charlton, & Carlen, 1999), and interesting new evidence has been reported that age-related impairment of FF may contribute to reduced LTP (Rosenzweig, Rao, McNaughton, & Barnes, 1997).

The facilitation mechanism itself has sometimes been viewed as a secondary phenomenon that arises not from enhanced excitatory synaptic processes but from suppression of the postsynaptic GABA-dependent IPSP (McCarren & Alger, 1985); however, there is substantial evidence against this view (Applegate & Landfield, 1988; Pitler & Landfield, 1987).

Single-Channel Mechanisms in Memory

Studies at still more basic electrophysiological levels (cell-attached patch clamp recording) have revealed another aging-related alteration in hippocampal neurons: Ca^{2+} currents are increased in aged animal hippocampal CA1 neurons (Landfield, Campbell, Hao, & Kerr, 1989) due primarily to an increased membrane density of L-type voltage-gated Ca^{2+} channels (L-VGCC) in pyramidal cells (Thibault & Landfield, 1996). Considerable evidence supports a potential involvement of L-VGCC in learning and memory. For example, Disterhoft and colleagues have shown that the Ca^{2+}-dependent, slow afterhyperpolarization (AHP) is inversely correlated with an animal's capacity to learn a conditioning task (Disterhoft, Golden, Read, Coulter, & Alkon, 1988), and the L-type antagonist nimodipine enhances learning in aging animals, possibly by reducing the AHP (see review in Disterhoft, Moyer, Thompson, & Kowalska, 1993). The AHP is larger in hippocampal CA1 neurons of aged rats (Kerr, Campbell, Hao, & Landfield, 1989; Landfield & Pitler, 1984) and aged rabbits (Disterhoft et al., 1993; Moyer, Thompson, Black, & Disterhoft, 1992) and is in part dependent on Ca^{2+} influx via L-VGCC (Mazzanti, Thibault, & Landfield, 1991; Moyer et al, 1992). Moreover, a greater density of L-VGCC in aged hippocampal neurons appears to alter LTP (Kapur, Yeckel, Gray, & Johnston, 1998; Norris, Halpain, & Foster, 1998; Shankar, Teyler, & Robbins, 1998) and long-term depression (Norris et al., 1998). Somewhat remarkably, given the large discrepancies in levels of biological organization, the ability to acquire a watermaze spatial task also was significantly correlated with L-type single-channel density across individual aged animals (Thibault & Landfield, 1996; see Figure 15.2C). As with the FF correlation (Figure 15.2B), this individual-subjects correlation pattern (Figure 15.2C) seemed reminiscent of the correlations of the HTR with memory processes (Figure 15.2A).

Hierarchical Interactions of Memory-Related Electrophysiological Systems

Thus, different organizational levels of hippocampal electrophysiological processes, from large synchronized population EEG responses (theta) to synaptic facilitation to single-channel density, have been observed to correlate across individual subjects with aspects of memory and learning processes. The possibility of functional linkage across these different organizational levels is suggested not only by the analogous patterns of correlation but also by the close similarities in the frequencies and temporal patterns that characterize these processes. For example, septal stimulation at 7 Hz induces EEG theta rhythms (Figure 15.4A), whereas synaptic stimulation at the same frequency induces large FF of the intracellular EPSP, with associated spike firing (Figure 15.4B). Thus, it has been suggested that theta may function as an endogenous mechanism for inducing FF, and potentially, LTP (see Landfield, 1977, 1988).

In addition, although it is well established that L-type VGCCs are activated throughout the soma and dendrites by a spike, it is less recognized that L-VGCC activity can continue for a significant period following spike repolarization (Thibault, Porter, & Landfield, 1993; Figure 15.4C). The inhibitory hyperpolarizing K^+ conductances underlying the AHP (Madison & Nicoll, 1984; Storm, 1990) are, as noted above, triggered in part by L-VGCC. Therefore, L-VGCCs may play an important role in pacing theta waves or FF by regulating the interburst intervals.

Thus, it is proposed here that these multiple processes are manifestations of a vertically integrated hierarchical system that serves to enhance the deposition, storage, and retrieval of memory traces. This hierarchical system, we suggest, provides the dynamic processes necessary for generating the neuroholographic traces in the model described in the following section. It seems highly intriguing, moreover, that several components of this system appear particularly susceptible to alteration during aging (review, Landfield, 1988; Thibault et al., 1998).

The Neuroholographic Model: Update and Extension

Collectively, the still expanding evidence in favor of a link between theta frequencies and the capacity for memory storage in rodent brain, as well as the correlations between impaired memory and altered function for several frequency-specific electrophysiological processes in aged animals, seems to indicate that the further development of a model of memory based on frequency-dependent interference patterns and a holographic analogy might have merit. Moreover, as we have worked to refine and extend the model, we have been intrigued by its apparent emergent properties and additional explanatory potential. Below we describe the extended model. The major new characteristics of this version include a system for storing ongoing temporally sequential "holoengrams" in ordered neural arrays, as well as considerably more detailed explanations of the principles, functions, and mechanisms of its operation. We also address several of the issues that were left vague or unresolved in the original model. Figure 15.5 summarizes operations of the extended, updated model.

Unresolved Questions

Several difficult and important questions on the specific operation and function of the interference–pattern holographic model were not dealt with in the original proposal (Landfield, 1976). The following sections attempt to clarify these unresolved questions and "flesh out" the model in the context of more recent findings.

What Essential Components of Neuronal Information Are Stored?

Whereas in optics the reflected object beam encodes the differences in phase (phase relationships) among the countless beams reflecting from different sites on the object, the thousands of axons projecting into the hippocampus instead

FIGURE 15.4

Vertical hierarchy of rhythmic electrophysiological patterns in rats that correspond to the correlates of learning and memory shown in Figure 15.2.

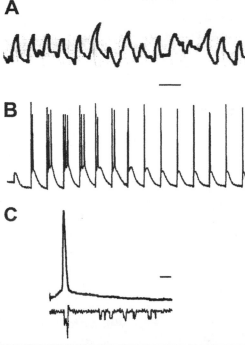

(A) Cortically recorded, hippocampally generated theta rhythms driven by 7.7 Hz electrical stimulation of the medial septum (slight curvature reflects electroencephalographic pen movements). Note the highly rhythmic and coherent theta waves activated by 7.7 Hz. From Figure 2 in "Different Effects of Posttrial Driving or Blocking of the Theta Rhythm on Avoidance Learning in Rats," by P. W. Landfield, 1977, *Physiology & Behavior, 18,* p. 439. Reprinted with permission from Elsevier Science. (B) Frequency facilitation in a hippocampal slice CA1 pyramidal neuron during 7 Hz synaptic stimulation (Schaffer collaterals). Note large potentiation of the excitatory postsynaptic potential (EPSP) above the first baseline EPSP and the bursts of multiple Na^+ spikes riding on the facilitated EPSP peaks. The brief spike bursts exhibited intraburst frequencies of approximately 100 Hz. Concomitantly, a large hyperpolarization accompanies the stimulation indicating that suppression of hyperpolarizing (e.g., inhibitory postsynaptic potential or IPSP) conductances does not account for facilitation. Facilitation of the EPSP occurs in the same stimulation frequency range as do spontaneous or driven theta rhythms. Calibration bar applies to A and B (150 milliseconds). (C) Single L-type Ca^{2+} channel activity during and following depolarization. Expanded time scale relative to A and B. Lower trace: L-type Ca^{2+} channels recorded in cell-attached mode from a cultured hippocampal neuron, activated by a 5-millisecond depolarization roughly mimicking an action potential. An EPSP and action potential from a slice neuron in the upper trace are included on the same expanded time base for illustration. Note the extensive Ca^{2+} channel activity that accompanies and follows repolarization differ among themselves in the frequencies of spike activity they sustain during some time window. It seems likely that it is these activity differences (activity relationships) that must be encoded in the projected theta object beam. Information from the primary sensory and association cortical areas reaches the hippocampus through entorhinal and other projections into the DG along the length of the hippocampus. Much of this information is then projected in the transverse direction along sheets of thousands of parallel mossy fibers to CA3–4 neurons. In turn, CA3 pyramids project to CA1 pyramidal cells via boutons en passage of the Schaffer collaterals, again along sheets of parallel fibers. Although many collateral and divergent pathways have been identified (Amaral & Witter, 1989; Soleng, Raastad, & Andersen, 1999), the originally defined transversely directed "trisynaptic" circuit (dentate, CA3, CA1) organized in parallel lamellae within the hippocampus (Andersen & Lomo, 1970) still appears to represent a major direction of information flow. Each transverse hippocampal axon can sequentially activate dozens to hundreds of neurons (and perhaps thousands when axonal divergence is considered; Soleng et al., 1999). Further, such sequential activation can apparently occur simultaneously in large numbers of parallel lines and lamellae along the entire longitudinal extent of the hippocampus. Thus, if information is transmitted along each lamellar line simultaneously, the information in the different lines will be at roughly similar distances along each axon at the same point in time. For example, if we envision a visual stimulus-triggered set of simultaneously activated fibers entering the DG from the entorhinal cortex, it can be inferred that the spatial representation encoded at a point in time is time-locked among the entire set of activated fibers at roughly a similar distance point along the axis of travel. Moreover, the relative activity (frequency of firing) obviously would vary greatly among different fibers in the set depending on their relative location in the visual representation. As the visual field continuously changed over time, so, too, would the activity among the many fibers, still in a time-locked fashion. Thus, it seems likely that, if a neural holo-engram is formed, it would encode at a point (or window) in time the relative activity relationships (frequencies of firing) among fibers activated simultaneously by an information representation.

("repolarization openings"), which may contribute to the Ca^{2+}-dependent AHP and thereby pace rhythmicity. To approximate physiological conditions, 5 mM Ca^{2+} was the charge carrier in the Ca^{2+} channel recordings. Calibration Bar (10 milliseconds). Data modified from Figure 5 in "Low Ba^{2+} and Ca^{2+} Induce a Sustained High Probability of Repolarization Openings of L-type Ca^{2+} Channels in Hippocampal Neurons: Physiological Implications," by O. Thibault, N. M. Porter, and P. W. Landfield, *Proceedings of the National Academy of Science (USA), 90,* p. 11792. Copyright 1993 by the National Academy of Sciences.

FIGURE 15.5

Extended version of the neuroholographic model of memory trace formation, storage, and retrieval.

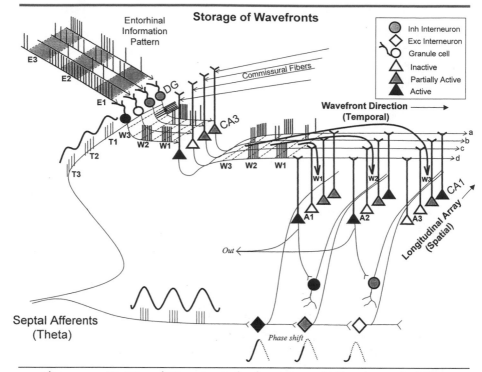

Theta waves T1, T2, and T3 moving to the dentate gyrus (DG) and entorhinal fiber activity episodes E1, E2, and E3 (shaded) represent neural activities of two inputs that will arrive at the DG granule cells in corresponding time windows (e.g., T1 with E1, T2 with E2, etc.). W1, W2, and W3 represent the bursts of activity that proportionally encode the entorhinal inputs and are projected as theta frequency wavefronts from the DG following the interference (summation) interactions in DG (i.e., W1 resulting from T1 and E1 interactions, etc.). Note that the activity relationships across parallel entorhinal input fibers in each time window are maintained in the projected bursts in parallel output fibers. The patterned shading of DG and CA3 neurons reflects the activity pattern generated by only the first encoded wavefront (W1). The emerging wavefronts only transmit quantitative information about the levels of relative activity sampled during the brief (e.g., 25–50 milliseconds) time windows at the excitatory phases of each theta wave. For simplicity, W1 is shown passing through CA3 unaltered. In CA1, a possible mechanism for storing temporally ordered information in spatially distinct and ordered arrays is shown. As each information-containing wavefront of relative activity (object beam) arrives in CA1 it will activate (and be encoded in) only one limited neural array on the transverse axis, the array that is simultaneously enabled (activated) by a transversely shifting peak of excitation from another input (e.g., either the excitatory phase of the CA1 reference theta rhythm or rebound excitation from shifting inhibition).

The schematic diagram illustrates the first wavefront (W1) activating and being encoded in the first neural array (A1) in which the CA1 theta excitatory phase is

What Are the Functional Advantages of a Neuroholographic Mechanism?

One simple but fundamental assumption appears to substantially assist in addressing this question: It is assumed here that, despite its billions of neurons and trillions of synapses, the brain's elements do not begin to approach the information storage capacity required to store the vast amounts of information that it constantly processes. As a corollary, therefore, one of the major functions of interference patterns and coherent rhythms in memory is proposed to be the sampling of continuous information patterns, both temporally and spatially, to greatly condense the amount of information to be stored.

We suggest that the HTR "temporally chunks" the continuous stream of relative activity relationships by periodically sampling the continuous information stream in DG at the frequency of theta and time-locking each information sample to the peak of an EEG wave. This time-locked sample then travels transversely across the hippocampus (from dentate to CA1) as a longitudinally extended (in the temporal to septal axis) theta wavefront. Each theta wave peak, then, can be viewed as a "window of excitation" of approximately 25–50 milliseconds, during which interactions in the DG with information-containing inputs are enabled. All digital bits (spikes) arriving over the informational input during one temporal window (theta wave excitatory phase) would be integrated into a single bit of information (e.g., the summed EPSP amplitude). Therefore, a hundred or more digital bits of information per second (e.g., 100 Hz spike activity) would be condensed to approximately 7 bits (waves per second). Clearly, this view also implies that, because of the overwhelming surfeit of information in the brain, sampling with 25–50-millisecond windows at 7 Hz is sufficient to capture the informational content of the activity relationships among activated inputs. In this view, loss of information between wave maxima may not only be acceptable but in fact essential for "noise" reduction. Although less total information than originally received would be transmitted in these samples, the range of relative activity across the multiple parallel input fibers would nevertheless be captured in the different relative intensities and

---

simultaneously maximal when W1 arrives. Subsequent arrays are not available for W1 because they have not yet reached the peak of theta or rebound activation. However, as W2 arrives in CA1, the neurons in A1 are no longer available for excitation because they are inhibited by a long afterhyperpolarization (AHP) or a recurrent inhibitory postsynaptic potential (IPSP), but A2 now becomes available because the theta peak has shifted to A2. An alternative mechanism is that rebound excitation in A2 follows inhibition induced by inhibitory neurons initially activated by A1 pyramidal neurons at the time of W1 and enables A2. Thus, W2 is able to trigger firing in the enabled A2 neurons and be encoded in A2. A similar set of conditions and additional peak phase shift allows the information patterns of W3 to most strongly activate neurons of A3 and so on. Exc = excitatory, Inh = inhibitory.

phases of the theta bursts projected from each DG neuron. Moreover, the conversion to a rhythmic output would both boost output intensity (e.g., by facilitation) and block extraneous inputs into relay neurons (by generating intervening AHPs and IPSPs) and, therefore, appears likely to enhance the fidelity, edge sharpness, and intensity of throughput in activated fibers.

Interference and summation effects in selected neurons are also proposed to fulfill a spatial sampling function. Because of the general damping effect on throughput of the digital-to-analog conversion in dendrites (e.g., presynaptic spikes are often converted to subthreshold EPSPs that do not generate spikes), postsynaptic spike generation in the model is limited to those cells in which multiple postsynaptic inputs (at least one of which is a theta peak) arrive in roughly the same time window. Cells activated strongly by one input in the absence of intense activity in the other would not be excited sufficiently to fire proportionally to the input activity. Because activated cells are presumably also the neurons in which lasting traces will be formed, this method of interference pattern encoding would limit the number of cells that store information to only those cells activated simultaneously by two peaks of activity. Presumably, this would represent a relatively small subset of all neurons in the array and would greatly reduce the number of units involved in storage.

How Can Sequential Temporal Information Be Stored and Retrieved?

The problem of how time and sequence are encoded in the brain of course involves many highly complex issues, many of which have been addressed recently in several models (e.g., Buzsaki & Chrobak, 1995; Churchland & Sejnowski, 1992; Gray & Singer, 1989; Kristan, 1998; McNaughton, 1998; Shadlen & Newsome, 1998). However, the corollary problem of how and where sequential information is saved in long-term storage after it has been encoded may be even more complex, given the potential for confounding by loss of time tagging during cumulative activation of the same neurons. Some models have proposed mechanisms through which the central nervous system (CNS) might prevent confounding by inhibiting the activation of previously stored patterns during acquisition of new traces (e.g., Hasselmo & Bower, 1993). A process such as that clearly seems necessary. In addition, however, the prevention of overlap and confounding among continuously arriving, differentially time-tagged information patterns is a separate and highly formidable problem with which the CNS must also cope.

Because of the apparent difficulty in maintaining "temporal tagging" in the same neuron we assume here that different time-tagged patterns are stored in different and spatially distinct neuronal arrays (although a single neuron presumably can participate in multiple arrays). We also propose that an anatomic organization that results in the sequential activation of multiple neurons by boutons en passage of a single fiber, such as is found along the long transverse projections of the trisynaptic circuit, is uniquely suited for the distribution of temporally distinct information to different neuronal arrays. Based on this, the CA1 region is proposed here as a likely region for storage arrays. This anatomic organization, also notably seen in parallel fibers of the cerebellum, is suggested to be specifically evolved for the storage and retrieval of rapid sequential patterns.

A certain amount of temporal spacing between time-tagged patterns along these fibers, in this view, is essential for their orderly distribution to adjacent arrays. In the model, it is proposed that the temporal spacing of sequential time-tagged patterns is governed by the spacing of theta waves, with sequential wavefronts being distributed into different but relatively adjacent neuronal arrays (Figure 15.5). This distribution into separate arrays is accomplished by a combination of AHP- and IPSP-induced silent periods in recently excited arrays and by an incrementally shifting peak phase of excitation along the transverse direction of information flow. This could be accomplished by an incremental shift of the peak of theta or by rebound (from inhibition) excitation, such that the excitatory peak shifts along the temporal (transverse) axis and is temporally synchronized to enable (activate) only the next adjacent spatial array just at the temporal point of arrival of the next succeeding wavefront over the Schaffer collaterals. Note that this incrementally shifting peak of excitation, synchronized to theta frequency, acts as a shifting reference beam in the holographic analogy, allowing only each sequentially selected array to be enabled for storage of one neural holo-engram in a temporal sequence.

Longitudinally projecting inhibitory interneurons maintain synchrony of theta in each array (Buckmaster & Schwartzkroin, 1995; Buzsaki & Chrobak, 1995), but may be slightly out of phase with other inhibitory interneurons controlling more lateral arrays along the transverse axis (e.g., Bland, Andersen, & Ganes, 1975; Bullock, Buzsaki, & McClune, 1990). Note that the information-containing dimension of the wavefront, which encodes relative activity, is envisioned to extend longitudinally in the hippocampus, whereas the time dimension (direction of wave travel) is proposed to extend in the transverse plane (along the trisynaptic circuit). Therefore, different time-slice wavefronts will be stored in different arrays along the transverse plane. An array might vary in width along this plane from a few to dozens or hundreds of neurons. Along the longitudinal extent, however, many thousands or more of parallel fibers and neurons could participate in a wavefront array.

Memory Consolidation and Retrieval

Memory consolidation would occur in this revised model much as it did in the original (e.g., by circulating bursts at theta frequency). Retrieval would occur subsequently through the sequential activation of the spatial arrays and would depend on recreation of the original temporal order. This would likely require some focusing or associative mechanism to trigger the recreation of the original sequence beginning at the first array. However, the essential element of retrieval of temporal memory in the model, such as for storage, is the rapid sequential enablement or activation of succeeding arrays in an orderly spatial pattern.

Conclusion

We have attempted to revisit and extend what appears to be a still promising neural model of memory mechanisms. This attempt has led to the apparent emergence of several new properties regarding the operations and functions of the proposed interference pattern or coherent rhythm model. In particular, three main functions in memory storage and retrieval appear to be clarified in the updated model:

1. *Temporal sampling function.* The model elaborates on the sampling function through which continuous streams of relative activity over primary informational inputs (sensory, associational, internal) are sampled by EEG waves and converted into a condensed output of sequential time-slices of activity relationships among parallel fibers.

2. *Spatial sampling function.* The model further develops a mechanism for temporally synchronizing two excitatory inputs to a restricted subset of neurons. Because only neurons in which summation of simultaneous excitatory inputs occurs store information, storage capacity is required only for the subset of neurons.

3. *Temporal storage and retrieval function.* A new element of the present version is a proposed method for the sequential storage of temporally ordered information waves in spatially adjacent neuronal arrays. This process depends on mechanisms and circuitry that produce a steadily incrementing shift in the spatial location at which synchronized inputs can occur. Consolidation occurs through repeated circulation of theta bursts over reactivated recently deposited traces. Retrieval depends on subsequent reactivation of the arrays in similar spatial order. Together, these mechanisms and functions appear to provide a means for repackaging continuous and overwhelming streams of information into more manageable quantities and for the temporal spacing needed for orderly spatial distribution and long-term storage of different time-slice patterns. The parallel fibers and boutons of passage of the hippocampus seem well-suited for this function, but similar prin-

ciples could well operate in a number of brain regions (e.g., the cerebellum).

A hierarchically integrated electrophysiological system that comprises theta rhythms and synaptic FF and is optimized at frequencies regulated in part by L-type Ca^{2+} channel-dependent inhibitory conductances (e.g., the AHP) is proposed to function to ensure signal intensification and maximal throughput in circuits activated at theta frequencies. Such maximal activation would clearly enhance summation effects and trace deposition. This system appears highly vulnerable to the effects of aging and, in the context of the model, its impaired function (e.g., in aging), should result in weaker neuronal interference patterns, reduced consolidation, and impaired retrieval.

The essential aspects of the model depend on the concept of interference pattern mechanisms more than on any specific EEG rhythm. Consequently, many of its patterned summation (interference) functions might well operate in the absence of large synchronous EEG waves or at different EEG frequencies. Localized excitatory–inhibitory cycles in much smaller circuits might well be able to accomplish similar interference pattern outcomes for more refined, rapid, or detailed patterns. For example, FF can occur at frequencies up to 20 to 30 Hz, although for much briefer durations. As noted (Landfield, 1976), similar interference effects on storage may also operate in other brain structures and for other EEG rhythms (e.g., alpha).

Theta rhythms are recognized to be less prominent in humans and monkeys (Stewart & Fox, 1990). Rodents depend extensively on information acquired by sniffing at theta frequencies and the prominent theta rhythm in rodents could therefore reflect a species-related mechanism for synchronizing the acquisition with the processing of sensory (olfactory) information. In primates, the importance of acquisition of sensory (e.g., visual) information at different frequencies may reduce the need for theta, or a larger brain with more complex and non-synchronized dipoles might reduce the detection of theta. Coherent waves at substantially higher frequencies can also be phase locked throughout the brain (e.g., Buzsaki & Chrobak, 1995; Gray & Singer, 1989) and could play a more significant role in primates. Some preliminary evidence suggests that the AHP may be briefer in monkey brain cells (Aou, Oomura, Woody, & Nishino, 1988) perhaps consistent with the view that higher frequencies of processing are favored. Further, many of the specific anatomic details or timing mechanisms proposed here are, of course, highly speculative.

Nevertheless, the prominence of the HTR in rodent hippocampus and its association with memory and LTP seem to make it an excellent synchronous EEG pattern with which to study and model underlying broader principles of summation and coherent brain activity in memory. Presumably, if the model is valid for rodent hippocampus, its basic principles can be generalized, with selected modifications, to information processing and storage in other brain structures and species.

References

Adey, W. R. (1966). Neurophysiological correlates of information transaction and storage in brain tissue. *Progress in Physiological Psychology, 1*, 1–43.

Amaral, D., & Witter, M. (1989). The three-dimensional organization of the hippocampal formation: A review of anatomical data. *Neuroscience, 31*, 571–591.

Andersen, P., & Andersson, S. A. (1968). *Physiological basis of the alpha rhythm.* New York: Appleton-Century-Crofts.

Andersen, P., & Lomo, T. (1970). Mode of control of hippocampal pyramidal cells discharges. In R. E. Whalen, R. F. Thompson, M. Verzeano, & N. M. Weinberger (Eds.), *The neural control of behavior* (pp. 3–25). New York: Academic Press.

Aou, S., Oomura, Y., Woody, C. D., & Nishino, H. (1988). Effects of behaviorally rewarding hypothalamic electrical stimulation on intacellularly recorded neuronal activity in the motor cortex of awake monkeys. *Brain Research, 439*, 31–38.

Applegate, M. D., & Landfield, P. W. (1988). Synaptic vesicle redistribution during hippocampal frequency potentiation and depression in young and aged rats. *Journal of Neuroscience, 8*, 1096–1111.

Bal, T., von Krosigk, M., & McCormick, D. A. (1994). From cellular to network mechanisms of a thalamic synchronized oscillation. In G. Buzsaki, R. Llinas, W. Singer, A. Berthoz, & Y. Christen (Eds.), *Temporal coding in the brain* (pp. 129–143). Berlin, Germany: Springer-Verlag.

Bland, B. H., Andersen, P., & Ganes, T. (1975). Two generators of hippocampal theta activity in rabbits. *Brain Research, 94*, 199–218.

Bliss, T. V. P., & Lomo, T. (1973). Long-lasting potentiation of synaptic transmission in the dentate gyrus area of anesthetized rabbit following stimulation of the perforant path. *Journal of Physiology, 232*, 331–336.

Buckmaster, P. S., & Schwartzkroin, P. A. (1995). Interneurons and inhibition in the dentate gyrus of the rat in vivo. *Journal of Neuroscience, 15*, 874–879.

Bullock, T. H., Buzsaki, G., & McClune, M. C. (1990). Coherence of compound field potentials reveals discontinuities in the CA1-subiculum of the hippocampus in freely-moving rats. *Neuroscience, 38*, 609–619.

Buzsaki, G., & Chrobak, J. J. (1995). Temporal structure in spatially organized neuronal ensembles: A role for interneuronal networks. *Current Opinion in Neurobiology, 5*, 504–510.

Churchland, P., & Sejnowski, T. (Eds.). (1992). *The computational brain.* Cambridge, MA: MIT Press.

Destrade, C. (1982). Two types of diencephalically driven RSA (theta) as a means of studying memory formation in mice. *Brain Research, 234*, 486–493.

Disterhoft, J. F., Golden, D. T., Read, H. L., Coulter, D. A., & Alkon, D. L. (1988). AHP reductions in rabbit hippocampal neurons during conditioning correlate with acquisition of the learned response. *Brain Research, 462,* 118–125.

Disterhoft, J. F., Moyer, J. R., Thompson, L. T., & Kowalska, M. (1993). Functional aspects of calcium-channel modulation. *Clinical Neuropharmacology, 16,* S12–S24.

Doyere, V., Errington, M. L., Laroche, S., & Bliss, T. V. P. (1996). Low-frequency trains of paired stimuli induce long-term depression in area CA1 but not in dentate gyrus of the intact rat. *Hippocampus, 6,* 52–57.

Gabor, D. (1972). Holography, 1948–1971. *Science, 177,* 299–313.

Gold, P. E., & McGaugh, J. L. (1975). Changes in learning and memory during aging. In J. M. Ordy & K. R. Brizzee (Eds.), *Neurobiology of aging* (pp. 145–158). New York: Plenum Press.

Gray, C. M., & Singer, W. (1989). Stimulus-specific neuronal oscillations in orientation columns of the cat visual cortex. *Proceedings of the National Academy of Science (USA), 86,* 1698–1702.

Guzowski, J. F., Lyford, G. L., Stevenson, G. D., Houston, F. P., McGaugh, J. L., Worley, P. F., & Barnes, C. A. (2000). Inhibition of activity-dependent arc protein expression in the rat hippocampus impairs the maintenance of long-term potentiation and the consolidation of long-term memory. *Journal of Neuroscience, 20,* 3993–4001.

Hasselmo, M. E., & Bower, J. M. (1993). Acetylcholine and memory. *Trends in Neurosciences, 16,* 218–222.

Hebb, C. O. (1949). *The organization of behavior.* New York: Wiley.

Holscher, C., Anwyl, R., & Rowan, M. J. (1997). Stimulation on the positive phase of theta rhythm induces long-term potentiation that can be depotentiated by stimulation on the negative phase in area CA1 in vivo. *Journal of Neuroscience, 17,* 6470–6477.

Huerta, P. T., & Lisman, J. E. (1995). Bidirectional synaptic plasticity induced by a single burst during cholinergic theta oscillation in CA1 in vivo. *Neuron, 15,* 1053–1063.

Kapur, A., Yeckel, M. W., Gray, R., & Johnston, D. (1998). L-type calcium channels are required for one form of hippocampal mossy fiber LTP. *Journal of Neurophysiology, 79,* 2181–2190.

Kerr, D. S., Campbell, L. W., Hao, S-Y., & Landfield, P. W. (1989). Corticosteroid modulation of hippocampal potentials: Increased effect with aging. *Science, 245,* 1505–1509.

Kristan, W. B., Jr. (1998). He's got rhythm: Single neurons signal timing on a scale of seconds. *Nature Neuroscience, 1,* 643–645.

Landfield, P. W. (1976). Synchronous EEG rhythms: Their nature and their possible functions in memory, information transmission and behavior. In W. H. Gispen (Ed.), *Molecular and functional neurobiology* (pp. 390–424). Amsterdam: Elsevier.

Landfield, P. W. (1977). Different effects of posttrial driving or blocking of the theta rhythm on avoidance learning in rats. *Physiology and Behavior, 18,* 439–445.

Landfield, P. W. (1980). Correlative studies of brain neurophysiology and behavior during aging. In D. G. Stein (Ed.), *The psychobiology of aging* (pp. 227–252). Amsterdam: Elsevier.

Landfield, P. W. (1988). Hippocampal neurobiological mechanisms of age-related memory dysfunction. *Neurobiology of Aging, 9,* 571–579.

Landfield, P. W., Campbell, L. W., Hao, S-Y., & Kerr, D. S. (1989). Aging-related increases in voltage-sensitive, inactivating calcium currents in rat hippocampus: Implications for mechanisms of brain aging and Alzheimer's disease. *Annals of the New York Academy of Science, 568,* 95–105.

Landfield, P. W., & Lynch, G. (1977). Impaired monosynaptic potentiation in in vitro hippocampal slices from aged, memory-deficient rats. *Journal of Gerontology, 32,* 523–533.

Landfield, P. W., McGaugh, J. L., & Lynch, G. (1978). Impaired synaptic potentiation processes in the hippocampus of aged, memory-deficient rats. *Brain Research, 150,* 85–101.

Landfield, P. W., McGaugh, J. L., & Tusa, R. J. (1972). Theta rhythm: A temporal correlate of memory storage processes in the rat. *Science, 175,* 87–89.

Landfield, P. W., & Morgan, G. A. (1984). Chronically elevating plasma Mg^{2+} improves hippocampal frequency potentiation and reversal learning in aged and young rats. *Brain Research, 322,* 167–171.

Landfield, P. W., & Pitler, T. A. (1984). Prolonged Ca^{2+}-dependent after hyperpolarizations in hippocampal neurons of aged rats. *Science, 226,* 1089–1092.

Landfield, P. W., Pitler, T. A., & Applegate, M. D. (1986). The effects of high Mg^{2+} to Ca^{2+} ratios on frequency potentiation in hippocampal slices of young and aged animals. *Journal of Neurophysiology, 56,* 797–811.

Larson, J., & Lynch, G. (1986). Induction of synaptic potentiation in hippocampus by patterned stimulation involves two events. *Science, 232,* 985–988.

Lashley, K. S. (1952). Functional interpretation of anatomic patterns. *Association for Research in Nervous and Mental Disease, Proceedings, 30,* 537–539.

Lisman, J. E. (1997). Bursts as a unit of neural information: Making unreliable synapses reliable. *Trends in Neuroscience, 20,* 38–43.

Madison, D. V., & Nicoll, R. A. (1984). Control of the repetitive discharge of rat CA1 pyramidal neurones in vitro. *Journal of Physiology, 354,* 319–331.

Markowska, A. L., Olton, D. S., & Givens, B. (1995). Cholinergic manipulation in the medial septal area: Age-related effects on working memory and hippocampal electrophysiology. *Journal of Neuroscience, 15,* 2063–2073.

Mazzanti, M. L., Thibault, O., & Landfield, P. W. (1991). Dihydropyridine modulation of normal hippocampal physiology in young and aged rats. *Neuroscience Research Communications, 9,* 117–125.

McCarren, M., & Alger, B. E. (1985). Use-dependent depression of the IPSPs in rat hippocampal pyramidal cells in vitro. *Journal of Physiology, 53,* 557–571.

McGaugh, J. L. (1966). Time-dependent processes in memory storage. *Science, 153,* 1351–1358.

McGaugh, J. L. (2000). Memory—A century of consolidation. *Science, 287,* 248–251.

McNaughton, B. L. (1998). The neurophysiology of reminiscence. *Neurobiology of Learning and Memory, 70,* 252–267.

Mitchell, S. J., Rawlins, J. N., Steward, O., & Olton, D. S. (1982). Medial septal area lesions disrupt theta rhythm and cholinergic staining in medial entorhinal cortex and produce impaired radial arm maze behavior in rats. *Journal of Neuroscience, 2,* 292–302.

Mizumori, S. J., Barnes, C. A., & McNaughton B. L. (1990). Behavioral correlates of theta-on and theta-off cells recorded from hippocampal formation of mature young and aged rats. *Experimental Brain Research, 80,* 365–373.

Moyer, J. R., Thompson, L. T., Black, J. P., & Disterhoft, J. F. (1992). Nimodipine increases excitability of rabbit CA1 pyramidal neurons in an age- and concentration-dependent manner. *Journal of Neurophysiology, 68,* 2100–2109.

Norris, C. M., Halpain, S., & Foster, T. C. (1998). Reversal of age-related alterations in synaptic plasticity by blockade of L-type Ca^{2+} channels. *Journal of Neuroscience, 18,* 3171–3179.

Otto, T., Eichenbaum, H., Wiener, S. L., & Wible, C. G. (1991). Learning-related patterns of CA1 spike trains parallel stimulation parameters optimal for inducing hippocampal long-term potentiation. *Hippocampus, 1,* 181–192.

Ouanounou, A., Zhang, L., Charlton, M. P., & Carlen, P. L. (1999). Differential modulation of synaptic transmission by calcium chelators in young and aged hippocampal CA1 neurons: Evidence for altered calcium homeostasis in aging. *Journal of Neuroscience, 19,* 906–915.

Pitler, T. A., & Landfield, P. W. (1987). Postsynaptic membrane shifts during frequency potentiation of the hippocampal EPSP. *Journal of Neurophysiology, 58,* 866–882.

Pribram, K. H. (1971). *Languages of the brain.* Englewood Cliffs, NJ: Prentice-Hall.

Rose, G. M., & Dunwiddie, T .V. (1986). Induction of hippocampal long-term potentiation using physiologically patterned stimulation. *Neuroscience Letters, 69,* 244–248.

Rosenzweig, E. S., Rao, G., McNaughton, B. L., & Barnes, C. A. (1997). Role of temporal summation in age-related long-term potentiation-induction deficits. *Hippocampus, 7,* 549–558.

Shadlen, M. N., & Newsome, W. T. (1998). The variable discharge of cortical neurons: Implications for connectivity, computation, and information encoding. *Journal of Neuroscience, 18,* 3870–3896.

Shankar, S., Teyler, T. J., & Robbins, N. (1998). Aging differentially alters forms of long-term potentiation in rat hippocampal area CA1. *Journal of Neurophysiology, 79,* 334–341.

Soleng, A. F., Raastad, M., & Andersen, P. (1999). Spatio–temporal properties of Schaffer collaterals allow activation of longitudinal strips of CA1 cells. *Society of Neuroscience Abstracts, 25,* 477.

Steriade, M. (1994). Coherent activities in corticothalamic networks during resting, sleep and their development into paroxysmal events. In G. Buzsaki, R. Llinas, W. Singer, A. Berthoz, & Y. Christen (Eds.), *Temporal coding in the brain* (pp. 115–128). Berlin. Germany: Springer-Verlag.

Stewart, M., & Fox, S. E. (1990). Do septal neurons pace the hippocampal theta rhythm? *Trends in Neurosciences, 13,* 163–168.

Storm, J. F. (1990). Potassium currents in hippocampal pyramidal cells. *Progress in Brain Research, 83,* 161–187.

Thibault, O., & Landfield, P. W. (1996). Increase in single L-type calcium channels in hippocampal neurons during aging. *Science, 272,* 1017–1020.

Thibault, O., Porter, N. M., Chen, K-C., Blalock, E. M., Kaminker, P. G., Clodfelter, G. V., Brewer, L. D., & Landfield, P. W. (1998). Calcium dysregulation in neuronal aging and Alzheimer's disease: History and new directions. *Cell Calcium, 24,* 417–433.

Thibault, O., Porter, N. M., & Landfield, P. W. (1993). Low Ba^{2+} and Ca^{2+} induce a sustained high probability of repolarization openings of L-type Ca^{2+} channels in hippocampal neurons: Physiological implications. *Proceedings of the National Academy of Science (USA), 90,* 11792–11796.

Thiels, E., Barrionuevo, G., & Berger, T. (1995). Excitatory stimulation during postsynaptic inhibition induces long-term depression in hippocampus in vivo. *Journal of Neurophysiology, 72,* 3009–3116.

Thomas, M. J., Watabe, A. M., Moody, T. D., Makhinson, M., & O'Dell, T. J. (1998). Postsynaptic complex spike bursting enables the induction of LTP by theta frequency synaptic stimulation. *Journal of Neuroscience, 18,* 7118–7126.

Verzeano, M. (1970). Evoked responses and network dynamics. In R. E. Whalen, R. F. Thompson, M. Verzeano, & N. M. Weinberger (Eds.), *The neural control of behavior* (pp. 27–54). New York: Academic Press.

Wetzel, W., Ott, T., & Matthies, H. (1977). Hippocampal rhythmic slow activity ("theta") and behavior elicited by medial septal stimulation in rats. *Behavioral Biology, 19,* 534–542.

Winson, J. (1978). Loss of hippocampal theta rhythm results in spatial memory deficit in the rat. *Science, 201,* 160–163.

Yeckel, M. F., & Berger, T. W. (1998). Spatial distribution of potentiated synapses in hippocampus: Dependence on cellular mechanisms and network properties. *Journal of Neuroscience, 18,* 438–450.

CHAPTER 16

Memory Codes:

New Concept for Old Problem

Norman M. Weinberger

A s the 21st century begins, few if any neuroscientists in the field of learning and memory would underestimate the extreme difficulties of achieving an understanding of how the brain acquires and stores information. That memory is highly complex and multifaceted is no longer doubted. Despite these difficulties, much has been achieved. Among the considerable advances, one can point to the use of powerful new methodologies that range from molecular genetics to functional recordings of the entire human brain. New ways of conceptualizing memory have likewise been a hallmark of the vast changes in the study of learning, memory, and the brain, although current memory taxonomies must be considered to be inadequate. For example, they fail to offer a place for processes as fundamental as the rapid stimulus–stimulus associative learning that develops as an initial stage in classical conditioning (Weinberger, 1998). The current and foreseeable burgeoning investigation of the neurobiology of learning and memory, which is characterized by the increasing attraction of scientists from other disciplines, promises ever more new methods and ideas.

However, as we rush to the future, this opportunity to formally honor James L. McGaugh is a particularly appropriate occasion[1] on which to address an

This research was supported by the following grants from the National Institutes of Health: MH-57235, DC 02346, and DC 02938. I thank Jacquie Weinberger for preparation of the manuscript and Gabriel Hui and Dewey McLin, III, for assistance with figures and insightful discussions.

[1] I cannot allow this festschrift to pass without including a personal statement about Jim McGaugh, who combines the best of science with consummate humanity. As a mentor to students and colleagues alike, he is unsurpassed. I am most fortunate to have been recruited by Jim in 1964 to help found the Department of Psychobiology (now the Department of Neurobiology and Behavior) at the University of California, Irvine. It has been and continues to be both a pleasure and an honor to be his colleague. Daily

important, neglected issue of long-standing, because McGaugh himself has repeatedly addressed and reinvigorated enduring issues in novel, insightful, and productive ways. His contributions include (a) the development of posttrial drug administration to attack memory without performance confounds, (b) reconceptualization of consolidation in terms of memory modulation, (c) integration of normal hormonal function with mnemonic processes, (d) discovery of amygdaloid involvement in regulating memory strength via hormonal feedback, and (e) revealing that sensitive behavioral assays show amygdaloid lesions do not prevent fear learning.

This chapter addresses the neglected topic of the codes for memory. By a *memory code* I mean *a relationship that describes the transformation of an experience into an enduring neural form.* As there seem to be no prior systematic writings about neurobiological memory codes, the concept may be highly novel, and this definition may seem vague. The rest of this chapter explicates memory codes, including the presentation of a candidate memory code for the learned behavioral importance of events. I suggest that the memory code for the acquired behavioral importance of a stimulus is the amount of receptive field retuning toward or to that stimulus. In short, more cells become tuned to important stimuli and fewer cells become tuned to less important stimuli.

First Considerations

Memory

It will prove helpful to begin by considering the concept of a memory code. By *memory* I refer to any type or form of memory, limited in no way to conscious, declarative, procedural, explicit, and implicit or any of the other terms in common use. The present approach does not demand that memory codes exist for every form or type of memory. However, it does assume the existence of at least one memory code for at least one form of moderate- to long-term memory. Without this reasonable assumption, there would be no issue.

Notice that I restrict memory codes to *moderate- or long-term memory.* By this, I intend memories that last for tens of minutes to lifetimes. There need be no absolute lower limit, because the lower limit can differ for various forms of memory or circumstance. I am really concerned with excluding short-term memories whose substrate can be "circulating" neuronal activity, such as continual neuronal discharges. Also, I want to distinguish memory codes from *sensory codes,* which describe the relationship between a sensory stimulus pa-

---

exposure to Jim's good humor and support, coupled with his exceptional knowledge, broad perspective, and tough-minded intellect, has shaped my professional and personal life in innumerable ways.

rameter and elicited neuronal activity (usually spike trains) that outlast the stimulus only for brief durations, for example, milliseconds to seconds. The working hypothesis is that memory codes do not exist for short-term memory. The fundamental question addressed is whether they actually exist for moderate- to long-term memory.

Codes

Whether one adheres to Occam's razor or common sense, the invention of new terms is inevitably suspect. So it may be with the introduction of the term *memory code*. In discussing brain and behavior, I am led inevitably to use words and metaphors from other walks of life. Although this has the advantage of promoting communication from the base of current common knowledge to a more esoteric, complex, and abstract discourse, it has the disadvantage of bringing "surplus meaning." For the present, it will be useful to use the term *code*, but a caveat is in order.

The common understanding of a code concerns cryptograms and the like. In this well-known case, there is a person who applies a code to a message, producing a product in an undecipherable form, until the appropriate "inverse code" is applied. In other words, communication requires both "encryption" and "decryption." I do not intend that the brain perform a decryption; there is no homunculus on the receiving end. However, encryption is part of the process under consideration. Certain basic properties of neurons (e.g., the ability of their synapses to change), the existence of different types of neurons (e.g., their morphology, transmitter, and other chemical systems), and the interconnections among neurons "blindly" instantiate memory codes.

Necessity of Encoding

Some readers may find it odd to have to justify the existence of memory encoding. However, others may find the concept unfathomable, and yet a third group seems to argue that encoding is not necessary (Freeman & Skarda, 1990). Therefore, we should consider the necessity of encoding at this point.

There are certainly different views on the nature of memories. Some regard them as veridical records of experiences. Others view a memory as merely a loose reconstruction based on bits and pieces, subject to conflation and a host of other processes in encoding and recall that compromise accuracy. Undoubtedly, different forms of memory are differentially subject to these problems, and the list of variables that affect memory strength and memory clarity is known to be long and is surely still incomplete. Nonetheless, whatever one's views about the veracity of memories, for memory as a fundamental competency of the brain to have any function at all, for organisms to derive any benefit from past experience, whatever the nature of the repository of experience in nervous systems, there must be the storage of sufficient correct detail to support future adaptive behavior. It can't all be a big muddle, even if inaccuracies abound.

The necessity of encoding is manifest whenever information in one form is transformed into another medium. For example, a tape recorder encodes patterns and amplitudes of sound levels as a pattern of magnetized particles on a plastic ribbon. A video camera encodes fluctuations of electromagnetic radiations into changes in the status of videotape. Strokes on a computer keyboard are encoded into bits in a computer's memory. Thus, it should not be surprising that experiences, in the form of sensory stimuli transduced into patterns of neuronal impulses, are encoded in the brain as enduring changes in neurons (and perhaps glia) that accurately reflect the stimuli.

Neural Bases of Encoding

Memory code may bring to mind the term *memory encoding*. Of course, encoding in memory is neither a new nor neglected topic. However, it has been approached mainly with respect to discovering which aspects of experience in humans (and sometimes other animals) attain memory. This important issue provides insight into the principles that govern what may be called the "contents" of memory or the "attributes of experience."

What has been neglected is a systematic consideration of the actual codes used by the brain to store cardinal features of experience. I hypothesize that encoding is governed by principles that are related to the type of information stored. This chapter discusses a code for stimulus importance, but I suggest other codes are used to represent other aspects of experience. There may be different memory codes for different classes of information. As discussed in more detail later, I suggest memory codes exist in the same sense that sensory codes exist. It just happens that although sensory codes have been the subject of intense research, memory codes seem to have been ignored. It is suggested that memory codes operate at the level of the transformation of current dynamic neural activity into long-lasting alterations of neural tissue, which are more latent in character. In short, I am concerned with a more reductionistic approach to the problem of encoding experience into memory than seems to have been done previously. Instead of seeking an understanding of what elements of experience are stored as memory in a given situation, I seek the neural principles by which experience becomes represented in the brain.

Attributes of Stored Experience

Given that the storage of experience must include some detail, it can be asked what attributes of an experience may be stored. Without attempting to be exhaustive, many of these attributes are

- *Background stimuli*—those stimuli relatively constant in the learning situation, including the location or place in which the experience occurs.

- *Changing stimuli*—which are usually brief (milliseconds to seconds).

- *Any and all sensory parameters of background and phasic stimuli*—sensory modality (e.g., visual), sensory dimension (e.g., sound frequency), location, intensity, duration, pattern, and so forth.

- *Physiological effects of receiving appetitive or aversive stimulation*—sensory feedback, hormonal release and feedback, and autonomic feedback.

- *Motivational/affective aspects of stimuli*—appetitive, aversive, or novel.

- *General physiological state*—as exemplified by state-dependent learning, state of general arousal, state of sexual arousal, state of hunger, and so forth.

- *Time*—of day, month, and season.

In short, attributes of experience include all afferentation to the brain plus various brain states themselves.

There is a paradoxical aspect of encoding. This is the fact that the encoding of experience into memory simultaneously encompasses both less and more than we directly sense. With regard to the "less" side, consider the construct of the *sensorium,* which is defined as the totality of sensory receptor epithelia. The state of the sensorium at any instant comprises a representation of all the sensory events that may attain processing within a nervous system and therefore ultimately may be stored as components of memory. However, on both reasonable empirical and conceptual grounds, the complete state of the sensorium at any one instant does not attain the status of memory, defined as enduring for minutes or longer. Not all sensory events are stored. Thus, memory, regardless of which type or form, contains less than did the sensorium. As to the "more" side, encoding includes factors that are not and never can be present in the sensorium. These are the more abstract features of experience. For example, a subject may encode whether or not a stimulus is novel or unexpected in a given context, by comparing it with stored information.

Another encoded abstraction is that of the acquired behavioral significance of a stimulus. This certainly occurs in associative conditioning, as when a conditional stimulus (CS) acquires significance by its predictive value as a signal for an unconditional stimulus (US). However, virtually all learning situations involve "tagging" or "assigning" significance or importance to experience, from the simplest habituation situation in invertebrates to the most sophisticated cognitive processes in humans. Neurophysiological evidence for a candidate memory code for the learned behavioral significance of stimuli will be presented later in this chapter. But first some other issues need to be considered.

Engrams As Particular Instances of the Operation of Memory Codes

To this point, the term *memory code* has not been clearly delineated from the term *engram*. It is now time to do so. The concept of an engram is well known; it is the term usually used to refer to the totality of neural changes that constitute a memory (Semon, 1921). It might be thought that memory code refers to engrams. However, engrams are not memory codes. To explicate each and their relationship, let's consider their characteristics.

Engrams

Five major features of engrams come readily to mind:

- *Form* may be static or dynamic (e.g., circulating patterns of neuronal discharges).
- *Place* refers to the degree of localization, extremes being completely localized or distributed throughout the brain.
- *Mobility* concerns the extent to which the engram stays in the same places once formed or rather is translocated in part or whole.
- *Lability* refers to whether or not the formed engram is essentially fixed or is subject to some sort of lawful "re-coding" over time and circumstance; an example would be a lawful or systematic change of the engram at times of retrieval (e.g., "ecphory"; Semon, 1921).
- *Stability* is intended to capture the dimension of strength over time, i.e., maintains its strength unchanged, becomes weaker or stronger.

In addition to these basic characteristics, engrams have another important feature—their uniqueness. If engrams are to have much adaptive significance, then they need to accurately reflect the particular experiences that give them rise. Each unique experience presumably could be stored as a unique engram. Failures of uniqueness compromise the accurate record of experience. In short, there should be as many engrams as there are memories in a brain.

Memory Codes

In contrast to engrams, memory codes are not unique to any experience. I suggest that they constitute a finite class that evolved to encode various attributes of experience. A memory code is not the actual neural substrate of a memory as is an engram. Rather, a memory code denotes a particular type of "input–output" function. A memory code describes the transform function from, for example, patterns of sensory-derived neuronal discharges (*input*) into long-lasting changes in neural organization (*output*). The long-lasting changes in neural organization constitute an engram (Figure 16.1). Because memory codes describe input–output functions, they are not physical entities as are engrams but rather are abstractions. Thus, unlike properties of engrams, memory codes cannot be said to have a potentially dynamic form, be localized in a particular place, have mobility or lability, or undergo a change in strength (property of stability) over time.

To help clarify the relationship between an engram and a memory code, consider the example of the auditory memory for your own name. This "sonic" engram presumably consists of various types of linked neuronal changes (at the levels of circuits, cells, and subcellular processes) perhaps localized mainly in the left hemisphere in one or more parts of the auditory cortex. What might be one of the involved memory codes? Because one's own name is very important, the memory needs to be encoded not only along acoustic dimensions but also in terms of relative behavioral importance. Therefore, a memory code for behavioral importance would be involved. It might be "increase the number of neurons that process and store highly important sensory stimuli."

Whether or not this is a memory code that would operate on one's own name is unknown. However, this may be the code for stimulus importance, based on evidence from the use of pure tone stimuli in guinea pigs and rats. We now turn to the findings that have led us to this hypothesis. We first consider the relationship between sensory and memory codes, next, how sensory codes may be used to seek memory codes; and then discuss our findings.

Sensory Codes and Memory Codes

Neuroscientists are familiar with neural codes within the domain of sensory physiology. A common example in the auditory system is the code for the loudness of sound; as stimulus intensity increases in decibels, the rate of discharge in the auditory nerve increases. Sensory codes and memory codes have both similarities and differences. The major difference involves sensory transduction. A sensory system must transform the type of energy that is appropriate for a given modality (e.g., electromagnetic for vision, mechanical for audition) into electrical energy that can be used by sensory systems in particular and nervous systems in general. In contrast, memory codes operate only on electrochemical events within nervous systems. That is, they are confined to interactions among neural elements, engaged minimally if at all with sensory receptors.

However, sensory codes also must confront electrochemical events, once past the stage of transduction. For example, within the auditory system, changes in mechanical energy are transduced into electrical energy within the hair cells of the cochlea. This change can be described by a transform function that

FIGURE 16.1

The hypothesized relationship among memory code, sensory neural activity, and engram.

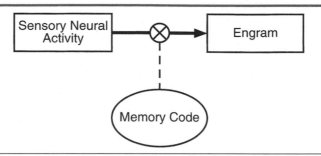

Some fraction of experience, represented by sensory neural activity, is stored as enduring changes in the brain, i.e., as an engram. Memory codes describe the function by which sensory activity is transformed into engrams. The memory code proposed here is that the number of neurons that become tuned to a stimulus is an increasing function of the degree of acquired behavioral importance of that stimulus.

encodes patterns of sound pressure levels into patterns of discharge within the auditory nerve. At a higher level of the auditory system, the patterns of discharge derived from the two ears converge on single cells at the level of the superior olivary complex of the brain stem. The outcome is a pattern of discharges that reflects parameters of relative sound pressure levels at the two ears, or times of arrival of stimulation from a distant sound source. The auditory system computes likely sources of sound in space based on this type of information. The superior olivary complex thus encodes a higher level of information than the 8th nerve, using a different sensory code.

As memory codes, like posttransduction sensory codes, concern neural-to-neural transformations, it seems reasonable to begin by using some knowledge from sensory codes to understand memory codes. But here we are likely to run into an obstacle that is not based in science; it is neither conceptual nor empirical, but rather attitudinal. Hence it ought to be easily overcome. But whether this is so is entirely the choice of the reader, because the barrier is the implicit assumption that sensory systems have little to offer to the study of memory. Most workers in the neurobiology of learning and memory remain uninterested in the learning-induced plasticity in primary sensory cortices that has been well documented over the past 50 years (e.g., see Weinberger & Diamond, 1987, for a review). The plasticity that is acknowledged, however, is generally narrowly viewed as limited to "perceptual learning," such as priming. But primary sensory cortical plasticity in learning is far more general and in no way limited to improvements in perceptual acuity. For example, improvements in perceptual acuity require thousands of trials over days or weeks (Karni, 1996; Karni &

Sagi, 1993; Recanzone, Jenkins, Hradek, & Merzenich, 1992). In contrast, specific receptive field plasticity in the primary auditory cortex develops in as few as five trials, the time required for a subject to form an association between a tone and a reinforcement (Edeline, Pham, & Weinberger, 1993; see also "Learning-Induced Receptive Field Plasticity in the Auditory Cortex" below).

Using Sensory Codes to Find Memory Codes

How can sensory codes be used to find memory codes? Let's take the case of a memory for a simple stimulus that is repeated alone. The subject responds (e.g., orients) to the stimulus initially but gradually fails to do so and finally may be said to ignore it. However, the introduction of a new stimulus produces a new orienting response. Given appropriate controls for receptor fatigue or adaptation, and given the assurance of a healthy, reactive state of the subject, readers will recognize this process as habituation. In habituation we recognize two sorts of processes, sensory and mnemonic. *Sensory processes* must be operative throughout, as without them one could not explain the elicitation of orienting responses or the selective response to a novel stimulus after habituation. *Mnemonic processes* must be operative throughout the experience, otherwise one could not explain the selective failure to respond to a stimulus that has no behavioral consequence or responding anew to a novel stimulus. It is at least quite reasonable to suppose that the subject stores the occurrences of the habituating stimulus and in some sense compares each incoming stimulus with this memory (Sokolov, 1963).

We come now to a critical distinction between sensory and memory codes. This is the difference of time domains. Sensory codes operate within a brief time domain, during and very shortly after (e.g., milliseconds to seconds) a sensory stimulus has been adequately transduced by an appropriate class of sensory receptor.

The neuronal transforms described by sensory codes may or may not endure. But if they do endure, then they become the province of memory codes, whose engrams may last from minutes to a lifetime. One thing seems certain: Mnemonic processes must have something to act on, so that if the sensory "traces" fade before mnemonic processes can access them, then a memory of those sensory events cannot be formed. This sequential linking of sensory and mnemonic processes has at least two very important implications.

- Memory codes most probably act on sensory activity. They may act on motor and other nonsensory outputs as well, but it is difficult to understand how sensory experience is remembered unless memory codes act on neurosensory activities.

- The search for memory codes can be given a starting locus. The input to a memory code "needle" can be sought in the "brain-as-haystack" by looking where the "products" of sensory codes are found, that is, in sensory systems.

Sensory codes and memory codes might be more closely related than is generally realized. Perhaps memory codes evolved from sensory codes. Mutations that greatly extended the lifetime of sensory traces that is, created memory, would have conferred a selective advantage to mnemonic life forms.

A Potential Code for Acquired Stimulus Significance

As discussed above, memory includes the acquired significance of stimuli, also referred to as the "learned behavioral importance of events." The two terms are used interchangably. The question at issue is whether or not there exists a code for stimulus significance. I present four hypotheses:

1. The brain has a specific memory code for the behavioral importance of experience.

2. The code for acquired behavioral significance is achieved through learning-induced, specific modifications of the receptive fields of neurons.

3. This memory code is increased significance of a stimulus is encoded as increased numbers of neurons whose receptive fields become tuned to or toward that stimulus.

4. The code for behavioral significance is most easily detected in sensory systems, particularly in sensory cortex, but is a general code in the brain.

In support of the first three hypotheses, I summarize findings from studies of primary auditory cortex conducted by me and my colleagues. The fourth hypothesis has not been tested.

Learning-Induced Receptive Field Plasticity in the Auditory Cortex

My colleagues and I have used the output of a sensory code to seek a memory code for acquired stimulus importance. The output in question is the receptive field for acoustic frequency in the primary auditory cortex. As commonly defined, a *sensory receptive field* of a neuron is comprised of all of the stimuli whose presence affects the neuron's activity. As used here, the *frequency receptive field* is the set of pure tone frequencies whose presentation alters neuronal discharge. The focus is on excitatory responses while recognizing that cells can be inhibited by stimuli. The frequency receptive field is commonly displayed as a graph of the number of discharges versus acoustic frequency. This graph is often called a *tuning curve,* and I use this term synonymously with frequency receptive field. The question we addressed was whether or not frequency receptive fields in the auditory cortex are systematically transformed when an animal learns that a single pure tone frequency is a signal for another event.

The first study was performed in secondary rather than primary auditory cortical fields of cats (Diamond & Weinberger, 1986, 1989). It revealed highly specific changes in receptive fields. However, receptive fields for tonal frequency in these secondary areas are not as distinct and sharp as in the primary auditory cortex, so it might have been expected that the type of marked receptive field plasticity observed would be found in the nonprimary auditory cortex, which some workers consider to be "association-type cortex." Therefore, to determine if receptive field plasticity might reflect the learned importance of tones, we subsequently investigated the primary auditory cortex.

The basic behavioral situation used to discover that learning specifically modifies neuronal receptive fields in the primary auditory cortex is rapid Pavlovian cardiac conditioning. An adult guinea pig receives a 6-second tone (CS) that is followed at tone offset by a brief, mild shock to the paw (US). Thirty trials are presented at approximately 1.5-minute intervals in a single session lasting approximately 45 minutes. Receptive field plasticity is also induced during two-tone discriminative Pavlovian conditioning. Moreover, it develops during instrumental avoidance conditioning, both for one-tone training and in two-tone discrimination training. This commonality across tasks and types of learning supports the view that the shifts in the tuning of receptive fields denote the operation of a general code for acquired stimulus significance. The findings have been published individually and in reviews (e.g., Weinberger, 1998) and therefore are summarized only briefly here.

The fundamental experiment consists of a hybrid design in which a sensory physiology paradigm is combined with a learning and memory paradigm. Following prior chronic implantation of microelectrodes in the primary auditory cortex, there are three basic stages:

- *Stage 1:* Receptive fields are obtained in an acoustic chamber by presenting brief tone pips (50–100 milliseconds) of many frequencies (and often many intensities) to the contralateral ear under conditions of acoustic control. The peak of the resultant frequency tuning curve (best frequency) is noted, and a non-best frequency is selected to serve as the CS; the rationale for choosing a non-best frequency is that this permits the detection of a shift in tuning toward or all the way to the frequency of the CS.

- *Stage 2:* The subject is moved to a different experimental room, where it undergoes classical (or instrumental avoidance) conditioning in a single session. For classical conditioning, heart rate is recorded. After several trials of habituation to the CS alone, the cardiac deceleration conditioned response develops within 5–10 trials (Edeline & Weinberger, 1993).

- *Stage 3:* The animal is returned to the acoustic chamber and receptive fields are obtained using the tone stimulus set identical to that used in Stage 1. Receptive fields may be obtained repeatedly over days; the longest time used has been about 60 days.

The findings can be summarized as follows. Receptive fields are changed in a systematic way to favor processing of the frequency of the CS; responses to the CS frequency are increased, whereas responses to the pretraining best frequency and many other frequencies are reduced (Bakin & Weinberger, 1990). These simultaneous opposite changes may be sufficient to change the tuning of the receptive field so that it shifts toward or even to the frequency of the CS (Figure 16.2).

This receptive field plasticity is associative because random presentation of the CS and US does not induce tuning shifts but only a general increase in response across frequency (Bakin, Lepan, & Weinberger, 1992). It is also discriminative—responses to a reinforced frequency (CS+) increase whereas responses to a nonreinforced frequency (CS−) and other frequencies decrease (Edeline & Weinberger, 1993). The tuning shifts are not spontaneous because the shifts are toward not away from the frequency of the CS. Finally, CS-specific receptive field plasticity is not due to putative arousal to the CS frequency during the posttraining determination of receptive fields for three reasons. First, subjects exhibit no behavioral arousal (e.g., cardiac response) to this frequency when it is presented in receptive field assays for 100 milliseconds instead of 6 seconds, intermixed with all the other frequencies. Second, neural responses to the tone presented only a few hundred milliseconds after the occurrence of the CS frequency do not exhibit increased responses, whereas arousal effects last for a longer period. Third, receptive field plasticity that is induced when animals are awake is expressed when they are under deep barbiturate anesthesia, during which state stimuli cannot and do not produce arousal (Weinberger, Javid, & Lepan, 1993).

Receptive field plasticity has other important characteristics in addition to being associative and stimulus specific. It is induced very rapidly, in as few as five trials (Edeline et al., 1993). Of particular importance, receptive field plasticity is retained for very long periods of time. It is present as long as 2 months after a single training session of 30 trials; this is the longest retention interval tested to date (Weinberger et al., 1993). Finally, it consolidates, that is, grows in strength and specificity over time (Edeline & Weinberger, 1993).

Table 16.1 summarizes the characteristics of receptive field plasticity with those of at least some forms of associative memory. This plasticity possesses all of these characteristics. Therefore, it is a viable candidate to encode specific attributes of a learning experience. As previously noted, the stimulus attribute that we believe is so encoded is the acquired behavioral importance of the frequency of the CS.

These findings show that acoustic frequencies that acquire behavioral importance as signals for a noxious stimulus or for the opportunity to avoid an aversive event achieve greater control of cortical processing than do frequencies that do not serve as relevant behavioral signals. At the level of single neurons, this is observed as increased response to signal frequencies and decreased response to nonsignal frequencies. But this individual retuning of receptive fields has implications for the overall functional organization of the primary auditory cortex because the frequency map is comprised of the receptive fields or, more specifically, is denoted by the best frequencies of cells at various loci. Therefore, after having found receptive field plasticity in the primary auditory cortex, we specifically hypothesized that learning would produce an increased representation of signal important frequencies across the map (Weinberger et al., 1990; see Figure 16.3). This prediction was subsequently fulfilled in a study of instrumental appetitive conditioning in the owl monkey (Recanzone, Schreiner, & Merzenich, 1993). The code for stimulus importance, then, may be the number of cells (i.e., amount of cortex) that becomes tuned to a stimulus.

Some Functional Implications of the Code for Acquired Stimulus Importance

There are several functional implications for a memory code that represents the behavioral significance of a stimulus by increasing the number of neurons that are tuned toward or to that stimulus, that is, biasing a cortical field to that stimulus. Four come readily to mind (Weinberger et al., 1990).

First, detection of that stimulus in a noisy situation could be increased because the probability of engaging cells that preferentially process that stimulus is increased. This does not mean that the cells are "grandmother" cells but only that the aggregate neuronal synaptic and spike activity to that stimulus will be greater than otherwise.

A second implication following from this is that the stimulus in question is more probable to gain attention in any situation, again on the hypothesis that the aggregate amount of response is positively related to the behavioral salience of a stimulus.

Third, there are more likely to be errors of perceptual commission for that stimulus because similar stimuli will also command greater neural response than

FIGURE 16.2

The effects of associative learning on the frequency receptive fields of a cell in the primary auditory cortex of a guinea pig.

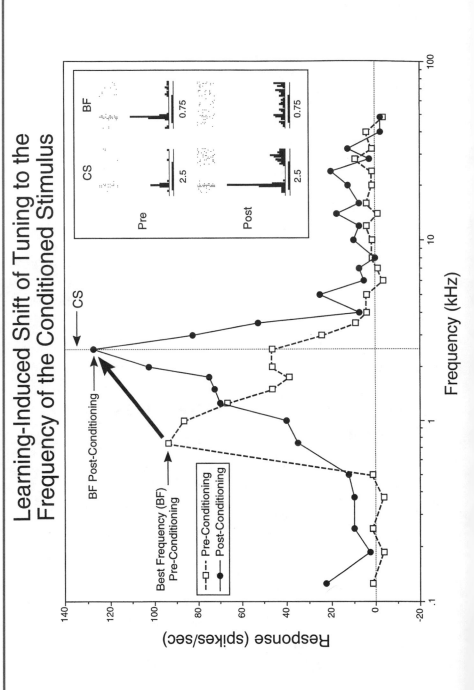

Learning-Induced Shift of Tuning to the Frequency of the Conditioned Stimulus

otherwise. A common example is that we often "hear" our name (particularly in a noisy environment) when it hasn't been called at all. Moreover, we are more likely to respond to words similar or identical to our name when they refer to something else. For example, with a nickname of "Norm," I find it difficult to listen to discussions about statistical "norms" without beginning to react as if to my name.

Fourth, the "safety" margin for processing and responding to important stimuli would be increased in the presence of some cerebral damage or other situation that compromises normal, full processing, such as fatigue, drugs states, and the like.

Testing the Hypothesis of Memory Codes

We have hypothesized that memory codes exist and that the code for acquired stimulus importance is increasing the number of cells tuned toward or to that stimulus. How might these hypotheses be tested? Obviously, it is insufficient to identify a neural correlate; this is merely an initial step. One method is to determine if related findings have been observed in other sensory systems. There is such evidence (Weinberger, 1995). Although such findings strengthen the generality of the relationship between learning and increased representation of behaviorally important stimuli, they are still correlative.

Behavioral validation would be a more direct test and it might be accomplished by several means. For example, the functional implications discussed above could be examined by training animals to a stimulus to various degrees and predicting that the more behaviorally important a stimulus, the greater will be its representation in sensory cortex. A more compelling approach would be

---

The subject underwent 30 trials of classical conditioning, during which a 6-second tone (conditioned stimulus, CS) was followed by a mild shock to the paw at stimulus offset. The subject developed a cardiac decelerative conditioned response, used to indicate that associative conditioning had been successful. Preconditioning, the cell's best frequency (BF) was 0.75 kHz. After conditioning with a CS of 2.5 kHz, the tuning had shifted so that the frequency of the CS became the peak of the tuning curve, i.e., the new BF. Note the opposite sign changes, with increased responses to the frequency of the CS and adjacent frequencies but decreased responses to the preconditioning BF and its adjacent frequencies. The inset shows the poststimulus time histograms (PSTHs) for the frequency of the CS and the BF pre- and postconditioning. Rasters show all spike discharges during the 20 repetitions of all frequencies used to determine the tuning curves. (Not illustrated are PSTHs for other frequencies.) Note the increased response to the frequency of the CS and the decreased response to the preconditioning BF; the consistency of response to the CS frequency in the postconditioning rasters shows that the increase of response was characteristic of each presentation of the CS frequency in the postconditioning receptive field.

TABLE 16.1

Some Characteristics of Associative Memory and Learning-Induced Receptive Field Plasticity

CHARACTERISTIC	ASSOCIATIVE MEMORY	RECEPTIVE FIELD PLASTICITY
Associative	Yes	Yes
Highly specific	Yes	Yes
Discriminative	Yes	Yes
Rapidly acquired	Yes	Yes
Long term retention	Yes	Yes
Consolidates	Yes	Yes

to induce increased tuning to a specific stimulus in primary sensory cortices in the absence of behavioral training and then predict that the specific stimulus will be treated behaviorally as if the increased tuning had occurred during normal learning. Such findings would speak to the issue of sufficiency. Necessity could be tested by reversibly changing the amount of preferential tuning and determining whether or not the behavior in question was degraded as a function of the amount of reduced tuning in the cortex.

Conclusion

The central issue in this chapter concerns the transformation of sensory experiences into memories of those experiences. I have set forth the idea that these transformations are unique at the level of the individual engrams that encode the details of each experience but that general principles govern the production of engrams. I suggest that these principles are embodied in memory codes, and I have presented evidence that the memory code for the learned behavioral importance of a stimulus is to increase the number of cells that preferentially process, that is, become tuned to, that stimulus.

To the best of my knowledge, the concept of memory codes has not been presented previously. Therefore, I provide a summary of the place of memory codes within a larger context. Figure 16.4 provides a simplified but useful hypothetical picture of the transformation of experience into memory. Three levels of processing are shown: psychological, neural systems, and neuronal. Also shown are the places within the processing stream at which two neural codes operate, sensory codes and memory codes (coding level).

At the psychological level, events occur in the environment, and these are experienced as percepts. Some fraction of percepts become memories, hence the arrow from percepts to memories is smaller than the arrow from events to percepts.

At the neural systems level, the events are treated as sensory stimuli. These are transduced in sensory receptors, but transduction is not viewed as part of perception. Rather, perception is seen as being coextensive with processing within central sensory systems; two parts are schematized, 1st and nth order processing, to indicate the hierarchical nature of sensory system operation. The highest order may be taken to be cortical processing. Some fractions of stimuli processed in sensory systems become engrams, the neural substrate of memories. Once again, as only fractions of sensory stimuli become engrams, the arrow to the latter is smaller than those within sensory processing proper.

The next reductionist level, the neuronal level, occurs entirely within the nervous system. Transduction at the systems level is more or less coextensive with generator potentials, which give rise to action potentials at all orders of a sensory system. Perception and sensory processing are coextensive at the neuronal level with the discharges (and, of course, synaptic potentials) of single cells in response to sensory stimuli (indicated by the bar below the illustrated spike train). Illustrated here are prelearning responses of a cell to a frequency that will later be used as the CS. The effects of learning are illustrated in the box to the right, in the memories/engrams column. This cell's response to the frequency of the CS is increased after learning because of presumptive increased synaptic strength for this stimulus. (Not illustrated are decreased responses to non-CS frequencies.)

At the coding level are illustrated a sensory code and a memory code. The sensory code is the relationship between the frequency of pure tones and the rate of discharge. Thus, the sensory code for frequency is given by the tuning curve or frequency receptive field. Illustrated to the right are receptive fields before (gray) and after (black) conditioning to the frequency labeled "CS." Note the shift in tuning from the original best frequency (BF) to the frequency of the CS. The memory code specifies the relationship between acquired stimulus importance and the amount of tuning change, which is illustrated as a monotonic increasing function. In short, the greater the acquired importance of a tonal frequency, the greater will be the magnitude of tuning shifts toward and to the frequency of the CS, and the number of cells that develop the tuning shifts. Thus, sensory codes are viewed as the initial specification of how an event is (transiently) encoded in sensory systems, whereas memory codes are considered to be engaged only when percepts are transformed into memories.[2]

This schematic summary is perhaps oversimplified but it is hoped not overly simplistic. This initial formulation of the concept of memory codes and

---

[2] Memory codes might also act on engrams previously formed from percepts, so that memory may be altered during recall, but space limitations preclude consideration of the full domain of the action of memory codes.

FIGURE 16.3

*Expanded representation of the frequency of the conditioned stimulus (CS)
that was predicted on the basis of associatively induced shifts of tuning
toward or to the frequency of the CS.*

A. Pre-Conditioning

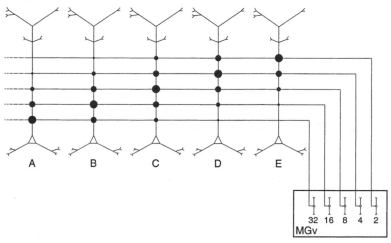

Post-Conditioning

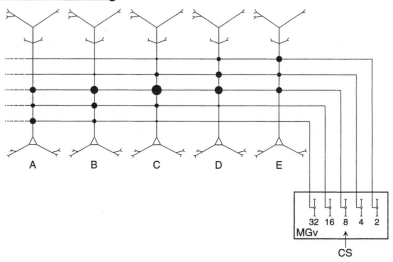

B.

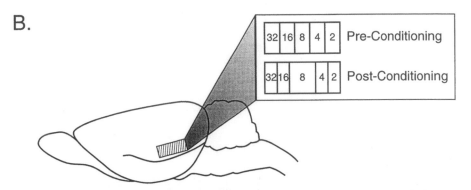

32	16	8	4	2	Pre-Conditioning

32	16	8	4	2	Post-Conditioning

(A) Hypothetical synaptic strengths for five cells in the primary auditory cortex (A–E) of inputs from five cells in the ventral medial geniculate nucleus (MGv, the thalamic tonotopic "relay"), each tuned to one of five frequency bands (2, 4, 8, 16, and 32 kHz). Synaptic strength for each thalamic input is proportional to the size of the black dots on the cortical cells. The largest dot shows the best frequency of each cell. Preconditioning, each cortical cell has a best frequency (greatest synaptic input) from a different frequency (A = 32 kHz, B = 16 kHz, C = 8 kHz, etc.). The subject underwent classical conditioning with a CS = 8 kHz. The rule applied is that the 8 kHz input was increased in strength for each cell (A–E), whereas the synaptic strengths for all other frequency inputs decreased during learning. Postconditioning, cells A, B, D, and E should exhibit shifted tuning. A and E would be shifted toward the CS frequency of 8 kHz, whereas B and D would have shifted to the frequency of the CS, i.e., 8 kHz. Cell C would show an increased response at 8 kHz relative to other frequencies but would not have shifted as its preconditioning BF was identical to the frequency of the CS. (B) The location of the primary auditory cortex showing the frequency "map" before and after conditioning. Preconditioning, the amount of representation of each frequency band was equal. Postconditioning, the representational space would have changed; the area tuned to the CS frequency of 8 kHz was predicted to increase, whereas areas tuned to the other frequencies would decrease. The predicted results were found by Recanzone, Schreiner, and Merzenich (1993). From Figure 13 on "Retuning Auditory Cortex by Learning: A Preliminary Model of Receptive Field Plasticity," by N. M. Weinberger, J. H. Ashe, & R. Metherate, 1990, *Concepts in Neuroscience, 6,* p. 122. Copyright 1990 by World Scientific Publishing Company. Modified with permission of the publisher.

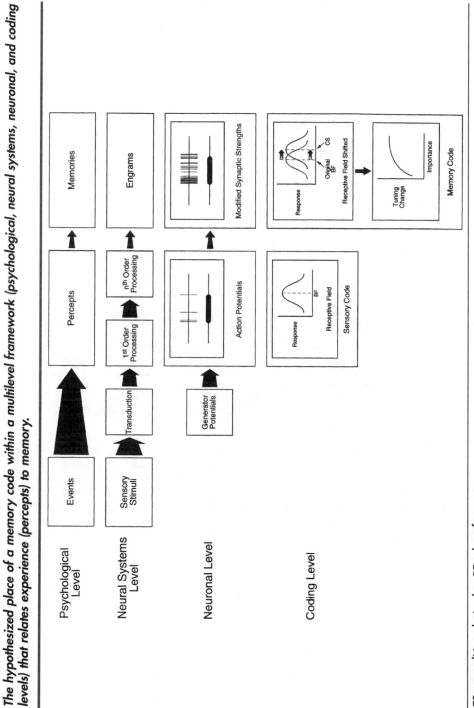

FIGURE 16.4

The hypothesized place of a memory code within a multilevel framework (psychological, neural systems, neuronal, and coding levels) that relates experience (percepts) to memory.

CS = conditioned stimulus; BF = best frequency.

the explication of findings that have led to postulating such codes is only an appropriate starting point. It is my hope that the concept of memory codes will engage others in theoretical and empirical studies of the neurobiology of memory encoding. It is surely worthwhile to seek general principles that have evolved to solve problems of the transformation of experience into enduring neural representations of the behaviorally meaningful world. If it turns out that the first neurobiological memory code has been discovered, there may be substantial implications for understanding memory and the brain. If not, perhaps the search to date will nonetheless prove illuminating.

References

Bakin, J. S., Lepan, B., & Weinberger, N. M. (1992). Sensitization induced receptive field plasticity in the auditory cortex is independent of CS-modality. *Brain Research, 577,* 226–235.

Bakin, J. S., & Weinberger, N. M. (1990). Classical conditioning induces CS-specific receptive field plasticity in the auditory cortex of the guinea pig. *Brain Research, 536,* 271–286.

Diamond, D. M., & Weinberger, N. M. (1986). Classical conditioning rapidly induces specific changes in frequency receptive fields of single neurons in secondary and ventral ectosylvian auditory cortical fields. *Brain Research, 372,* 357–360.

Diamond, D. M., & Weinberger, N. M. (1989). Role of context in the expression of learning-induced plasticity of single neurons in auditory cortex. *Behavioral Neuroscience, 103,* 471–494.

Edeline, J. M., Pham, P., & Weinberger, N. M. (1993). Rapid development of learning-induced receptive field plasticity in the auditory cortex. *Behavioral Neuroscience, 107,* 539–551.

Edeline, J. M., & Weinberger, N. M. (1993). Receptive field plasticity in the auditory cortex during frequency discrimination training: Selective retuning independent of task difficulty. *Behavioral Neuroscience, 107,* 82–103.

Freeman, W. J., & Skarda, C. A. (1990). Representations: Who needs them? In J. L. McGaugh, N. M. Weinberger, & G. Lynch (Eds.), *Brain organization and memory: Cells, systems, and circuits* (pp. 375–381). New York: Oxford University Press.

Karni, A. (1996). The acquisition of perceptual and motor skills: A memory system in the adult human cortex. *Brain Research: Cognitive Brain Research, 5,* 39–48.

Karni, A., & Sagi, D. (1993). The time course of learning a visual skill. *Nature, 365,* 250–252.

Recanzone, G. H., Jenkins, W. M., Hradek, G. T., & Merzenich, M. M. (1992). Progressive improvement in discriminative abilities in adult owl monkeys performing a tactile frequency discrimination task. *Journal of Neurophysiology, 67,* 1015–1030.

Recanzone, G. H., Schreiner, C. E., & Merzenich, M. M. (1993). Plasticity in the frequency representation of primary auditory cortex following discrimination training in adult owl monkeys. *Journal of Neuroscience, 13,* 87–103.

Semon, R. W. (1921). *The mneme.* New York: Macmillan.

Sokolov, E. N. (1963). *Perception and the conditional reflex.* New York: Macmillan.

Weinberger, N. M. (1995). Dynamic regulation of receptive fields and maps in the adult sensory cortex. *Annual Review of Neuroscience, 18,* 129–158.

Weinberger, N. M. (1998). Physiological memory in primary auditory cortex: Characteristics and mechanisms. *Neurobiology of Learning and Memory, 70,* 226–251.

Weinberger, N. M., Ashe, J. H., Metherate, R., McKenna, T. M., Diamond, D. M., Bakin, J. S., Lennartz, R. C., & Cassady, J. M. (1990). Neural adaptive information processing: A preliminary model of receptive field plasticity in auditory cortex during Pavlovian conditioning. In M. Gabriel & J. Moore (Eds.), *Neurocomputation and learning: Foundations of adaptive networks* (pp. 91–138). Cambridge, MA: Bradford Books/MIT Press.

Weinberger, N. M., & Diamond, D. M. (1987). Physiological plasticity in auditory cortex: Rapid induction by learning. *Progress in Neurobiology, 29,* 1–55.

Weinberger, N. M., Javid, R., & Lepan, B. (1993). Long-term retention of learning-induced receptive-field plasticity in the auditory cortex. *Proceedings of the National Academy of Sciences, 90,* 2394–2398.

Appendix:

The Publications by James L. McGaugh

McGaugh, J. L., & Petrinovich, L. (1956). An apparatus for the study of instrumental learning in the rat. *American Journal of Psychology, 69,* 660–663.

McGaugh, J. L. (1958). *Student workbook for elements of psychology.* New York: Alfred A. Knopf.

McGaugh, J. L., & Petrinovich, L. (1959). The effect of strychnine sulphate on maze-learning. *American Journal of Psychology, 72,* 99–102.

Breen, R. A., & McGaugh, J. L. (1961). Facilitation of maze learning with posttrial injections of picrotoxin. *Journal of Comparative and Physiological Psychology, 54,* 498–501.

Fehmi, L., & McGaugh, J. L. (1961). Discrimination learning by descendants of Tryon maze bright and maze dull strains. *Psychological Reports, 8,* 122.

Madsen, M. C., & McGaugh, J. L. (1961). The effect of ECS on one-trial avoidance learning. *Journal of Comparative and Physiological Psychology, 54,* 522–523.

McGaugh, J. L. (1961). Facilitative and disruptive effects of strychnine sulphate on maze learning. *Psychological Reports, 8,* 99–104.

McGaugh, J. L., Westbrook, W., & Burt, G. (1961). Strain differences in the facilitative effects of 5-7-diphenyl-1-3-diazadamantan-6-ol (1757 I.S.) on maze learning. *Journal of Comparative and Physiological Psychology, 54,* 502–505.

Thomson, C. W., McGaugh, J. L., Smith, C. E., Hudspeth, W. J., & Westbrook, W. H. (1961). Strain differences in the retroactive effects of electroconvulsive shock on maze learning. *Canadian Journal of Psychology, 15,* 69–74.

McGaugh, J. L., Jennings, R. D., & Thomson, C. W. (1962). Effect of distribution of practice on the maze learning of descendants of the Tryon maze bright and maze dull strains. *Psychological Reports, 11,* 147–150.

McGaugh, J. L., & Thomson, C. W. (1962). Facilitation of simultaneous discrimination learning with strychnine sulphate. *Psychopharmacologia, 3,* 166–172.

McGaugh, J. L., Thomson, C. W., Westbrook, W. H., & Hudspeth, W. J. (1962). A further study of learning facilitation with strychnine sulphate. *Psychopharmacologia, 3*, 352–360.

McGaugh, J. L., Westbrook, W. H., & Thomson, C. W. (1962). Facilitation of maze learning with posttrial injections of 5-7-diphenyl-1-3-diazadamantan-6-ol (1757 I.S.). *Journal of Comparative and Physiological Psychology, 55*, 710–713.

Cooper, J. B., & McGaugh, J. L. (1963). *Integrating principles of social psychology.* Cambridge, MA: Schenkman.

McGaugh, J. L., DeBaran, L., & Longo, V. G. (1963). Electroencephalographic and behavioral analysis of drug effects on an instrumental reward discrimination in rabbits. *Psychopharmacologia, 4*, 126–138.

McGaugh, J. L., & Petrinovich, L. (1963). Comments concerning the basis of learning enhancement with central nervous system stimulants. *Psychological Reports, 12*, 211–214.

Robustelli, F., McGaugh, J. L., & Bovet, D. (1963). Relationship between avoidance conditioning and maze learning. *Psychological Reports, 13*, 103–106.

Hudspeth, W. J., McGaugh, J. L., & Thomson, C. W. (1964). Aversive and amnesic effects of electroconvulsive shock. *Journal of Comparative and Physiological Psychology, 57*, 61–64.

McGaugh, J. L. (1964). Neural "efficiency" and the adaptiveness of behavior. *Acta Physiologica, 23*, 166–167.

McGaugh, J. L., & Madsen, M. C. (1964). Amnesic and punishing effects of electroconvulsive shock. *Science, 144*, 182–183.

Westbrook, W. H., & McGaugh, J. L. (1964). Drug facilitation of latent learning. *Psychopharmacologia, 5*, 440–446.

Breger, L., & McGaugh, J. L. (1965). Critique and reformulation of "learning-theory" approaches to psychotherapy and neurosis. *Psychological Bulletin, 63*, 338–358.

Greenough, W. T., & McGaugh, J. L. (1965). The effect of strychnine sulphate on learning as a function of time of administration. *Psychopharmacologia, 8*, 290–294.

McGaugh, J. L. (1965). Facilitation and impairment of memory storage processes. In D. P. Kimble (Ed.), *The anatomy of memory* (pp. 240–292). Palo Alto, CA: Science & Behavior Books.

McGaugh, J. L. (1965). Memory traces. In *McGraw-Hill yearbook of science and technology* (pp. 249–252). New York: McGraw-Hill.

McGaugh, J. L., & Cole, J. M. (1965). Age and strain differences in the effect of distribution of practice on maze learning. *Psychonomic Science, 2*, 253–254.

McGaugh, J. L., & Petrinovich, L. F. (1965). Effects of drugs on learning and memory. *International Review of Neurobiology, 8*, 139–196.

Petrinovich, L., Bradford, D., & McGaugh, J. L. (1965). Drug facilitation of memory in rats. *Psychonomic Science, 2,* 191–192.

Bovet, D., McGaugh, J. L., & Oliverio, A. (1966). Effects of posttrial administration of drugs on avoidance learning of mice. *Life Sciences, 5,* 1309–1315.

Breger, L., & McGaugh, J. L. (1966). Learning theory and behavior therapy: A reply to Rachman and Eysenck. *Psychological Bulletin, 65,* 170–173.

Luttges, M., Johnson, T., Buck, C., Holland, J., & McGaugh, J. L. (1966). An examination of "transfer of learning" by nucleic acid. *Science, 151,* 834–837.

McGaugh, J. L. (1966, August). *Discussion comments.* Symposium on Biological Bases of Memory Traces, XVII International Congress of Psychology, Moscow.

McGaugh, J. L. (1966). Drug facilitation of memory storage. In *Proceedings of the Fifth International Congress of the Colloquium Internationale Neuro-psychopharmacologicum.* Washington, DC: Excerpta Medica Foundation.

McGaugh, J. L. (1966, August). *Memory storage processes.* Symposium on the Relationship Between Long-Term and Short-Term Memory, XVII International Congress of Psychology, Moscow.

McGaugh, J. L. (1966). Time-dependent processes in memory storage. *Science, 153,* 1351–1358.

McGaugh, J. L., & Alpern, H. P. (1966). Effects of electroshock on memory: Amnesia without convulsions. *Science, 152,* 665–666.

McGaugh, J. L., & Petrinovich, L. F. (1966). Neural consolidation and electro-convulsive shock re-examined. *Psychological Review, 73,* 382–387.

McGaugh, J. L., Weinberger, N. M., & Whalen, R. E. (Eds.). (1966). *Psychobiology: Readings from* Scientific American. San Francisco, CA: W. H. Freeman.

Luttges, M. W., & McGaugh, J. L. (1967). Permanence of retrograde amnesia produced by electroconvulsive shock. *Science, 156,* 408–410.

McGaugh, J. L. (1967). Analysis of memory transfer and enhancement. *Proceedings of the American Philosophical Society, 111,* 347–351.

McGaugh, J. L. (1967). Biological aspects of learning and memory. *Proceedings of the Educational Records Bureau,* 47–57.

McGaugh, J. L. (1967). Chemical influences on memory. *Industrial Research, 9,* 81–83.

McGaugh, J. L. (1967). Experimental modification of memory storage. In F. L. Ruch (Ed.), *Psychology and life* (pp. 666–671). Glenview, IL: Scott, Foresman.

McGaugh, J. L. (1967). Where is the engram? *Contemporary Psychology, 2,* 115–116.

Stephens, G., McGaugh, J. L., & Alpern, H. P. (1967). Periodicity and memory in mice. *Psychonomic Science, 8,* 201–202.

Alpern, H. P., & McGaugh, J. L. (1968). Retrograde amnesia as a function of duration of electroshock stimulation. *Journal of Comparative and Physiological Psychology, 65,* 265–269.

Krivanek, J., & McGaugh, J. L. (1968). Effects of pentylenetetrazol on memory storage in mice. *Psychopharmacologia, 12,* 303–321.

McGaugh, J. L. (1968). A multi-trace view of memory storage processes. In D. Bovet, F. Bovet-Nitti, & A. Oliverio (Eds.), *Recent advances in learning and retention* (No. 109, pp. 13–24). Rome: Roma Accademia Nazionale Dei Lincei.

McGaugh, J. L. (1968). An alternative view of memory storage. *Science, 160,* 1097–1098.

McGaugh, J. L. (1968). Changing concepts of learning and memory. *NEA Journal, 57,* 8–9, 51, 52, 54.

McGaugh, J. L. (1968). Drug facilitation of memory and learning. In D. H. Efron (Ed.), *Psychopharmacology: A review of progress* (PHS Pub. No. 1836, pp. 891–904). Washington, DC: U.S. Government Printing Office.

McGaugh, J. L. (1968). Electroconvulsive shock. *International Encyclopedia of the Social Sciences, 5,* 21–25.

McGaugh, J. L. (1968). Wie funktioniert das Gedachtnis? [How does memory work? Experimental analysis of the processes involved in the storage of memory contents.] *Umshau in Wissenschaft und Technik, 10,* 289–294.

Stephens, G. J., & McGaugh, J. L. (1968). Periodicity and memory in mice: A supplementary report. *Communications in Behavioral Biology, 2,* 59–63.

Stephens, G., & McGaugh, J. L. (1968). Retrograde amnesia: Effects of periodicity and degree of training. *Communications in Behavioral Biology, 1,* 267–275.

Dawson, R. G., & McGaugh, J. L. (1969). Electroconvulsive shock effects on a reactivated memory trace: Further examination. *Science, 166,* 525–527.

Dawson, R. G., & McGaugh, J. L. (1969). Electroconvulsive shock-produced retrograde amnesia: Analysis of the familiarization effect. *Communications in Behavioral Biology, Part A, 4,* 91–95.

Dawson, R. G., & McGaugh, J. L. (1969). Familiarization and retrograde amnesia: A re-evaluation re-evaluated. *Communications in Behavioral Biology, Part A, 4,* 257–259.

Krivanek, J. A., & McGaugh, J. L. (1969). Facilitating effects of pre- and posttrial amphetamine administration on discrimination learning in mice. *Agents and Actions, 1,* 36–42.

McGaugh, J. L. (1969). Drug effects on learning and memory. *Memory Documenta Geigy,* 8.

McGaugh, J. L. (1969). Effects of analeptics on learning and memory in infrahumans. In P. Black (Ed.), *Drugs and the brain* (pp. 241–250). Baltimore: Johns Hopkins University Press.

McGaugh, J. L. (1969). Facilitation of memory storage processes. In S. Bogoch (Ed.), *The future of the brain sciences* (pp. 355–370). New York: Plenum Press.

McGaugh, J. L. (1969). Le basi biologiche della memoria [Biological bases of memory]. *Enciclopedia Della Scienza E Della Tecnica Mondadori, 23,* 313–320.

McGaugh, J. L., & Longacre, B. (1969). Effect of electroconvulsive shock on performance of a well-learned avoidance response: Contribution of the convulsion. *Communications in Behavioral Biology, Part A, 4,* 177–181.

Stephens, G. J., & McGaugh, J. L. (1969). Retrograde amnesia in mice: Alteration in temporal gradients with phase-shifting of the temperature rhythm. *Communications in Behavioral Biology, Part A, 3,* 253–257.

Swanson, R., McGaugh, J. L., & Cotman, C. (1969). Acetoxycycloheximide effects on one-trial inhibitory avoidance learning. *Communications in Behavioral Biology, Part A, 4,* 239–245.

Zornetzer, S., & McGaugh, J. L. (1969). Effects of electroconvulsive shock upon inhibitory avoidance: The persistence and stability of amnesia. *Communications in Behavioral Biology, Part A, 3,* 173–180.

Denti, A., McGaugh, J. L., Landfield, P. W., & Shinkman, P. (1970). Effects of posttrial electrical stimulation of the mesencephalic reticular formation on avoidance learning in rats. *Physiology and Behavior, 5,* 659–662.

Luttges, M. W., & McGaugh, J. L. (1970). Facilitating effects of bemegride on retention of a visual discrimination task. *Agents and Actions, 1,* 234–239.

McGaugh, J. L. (1970). Chairman's report: A summary of the discussion group on "behavior," especially as regards learning and memory. *Proceedings of the Fourth International Congress of Pharmacology, 1,* 159–167.

McGaugh, J. L. (1970). Memory storage processes. In K. H. Pribram & D. Broadbent (Eds.), *Biology of memory* (pp. 51–61). New York: Academic Press.

McGaugh, J. L., & Krivanek, J. (1970). Strychnine effects on discrimination learning in mice: Effects of dose and time of administration. *Physiology and Behavior, 5,* 1437–1442.

McGaugh, J. L., & Landfield, P. W. (1970). Delayed development of amnesia following electroconvulsive shock. *Physiology and Behavior, 5,* 1109–1113.

McGaugh, J. L., & Zornetzer, S. (1970). Amnesia and brain seizure activity in mice: Effects of diethyl ether anesthesia prior to electroshock stimulation. *Communications in Behavioral Biology, Part A, 5,* 243–248.

Zornetzer, S., & McGaugh, J. L. (1970). Effects of frontal brain electroshock stimulation on EEG activity and memory in rats: Relationship to ECS-produced retrograde amnesia. *Journal of Neurobiology, 1,* 379–394.

Cotman, C., Banker, G., Zornetzer, S., & McGaugh, J. L. (1971). Electroshock effects on brain protein synthesis: Relation to brain seizures and retrograde amnesia. *Science, 173,* 454–456.

Fishbein, W., McGaugh, J. L., & Swarz, J. R. (1971). Retrograde amnesia: Electroconvulsive shock effects after termination of rapid eye movement sleep deprivation. *Science, 172,* 80–82.

Harlow, H. F., McGaugh, J. L., & Thompson, R. F. (1971). *Psychology.* San Francisco, CA: Albion.

Luttges, M. W., & McGaugh, J. L. (1971). Facilitation of avoidance conditioning in mice by posttraining administration of bemegride. *Agents and Actions, 3,* 118–121.

McGaugh, J. L. (1971). Electroconvulsive shock. In *Encyclopedia of science and technology* (Vol. 4, pp. 534–535). New York: McGraw-Hill.

McGaugh, J. L. (1971). Learning: A biological perspective. *Contemporary Psychology, 16,* 206–207.

McGaugh, J. L. (Ed.). (1971). *Psychobiology: Behavior from a biological perspective.* New York: Academic Press.

McGaugh, J. L., & Dawson, R. G. (1971). Modification of memory storage processes. In W. K. Honig & P. H. R. James (Eds.), *Animal memory* (pp. 215–242). New York: Academic Press.

McGaugh, J. L., Dawson, R. G., Coleman, R., & Rawie, J. (1971). Electroshock effects on memory in Diethyl ether-treated mice: Analysis of the CER-incubation hypothesis of retrograde amnesia. *Communications in Behavioral Biology, Part A, 6,* 227–232.

Zornetzer, S., & McGaugh, J. L. (1971). Retrograde amnesia and brain seizures in mice. *Physiology and Behavior, 7,* 401–408.

Zornetzer, S., & McGaugh, J. L. (1971). Retrograde amnesia and brain seizures in mice: A further analysis. *Physiology and Behavior, 7,* 841–845.

Gold, P. E., & McGaugh, J. L. (1972). Effect of recent footshock on brain seizures and behavioral convulsions induced by electrical stimulation of the brain. *Behavioral Biology, 7,* 421–426.

Landfield, P. W., & McGaugh, J. L. (1972). Effects of electroconvulsive shock and brain stimulation on EEG cortical theta rhythms in rats. *Behavioral Biology, 7,* 271–278.

Landfield, P. W., McGaugh, J. L., & Tusa, R. J. (1972). Theta rhythm: A temporal correlate of memory storage processes in the rat. *Science, 175,* 87–89.

Landfield, P. W., McGaugh, J. L., & Tusa, R. J. (1972). Theta rhythm and memory. *Science, 176,* 1449.

McGaugh, J. L. (1972). Impairment and facilitation of memory consolidation. *Activitas Nervosa Superior (Praha), 14,* 64–74.

McGaugh, J. L. (1972). Learning and memory. In *Biology today.* Del Mar, CA: CRM Books.

McGaugh, J. L. (Ed.). (1972). *The chemistry of mood, motivation, and memory.* New York: Plenum Press.

McGaugh, J. L. (1972). The search for the memory trace. *Annals of the New York Academy of Sciences, 193,* 112–123.

McGaugh, J. L., & Herz, M. J. (1972). *Memory consolidation.* San Francisco, CA: Albion.

McGaugh, J. L., Zornetzer, S. F., Gold, P. E., & Landfield, P. W. (1972). Modification of memory systems: Some neurobiological aspects. *Quarterly Reviews of Biophysics, 5,* 163–186.

Stephens, G., & McGaugh, J. L. (1972). Biologic factors related to learning in the land snail *Helix aspersa Muller. Animal Behaviour, 20,* 309–315.

Zornetzer, S., & McGaugh, J. L. (1972). Electrophysiological correlates of frontal cortex-induced retrograde amnesia in rats. *Physiology and Behavior, 8,* 233–238.

Dawson, R. G., & McGaugh, J. L. (1973). Drug facilitation of learning and memory. In J. A. Deutsch (Ed.), *The physiological basis of memory* (pp. 77–111). New York: Academic Press.

Gold, P. E., Bueno, O. F., & McGaugh, J. L. (1973). Training and task-related differences in retrograde amnesia thresholds determined by direct electrical stimulation of the cortex in rats. *Physiology and Behavior, 11,* 57–63.

Gold, P. E., Haycock, J. W., Macri, J., & McGaugh, J. L. (1973). Retrograde amnesia and the "reminder effect": An alternative interpretation. *Science, 180,* 1199–1201.

Gold, P. E., Macri, J., & McGaugh, J. L. (1973). Retrograde amnesia gradients: Effects of direct cortical stimulation. *Science, 179,* 1343–1345.

Gold, P. E., Macri, J., & McGaugh, J. L. (1973). Retrograde amnesia produced by sub-seizure amygdala stimulation. *Behavioral Biology, 9,* 671–680.

Gold, P. E., & McGaugh, J. L. (1973). Relationship between amnesia and brain seizures in rats. *Physiology and Behavior, 9,* 41–46.

Haycock, J. W., Deadwyler, S. A., Sideroff, S. I., & McGaugh, J. L. (1973). Retrograde amnesia and cholinergic systems in the caudate-putamen complex and dorsal hippocampus of the rat. *Experimental Neurology, 41,* 201–213.

Haycock, J. W., Gold, P. E., Macri, J., & McGaugh, J. L. (1973). Noncontingent foot-shock attenuation of retrograde amnesia: A generalization effect. *Physiology and Behavior, 11,* 99–102.

Haycock, J. W., & McGaugh, J. L. (1973). Retrograde amnesia gradients as a function of ECS-intensity. *Behavioral Biology, 9,* 123–127.

Izquierdo, J. A., Baratti, C. M., Torrelio, M., Arevalo, L., & McGaugh, J. L. (1973). Effects of food deprivation, discrimination experience and physostigmine on choline acetylase and acetylcholinesterase in the dorsal hippocampus and frontal cortex of rats. *Psychopharmacologia (Berlin), 33,* 103–110.

Landfield, P. W., Tusa, R., & McGaugh, J. L. (1973). Effects of posttrial hippocampal stimulation on memory storage and EEG activity. *Behavioral Biology, 8,* 485–505.

McGaugh, J. L. (1973). Drug facilitation of learning and memory. *Annual Review of Pharmacology, 13,* 229–241.

McGaugh, J. L. (1973). *Learning and memory: An introduction.* San Francisco, CA: Albion.

McGaugh, J. L. (1973). Modification of learning and memory by CNS stimulants and electrical stimulation of the brain. In F. E. Bloom & G. H. Acheson (Eds.), *Brain, nerves, and synapses* (Proceedings of the 5th International Congress of Pharmacology, Vol. 4, pp. 39–45). Basel, Switzerland: Karger.

McGaugh, J. L. (1973). Report of the discussion of the symposium on pharmacological agents on memory and learning. In F. E. Bloom & G. H. Acheson, (Eds.), *Brain, nerves, and synapses* (Proceedings of the 5th International Congress of Pharmacology, Vol. 4, pp. B7/1–B7/3). Basel, Switzerland: Karger.

McGaugh, J. L., & Gold, P. E. (1973). Impairment of memory storage processes by electrical stimulation of the brain. In S. Bogoch (Ed.), *Biological diagnosis of brain disorders* (pp. 153–164). New York: Spectrum.

Fink, M., Kety, S. S., McGaugh, J. L., & Williams, T. A. (Eds.). (1974). *Psychobiology of convulsive therapy.* Washington, DC: V. H. Winston & Sons.

Gold, P. E., Haycock, J. W., & McGaugh, J. L. (1974). Retrograde amnesia and the "reminder effect." *Science, 186,* 1136.

Gold, P. E., McDonald, R., & McGaugh, J. L. (1974). Direct cortical stimulation: A further study of treatment intensity effects on retrograde amnesia gradients. *Behavioral Biology, 10,* 485–490.

Gold, P. E., Zornetzer, S. F., & McGaugh, J. L. (1974). Electrical stimulation of the brain: Effects on memory storage. In G. Newton & A. Riesen (Eds.), *Advances in psychobiology* (Vol. 2, pp. 193–224). New York: Wiley Interscience.

Handwerker, M. J., Gold, P. E., & McGaugh, J. L. (1974). Impairment of active avoidance learning with posttraining amygdala stimulation. *Brain Research, 75,* 324–327.

McGaugh, J. L. (1974). Electroconvulsive shock: Effects on learning and memory in animals. In M. Fink, S. S. Kety, J. L. McGaugh, & T. A. Williams (Eds.), *Psychobiology of convulsive therapy* (pp. 85–97). Washington, DC: V. H. Winston & Sons.

McGaugh, J. L. (1974). In memoriam: Ralph Waldo Gerard, 1900–1974. *Behavioral Biology, 11,* 285–286.

McGaugh, J. L. (1974). Modification of learning and memory by chemical and electrical stimulation of the brain. In J. Knoll & B. Knoll (Eds.), *Symposium on pharmacology of learning and retention* (pp. 931–942). Budapest, Hungary: Akademiai Kiado.

McGaugh, J. L., & Gold, P. E. (1974). Conceptual and neurobiological issues in studies of treatments affecting memory storage. In G. H. Bower (Ed.), *The psychology of learning and motivation* (Vol. 8, pp. 233–264). New York: Academic Press.

McGaugh, J. L., & Gold, P. E. (1974). The effects of drugs and electrical stimulation of the brain on memory storage processes. In R. D. Myers & R. R. Drucker-Colin (Eds.), *Neurohumoral coding of brain function* (pp. 189–206). New York: Plenum Press.

McGaugh, J. L., & Williams, T. A. (1974). Summary: Neurophysiological and behavioral effects of convulsive phenomena. In M. Fink, S. S. Kety, J. L. McGaugh, & T. A. Williams (Eds.), *Psychobiology of convulsive therapy* (pp. 279–283). Washington, DC: V. H. Winston & Sons.

Sideroff, S., Bueno, O., Hirsch, A., Weyand, T., & McGaugh, J. L. (1974). Retrograde amnesia initiated by low-level stimulation of hippocampal cytoarchitectonic areas. *Experimental Neurology, 43,* 285–297.

van Buskirk, R., & McGaugh, J. L. (1974). Pentylenetetrazol-induced retrograde amnesia and brain seizures in mice. *Psychopharmacologia, 40,* 77–90.

Drucker-Colin, R. R., Spanis, C. W., Cotman, C. W., & McGaugh J. L. (1975). Changes in protein levels in perfusates of freely moving cats: Relation to behavioral state. *Science, 187,* 963–965.

Drucker-Colin, R. R., Spanis, C. W., Cotman, C. W., & McGaugh, J. L. (1975). Proteins and REM sleep. In P. Levin & W. P. Koella, (Eds.), *Sleep, 1974: Instinct, neurophysiology, endocrinology, episodes, dreams, epilepsy, and intracranial pathology* (pp. 55–59). Basel, Switzerland: Karger.

Drucker-Colin, R. R., Spanis, C. W., Hunyadi, J., Sassin, J. F., & McGaugh, J. L. (1975). Growth hormone effects on sleep and wakefulness in the rat. *Neuroendocrinology, 18,* 1–8.

Gold, P. E., Edwards, R. M., & McGaugh, J. L. (1975). Amnesia produced by unilateral, subseizure, electrical stimulation of the amygdala in rats. *Behavioral Biology, 15,* 95–105.

Gold, P. E., Hankins, L., Edwards, R. M., Chester, J., & McGaugh, J. L. (1975). Memory interference and facilitation with posttrial amygdala stimulation: Effect on memory varies with footshock level. *Brain Research, 86,* 509–513.

Gold, P. E., & McGaugh, J. L. (1975). A single-trace, two-process view of memory storage processes. In D. Deutsch & J. A. Deutsch (Eds.), *Short-term memory* (pp. 355–378). New York: Academic Press.

Gold, P. E., & McGaugh, J. L. (1975). Changes in learning and memory during aging. In J. M. Ordy & K. R. Brizzee (Eds.), *Neurobiology of aging* (pp. 145–158). New York: Plenum Press.

Gold, P. E., van Buskirk, R. B., & McGaugh, J. L. (1975). Age-related changes in learning and memory. In G. J. Maletta (Ed.), *Survey report on the aging nervous system* (pp. 169–178). Washington, DC: U.S. Government Printing Office.

Gold, P. E., van Buskirk, R. B., & McGaugh, J. L. (1975). Effects of hormones on time-dependent memory storage processes. In W. H. Gispen, Tj. B. van Wimersma Greidanus, B. Bohus, & D. de Wied (Eds.), *Hormones, homeostasis, and the brain* (Progress in Brain Research, Vol. 42, pp. 210–211). Amsterdam: Elsevier.

McGaugh, J. L. (1975). Biological bases of memory storage processes: The state of the art. In J. R. Nazzaro (Ed.), *Master lectures on physiological psychology* (Tape Series). New York: American Psychological Association.

McGaugh, J. L., Gold, P. E., van Buskirk, R. B., & Haycock, J. W. (1975). Modulating influences of hormones and catecholamines on memory storage processes. In W. H. Gispen, Tj. B. van Wimersma Greidanus, B. Bohus, & D. de Wied (Eds.), *Hormones, homeostasis, and the brain* (Progress in Brain Research, Vol. 42, pp. 151–162). Amsterdam: Elsevier.

van Buskirk, R. B., Gold, P. E., & McGaugh, J. L. (1975). Mediation of epinephrine effects on memory processes by alpha and beta receptors. In W. H. Gispen, Tj. B. van Wimersma Greidanus, B. Bohus, & D. de Wied (Eds.), *Hormones, homeostasis, and the brain* (Progress in Brain Research, Vol. 42, p. 210). Amsterdam: Elsevier.

Haycock, J. W., van Buskirk, R., & McGaugh, J. L. (1976). Facilitation of retention performance in mice by posttraining diethyldithiocarbamate. *Pharmacology Biochemistry and Behavior, 5,* 525–528.

McGaugh, J. L. (1976). Cognition and consolidation. In L. Petrinovich & J. L. McGaugh (Eds.), *Knowing, thinking, and believing* (Festschrift for Professor David Krech; pp. 117–141). New York: Plenum Press.

McGaugh, J. L. (1976). Neurobiological aspects of memory. In R. G. Grenell & S. Gabay (Eds.), *Biological foundations of psychiatry* (pp. 499–525). New York: Raven Press.

McGaugh, J. L. (1976). Neurobiology and the future of education. *School Review, 85,* 166–175.

McGaugh, J. L., & Gold, P. E. (1976). Modulation of memory by electrical stimulation of the brain. In M. R. Rosenzweig & E. L. Bennett (Eds.), *Neural mechanisms of learning and memory* (pp. 549–560). Cambridge, MA: MIT Press.

Petrinovich, L., & McGaugh, J. L. (Eds.). (1976). *Knowing, thinking, and believing* (Festschrift for Professor David Krech). New York: Plenum Press.

van Buskirk, R. B., & McGaugh, J. L. (1976). Retrograde amnesia and brain seizure activity in mice: Strain differences. *Experimental Neurology, 51,* 150–159.

Drucker-Colin, R. R., & McGaugh, J. L. (Eds.); Jensen, R. A., & Martinez, J.L., Jr. (Assoc. Eds.). (1977). *Neurobiology of sleep and memory.* New York: Academic Press.

Gold, P. E., & McGaugh, J. L. (1977). Hormones and memory. In L. H. Miller, C. A. Sandman, & A. J. Kastin (Eds.), *Neuropeptide influences on the brain and behavior* (pp. 127–143). New York: Raven Press.

Haycock, J. W., van Buskirk, R., & McGaugh, J. L. (1977). Effects of catecholaminergic drugs upon memory storage processes in mice. *Behavioral Biology, 20,* 281–310.

Haycock, J. W., van Buskirk, R., Ryan, J. R., & McGaugh, J. L. (1977). Enhancement of retention with centrally administered catecholamines. *Experimental Neurology, 54,* 199–208.

Haycock, J. W., White, W. F., McGaugh, J. L., & Cotman, C. W. (1977). Enhanced stimulus-secretion coupling from brains of aged mice. *Experimental Neurology, 57,* 873–882.

Hunter, B., Zornetzer, S. F., Jarvik, M. E., & McGaugh, J. L. (1977). Modulation of learning and memory: Effects of drugs influencing neurotransmitters. In L. Iversen, S. Iversen, & S. Snyder (Eds.), *Handbook of psychopharmacology* (Vol. 8, Drugs, Neurotransmitters, and Behavior, pp. 531–577). New York: Plenum Press.

Martinez, Jr., J. L., McGaugh, J. L., Hanes, C. L., & Lacob, J. S. (1977). Modulation of memory processes induced by stimulation of the entorhinal cortex. *Physiology and Behavior, 19,* 139–144.

Martinez, Jr., J. L., Vasquez, B. J., Jensen, R. A., & McGaugh, J. L. (1977). Facilitation by reserpine of retention in an inhibitory avoidance task in mice. *Behavioral Biology, 21,* 151–156.

McGaugh, J. L., Thompson, R. F., & Nelson, T. O. (1977). *Psychology I: An experimental approach.* San Francisco, CA: Albion.

Spanis, C. W., Haycock, J. W., Handwerker, M. J., Rose, R. P., & McGaugh, J. L. (1977). Impairment of retention of avoidance responses in rats by posttraining diethyldithiocarbamate. *Psychopharmacology, 53,* 213–215.

Vasquez, B. J., Martinez, J. L., Jr., Jensen, R. A., & McGaugh, J. L. (1977). Amnestic effects of propylene glycol in mice. *Proceedings of the Western Pharmacological Society, 20,* 179–183.

Gold, P. E., & McGaugh, J. L. (1978). Endogenous modulators of memory storage processes. In L. Carenza, P. Pancheri, & L. Zichella (Eds.), *Clinical psychoneuroendocrinology in reproduction* (pp. 25–46). London: Academic Press.

Gold, P. E., & McGaugh, J. L. (1978). Neurobiology and memory: Modulators, correlates, and assumptions. In T. Teyler (Ed.), *Brain and learning* (pp. 93–103). Stamford, CT: Greylock.

Haycock, J. W., van Buskirk, R., Gold, P. E., & McGaugh, J. L. (1978). Effects of diethyldithiocarbamate and fusaric acid upon memory storage processes in rats. *European Journal of Pharmacology, 51,* 261–273.

Jarvik, M. E., & McGaugh, J. L. (1978). Drug influences on learning and memory: Progress in research, 1967–1977. In M. A. Lipton, A. DeMascio, & K. F. Killam (Eds.), *Psychopharmacology: A generation of progress* (pp. 621–622). New York: Raven Press.

Landfield, P. W., McGaugh, J. L., & Lynch, G. (1978). Impaired synaptic potentiation processes in the hippocampus of aged, memory-deficient rats. *Brain Research, 150,* 85–101.

Martinez, Jr., J. L., Jensen, R. A., Vasquez, B. J., McGuinness, T., & McGaugh, J. L. (1978). Methylene blue alters retention of inhibitory avoidance responses. *Physiological Psychology, 6,* 387–390.

Meligeni, J. A., Ledergerber, S. A., & McGaugh, J. L. (1978). Norepinephrine attenuation of amnesia produced by diethyldithiocarbamate. *Brain Research, 149,* 155–164.

Jensen, R. A., Martinez, J. L., Jr., Vasquez, B. J., & McGaugh, J. L. (1979). Benzodiazepines alter acquisition and retention of an inhibitory avoidance response in mice. *Psychopharmacology, 64,* 125–126.

Martinez, J. L., Jr., Jensen, R. A., Creager, R., Veliquette, J., Messing, R. B., McGaugh, J. L., & Lynch, G. (1979). Selective effects of enkephalin on electrical activity of the in vitro hippocampal slice. *Behavioral and Neural Biology, 26,* 128–131.

Martinez, J. L., Jr., Jensen, R. A., Vasquez, B. J., Lacob, J. S., McGaugh, J. L., & Purdy, R. E. (1979). Acquisition deficits induced by sodium nitrite in rats and mice. *Psychopharmacology, 60,* 221–228.

Martinez, J. L., Jr., Vasquez, B. J., Jensen, R. A., Soumireu-Mourat, B., & McGaugh, J. L. (1979). ACTH4-9 analog (ORG 2766) facilitates acquisition of an inhibitory avoidance response in rats. *Pharmacology Biochemistry and Behavior, 10,* 145–147.

McGaugh, J. L., Gold, P. E., Handwerker, M. J., Jensen, R. A., Martinez, J. L., Jr., Meligeni, J. A., & Vasquez, B. J. (1979). Altering memory by electrical and chemical stimulation of the brain. In M. A. B. Brazier (Ed.), *Brain mechanisms in memory and learning: From the single neuron to man* (IBRO Monograph Series, Vol. 4, pp. 151–164). New York: Raven Press.

McGaugh, J. L., Jensen, R. A., & Martinez, J. L., Jr. (1979). Sleep, brain state and memory. In M. Shkurovich, R. Drucker-Colin, & M. B. Sterman (Eds.), *The functions of sleep* (pp. 295–301). New York: Academic Press.

Messing, R. B., Jensen, R. A., Martinez, J. L., Jr., Spiehler, V. R., Vasquez, B. J., Soumireu-Mourat, B., Liang, K. C., & McGaugh, J. L. (1979). Naloxone enhancement of memory. *Behavioral and Neural Biology, 27,* 266–275.

Rigter, H., Messing, R. B., Vasquez, B. J., Jensen, R. A., Martinez, J. L., Jr., Crabbe, Jr., J. C., & McGaugh, J. L. (1979). Regional analysis of brain opiate receptors in rats with hereditary hypothalamic diabetes insipidus. *Life Sciences, 25,* 1137–1144.

Cotman, C. W., & McGaugh, J. L. (1980). *Behavioral neuroscience.* New York: Academic Press.

Jensen, R. A., Martinez, J. L., Jr., McGaugh, J. L., Messing, R. B., & Vasquez, B. J. (1980). The psychobiology of aging. In G. J. Maletta & F. J. Pirozzolo (Eds.), *The aging nervous system* (pp. 110–125). New York: Praeger.

Jensen, R. A., Messing, R. B., Martinez, J. L., Jr., Vasquez, B. J., & McGaugh, J. L. (1980). Opiate modulation of learning and memory in the rat. In L. Poon (Ed.), *Aging in the 1980s: Psychological issues* (pp. 191–200). Washington, DC: American Psychological Association.

Jensen, R. A., Messing, R. B., Spiehler, V. R., Martinez, J. L., Jr., Vasquez, B. J., & McGaugh, J. L. (1980). Memory, opiate receptors, and aging. *Peptides, 1*(Suppl. 1), 197–201.

Martinez, J. L., Jr., Jensen, R. A., Messing, R. B., Vasquez, B. J., Soumireu-Mourat, B., Geddes, D., Liang, K. C., & McGaugh, J. L. (1980). Central and peripheral actions of amphetamine on memory storage. *Brain Research, 182,* 157–166.

Martinez, J. L., Jr., Vasquez, B. J., Rigter, H., Messing, R. B., Jensen, R. A., Liang, K. C., & McGaugh, J. L. (1980). Attenuation of amphetamine-induced enhancement of learning by adrenal demedullation. *Brain Research, 195,* 433–443.

Martinez, J. L., Jr., Vasquez, B. J., Jensen, R. A., & McGaugh, J. L. (1980). L-dopa enhances acquisition of an inhibitory avoidance response. *Communications in Psychopharmacology, 4*, 215–218.

McGaugh, J. L. (1980). Adrenaline: A secret agent in memory. *Psychology Today, 14*, 132.

McGaugh, J. L., Martinez, J. L., Jr., Jensen, R. A., Messing, R. B., & Vasquez, B. J. (1980). Central and peripheral catecholamine function in learning and memory processes. In R. F. Thompson, L. H. Hicks, & V. B. Shvyrkov (Eds.), *Neural mechanisms of goal-directed behavior and learning* (pp. 75–91). New York: Academic Press.

Messing, R. B., Vasquez, B. J., Spiehler, V. R., Martinez, J. L., Jr., Jensen, R. A., Rigter, H., & McGaugh, J. L. (1980). 3H-dihydromorphine binding in brain regions of young and aged rats. *Life Sciences, 26*, 921–927.

Rigter, H., Hannan, T. J., Messing, R. B., Martinez, J. L., Jr., Vasquez, B. J., Jensen, R. A., Veliquette, J., & McGaugh, J. L. (1980). Enkephalins interfere with acquisition of an active avoidance response. *Life Sciences, 26*, 337–345.

Rigter, H., Jensen, R. A., Martinez, J. L., Jr., Messing, R. B., Vasquez, B. J., Liang, K. C., & McGaugh, J. L. (1980). Enkephalin and fear-motivated behavior. *Proceedings of the National Academy of Sciences, 77*, 3729–3732.

Soumireu-Mourat, B., Martinez, J. L., Jr., Jensen, R. A., & McGaugh, J. L. (1980). Facilitation of memory processes in aged rats by subseizure hippocampal stimulation. *Physiology and Behavior, 25*, 263–265.

Gold, P. E., McGaugh, J. L., Hankins, L. L., Rose, R. P., & Vasquez, B. J. (1981). Age dependent changes in retention in rats. *Experimental Aging Research, 8*, 53–58.

Ishikawa, K., Ott, T., & McGaugh, J. L. (1981). Evidence for dopamine as a transmitter in dorsal hippocampus. *Brain Research, 232*, 222–226.

Jensen, R. A., Messing, R. B., Martinez, J. L., Jr., Vasquez, B. J., Spiehler, V. R., & McGaugh, J. L. (1981). Changes in brain peptide systems and altered learning and memory processes in aged animals. In J. L. Martinez, Jr., R. A. Jensen, R. B. Messing, H. Rigter, & J. L. McGaugh (Eds.), *Endogenous peptides and learning and memory processes* (pp. 463–477). New York: Academic Press.

Lynch, G. S., Jensen, R. A., McGaugh, J. L., Davila, K., & Oliver, M. W. (1981). Effects of enkephalin, morphine, and naloxone on the electrical activity of the in vitro hippocampal slice preparation. *Experimental Neurology, 71*, 527–540.

Martinez, J. L., Jr., Jensen, R. A., & McGaugh, J. L. (1981). Attenuation of experimentally-induced amnesia. *Progress in Neurobiology, 16*, 155–186.

Martinez, J. L., Jr., Jensen, R. A., Messing, R. B., Rigter, H., & McGaugh, J. L. (Eds.). (1981). *Endogenous peptides and learning and memory processes*. New York: Academic Press.

Martinez, J. L., Jr., Rigter, H., Jensen, R. A., Messing, R. B., Vasquez, B. J., & McGaugh, J. L. (1981). Endorphin and enkephalin effects on avoidance conditioning: The other side of the pituitary-adrenal axis. In J. L. Martinez, Jr., R. A. Jensen, R. B.

Messing, H. Rigter, & J. L. McGaugh (Eds.), *Endogenous peptides and learning and memory processes* (pp. 305–324). New York: Academic Press.

Martinez, J. L., Jr., Vasquez, B. J., Messing, R. B., Jensen, R. A., Liang, K. C., & McGaugh, J. L. (1981). Age-related changes in the catecholamine content of peripheral organs in male and female F344 rats. *Journal of Gerontology, 36,* 280–284.

McGaugh, J. L. (1981). Psicologia del comportamento (Behaviorism). In G. Bedeschi (Ed.), *Twentieth century encyclopedia* (pp. 828–837). Rome: Istituto dell'Enciclopedia Italiana.

McGaugh, J. L., & Kiesler, S. B. (Eds.). (1981). *Aging: Biology and behavior.* New York: Academic Press.

McGaugh, J. L. & Martinez, J. L., Jr. (1981). Learning modulatory hormones: An introduction to endogenous peptides and learning and memory processes. In J. L. Martinez, Jr., R. A. Jensen, R. B. Messing, H. Rigter, & J. L. McGaugh (Eds.), *Endogenous peptides and learning and memory processes* (pp. 1–3). New York: Academic Press.

Messing, R. B., Jensen, R. A., Vasquez, B. J., Martinez, J. L., Jr., Spiehler, V. R., & McGaugh, J. L. (1981). Opiate modulation of memory. In J. L. Martinez, Jr., R. A. Jensen, R. B. Messing, H. Rigter, & J. L. McGaugh (Eds.), *Endogenous peptides and learning and memory processes* (pp. 431–443). New York: Academic Press.

Messing, R. B., Vasquez, B. J., Samaniego, B., Jensen, R. A., Martinez, J. L., Jr., & McGaugh, J. L. (1981). Alterations in dihydromorphine binding in cerebral hemispheres of aged male rats. *Journal of Neurochemistry, 36,* 784–787.

Ishikawa, K., & McGaugh, J. L. (1982). Simultaneous determination of monoamine transmitters, precursors, and metabolites in a single mouse brain. *Journal of Chromatography, 229,* 35–46.

Ishikawa, K., Martinez, J. L., Jr., & McGaugh, J. L. (1982). Simultaneous determination of morphine and monoamine transmitters in a single mouse brain. *Journal of Chromatography, 231,* 255–264.

Ishikawa, K., McGaugh, J. L., Shibanoki, S., & Kubo, T. (1982). A sensitive procedure for determination of morphine in mouse whole blood by high performance liquid chromatography with electrochemical detection. *Japanese Journal of Pharmacology, 32,* 969–971.

Ishikawa, K., Shibanoki, S., Saito, S., & McGaugh, J. L. (1982). Effect of microwave irradiation on monoamine metabolism in dissected rat brain. *Brain Research, 240,* 158–161.

Liang, K. C., McGaugh, J. L., Martinez, J. L., Jr., Jensen, R. A., Vasquez, B. J., & Messing, R. B. (1982). Posttraining amygdaloid lesions impair retention of an inhibitory avoidance response. *Behavioural Brain Research, 4,* 237–249.

McGaugh, J. L. (1982). Citation and biography for the 1981 Distinguished Scientific Contribution Award. *American Psychologist, 37,* 43–51.

McGaugh, J. L., Liang, K. C., Bennett, C., Martinez, J. L., Jr., Messing, R. B., & Ishikawa, K. (1982). Modulating influences of peripheral hormones on memory storage. In

S. Saito & T. Yanagita (Eds.), *Learning and memory drugs as reinforcer* (pp. 70–82). Amsterdam: Excerpta Medica.

McGaugh, J. L., Martinez, J. L., Jr., Jensen, R. A., Hannan, T. J., Vasquez, B. J., Messing, R. B., Liang, K. C., Brewton, C. B., & Spiehler, V. R. (1982). Modulation of memory storage by treatments affecting peripheral catecholamines. In C. Ajmone Marsan & H. Matthies (Eds.), *Neuronal plasticity and memory formation* (pp. 311–325). New York: Raven Press.

McGaugh, J. L., Martinez, J. L., Jr., Messing, R. B., Liang, K. C., Jensen, R. A., Vasquez, B. J., & Rigter, H. (1982). Role of neurohormones as modulators of memory storage. In E. Costa & M. Trabucchi (Eds.), *Regulatory peptides: From molecular biology to function* (pp. 123–130). New York: Raven Press.

Sternberg, D. B., Gold, P. E., & McGaugh, J. L. (1982). Noradrenergic sympathetic blockade: Lack of effect on memory or retrograde amnesia. *European Journal of Pharmacology, 81,* 133–136.

Ishikawa, K., Shibanoki, S., & McGaugh, J. L. (1983). Direct correlation between levels of morphine and its biochemical changes on monoamine systems in mouse brain: An evidence for involvement of dopaminergic neurons in the pharmacological action of acute morphine. *Biochemical Pharmacology, 32,* 1473–1478.

Liang, K. C., & McGaugh, J. L. (1983). Lesions of the stria terminalis attenuate the amnestic effect of amygdaloid stimulation on avoidance responses. *Brain Research, 274,* 309–318.

Liang, K. C., & McGaugh, J. L. (1983). Lesions of the stria terminalis attenuate the enhancing effect of post-training epinephrine on retention of an inhibitory avoidance response. *Behavioural Brain Research, 9,* 49–58.

Liang, K. C., Messing, R. B., & McGaugh, J. L. (1983). Naloxone attenuates amnesia caused by amygdaloid stimulation: The involvement of a central opioid system. *Brain Research, 271,* 41–49.

Martinez, J. L., Jr., Ishikawa, K., Liang, K. C., Jensen, R. A., Bennett, C., Sternberg, D. B., & McGaugh, J. L. (1983). 4-OH Amphetamine enhances retention of an active avoidance response in rats and decreases regional brain concentrations of norepinephrine and dopamine. *Behavioral Neuroscience, 97,* 962–969.

Martinez, J. L., Jr., Jensen, R. A., & McGaugh, J. L. (1983). Facilitation of memory consolidation. In J. A. Deutsch (Ed.), *The physiological basis of memory* (pp. 49–70). New York: Academic Press.

McGaugh, J. L. (1983). Hormonal influences on memory. *Annual Review of Psychology, 34,* 297–323.

McGaugh, J. L. (1983). Preserving the presence of the past: Hormonal influences on memory storage. *American Psychologist, 38,* 161–174.

Sternberg, D. B., Gold, P. E., & McGaugh, J. L. (1983). Memory facilitation and impairment with supraseizure electrical brain stimulation: Attenuation with pretrial propranolol injections. *Behavioral and Neural Biology, 38,* 261–268.

Vasquez, B. J., Martinez, J. L., Jr., Jensen, R. A., Messing, R. B., Rigter, H., & McGaugh, J. L. (1983). Learning and memory in young and aged Fischer 344 rats. *Archives of Gerontology and Geriatrics, 2,* 279–291.

Bennett, C. B., Hock, F., & McGaugh, J. L. (1984). Dose and time dependence of noradrenergic depletion after N-(2-chloroethyl)-N-ethyl-2-bromobenzylamine. *IRCS Medical Science, 12,* 181–182.

Gold, P. E. & McGaugh, J. L. (1984). Endogenous processes in memory consolidation. In H. Weingartner & E. Parker (Eds.), *Memory consolidation* (pp. 65–83). Hillsdale, NJ: Erlbaum.

Ishikawa, K., Martinez, J. L., Jr., & McGaugh, J. L. (1984). Simple determination of p-hydroxyamphetamine by high performance liquid chromatography with electrochemical detection. *Journal of Chromatography, 306,* 394–397.

Lynch, G., McGaugh, J. L., & Weinberger, N. M. (Eds.). (1984). *Neurobiology of learning and memory.* New York: Guilford Press.

McGaugh, J. L. (1984). Commentary for citation classic: Time-dependent processes in memory storage. *Current Contents, 27*(33), 22.

McGaugh, J. L., Liang, K. C., Bennett, C., & Sternberg, D. B. (1984). Adrenergic influences on memory storage: Interaction of peripheral and central systems. In G. Lynch, J. L. McGaugh, & N. M. Weinberger (Eds.), *Neurobiology of learning and memory* (pp. 313–333). New York: Guilford Press.

Bennett, C. B., Kaleta, S., & McGaugh, J. L. (1985). Dose and time response characteristics of whole brain monoamines to yohimbine after central norepinephrine depletion with DSP4. *IRCS Medical Science, 13,* 36–37.

Bennett, C., Liang, K. C., & McGaugh, J. L. (1985). Depletion of adrenal catecholamines alters the amnestic effect of amygdala stimulation. *Behavioural Brain Research, 15,* 83–91.

Hock, F. J., & McGaugh, J. L. (1985). Enhancing effects of HOE 175 on memory in mice. *Psychopharmacology, 86,* 114–117.

Introini, I. B., McGaugh, J. L., & Baratti, C. M. (1985). Pharmacological evidence of a central effect of naltrexone, morphine and beta-endorphin and a peripheral effect of Met-and Leu-enkephalin on retention of an inhibitory response in mice. *Behavioral and Neural Biology, 44,* 434–446.

Izquierdo, I., & McGaugh, J. L. (1985). Delayed onset of the amnestic effect of post-training beta-endorphin: Effects of propranolol administered prior to retention testing. *European Journal of Pharmacology, 113,* 105–108.

Izquierdo, I., & McGaugh, J. L. (1985). Effect of a novel experience prior to training or testing on retention of an inhibitory avoidance response in mice: Involvement of an opioid system. *Behavioral and Neural Biology, 44,* 228–238.

Leslie, F. M., Loughlin, S. E., Sternberg, D. B., McGaugh, J. L., Young, L. E., & Zornetzer, S. F. (1985). Noradrenergic changes and memory loss in aged mice. *Brain Research, 359,* 292–299.

Liang, K. C., Bennett, C., & McGaugh, J. L. (1985). Peripheral epinephrine modulates the effects of posttraining amygdala stimulation on memory. *Behavioural Brain Research, 15,* 93–100.

McGaugh, J. L. (1985). Peripheral and central adrenergic influences on brain systems involved in the modulation of memory storage. In D. S. Olton, E. Gamzu, & S. Corkin (Eds.), *Memory dysfunctions: An integration of animal and human research from preclinical and clinical perspectives* (pp. 150–161). New York: New York Academy of Sciences.

McGaugh, J. L., Liang, K. C., Bennett, M. C., & Sternberg, D. B. (1985). Hormonal influences on memory: Interaction of central and peripheral systems. In B. E. Will, P. Schmitt, & J. C. Dalrymple-Alford (Eds.), *Brain plasticity, learning and memory* (pp. 253–259). New York: Plenum Press.

McGaugh, J. L., Weinberger, N. M., Lynch, G., & Granger, R. (1985). Neural mechanisms of learning and memory: Cells, systems and computations. *Naval Research Review, 37,* 15–29.

Sternberg, D. B., Isaacs, K., Gold, P. E., & McGaugh, J. L. (1985). Epinephrine facilitation of appetitive learning: Attenuation with adrenergic receptor antagonists. *Behavioral and Neural Biology, 44,* 447–453.

Sternberg, D. B., Martinez, J. L., Jr., Gold, P. E., & McGaugh, J. L. (1985). Age-related memory deficits in rats and mice: Enhancement with peripheral injections of epinephrine. *Behavioral and Neural Biology, 44,* 213–220.

Weinberger, N. M., McGaugh, J. L., & Lynch, G. (Eds.). (1985). *Memory systems of the brain: Animal and human cognitive processes.* New York: Guilford Press.

Introini-Collison, I. B., & McGaugh, J. L. (1986). Epinephrine modulates long-term retention of an aversively-motivated discrimination task. *Behavioral and Neural Biology, 45,* 358–365.

Liang, K. C., Juler, R. G., & McGaugh, J. L. (1986). Modulating effects of post-training epinephrine on memory: Involvement of the amygdala noradrenergic system. *Brain Research, 368,* 125–133.

McGaugh, J. L. (Ed.). (1986). *Contemporary psychology: Biological processes and theoretical issues.* Amsterdam: Elsevier/North Holland.

McGaugh, J. L., & Introini-Collison, I. B. (1986). Memory: Peptide, neurotransmitters and drug influences. *Clinical Neuropharmacology, 9,* 289–291.

McGaugh, J. L., Introini-Collison, I. B., Juler, R. G., & Izquierdo, I. (1986). Stria terminalis lesions attenuate the effects of posttraining naloxone and β-endorphin on retention. *Behavioral Neuroscience, 100,* 839–844.

Sternberg, D. B., Korol, D., Novack, G. D., & McGaugh, J. L. (1986). Epinephrine-induced memory facilitation: Attenuation by adrenergic receptor antagonists. *European Journal of Pharmacology, 129,* 189–193.

Introini-Collison, I. B., Cahill, L., Baratti, C. M., & McGaugh, J. L. (1987). Dynorphin induces task-specific impairment of memory. *Psychobiology, 15,* 171–174.

Introini-Collison, I. B., & McGaugh, J. L. (1987). Naloxone and beta-endorphin alter the effects of posttraining epinephrine on memory. *Psychopharmacology, 92,* 229–235.

Izquierdo, I. B., & McGaugh, J. L. (1987). Effect of novel experiences on retention of inhibitory avoidance behavior in mice: The influence of previous exposure to the same or another experience. *Behavioral and Neural Biology, 47,* 109–115.

Izquierdo, I. B., & McGaugh, J. L. (1987). Retention impairment by posttraining epinephrine: Role of state dependency and of endogenous opioid mechanisms. *Behavioral Neuroscience, 101,* 778–781.

Liang, K. C., & McGaugh, J. L. (1987). Effects of adrenal demedullation and stria terminalis lesions on retention of an inhibitory avoidance response. *Psychobiology, 15,* 154–160.

McGaugh, J. L. (1987). *Making memories* (Distinguished Faculty Lecture). Irvine: University of California, Academic Senate.

McGaugh, J. L. (1987). Memory consolidation. In G. Adelman (Ed.), *Encyclopedia of neuroscience* (pp. 636–637). Boston: Birkhauser Boston.

McGaugh, J. L. (1987). Memory, hormone influences. In G. Adelman (Ed.), *Encyclopedia of neuroscience* (pp. 636–637). Boston: Birkhauser Boston.

McGaugh, J. L., Bennett, M. C., Liang, K. C., Juler, R. G., & Tam, D. (1987). Memory-enhancing effect of posttraining epinephrine is not blocked by dexamethasone. *Psychobiology, 15,* 343–344.

McGaugh, J. L., & Introini-Collison, I. B. (1987). Novel experience prior to training attenuates the amnestic effects of posttraining ECS. *Behavioral Neuroscience, 101,* 296–299.

Zhang, S., McGaugh, J. L., Juler, R. G., & Introini-Collison, I. B. (1987). Naloxone and [Met^5]-enkephalin effects on retention: Attenuation by adrenal denervation. *European Journal of Pharmacology, 138,* 37–44.

McGaugh, J. L., & Introini-Collison, I. B. (1987–1988). Hormonal and neurotransmitter interactions in the modulation of memory storage: Involvement of the amygdala. *International Journal of Neurology, 21–22,* 58–72.

Brioni, J. D., & McGaugh, J. L. (1988). Posttraining administration of GABAergic antagonists enhance retention of aversively motivated tasks. *Psychopharmacology, 96,* 505–510.

Cornwell-Jones, C. A., Velasquez, P., Wright, E. L., & McGaugh, J. L. (1988). Early experience influences adult retention of aversively-motivated tasks in normal, but not DSP4-treated rats. *Developmental Psychobiology, 21,* 177–185.

Introini-Collison, I. B., & McGaugh, J. L. (1988). Modulation of memory by posttraining epinephrine: Involvement of cholinergic mechanisms. *Psychopharmacology, 94,* 379–385.

McGaugh, J. L., Introini-Collison, I. B., & Nagahara, A. H. (1988). Memory-enhancing effects of posttraining naloxone: Involvement of B-noradrenergic influences in the amygdaloid complex. *Brain Research, 446,* 37–49.

Oscos, A., Martinez, J. L., Jr., & McGaugh, J. L. (1988). Effects of posttraining d-amphetamine on acquisition of an appetitive autoshaped lever press response in rats. *Psychopharmacology, 95,* 132–134.

Woody, C. D., Alkon, D. L., & McGaugh, J. L. (Eds.). (1988). *Cellular mechanisms of conditioning and behavioral plasticity.* New York: Plenum Press.

Brioni, J. D., McGaugh, J. L., & Izquierdo, I. (1989). Amnesia induced by short-term treatment with ethanol: Attenuation by pre-test oxotremorine. *Pharmacology, Biochemistry and Behavior, 33,* 27–29.

Brioni, J. D., Nagahara, A. H., & McGaugh, J. L. (1989). Involvement of the amygdala GABAergic system in the modulation of memory storage. *Brain Research, 487,* 105–112.

Castellano, C., Brioni, J. D., Nagahara, A. H., & McGaugh, J. L. (1989). Posttraining systemic and intra-amygdala administration of the gaba-b agonist baclofen impair retention. *Behavioral and Neural Biology, 52,* 170–179.

Castellano, C., Introini-Collison, I. B., Pavone, F., & McGaugh, J. L. (1989). Effects of naloxone and naltrexone on memory consolidation in CD1 mice: Involvement of GABAergic mechanisms. *Pharmacology, Biochemistry and Behavior, 32,* 563–567.

Castellano, C., & McGaugh, J. L. (1989). Effect of morphine on one-trial inhibitory avoidance in mice: Lack of state dependency. *Psychobiology, 17,* 89–92.

Castellano, C., & McGaugh, J. L. (1989). Retention enhancement with posttraining picrotoxin: Lack of state dependency. *Behavioral and Neural Biology, 51,* 165–170.

Cornwell-Jones, C. A., Decker, M. W., Chang, J. W., Cole, B., Goltz, K. M., Tran, T., & McGaugh, J. L. (1989). Neonatal 6-Hydroxydopa, but not DSP4, elevates brainstem monoamines and impairs inhibitory avoidance learning in developing rats. *Brain Research, 493,* 258–268.

Decker, M. W., Introini-Collison, I. B., & McGaugh, J. L. (1989). Effects of naloxone on Morris water maze learning in the rat: Enhanced acquisition with pretraining but not posttraining administration. *Psychobiology, 17,* 270–275.

Decker, M. W., & McGaugh, J. L. (1989). Effects of concurrent manipulations of cholinergic and noradrenergic function on learning and retention in mice. *Brain Research, 477,* 29–37.

Introini-Collison, I. B., Arai, Y., & McGaugh, J. L. (1989). Stria terminalis lesions attenuate the effects of posttraining oxotremorine and atropine on retention. *Psychobiology, 17,* 397–401.

Introini-Collison, I. B., & McGaugh, J. L. (1989). Cocaine enhances memory storage in mice. *Psychopharmacology, 99,* 537–541.

Introini-Collison, I. B., Nagahara, A. H., & McGaugh, J. L. (1989). Memory-enhancement with intra-amygdala posttraining naloxone is blocked by concurrent administration of propranolol. *Brain Research, 476,* 94–101.

McGaugh, J. L. (1989). Dissociating learning and performance: Drug and hormone enhancement of memory storage. *Brain Research Bulletin, 23,* 339–345.

McGaugh, J. L. (1989). Involvement of hormonal and neuromodulatory systems in the regulation of memory storage. *Annual Review of Neuroscience, 12,* 255–287.

McGaugh, J. L. (1989). Modulation of memory storage processes. In P. R. Solomon, G. R. Goethals, C. M. Kelley, & B. R. Stephens (Eds.), *Memory: Interdisciplinary approaches* (pp. 33–64). New York: Springer-Verlag.

McGaugh, J. L., & Gold, P. E. (1989). Hormonal modulation of memory. In R. B. Brush & S. Levine (Eds.), *Psychoendocrinology* (pp. 305–339). New York: Academic Press.

McGaugh, J. L., Introini-Collison, I. B., Nagahara, A. H., & Cahill, L. (1989). Involvement of the amygdala in hormonal and neurotransmitter interactions in the modulation of memory storage. In T. Archer & L.-G. Nilsson (Eds.), *Aversion, avoidance, and anxiety, perspectives on aversively motivated behavior* (pp. 231–249). Hillsdale, NJ: Erlbaum.

Zhang, S., Introini-Collison, I. B., & McGaugh, J. L. (1989). Effect of bestatin, an aminopeptidase inhibitor, on memory in inhibitory avoidance and y-maze discrimination tasks. *Psychobiology, 17,* 323–325.

Bennett, M. C., Kaleta, S., Arnold, M., & McGaugh, J. L. (1990). Impairment of active avoidance by the noradrenergic neurotoxin, DSP4: Attenuation by post-training epinephrine. *Psychopharmacology, 101,* 505–510.

Brioni, J. D., Decker, M. W., Gamboa, L. P., Izquierdo, I., & McGaugh, J. L. (1990). Muscimol injections in the medial septum impair spatial learning. *Brain Research, 522,* 227–234.

Cahill, L., & McGaugh, J. L. (1990). Amygdaloid complex lesions differentially affect retention of tasks using appetitive and aversive reinforcement. *Behavioral Neuroscience, 104,* 532–543.

Castellano, C., Brioni, J. D., & McGaugh, J. L. (1990). GABAergic modulation of memory. In L. Squire & E. Lindenlaub (Eds.), *Biology of memory* (pp. 361–378). New York: Schattauer-Verlag.

Castellano, C., & McGaugh, J. L. (1990). Effects of post-training bicuculline and muscimol on retention: Lack of state dependency. *Behavioral and Neural Biology, 54,* 156–164.

Cornwell-Jones, C. A., Decker, M. W., Gianulli, T., Wright, E. L., & McGaugh, J. L. (1990). Norepinephrine depletion reduces the effects of social and olfactory experience. *Brain Research Bulletin, 25,* 643–649.

Decker, M. W., Gill, T. M., & McGaugh, J. L. (1990). Concurrent muscarinic and beta-adrenergic blockade in rats impairs place-learning in a water maze and retention of inhibitory avoidance. *Brain Research, 513,* 81–85.

Decker, M. W., Tran, T., & McGaugh, J. L. (1990). A comparison of the effects of scopolamine and diazepam on acquisition and retention of inhibitory avoidance in mice. *Psychopharmacology, 100,* 515–521.

Liang, K. C., McGaugh, J. L., & Yao, H.-Y. (1990). Involvement of amygdala pathways in the influence of post-training intra-amygdala norepinephrine and peripheral epinephrine on memory storage. *Brain Research, 508,* 225–233.

McGaugh, J. L. (1990). Involvement of the amygdala in the influence of neuromodulatory systems on memory storage. In L. Squire, M. Mishkin, & A. Shimamura (Eds.), *Discussions in neurosciences* (Vol. 7, pp. 56–64). Amsterdam, North Holland: Elsevier.

McGaugh, J. L. (1990). Significance and remembrance: The role of neuromodulatory systems. *Psychological Science, 1,* 15–25.

McGaugh, J. L., Castellano, C., & Brioni, J. D. (1990). Picrotoxin enhances latent extinction of conditioned fear. *Behavioral Neuroscience, 104,* 262–265.

McGaugh, J. L., Introini-Collison, I. B., Nagahara, A. H., Cahill, L., Brioni, J. D., & Castellano, C. (1990). Involvement of the amygdaloid complex in neuromodulatory influences on memory storage. *Neuroscience and Biobehavioral Reviews, 14,* 425–431.

McGaugh, J. L., Weinberger, N. M., & Lynch, G. (Eds.). (1990). *Brain organization and memory: Cells, systems and circuits.* New York: Oxford University Press.

Shaw, G., McGaugh, J. L., & Rose, S. (Eds.). (1990). *Neurobiology of learning and memory* (World Scientific Advanced Series in Neuroscience, Vol. 2). Singapore: World Scientific.

Ammassari-Teule, M., Pavone, F., Castellano, C., & McGaugh, J. L. (1991). Amygdala and dorsal hippocampus lesions block the effects of GABAergic drugs on memory storage. *Brain Research, 551,* 104–109.

Bermudez-Rattoni, F., Introini-Collison, I. B., & McGaugh, J. L. (1991). Reversible inactivation of the insular cortex by tetrodotoxin produces retrograde and anterograde amnesia for inhibitory avoidance and spatial learning. *Proceedings of the National Academy of Sciences, 88,* 5379–5382.

Bermudez-Rattoni, F., & McGaugh, J. L. (1991). Insular cortex and amygdala lesions differentially affect acquisition of inhibitory avoidance and conditioned taste aversion. *Brain Research, 549,* 165–170.

Cahill, L., & McGaugh, J. L. (1991). NMDA-induced lesions of the amygdaloid complex block the retention enhancing effect of posttraining epinephrine. *Psychobiology, 19,* 206–210.

Castellano, C., & McGaugh, J. L. (1991). Oxotremorine attenuates retrograde amnesia induced by posttraining administration of the GABAergic agonists muscimol and baclofen. *Behavioral and Neural Biology, 56,* 25–31.

Decker, M. W., & McGaugh, J. L. (1991). The role of interactions between the cholinergic system and other neuromodulatory systems in learning and memory. *Synapse, 7,* 151–168.

Frederickson, R. C. A., McGaugh, J. L., & Felten, D. L. (Eds.). (1991). *Peripheral signaling of the brain: Role in neural–immune interactions, learning and memory.* Toronto, Ontario, Canada: Hogrefe & Huber.

Introini-Collison, I. B., & McGaugh, J. L. (1991). Interaction of hormones and neuro-transmitter systems in the modulation of memory storage. In R. C. A. Frederickson, J. L. McGaugh, & D. L. Felten (Eds.), *Peripheral signaling of the brain: Role in neural–immune interactions, learning and memory* (pp. 275–302). Toronto, Ontario, Canada: Hogrefe & Huber.

Introini-Collison, I. B., Miyasaki, B., & McGaugh, J. L. (1991). Involvement of the amygdala in the memory-enhancing effects of clenbuterol. *Psychopharmacology, 104,* 541–544.

McGaugh, J. L. (1991). Neuromodulation and the storage of information: Involvement of the amygdaloid complex. In R. G. Lister & H. J. Weingartner (Eds.), *Perspectives in cognitive neuroscience* (pp. 279–299). New York: Oxford University Press.

Sullivan, R. M., McGaugh, J. L., & Leon, M. (1991). Norepinephrine induced plasticity and one-trial olfactory learning in neonatal rats. *Developmental Brain Research, 60,* 219–228.

Squire, L., Lynch, G., Weinberger, N. M., & McGaugh, J. L. (Eds.). (1991). *Memory: Organization and locus of change.* New York: Oxford University Press.

Tomaz, C., Dickinson-Anson, H., & McGaugh, J. L. (1991). Amygdala lesions block the amnestic effects of diazepam. *Brain Research, 568,* 85–91.

Introini-Collison, I. B., Saghafi, D., Novack, G., & McGaugh, J. L. (1992). Memory-enhancing effects of posttraining dipivefrin and epinephrine: Involvement of peripheral and central adrenergic receptors. *Brain Research, 572,* 81–86.

Introini-Collison, I. B., To, S., & McGaugh, J. L. (1992). Fluoxetine effects on retention of inhibitory avoidance and water-maze spatial learning: Enhancement by systemic but not intra-amygdala injections. *Psychobiology, 20,* 28–32.

Kim, M., & McGaugh, J. L. (1992). Effects of intra-amygdala injections of NMDA receptor antagonists on acquisition and retention of inhibitory avoidance. *Brain Research, 585,* 35–48.

McGaugh, J. L. (1992). Affect, neuromodulatory systems and memory storage. In S.-A. Christianson (Ed.), *Handbook of emotion and memory: Current research and theory* (pp. 245–268). Hillsdale, NJ: Erlbaum.

McGaugh, J. L. (1992). Enhancing cognitive performance. *Southern California Law Review (USC), 65,* 383–395.

McGaugh, J. L. (1992). Hormones and memory. In *The encyclopedia of learning and memory* (pp. 248–250). New York: Macmillan.

McGaugh, J. L. (1992). Neuromodulatory systems and the regulation of memory storage. In L. R. Squire & N. Butters (Eds.) *Neuropsychology of memory* (pp. 386–401). New York: Guilford Press.

McGaugh, J. L., & Gold, P. E. (1992). Memory consolidation. In *The encyclopedia of learning and memory* (pp. 395–398). New York: Macmillan.

McGaugh, J. L., Introini-Collison, I. B., Cahill, L., Kim, M., & Liang, K. C. (1992).

Involvement of the amygdala in neuromodulatory influences on memory storage. In J. Aggleton (Ed.), *The amygdala* (pp. 431–451). New York: John Wiley & Sons.

McGaugh, J. L., Introini-Collison, I. B., & Decker, M. W. (1992). Interaction of hormones and neurotransmitters in the modulation of memory storage. In J. E. Morley, R. M. Coe, R. Strong, & G. T. Grossberg (Eds.), *Memory function and aging-related disorders* (pp. 37–64). New York: Springer.

Nagahara, A. H., Brioni, J. D., & McGaugh, J. L. (1992). Effects of intraseptal infusion of muscimol on inhibitory avoidance and spatial learning: Differential effects of pretraining and posttraining administration. *Psychobiology, 20,* 198–204.

Nagahara, A. H., & McGaugh, J. L. (1992). Muscimol infused into the medial septal area impairs long-term memory but not short-term memory in inhibitory avoidance, water maze place learning and rewarded alternation tasks. *Brain Research, 591,* 54–61.

Packard, M. G., & McGaugh, J. L. (1992). Double dissociation of fornix and caudate nucleus lesions on acquisition of two water maze tasks: Further evidence for multiple memory systems. *Behavioral Neuroscience, 106,* 439–446.

Packard, M. G., Williams, C. L., & McGaugh, J. L. (1992). Enhancement of win-shift radial maze retention by peripheral post-training administration of d-amphetamine and 4-OH amphetamine. *Psychobiology, 20,* 280–285.

Parent, M. B., Tomaz, C., & McGaugh, J. L. (1992). Increased training in an aversively motivated task attenuates the memory impairing effects of posttraining N-Methyl-D-Aspartic Acid-induced amygdala lesions. *Behavioral Neuroscience, 106,* 791–799.

Tomaz, C., Dickinson-Anson, H., & McGaugh, J. L. (1992). Basolateral amygdala lesions block diazepam-induced anterograde amnesia in an inhibitory avoidance task. *Proceedings National Academy of Science, 89,* 3615–3619.

Williams, C. L., & McGaugh, J. L. (1992). Reversible inactivation of the nucleus of the solitary tract impairs retention performance in an inhibitory avoidance task. *Behavioral and Neural Biology, 58,* 204–210.

Castellano, C., Introini-Collison, I. B., & McGaugh, J. L. (1993). Interaction of β-endorphin and GABAergic drugs in the regulation of memory storage. *Behavioral and Neural Biology, 60,* 123–128.

Dalmaz, C., Introini-Collison, I. B., & McGaugh, J. L. (1993). Noradrenergic and cholinergic interactions in the amygdala and the modulation of memory storage. *Behavioral Brain Research, 58,* 167–174.

Dickinson-Anson, H., & McGaugh, J. L. (1993). Midazolam administered into the amygdala impairs retention of an inhibitory avoidance task. *Behavioral and Neural Biology, 60,* 84–87.

Dickinson-Anson, H., Mesches, M. H., Coleman, K., & McGaugh, J. L. (1993). Bicuculline administered into the amygdala blocks benzodiazepine-induced amnesia. *Behavioral and Neural Biology, 60,* 1–4.

Gasbarri, A., Introini-Collison, I. B., Packard, M. G., Pacitti, C., & McGaugh, J. L.

(1993). Interaction of cholinergic–dopaminergic systems in the regulation of memory storage in aversively motivated learning tasks. *Brain Research, 627,* 72–78.

McGaugh, J. L., Introini-Collison, I. B., Cahill, L. F., Castellano, C., Dalmaz, C., Parent, M. B., & Williams, C. L. (1993). Neuromodulatory systems and memory storage: Role of the amygdala. *Behavioural Brain Research, 58,* 81–90.

McGaugh, J. L., Introini-Collison, I. B., & Castellano, C. (1993). Involvement of opioid peptides in learning and memory. In A. Herz, H. Akil, & E. J. Simon (Eds.), *Handbook of experimental pharmacology, opioids* (Part II, pp. 429–447). Heidelberg, Germany: Springer-Verlag.

Salinas, J. A., Packard, M. G., & McGaugh, J. L. (1993). Amygdala modulates memory for changes in reward magnitude: Reversible post-training inactivation with lidocaine attenuates the response to a reduction reward. *Behavioural Brain Research, 59,* 153–159.

Tomaz, C., Dickinson-Anson, H., McGaugh, J. L., Souza-Silva, M. A., Viana, M. B., & Graeff, F. G. (1993). Localization in the amygdala of the amnestic action of diazepam on emotional memory. *Behavioral Brain Research, 58,* 99–105.

Williams, C. L., & McGaugh, J. L. (1993). Reversible lesions of the nucleus of the solitary tract attenuate the memory-modulating effects of posttraining epinephrine. *Behavioral Neuroscience, 107,* 955–962.

Cahill, L., Prins, B., Weber, M., & McGaugh, J. L. (1994). β-adrenergic activation and memory for emotional events. *Nature, 371,* 702–704.

Dickinson-Anson, H., & McGaugh, J. L. (1994). Infusion of the GABAergic antagonist bicuculline into the medial septal area does not block the impairing effects of systemically administered midazolam on inhibitory avoidance retention. *Behavioral and Neural Biology, 62,* 253–258.

Introini-Collison, I. B., Castellano, C., & McGaugh, J. L. (1994). Interaction of GABAergic and β-noradrenergic drugs in the regulation of memory storage. *Behavioral and Neural Biology, 61,* 150–155.

Packard, M. G., Cahill, L., & McGaugh, J. L. (1994). Amygdala modulation of hippocampal-dependent and caudate nucleus-dependent memory processes. *Proceedings of the National Academy of Sciences, 91,* 8477–8481.

Packard, M. G., & McGaugh, J. L. (1994). Quinpirole and d-amphetamine administration post-training enhance memory on spatial and cued water maze tasks. *Psychobiology, 22,* 54–60.

Parent, M. B., & McGaugh, J. L. (1994). Posttraining infusion of lidocaine into the amygdala basolateral complex impairs retention of inhibitory avoidance training. *Brain Research, 661,* 97–103.

Parent, M. B., West, M., & McGaugh, J. L. (1994). Memory of rats with amygdala lesions induced 30 days after footshock-motivated escape training reflects degree of original training. *Behavioral Neuroscience, 6,* 1080–1087.

Russell, R. W., McGaugh, J. L., & Isaacson, R. (1994). Nitrates, nitrites, nitroso compounds: Balancing benefits and risks. In R. Isaacson & K. Jensen (Eds.), *The vulnerable brain and environmental risks* (Vol. 3, Toxins in Air and Water, pp. 323–340). New York: Plenum Press,.

Salinas, J. A., Dickinson-Anson, H. A., & McGaugh, J. L. (1994). Midazolam administered to rats induces anterograde amnesia for changes in reward magnitude. *Behavioral Neuroscience, 6,* 1059–1064.

Williams, C. L., & McGaugh, J. L. (1994). Enhancement of memory processing in an inhibitory avoidance and radial maze task by posttraining infusion of bombesin into the nucleus tractus solitarius. *Brain Research, 654,* 251–256.

Williams, C. L., Packard, M. G., & McGaugh, J. L. (1994). Amphetamine facilitation of win-shift radial arm maze retention: The involvement of peripheral adrenergic and central dopaminergic systems. *Psychobiology, 22,* 141–148.

Cahill, L., Babinsky, R., Markowitsch, H. J., & McGaugh, J. L. (1995). The amygdala and emotional memory. *Nature, 377,* 295–296.

Cahill, L., & McGaugh, J. L. (1995). A novel demonstration of enhanced memory associated with emotional arousal. *Consciousness and Cognition, 4,* 410–421.

Coleman-Mesches, K., & McGaugh, J. L. (1995). Differential effects of pre-training inactivation of the right or left amygdala on retention of inhibitory avoidance training. *Behavioral Neuroscience, 109,* 642–647.

Coleman-Mesches, K., & McGaugh, J. L. (1995). Differential involvement of the right and left amygdalae in expression of memory for aversively motivated training. *Brain Research, 670,* 75–81.

Coleman-Mesches, K., & McGaugh, J. L. (1995). Muscimol injected into the right or left amygdaloid complex differentially affects retention performance following aversively motivated training. *Brain Research, 676,* 183–188.

Introini-Collison, I. B., Ford, L., & McGaugh, J. L. (1995). Memory impairment induced by intra-amygdala β-endorphin is mediated by noradrenergic influences. *Neurobiology of Learning and Memory, 63,* 200–205.

Izquierdo, I., & McGaugh, J. L. (1995). Effects of drugs and alcohol on memory. In J. H. Jaffe, R. R. Clayton, C. E. Johanson, M. J. Kuhar, M. H. Moore, & E. M. Sellars (Eds.), *The encyclopedia of drugs and alcohol* (Vol. 2, 666–669). New York: Macmillan.

McGaugh, J. L. (1995). Emotional activation, neuromodulatory systems and memory strength. In D. L. Schacter, J. T. Coyle, M.-M. Mesulam, & L. E. Sullivan (Eds.), *Memory distortion: How minds, brains, and societies reconstruct the past* (pp. 255–273). Cambridge, MA: Harvard University Press.

McGaugh, J. L., Bermudez-Rattoni, F., & Prado-Alcala, R. (1995). *Plasticity in the central nervous system: Learning and memory.* Hillsdale, NJ: Erlbaum.

McGaugh, J. L., Cahill, L., Parent, M. B., Mesches, M. H., Coleman-Mesches, K., & Salinas, J. A. (1995). Involvement of the amygdala in the regulation of memory storage. In J. L. McGaugh, F. Bermudez-Rattoni, & R. A. Prado-Alcala (Eds.), *Plas-*

ticity in the central nervous system: Learning and memory (pp. 17–40). Hillsdale, NJ: Erlbaum.

McGaugh, J. L., Weinberger, N. M., & Lynch, G. (Eds.). (1995). *Brain and memory: Modulation and mediation of neuroplasticity.* New York: Oxford University Press.

Packard, M. G., Williams, C. L., Cahill, L., & McGaugh, J. L. (1995). The anatomy of a memory modulatory system: From periphery to brain. In N. E. Spear, L. P. Spear, & M. L. Woodruff (Eds.), *Neurobehavioral plasticity: Learning, development and response to brain insults* (pp. 149–184). Hillsdale, NJ: Erlbaum.

Parent, M. B., Avila, E., & McGaugh, J. L. (1995). Footshock facilitates the expression of aversively motivated memory in rats given post-training amygdala basolateral complex lesions. *Brain Research, 676,* 235–244.

Parent, M. B., Quirarte, G. L., Cahill, L., & McGaugh, J. L. (1995). Spared retention of inhibitory avoidance learning following posttraining amygdala lesions. *Behavioral Neuroscience, 109,* 803–807.

Salinas, J. A., & McGaugh, J. L. (1995). Muscimol induces retrograde amnesia for changes in reward magnitude. *Neurobiology of Learning and Memory, 63,* 277–285.

Cahill, L., Haier, R. J., Fallon, J., Alkire, M., Tang, C., Keator, D., Wu, J., & McGaugh, J. L. (1996). Amygdala activity at encoding correlated with long-term, free recall of emotional information. *Proceedings of the National Academy of Sciences, 93,* 8016–8021.

Cahill, L., & McGaugh, J. L. (1996). Modulation of memory storage. *Current Opinion in Neurobiology, 6,* 237–242.

Cahill, L., & McGaugh, J. L. (1996). The neurobiology of memory for emotional events: Adrenergic activation and the amygdala. *Proceedings of the Western Pharmacological Society, 39,* 81–84.

Coleman-Mesches, K., Salinas, J. A., & McGaugh, J. L. (1996). Unilateral amygdala inactivation after training attenuates memory for reduced reward. *Behavioural Brain Research, 77,* 175–180.

Cornwell-Jones, C., Chang, J. W., Cole, B., Fukada, Y., Gianulli, T., Rathbone, E. A., McFarlane, H., & McGaugh, J. L. (1996). DSP-4 treatment influences olfactory preferences of developing rats. *Brain Research, 711,* 26–33.

Galvez, R., Mesches, M. H., & McGaugh, J. L. (1996). Norepinephrine release in the amygdala in response to footshock stimulation. *Neurobiology of Learning and Memory, 66,* 253–257.

Introini-Collison, I. B., Dalmaz, C., & McGaugh, J. L. (1996). Amygdala β-noradrenergic influences on memory storage involve cholinergic activation. *Neurobiology of Learning and Memory, 65,* 57–64.

Ishikawa, K., McGaugh, J. L., & Sakata, H. (Eds.). (1996). *Brain processes and memory* (Excerpta Medica, International Congress Series 1108). Amsterdam: Elsevier.

McGaugh, J. L., Cahill, L., & Roozendaal, B. (1996). Involvement of the amygdala in memory storage: Interaction with other brain systems. *Proceedings of the National Academy of Sciences, 93,* 13508–13514.

Mesches, M. H., Bianchin, M., & McGaugh, J. L. (1996). The effects of intra-amygdala infusion of the AMPA receptor antagonist CNQX on retention performance following aversive training. *Neurobiology of Learning and Memory, 66,* 324–340.

Packard, M. G., Introini-Collison, I. B., & McGaugh, J. L. (1996). Stria terminalis lesions attenuate memory enhancement produced by intra-caudate nucleus injections of oxotremorine. *Neurobiology of Learning and Memory, 65,* 278–282.

Packard, M. G., & McGaugh, J. L. (1996). Inactivation of hippocampus or caudate nucleus with lidocaine differentially affects expression of place and response learning. *Neurobiology of Learning and Memory, 65,* 65–72.

Roozendaal, B., Bohus, B., & McGaugh, J. L. (1996). Dose-dependent suppression of adreno-cortical activity with metyrapone: Effects on emotion and learning. *Psychoneuroendocrinology, 21,* 681–693.

Roozendaal, B., Cahill, L., & McGaugh, J. L. (1996). Interaction of emotionally activated neuromodulatory systems in regulating memory storage. In K. Ishikawa, J. L. McGaugh, & H. Sakata (Eds.), *Brain processes and memory* (Excerpta Medica, International Congress Series 1108). Amsterdam, The Netherlands: Elsevier.

Roozendaal, B., Carmi, O., & McGaugh, J. L. (1996). Adrenocortical suppression blocks the memory-enhancing effects of amphetamine and epinephrine. *Proceedings of the National Academy of Sciences, 93,* 1429–1433.

Roozendaal, B., & McGaugh, J. L. (1996). Amygdaloid nuclei lesions differentially affect glucocorticoid-induced memory enhancement in an inhibitory avoidance task. *Neurobiology of Learning and Memory, 65,* 1–8.

Roozendaal, B., & McGaugh, J. L. (1996). The memory-modulatory effects of glucocorticoids depend on an intact stria terminalis. *Brain Research, 709,* 243–250.

Roozendaal, B., Portillo-Marquez, G., & McGaugh, J. L. (1996). Basolateral amygdala lesions block glucocorticoid-induced modulation of memory for spatial learning. *Behavioral Neuroscience, 110,* 1074–1083.

Salinas, J. A., & McGaugh, J. L. (1996). The amygdala modulates memory for changes in reward magnitude: Involvement of the amygdaloid gabaergic system. *Behavioural Brain Research, 80,* 87–98.

Salinas, J. A., Parent, M. B., & McGaugh, J. L. (1996). Ibotenic acid lesions of amygdala nuclei differentially effect the response to reductions in reward. *Brain Research, 742,* 283–293.

Salinas, J. A., Williams, C. L., & McGaugh, J. L. (1996). Peripheral posttraining administration of 4-OH amphetamine enhances retention of a reduction in reward magnitude. *Neurobiology of Learning and Memory, 65,* 192–195.

Bermudez-Rattoni, F., Introini-Collison, I. B., Coleman-Mesches, K., & McGaugh, J. L. (1997). Insular cortex and amygdala lesions induced after aversive training impair retention: Effects of degree of training. *Neurobiology of Learning and Memory, 67,* 57–63.

Brioni, J. D., Hock, F. J., Huger, F. P., & McGaugh, J. L. (1997). Drug effects on learning and memory. In H. G. Vogel & W. H. Vogel (Eds.), *Drug discovery and evaluation* (pp. 317–349). Berlin, Germany: Springer.

Cahill, L., & McGaugh, J. L. (1997). Commentary on paper by Furmark et al., The amygdala and individual differences in human fear conditioning. *Neuroreport, 8,* R1.

Cahill, L., Roozendaal, B. R., & McGaugh, J. L (1997). The neurobiology of memory for aversive emotional events. In M. E. Bouton & M. S. Fanselow (Eds.), *Learning, motivation and cognition: The functional behaviorism of Robert C. Bolles* (pp. 369–384). Washington, DC: American Psychological Association.

Coleman-Mesches, K., West, M. A., & McGaugh, J. L. (1997). Opposite effects on two different measures of retention following unilateral inactivation of the amygdala. *Behavioural Brain Research, 86,* 17–23.

Dickinson-Anson, H., & McGaugh, J. L. (1997). Bicuculline administered into the amygdala after training blocks benzodiazepine-induced amnesia. *Brain Research, 752,* 197–202.

Gasbarri, A., Sulli, A., Pacitti, C., Puglisi-Allegra, S., Cabib, S., Castellano, C., Introini-Collison, I. B., & McGaugh, J. L. (1997). Strain-dependent effects of D_2 dopaminergic and muscarinic-cholinergic agonists and antagonists on memory consolidation processes in mice. *Behavioural Brain Research, 86,* 97–104.

Guzowski, J. F., & McGaugh, J. L. (1997). Antisense oligodeoxynucleotide-mediated disruption of hippocampal CREB protein levels impairs memory of a spatial task. *Proceedings of the National Academy of Sciences, 94,* 2693–2698.

Guzowski, J. F., & McGaugh, J. L. (1997). Interaction of neuromodulatory systems regulating memory storage. In J. D. Brioni & M. W. Decker (Eds.), *Pharmacological treatment of Alzheimer's disease: Molecular and neurobiological foundation* (pp. 37–61). New York: Wiley-Liss.

Hamann, S. B., Cahill, L., McGaugh, J. L., & Squire, L. R. (1997). Intact enhancement of declarative memory for emotional material in amnesia. *Learning and Memory, 4,* 301–309.

McGaugh, J. L., & Cahill, L. (1997). Interaction of neuromodulatory systems in modulating memory storage. *Behavioural Brain Research, 83,* 31–38.

Quirarte, G. L., Roozendaal, B., & McGaugh, J. L. (1997). Glucocorticoid enhancement of memory storage involves noradrenergic activation in the basolateral amygdala. *Proceedings of the National Academy of Sciences, 94,* 14048–14053.

Roozendaal, B., & McGaugh, J. L. (1997). Basolateral amygdala lesions block the memory-enhancing effect of glucocorticoid administration in the dorsal hippocampus of rats. *European Journal of Neuroscience, 9,* 76–83.

Roozendaal, B., & McGaugh, J. L. (1997). Glucocorticoid receptor agonist and antagonist administration into the basolateral but not central amygdala modulates memory storage. *Neurobiology of Learning and Memory, 67,* 176–179.

Roozendaal, B., Quirarte, G. L., & McGaugh, J. L. (1997). Stress-activated hormonal systems and the regulation of memory storage. In R. Yehuda & A. C. McFarlane (Eds.), *Psychobiology of posttraumatic stress disorder* (pp. 247–258). New York: New York Academy of Sciences.

Salinas, J. A., Introini-Collison, I. B., Dalmaz, C., & McGaugh, J. L. (1997). Posttraining intra-amygdala infusion of oxotremorine and propranolol modulate storage of memory for reductions in reward magnitude. *Neurobiology of Learning and Memory, 68,* 51–59.

Cahill, L., & McGaugh, J. L. (1998). Mechanisms of emotional arousal and lasting declarative memory. *Trends in Neuroscience, 21,* 294–299.

Cahill, L., & McGaugh, J. L. (1998). Modulation of memory storage. In L. R. Squire & S. M. Kosslyn (Eds.), *Findings and current opinion in cognitive neuroscience* (pp. 85–90). Cambridge, MA: MIT Press.

de Quervain, D. J.-F., Roozendaal, B., & McGaugh, J. L. (1998). Stress and glucocorticoids impair retrieval of long-term spatial memory. *Nature, 394,* 787–790.

McGaugh, J. L. (1998). Memory consolidation. In G. Adelman & B. H. Smith (Eds.), *Encyclopedia of neuroscience* (2nd ed., CD-ROM). Amsterdam, The Netherlands: Elsevier.

McGaugh, J. L. (1998). Memory, hormone influences. In G. Adelman & B. H. Smith (Eds.), *Encyclopedia of neuroscience* (2nd ed., CD-ROM). Amsterdam, The Netherlands: Elsevier.

Quirarte, G. L., Galvez, R., Roozendaal, B., & McGaugh, J. L. (1998). Norepinephrine release in the amygdala in response to footshock and opioid peptidergic drugs. *Brain Research, 808,* 134–140.

Roozendaal, B., Sapolsky, R. M., & McGaugh, J. L. (1998). Basolateral amygdala lesions block the disruptive effects of long-term adrenalectomy on spatial memory. *Neuroscience, 84,* 453–465.

Setlow, B., & McGaugh, J. L. (1998). Sulpiride infused into the nucleus accumbens post-training impairs retention in the spatial water maze. *Behavioral Neuroscience, 112,* 603–610.

van Stegeren, A. H., Everaerd, W., Cahill, L., McGaugh, J. L., & Gooren, L. J. G. (1998). Memory for emotional events: Differential effects of centrally versus peripherally acting β-blocking agents. *Psychopharmacology, 138,* 305–310.

Vazdarjanova, A., & McGaugh, J. L. (1998). Basolateral amygdala is not critical for cognitive memory of contextual fear conditioning. *Proceedings of the National Academy of Sciences, 95,* 15003–15007.

Barros, D. M., Izquierdo, L. A., Sant'Anna, M. K., Quevedo, J., Medina, J. H., McGaugh, J. L., & Izquierdo, I. B. (1999). Stimulators of the cAMP cascade reverse amnesia induced by intra-amygdala but not intrahippocampal KN-62 administration. *Neurobiology of Learning and Memory, 71,* 94–103.

Cahill, L., McGaugh, J. L., Roozendaal, B., & Williams, C. L. (1999). Modulation of memory storage. In M. J. Zigmond, F. E. Bloom, S. C. Landis, J. L. Roberts, &

L. R. Squire (Eds.), *Fundamental neuroscience* (pp. 1455–1486). New York: Academic Press.

Cahill, L., Weinberger, N. M., Roozendaal, B., & McGaugh, J. L. (1999). Is the amygdala a locus of "conditioned fear"? Some Questions and Caveats. *Neuron, 23,* 227–228.

Castellano, C., Cabib, S., Puglisi-Allegra, S., Gasbarri, A., Sulli, A., Pacitti, C., Introini-Collison, I. B., & McGaugh, J. L. (1999). Strain-dependent involvement of D1 and D2 dopamine receptors in the effects of oxotremorine and atropine on memory storage. *Behavioural Brain Research, 98,* 17–26.

DaCunha, C., Roozendaal, B., Vazdarjanova, A., & McGaugh, J. L. (1999). Microinfusions of flumazenil into the basolateral but not the central nucleus of the amygdala enhance memory consolidation in rats. *Neurobiology of Learning and Memory, 72,* 1–7.

Ferry, B., & McGaugh, J. L. (1999). Clenbuterol administration into the basolateral amygdala post-training enhances retention in an inhibitory avoidance task. *Neurobiology of Learning and Memory, 72,* 8–12.

Ferry, B., Roozendaal, B., & McGaugh, J. L. (1999). Basolateral amygdala noradrenergic influences on memory storage are mediated by an interaction between beta- and alpha$_1$-receptors. *Journal of Neuroscience, 19,* 5119–5123.

Ferry, B., Roozendaal, B., & McGaugh, J. L. (1999). Involvement of alpha$_1$-adrenergic receptors in the basolateral amygdala in modulation of memory storage. *European Journal of Pharmacology, 372,* 9–16.

Ferry, B., Roozendaal, B., & McGaugh, J. L. (1999). Role of norepinephrine in mediating stress hormone regulation of long-term memory storage: A critical involvement of the amygdala. *Biological Psychiatry, 46,* 1140–1152.

Gasbarri, A., Sulli, A., Pacitti, C., & McGaugh, J. L. (1999). Serotonergic input to cholinergic neurons in the substantia innominata and nucleus basalis magnocellularis in the rat. *Neuroscience, 91,* 1129–1142.

Hatfield, T., & McGaugh, J. L. (1999). Norepinephrine infused into the basolateral amygdala posttraining enhances retention in a spatial water maze task. *Neurobiology of Learning and Memory, 71,* 232–239.

Hatfield, T., Spanis, C., & McGaugh, J. L. (1999). Response of amygdalar norepinephrine to footshock and GABAergic drugs using in vivo microdialysis and HPLC. *Brain Research, 835,* 340–345.

Izquierdo, I., & McGaugh, J. L. (2000). Behavioural pharmacology and its contribution to the molecular basis of memory consolidation. *Behavioural Pharmacology, 11,* 517–534.

McGaugh, J. L. (1999). Memory consolidation. In G. Adelman & B. H. Smith (Eds.), *Encyclopedia of neuroscience* (2nd ed., pp. 1137–1138). Amsterdam, The Netherlands: Elsevier.

McGaugh, J. L. (1999). Memory, hormone influences. In G. Adelman & B. H. Smith (Eds.), *Encyclopedia of neuroscience* (2nd ed., pp. 1133–1134). Amsterdam, The Netherlands: Elsevier.

McGaugh, J. L. (1999). Memory storage, modulation of. In R. A. Wilson & F. C. Keil

(Eds.), *The MIT encyclopedia of the cognitive sciences* (pp. 522–524). Cambridge, MA: MIT Press.

McGaugh, J. L. (1999). The perseveration–consolidation hypothesis: Mueller and Pilzecker, 1900. *Brain Research Bulletin, 50,* 445–446.

McGaugh, J. L. (1999). Why I came to study the brain. In *The Dana Brain Science Guide: Resources for secondary and post-secondary teachers and students* (pp. 4–6). New York: Dana Press.

McGaugh, J. L., Roozendaal, B., & Cahill, L. (1999). Modulation of memory storage by stress hormones and the amygdaloid complex. In M. Gazzaniga (Ed.), *Cognitive neuroscience* (2nd ed., pp. 1081–1098). Cambridge, MA: MIT Press.

Roozendaal, B., Nguyen, B. T., Power, A., & McGaugh, J. L. (1999). Basolateral amygdala noradrenergic influence enables enhancement of memory consolidation induced by hippocampal glucocorticoid receptor activation. *Proceedings of the National Academy of Sciences, 96,* 11642–11647.

Roozendaal, B., Williams, C. L., & McGaugh, J. L. (1999). Glucocorticoid receptor activation in the rat nucleus of the solitary tract facilitates memory consolidation: Involvement of the basolateral amygdala. *European Journal of Neuroscience, 11,* 1317–1323.

Setlow, B., & McGaugh, J. L. (1999). Differential effects of immediate posttraining sulpiride microinfusions into the nucleus accumbens shell and core on Morris water maze memory. *Psychobiology, 27,* 248–255.

Setlow, B., & McGaugh, J. L. (1999). Involvement of the posteroventral caudate-putamen in memory consolidation in the Morris water maze. *Neurobiology of Learning and Memory, 71,* 240–247.

Spanis, C. W., Bianchin, M. M., Izquierdo, I., & McGaugh, J. L. (1999). Excitotoxic basolateral amygdala lesions potentiate the memory impairment effect of muscimol injected into the medial septal area. *Brain Research, 816,* 329–336.

Vazdarjanova, A., & McGaugh, J. L. (1999). Basolateral amygdala is involved in modulating consolidation of memory for classical fear conditioning. *Journal of Neuroscience, 19,* 6615–6622.

Baddeley, A., Bueno, O., Cahill, L., Fuster, J., Izquierdo, I., McGaugh, J. L., Morris, R. G. M., Nadel, L., Routtenberg, A., Xavier, G., & Da Cunha, C. (2000). The brain decade in debate: I. Neurobiology of learning and memory. *Brazilian Journal of Medical and Biological Research, 33,* 993–1002.

Bianchin, M. M., Spanis, C. W., Roesler, R., Izquierdo, I., & McGaugh, J. L. (2000). (+)-a-Methyl-4-Carboxyphenylglycine, a metabotropic receptor blocker, impairs retention of an inhibitory avoidance task in rats when infused into the basolateral nucleus of the amygdala. *Brain Research, 852,* 436–443.

de Quervain, D. J.-F., Roozendaal, B., Nitsch, R. M., McGaugh, J. L., & Hock, C. (2000). Acute cortisone administration impairs retrieval of long-term declarative memory in healthy subjects. *Nature Neuroscience, 3,* 313–314.

Ferry, B., & McGaugh, J. L. (2000). Role of the amygdala norepinephrine in mediating stress hormone regulation of memory storage. *Acta Pharmacologica Sinica, 21*, 481–493.

Guzowski, J. F., Lyford, G. L., Stevenson, G. D., Houston, F. P., McGaugh, J. L., Worley, P. F., & Barnes, C. A. (2000). Inhibition of activity-dependent arc protein expression in the rat hippocampus impairs the maintenance of long-term potentiation and consolidation of long-term memory. *Journal of Neuroscience, 20*, 3993–4001.

McLaughlin, J., Roozendaal, B., Gupta, A., Ajilore, O., Dumas, T., Heieh, J., Ho, D., Lawrence, M. McGaugh, J. L., & Sapolsky, R. (2000). Sparing of neuronal function postseizure with gene therapy. *Proceedings, National Academy of Sciences, 97*, 12804–12809.

McGaugh, J. L. (2000). Biography. In W. E. Craighead & C. B. Nermeroff (Eds.), *The Corsini encyclopedia of psychology and behavioral science* (3rd ed., pp. 926–927). New York: Wiley.

McGaugh, J. L. (2000). Memory: A century of consolidation. *Science, 287*, 248–251.

McGaugh, J. L., Cahill, L., Ferry, B., & Roozendaal, R. (2000). Brain systems and the regulation of memory consolidation. In J. J. Bolhuis (Ed.), *Brain, perception, memory: Advances in cognitive neuroscience* (pp. 233–251). London: Oxford University Press.

McGaugh, J. L., Ferry, B., Vazdarjanova, A., & Roozendaal, B. (2000). Amygdala: Role in modulation of memory storage. In J. P. Aggleton, (Ed.), *The amygdala: A functional analysis* (pp. 391–423). London: Oxford University Press.

McGaugh, J. L., & Izquierdo, I. (2000). Pharmacology's contribution to research on the mechanisms of memory formation. *Trends in Pharmacological Sciences, 21*, 208–210.

Power, A. E., Roozendaal, B., & McGaugh, J. L. (2000). Glucocorticoid enhancement of memory consolidation in the rat is blocked by muscarinic receptor antagonism in the basolateral amygdala. *European Journal of Neuroscience, 12*, 3481–3487.

Setlow, B., & McGaugh, J. L. (2000). D2 dopamine receptor blockade immediately post-training enhances retention in hidden and visible platform versions of the water maze. *Learning and Memory, 7*, 187–191.

Setlow, B., Roozendaal, B., & McGaugh, J. L. (2000). Involvement of a basolateral amygdala complex-nucleus accumbens pathway in glucocorticoid-induced modulation of memory storage. *European Journal of Neuroscience, 12*, 367–375.

Author Index

Subject Index

About the Editors

Paul E. Gold, professor of psychology and neuroscience faculty member at the University of Illinois at Urbana–Champaign, is a leading authority on pharmacological enhancement of learning and memory in rodents and humans. He received a BA from the University of Michigan in 1966 and a PhD from the University of North Carolina at Chapel Hill in 1971. He was a postdoctoral fellow in Dr. James L. McGaugh's laboratory at the University of California at Irvine until 1976. He then joined the faculty of the University of Virginia, where he was Commonwealth Professor of Psychology, head of the Psychobiology Program, and director of the Neuroscience Program. He was also a member of the university's Program in Cognitive Science and of the Center on Aging and Health, chairing the section on Neuroscience of Aging, Memory, and Behavior. In 1998, he was appointed to the Governor's Commission on Alzheimer's Disease and Related Disorders for the Commonwealth of Virginia. He was at State University of New York–Binghamton from 1999 to 2000, where he served as head of the Behavioral Neuroscience Program, before moving to the University of Illinois. In 2000, Dr. Gold received the Distinguished Alumnus Award from the Department of Psychology at the University of North Carolina at Chapel Hill. He is a fellow of the American Psychological Association, the American Psychological Society, and the American Association for the Advancement of Science. He coedits the journal *Neurobiology of Learning and Memory* with William T. Greenough and has served on editorial boards of numerous other journals. He is currently director of the Medical Scholars Program at the University of Illinois College of Medicine.

William T. Greenough is Swanlund and Center for Advanced Study Professor of Psychology, a professor of psychiatry and cell and structural biology, and a neuroscience faculty member at the University of Illinois at Urbana–Champaign. He is a leading authority on the effects of experience (including physical exercise) and learning on the structure and function of the developing and adult mammalian brain. He received a BA from the University of Oregon in 1964, conducted thesis research under the direction of Jim McGaugh, a PhD from the University of California at Los Angeles in 1969, and has been at the University of Illinois since then. He has held elective office in the Society for Neuroscience; the Winter Conference on Brain Research; the Society for Developmental Psychobiology; and the Federation of Behavioral, Psychological, and Cognitive Societies. He has served on the Advisory Committee of the Biological Sciences Directorate of the National Science Foundation and was a member of the Office of Science and Technology Policy Forum on Science in the National Interest that helped to lay out the Clinton administration's science policy document released in 1994. He is a member of the National Academy of Sciences and a Fellow of the American Association for the Advancement of Science, the American Psychological Association (APA), the American Psychological Society (APS), and the Society for Experimental Psychology. In 1996, he received the APS William James Award, and in 1998–1999 he received the APA Distinguished Scientific Contribution Award. He coedits the journal *Neurobiology of Learning and Memory* with Paul E. Gold and has served on editorial boards of numerous other journals. He currently directs the University of Illinois Neuroscience PhD program, directs the University of Illinois Center for Advanced Study, and codirects the Beckman Institute Main Research Theme Group on Biological Intelligence.